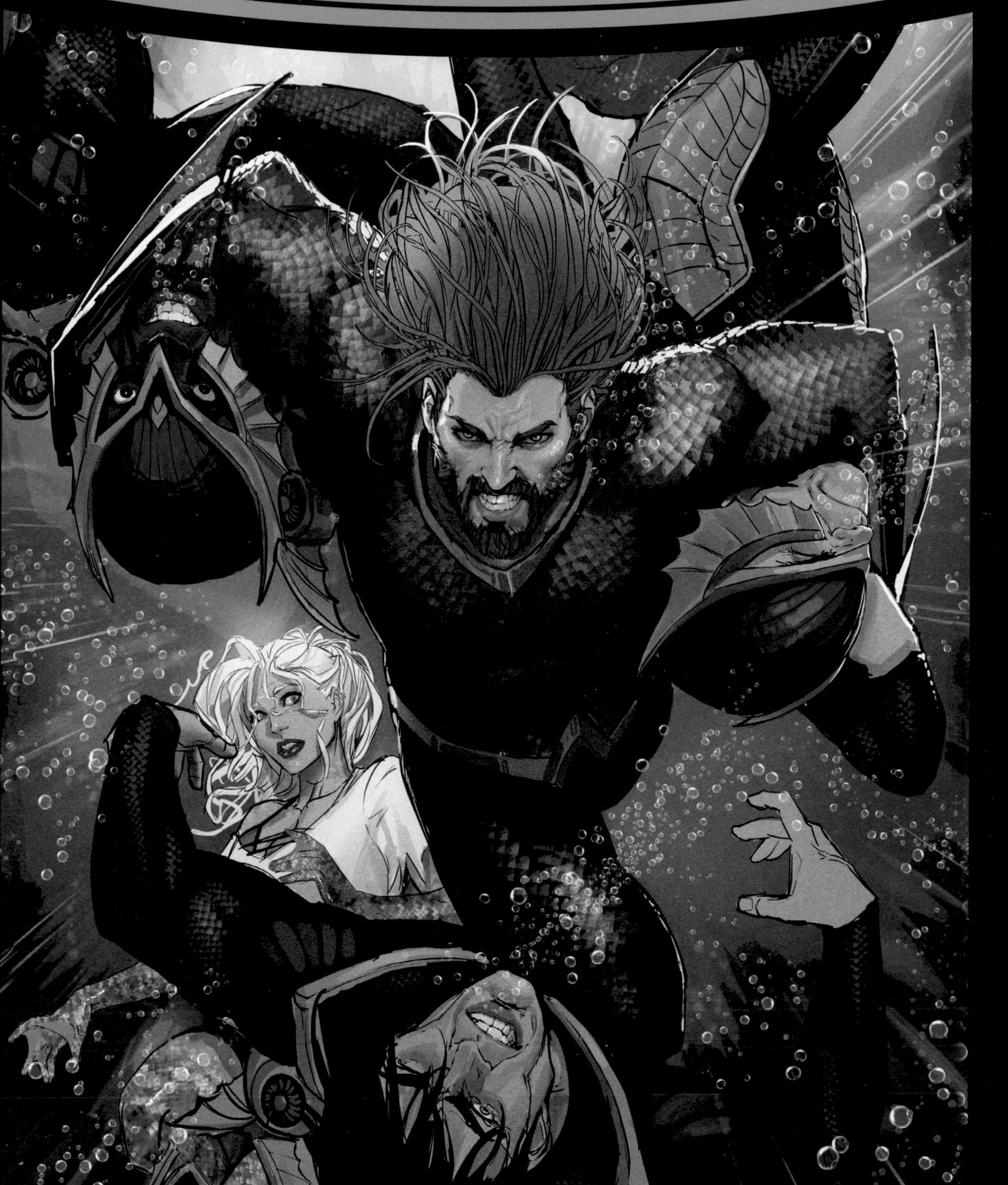

AQUAMAN

VOL.4 UNDERWORLD

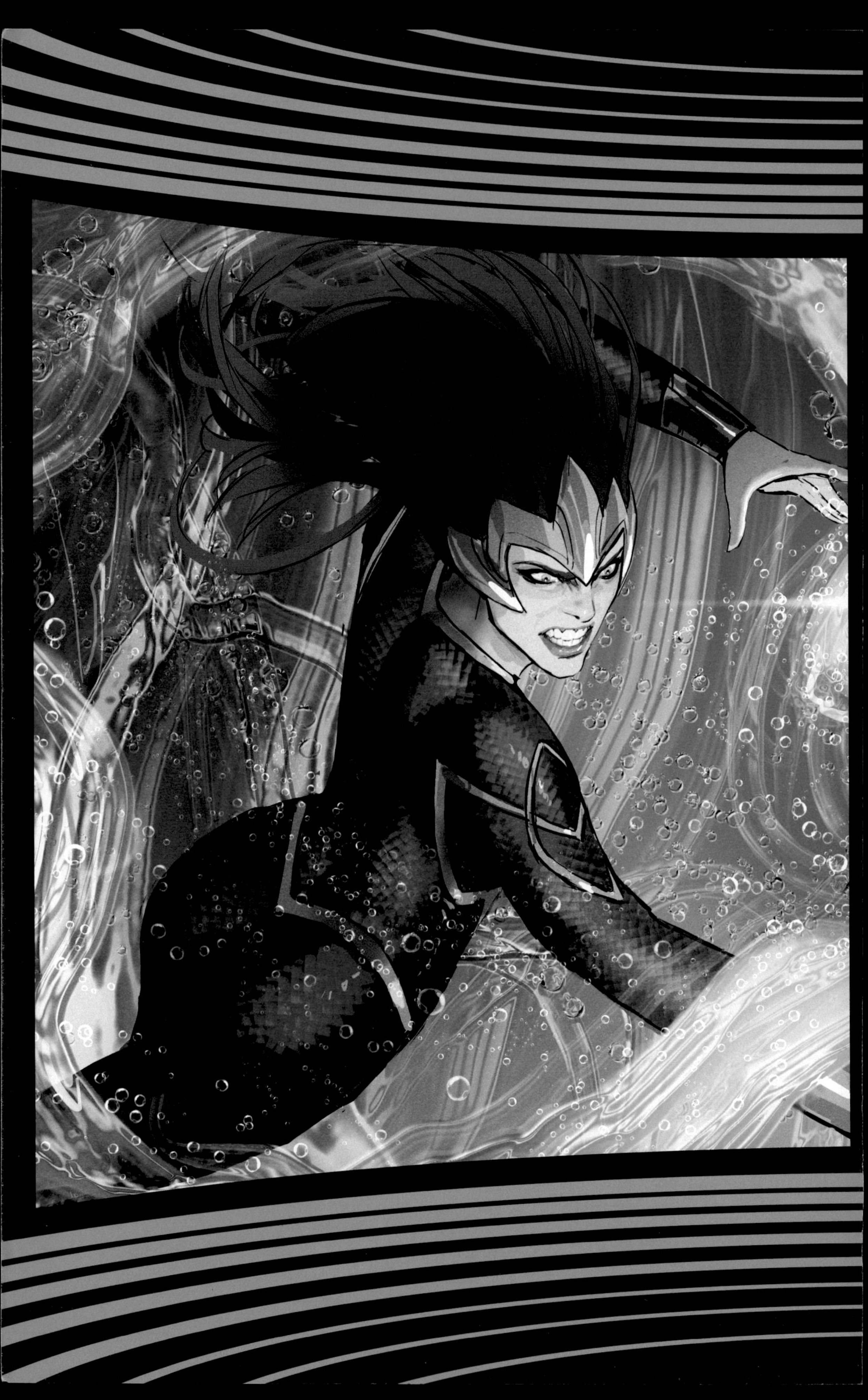

AQUAMAN
VOL.4 UNDERWORLD

DAN ABNETT
writer

STJEPAN SEJIC
artist

STEVE WANDS
letterer

STJEPAN SEJIC
collection cover artist

AQUAMAN created by **PAUL NORRIS**

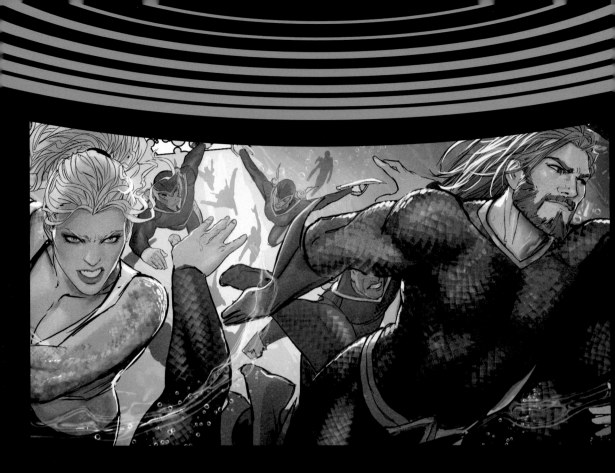

ALEX ANTONE, ANDY KHOURI Editors - Original Series
HARVEY RICHARDS Associate Editor - Original Series * **DAVE WIELGOSZ** Assistant Editor - Original Series
JEB WOODARD Group Editor - Collected Editions * **BETSY GOLDEN** Editor - Collected Edition
STEVE COOK Design Director - Books * **SHANNON STEWART** Publication Design

BOB HARRAS Senior VP - Editor-in-Chief, DC Comics * **PAT McCALLUM** Executive Editor, DC Comics

DIANE NELSON President * **DAN DiDIO** Publisher * **JIM LEE** Publisher * **GEOFF JOHNS** President & Chief Creative Officer
AMIT DESAI Executive VP - Business & Marketing Strategy, Direct to Consumer & Global Franchise Management
SAM ADES Senior VP & General Manager, Digital Services * **BOBBIE CHASE** VP & Executive Editor, Young Reader & Talent Development
MARK CHIARELLO Senior VP - Art, Design & Collected Editions * **JOHN CUNNINGHAM** Senior VP - Sales & Trade Marketing
ANNE DePIES Senior VP - Business Strategy, Finance & Administration * **DON FALLETTI** VP - Manufacturing Operations
LAWRENCE GANEM VP - Editorial Administration & Talent Relations * **ALISON GILL** Senior VP - Manufacturing & Operations
HANK KANALZ Senior VP - Editorial Strategy & Administration * **JAY KOGAN** VP - Legal Affairs
JACK MAHAN VP - Business Affairs * **NICK J. NAPOLITANO** VP - Manufacturing Administration
EDDIE SCANNELL VP - Consumer Marketing * **COURTNEY SIMMONS** Senior VP - Publicity & Communications
JIM (SKI) SOKOLOWSKI VP - Comic Book Specialty Sales & Trade Marketing
NANCY SPEARS VP - Mass, Book, Digital Sales & Trade Marketing * **MICHELE R. WELLS** VP - Content Strategy

AQUAMAN VOL.4: UNDERWORLD

DC Comics, 2900 West Alameda Ave., Burbank, CA 91505
Printed by LSC Communications, Kendallville, IN, USA. 12/22/17. First Printing.
ISBN: 978-1-4012-7542-6

Library of Congress Cataloging-in-Publication Data is available.

PEFC Certified
Printed on paper from sustainably managed forests, controlled sources
PEFC
PEFC/29-31-337
www.pefc.org

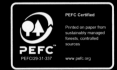

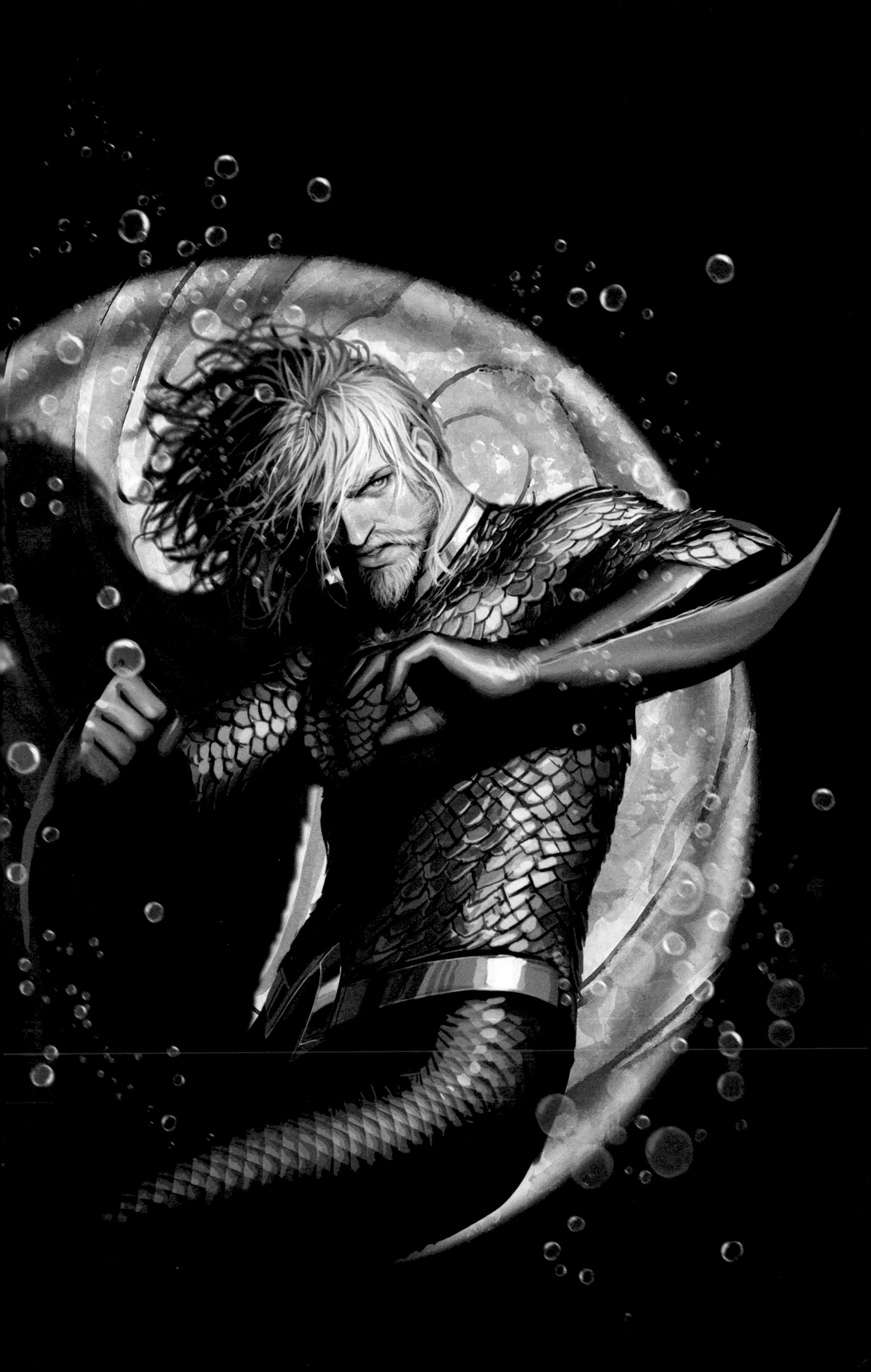

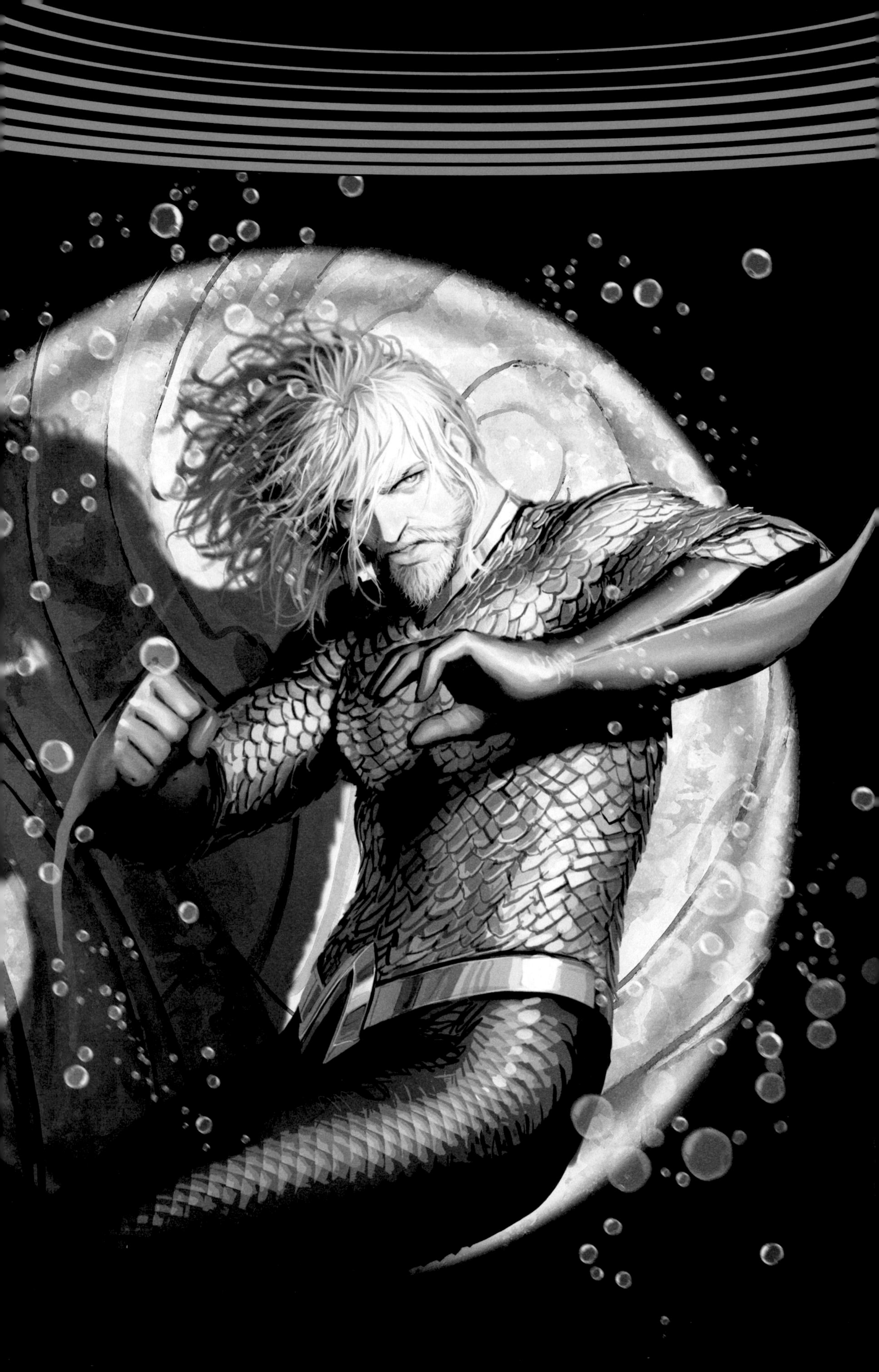

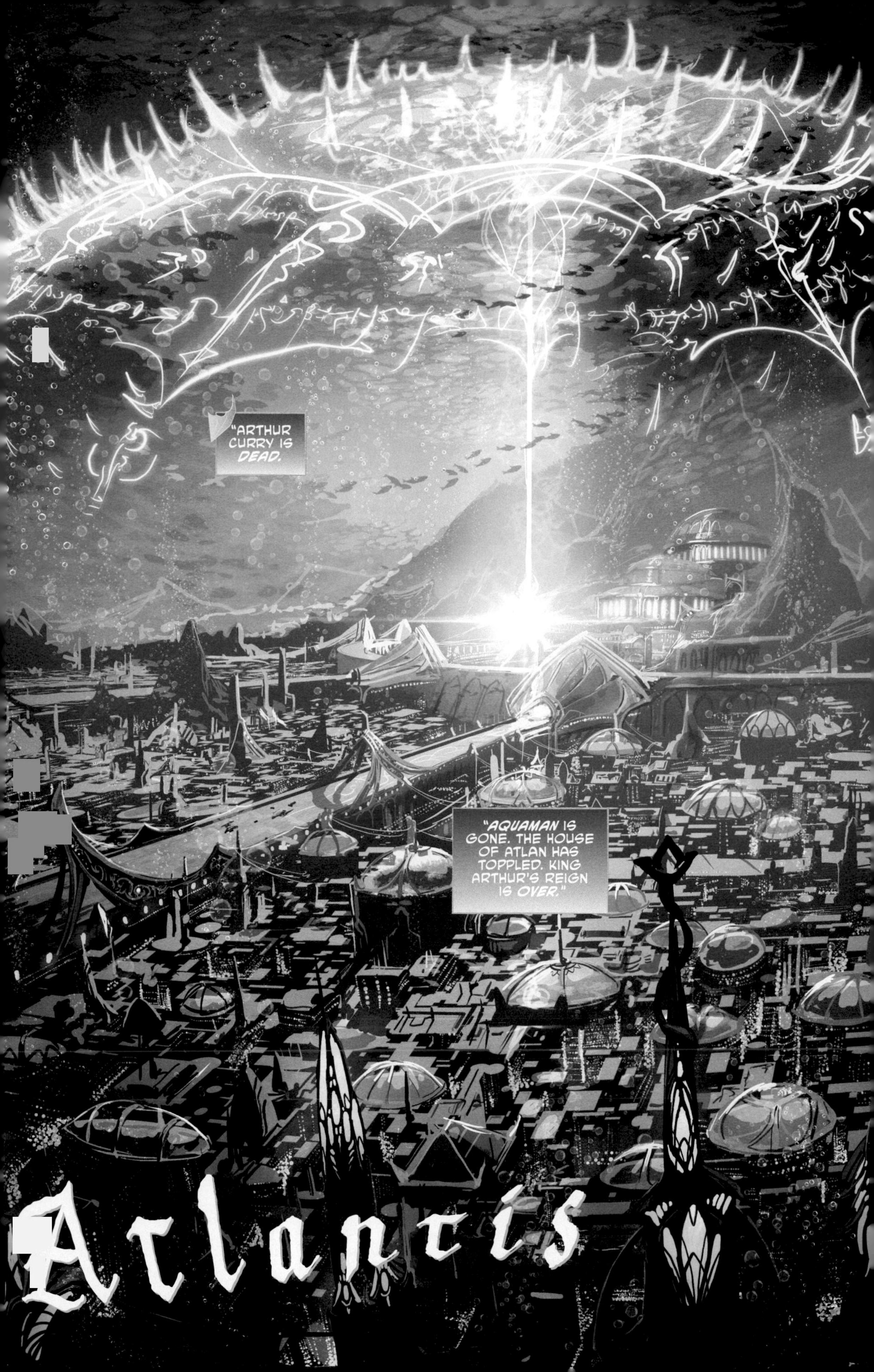
"ARTHUR CURRY IS DEAD.
"AQUAMAN IS GONE. THE HOUSE OF ATLAN HAS TOPPLED. KING ARTHUR'S REIGN IS OVER."
Atlantis

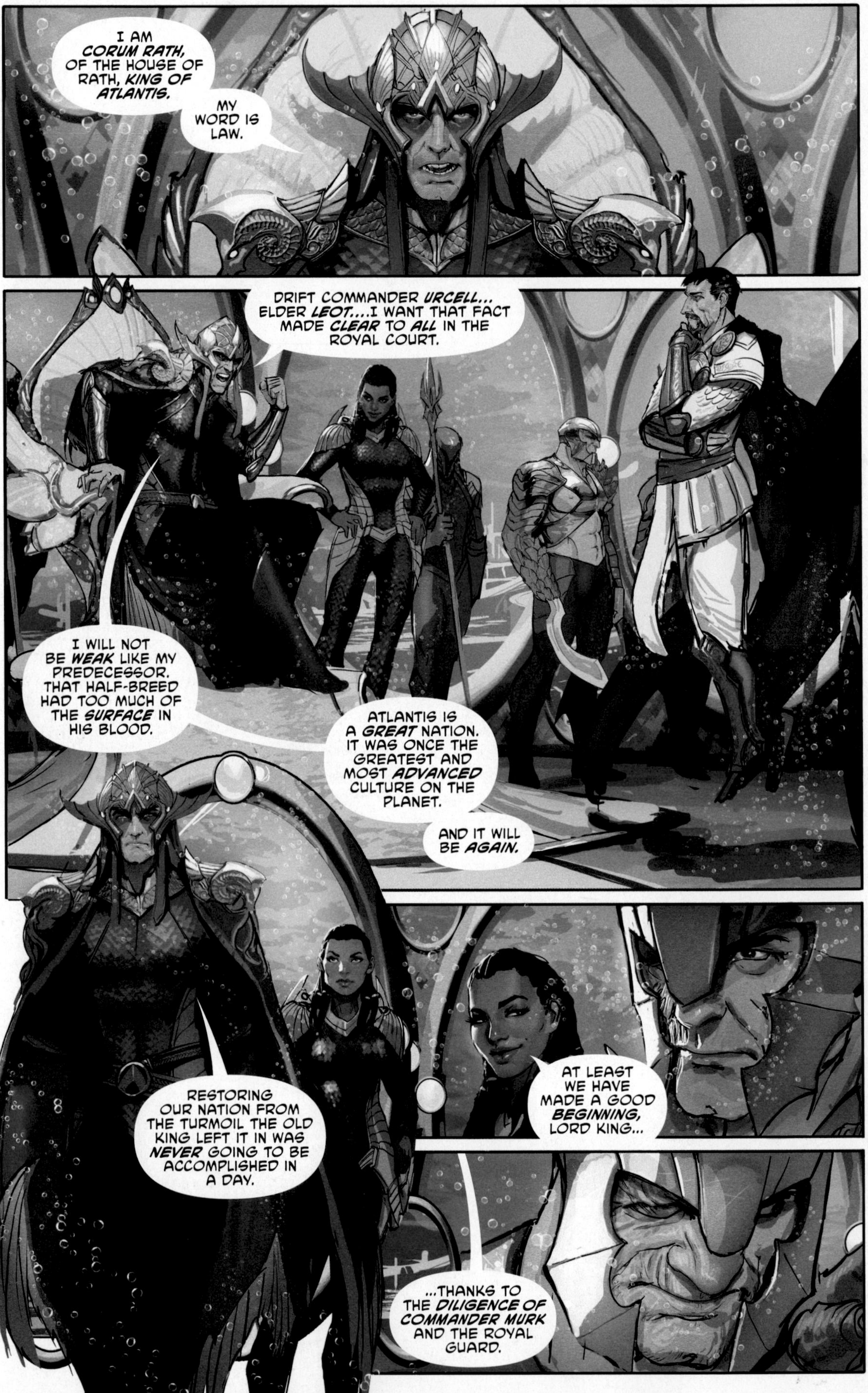

I AM CORUM RATH, OF THE HOUSE OF RATH, KING OF ATLANTIS.
MY WORD IS LAW.
DRIFT COMMANDER URCELL... ELDER LEOT....I WANT THAT FACT MADE CLEAR TO ALL IN THE ROYAL COURT.
I WILL NOT BE WEAK LIKE MY PREDECESSOR. THAT HALF-BREED HAD TOO MUCH OF THE SURFACE IN HIS BLOOD.
ATLANTIS IS A GREAT NATION. IT WAS ONCE THE GREATEST AND MOST ADVANCED CULTURE ON THE PLANET.
AND IT WILL BE AGAIN.
RESTORING OUR NATION FROM THE TURMOIL THE OLD KING LEFT IT IN WAS NEVER GOING TO BE ACCOMPLISHED IN A DAY.
AT LEAST WE HAVE MADE A GOOD BEGINNING, LORD KING...
...THANKS TO THE DILIGENCE OF COMMANDER MURK AND THE ROYAL GUARD.

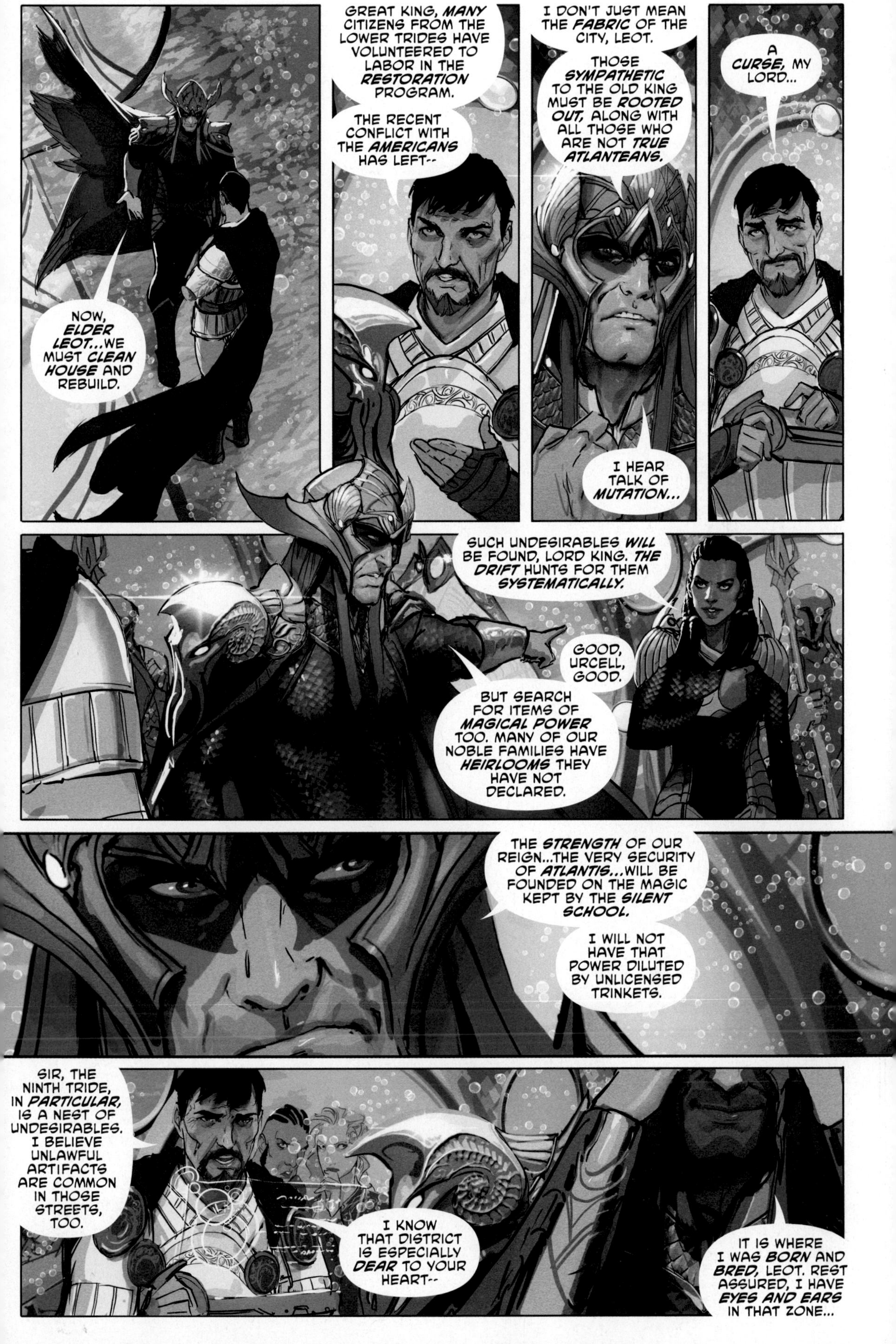
NOW, ELDER LEOT...WE MUST CLEAN HOUSE AND REBUILD.
GREAT KING, MANY CITIZENS FROM THE LOWER TRIDES HAVE VOLUNTEERED TO LABOR IN THE RESTORATION PROGRAM.
THE RECENT CONFLICT WITH THE AMERICANS HAS LEFT--
I DON'T JUST MEAN THE FABRIC OF THE CITY, LEOT.
THOSE SYMPATHETIC TO THE OLD KING MUST BE ROOTED OUT, ALONG WITH ALL THOSE WHO ARE NOT TRUE ATLANTEANS.
I HEAR TALK OF MUTATION...
A CURSE, MY LORD...
SUCH UNDESIRABLES WILL BE FOUND, LORD KING. THE DRIFT HUNTS FOR THEM SYSTEMATICALLY.
GOOD, URCELL, GOOD.
BUT SEARCH FOR ITEMS OF MAGICAL POWER TOO. MANY OF OUR NOBLE FAMILIES HAVE HEIRLOOMS THEY HAVE NOT DECLARED.
THE STRENGTH OF OUR REIGN...THE VERY SECURITY OF ATLANTIS...WILL BE FOUNDED ON THE MAGIC KEPT BY THE SILENT SCHOOL.
I WILL NOT HAVE THAT POWER DILUTED BY UNLICENSED TRINKETS.
SIR, THE NINTH TRIDE, IN PARTICULAR, IS A NEST OF UNDESIRABLES. I BELIEVE UNLAWFUL ARTIFACTS ARE COMMON IN THOSE STREETS, TOO.
I KNOW THAT DISTRICT IS ESPECIALLY DEAR TO YOUR HEART--
IT IS WHERE I WAS BORN AND BRED, LEOT. REST ASSURED, I HAVE EYES AND EARS IN THAT ZONE...

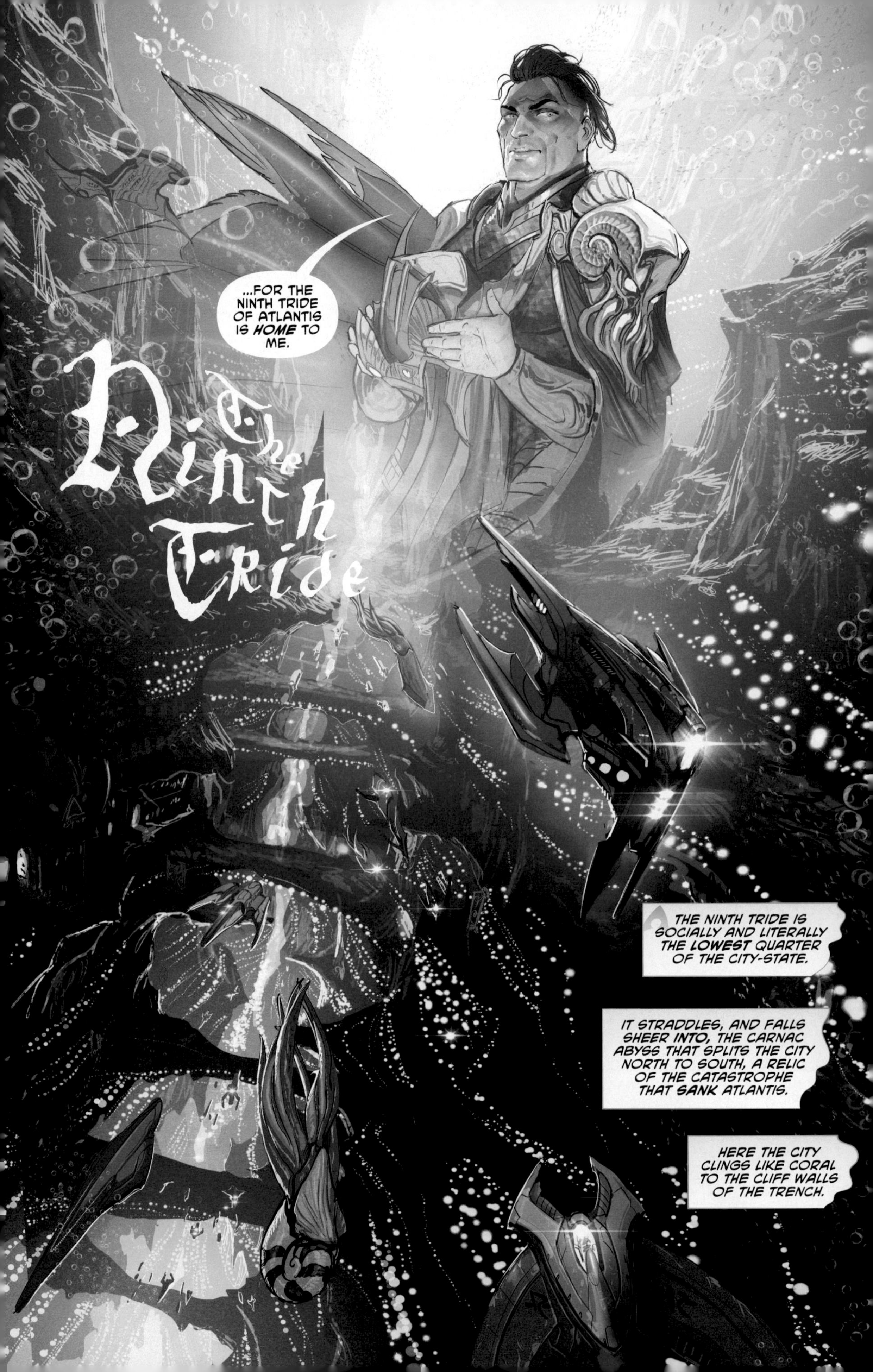

...FOR THE NINTH TRIDE OF ATLANTIS IS HOME TO ME.
The Ninth Tride
THE NINTH TRIDE IS SOCIALLY AND LITERALLY THE LOWEST QUARTER OF THE CITY-STATE.
IT STRADDLES, AND FALLS SHEER INTO, THE CARNAC ABYSS THAT SPLITS THE CITY NORTH TO SOUTH, A RELIC OF THE CATASTROPHE THAT SANK ATLANTIS.
HERE THE CITY CLINGS LIKE CORAL TO THE CLIFF WALLS OF THE TRENCH.

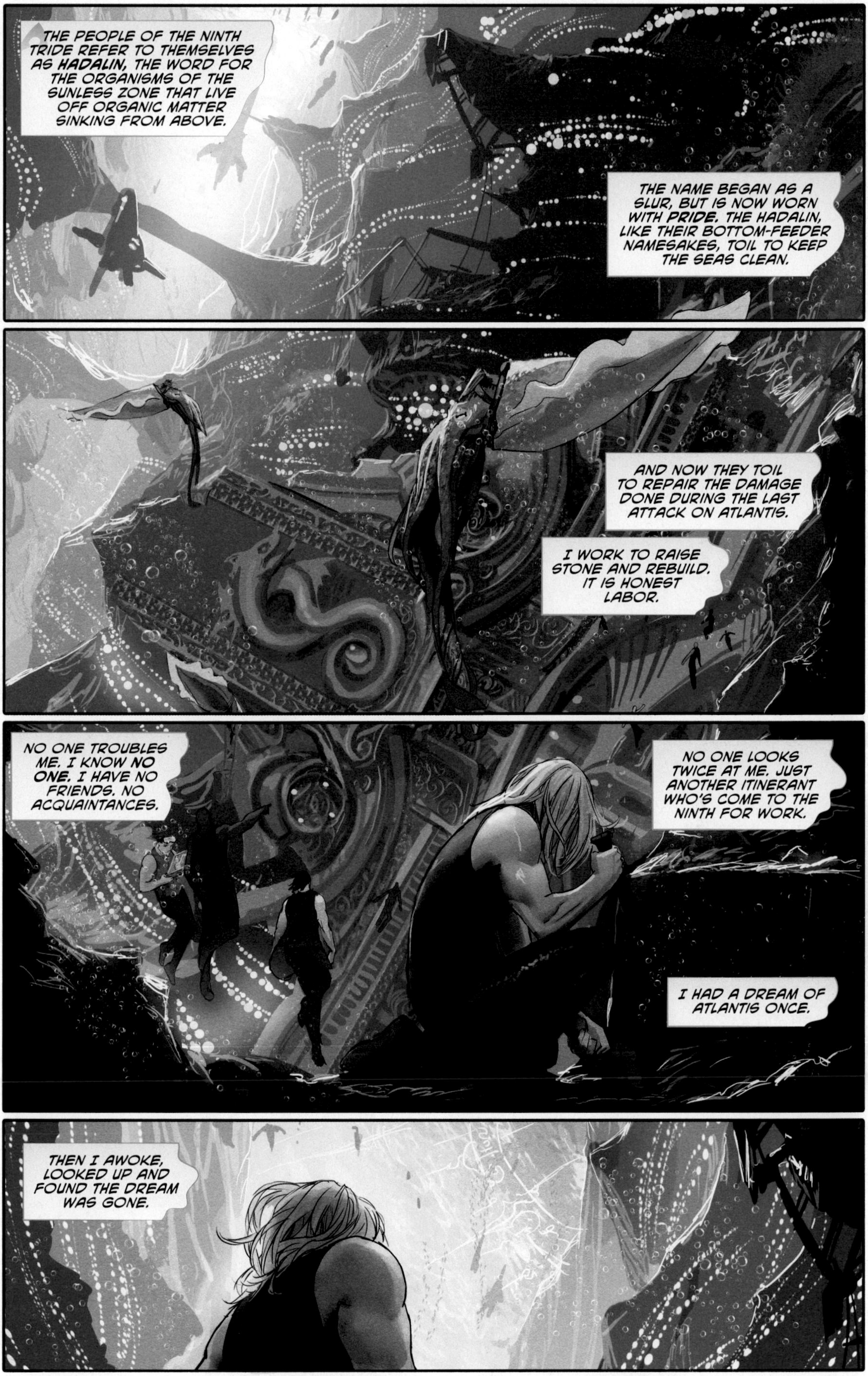
THE PEOPLE OF THE NINTH TRIDE REFER TO THEMSELVES AS **HADALIN**, THE WORD FOR THE ORGANISMS OF THE SUNLESS ZONE THAT LIVE OFF ORGANIC MATTER SINKING FROM ABOVE.
THE NAME BEGAN AS A SLUR, BUT IS NOW WORN WITH **PRIDE.** THE HADALIN, LIKE THEIR BOTTOM-FEEDER NAMESAKES, TOIL TO KEEP THE SEAS CLEAN.
AND NOW THEY TOIL TO REPAIR THE DAMAGE DONE DURING THE LAST ATTACK ON ATLANTIS.
I WORK TO RAISE STONE AND REBUILD. IT IS HONEST LABOR.
NO ONE TROUBLES ME. I KNOW **NO ONE.** I HAVE NO FRIENDS. NO ACQUAINTANCES.
NO ONE LOOKS TWICE AT ME. JUST ANOTHER ITINERANT WHO'S COME TO THE NINTH FOR WORK.
I HAD A DREAM OF ATLANTIS ONCE.
THEN I AWOKE, LOOKED UP AND FOUND THE DREAM WAS GONE.

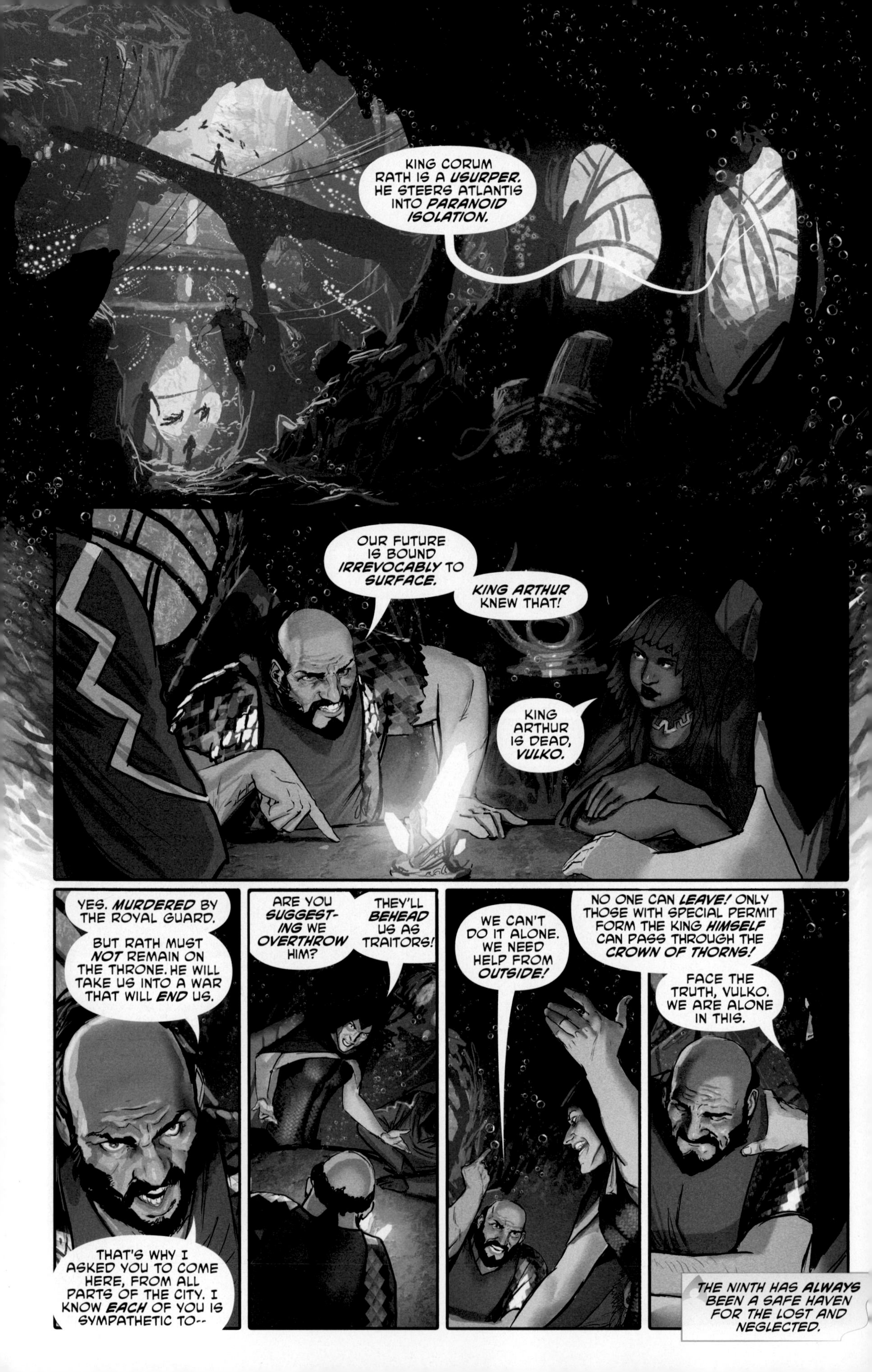

KING CORUM RATH IS A USURPER. HE STEERS ATLANTIS INTO PARANOID ISOLATION.
OUR FUTURE IS BOUND IRREVOCABLY TO SURFACE.
KING ARTHUR KNEW THAT!
KING ARTHUR IS DEAD, VULKO.
YES. MURDERED BY THE ROYAL GUARD.
BUT RATH MUST NOT REMAIN ON THE THRONE. HE WILL TAKE US INTO A WAR THAT WILL END US.
THAT'S WHY I ASKED YOU TO COME HERE, FROM ALL PARTS OF THE CITY. I KNOW EACH OF YOU IS SYMPATHETIC TO--
ARE YOU SUGGEST-ING WE OVERTHROW HIM?
THEY'LL BEHEAD US AS TRAITORS!
WE CAN'T DO IT ALONE. WE NEED HELP FROM OUTSIDE!
NO ONE CAN LEAVE! ONLY THOSE WITH SPECIAL PERMIT FORM THE KING HIMSELF CAN PASS THROUGH THE CROWN OF THORNS!
FACE THE TRUTH, VULKO. WE ARE ALONE IN THIS.
THE NINTH HAS ALWAYS BEEN A SAFE HAVEN FOR THE LOST AND NEGLECTED.

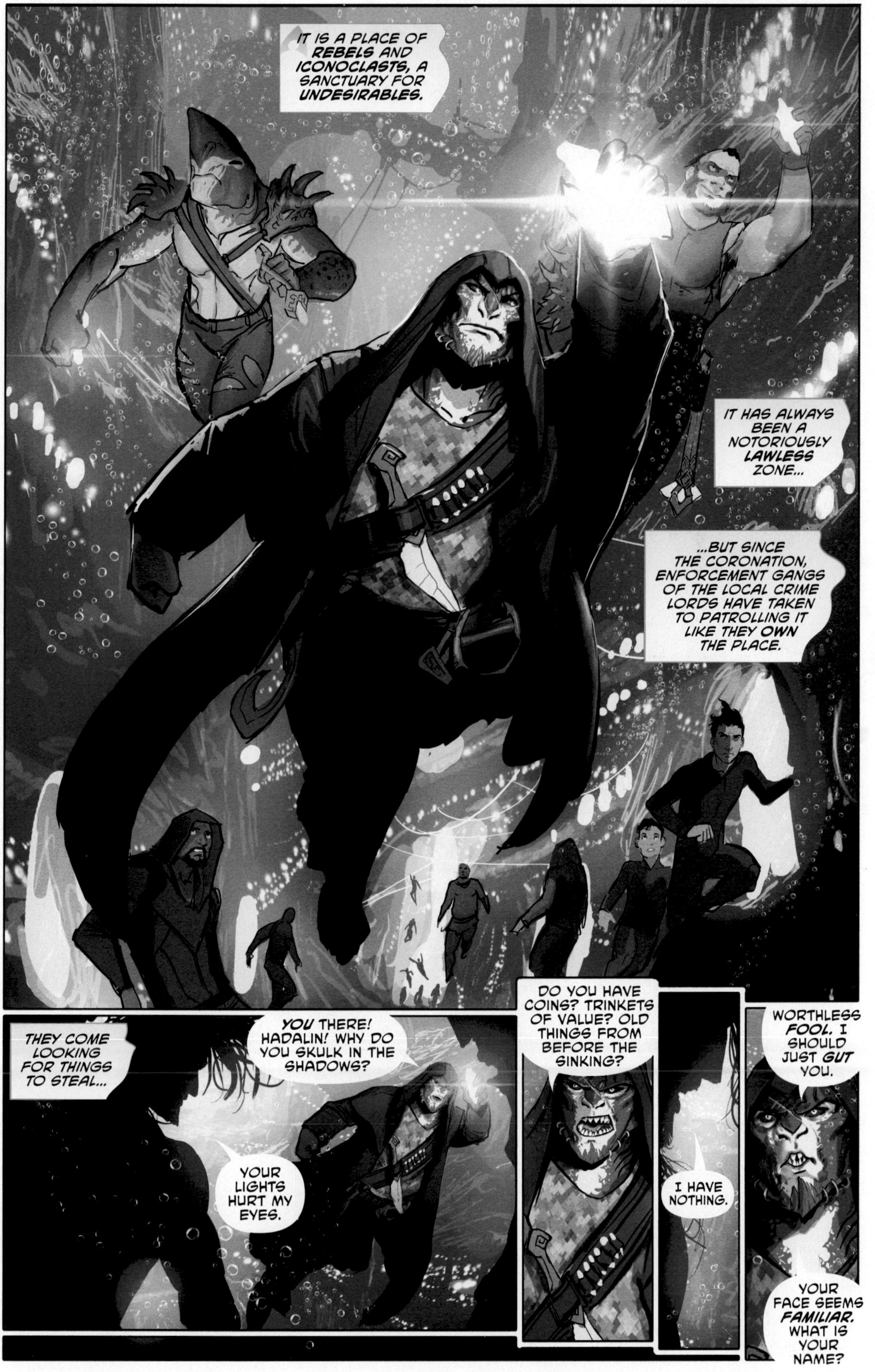
IT IS A PLACE OF REBELS AND ICONOCLASTS, A SANCTUARY FOR UNDESIRABLES.
IT HAS ALWAYS BEEN A NOTORIOUSLY LAWLESS ZONE...
...BUT SINCE THE CORONATION, ENFORCEMENT GANGS OF THE LOCAL CRIME LORDS HAVE TAKEN TO PATROLLING IT LIKE THEY OWN THE PLACE.
THEY COME LOOKING FOR THINGS TO STEAL...
YOU THERE! HADALIN! WHY DO YOU SKULK IN THE SHADOWS?
YOUR LIGHTS HURT MY EYES.
DO YOU HAVE COINS? TRINKETS OF VALUE? OLD THINGS FROM BEFORE THE SINKING?
I HAVE NOTHING.
WORTHLESS FOOL. I SHOULD JUST GUT YOU.
YOUR FACE SEEMS FAMILIAR. WHAT IS YOUR NAME?

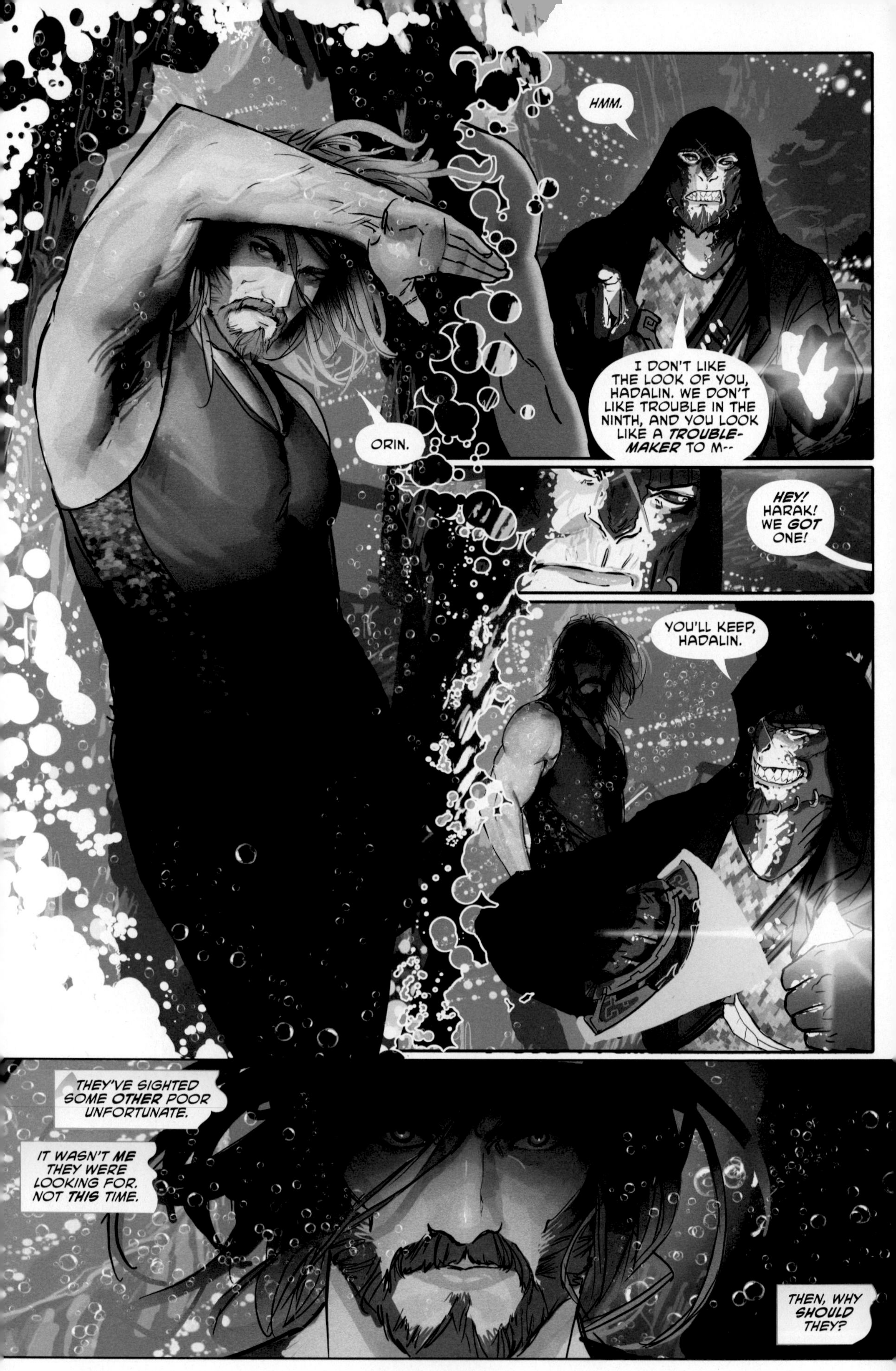
HMM.
ORIN.
I DON'T LIKE THE LOOK OF YOU, HADALIN. WE DON'T LIKE TROUBLE IN THE NINTH, AND YOU LOOK LIKE A TROUBLE-MAKER TO M--
HEY! HARAK! WE GOT ONE!
YOU'LL KEEP, HADALIN.
THEY'VE SIGHTED SOME OTHER POOR UNFORTUNATE.
IT WASN'T ME THEY WERE LOOKING FOR. NOT THIS TIME.
THEN, WHY SHOULD THEY?

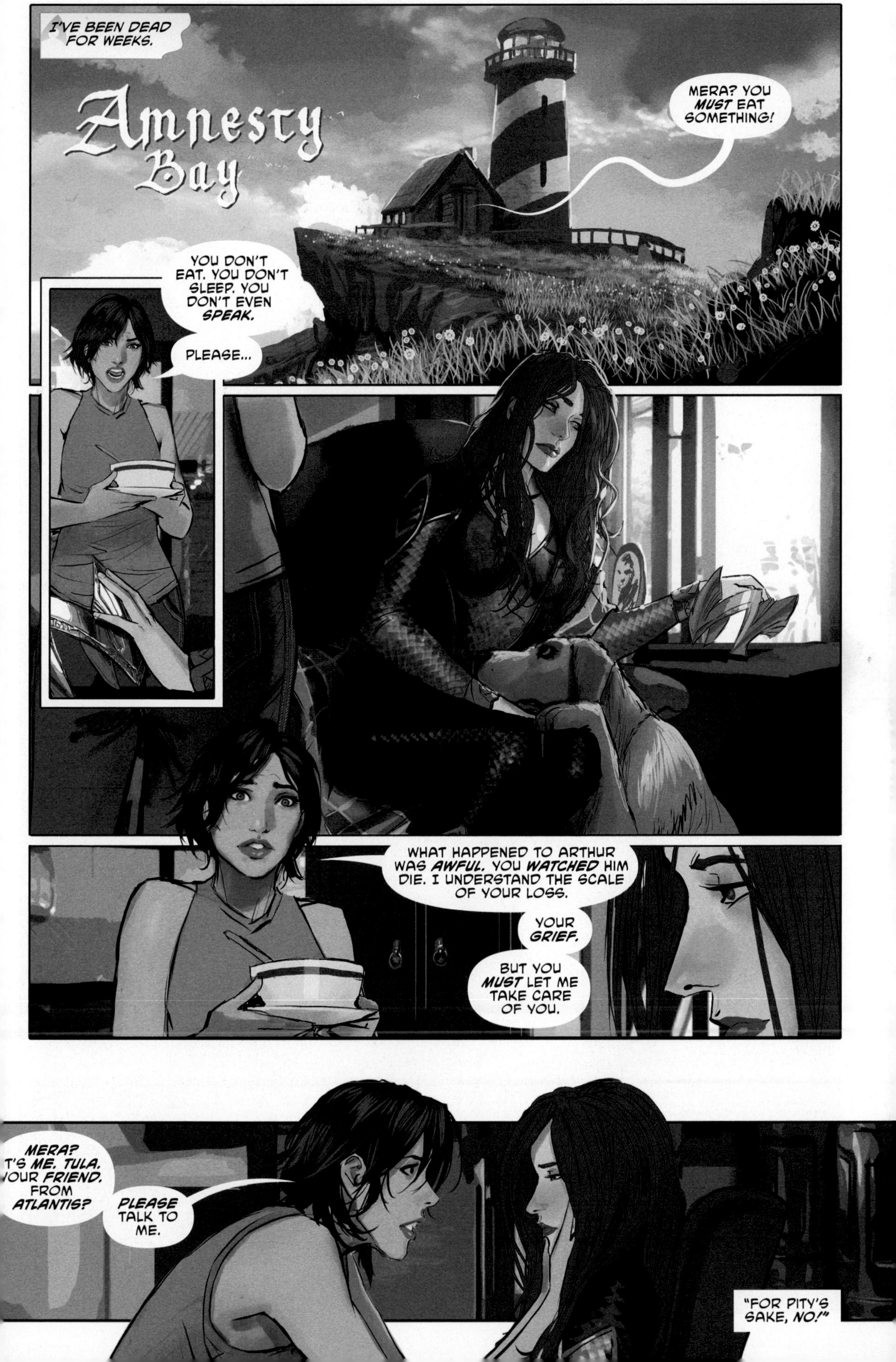
I'VE BEEN DEAD FOR WEEKS.
Amnesty Bay
MERA? YOU *MUST* EAT SOMETHING!
YOU DON'T EAT. YOU DON'T SLEEP. YOU DON'T EVEN *SPEAK.*
PLEASE...
WHAT HAPPENED TO ARTHUR WAS *AWFUL.* YOU *WATCHED* HIM DIE. I UNDERSTAND THE SCALE OF YOUR LOSS.
YOUR *GRIEF.*
BUT YOU *MUST* LET ME TAKE CARE OF YOU.
MERA? IT'S *ME.* TULA. YOUR *FRIEND.* FROM *ATLANTIS?*
PLEASE TALK TO ME.
"FOR PITY'S SAKE, *NO!*"

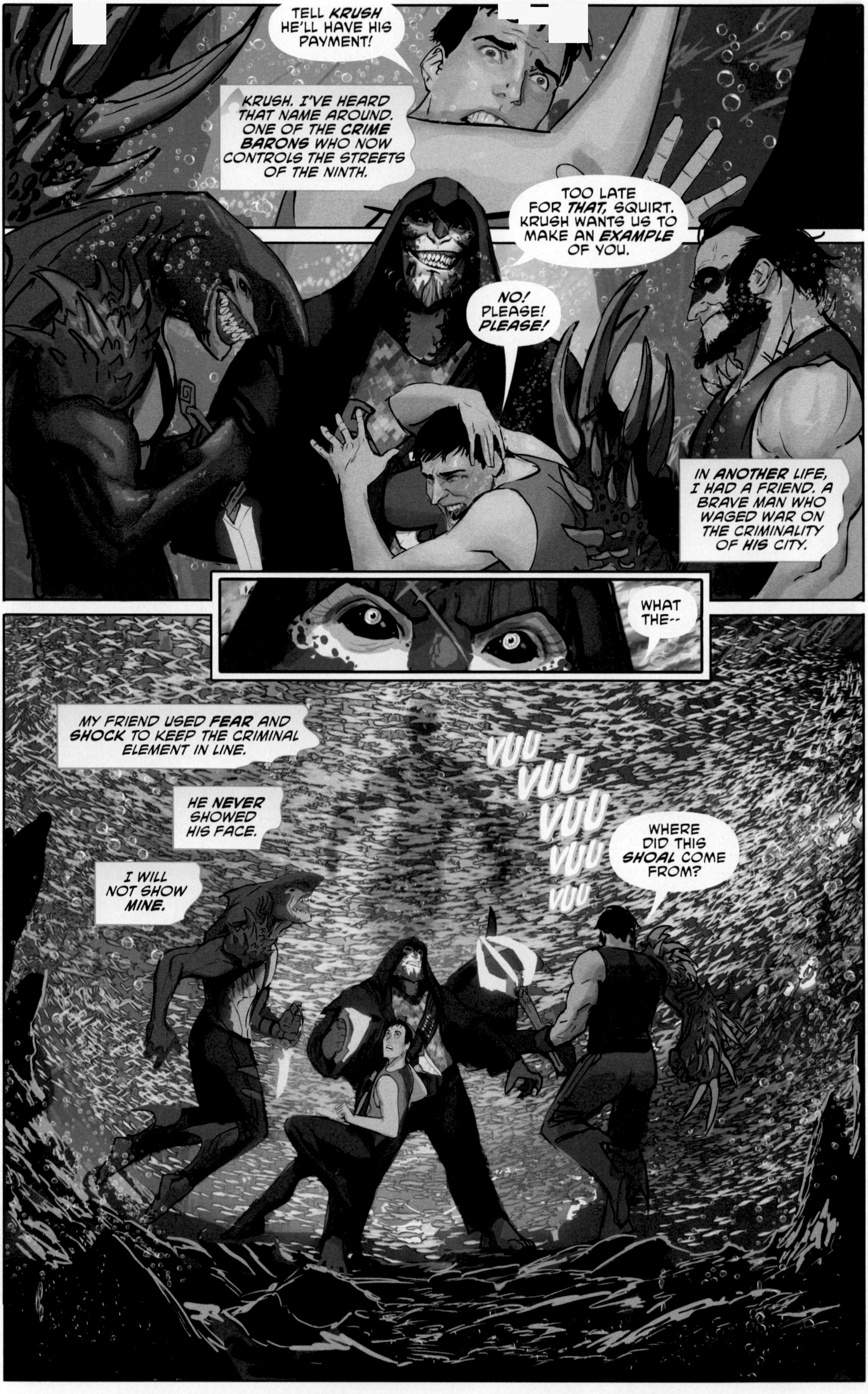
TELL KRUSH HE'LL HAVE HIS PAYMENT!
KRUSH. I'VE HEARD THAT NAME AROUND. ONE OF THE CRIME BARONS WHO NOW CONTROLS THE STREETS OF THE NINTH.
TOO LATE FOR THAT, SQUIRT. KRUSH WANTS US TO MAKE AN EXAMPLE OF YOU.
NO! PLEASE! PLEASE!
IN ANOTHER LIFE, I HAD A FRIEND. A BRAVE MAN WHO WAGED WAR ON THE CRIMINALITY OF HIS CITY.
WHAT THE--
MY FRIEND USED FEAR AND SHOCK TO KEEP THE CRIMINAL ELEMENT IN LINE.
HE NEVER SHOWED HIS FACE.
I WILL NOT SHOW MINE.
VUU VUU VUU VUU VUU
WHERE DID THIS SHOAL COME FROM?

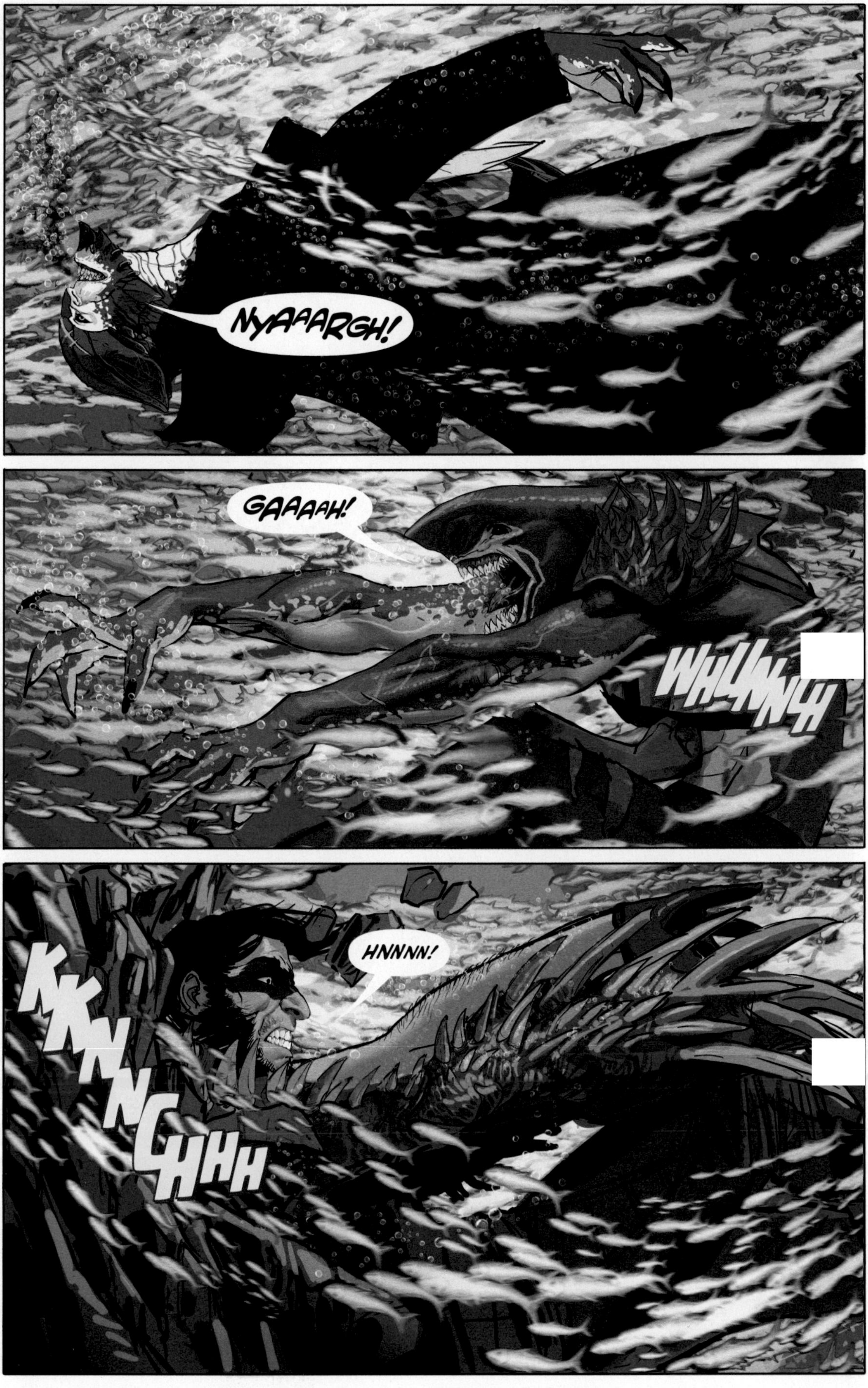
NYAAARGH!
GAAAAH!
WHUMNCH
HNNNN!
KKNNCHHH

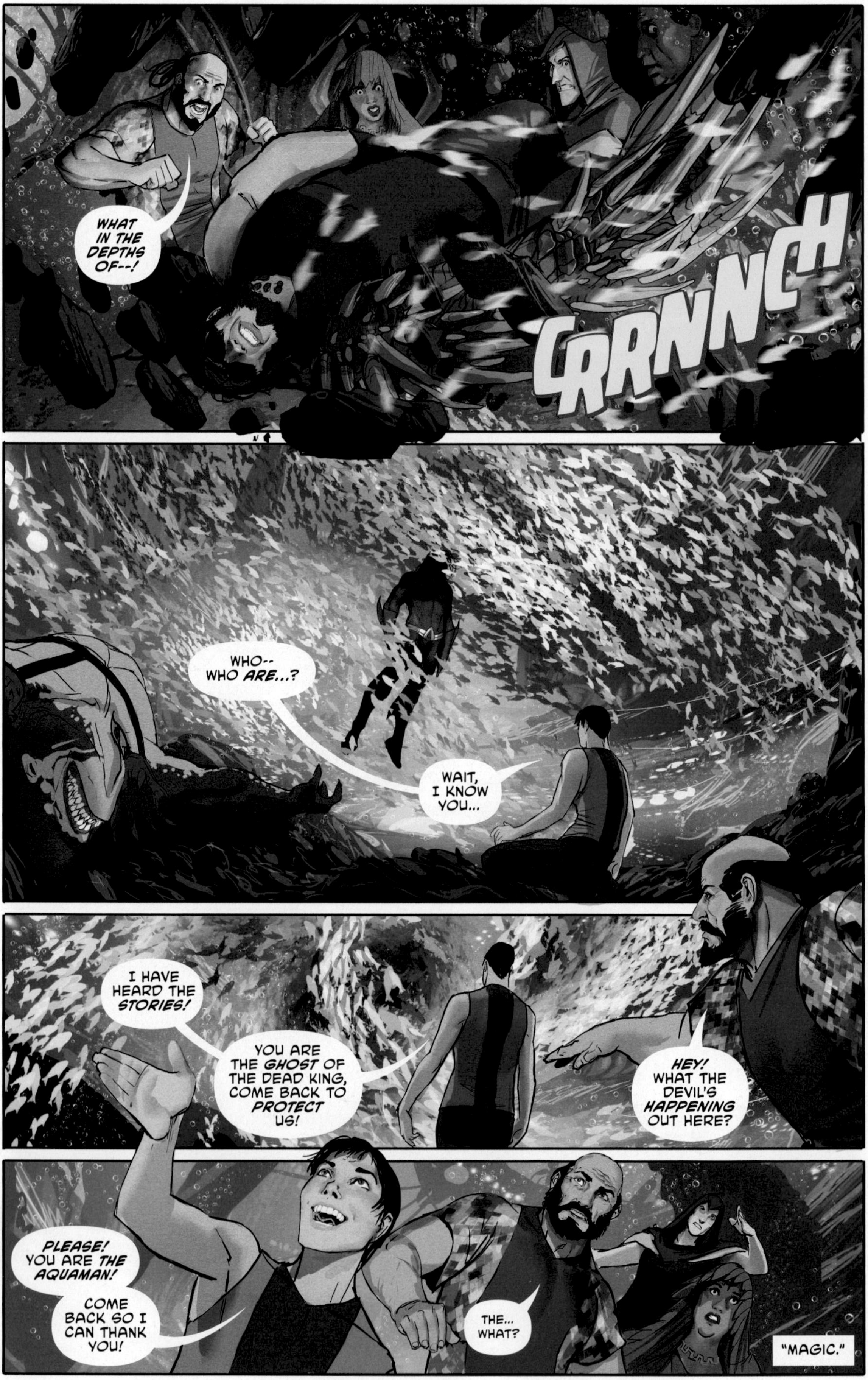
WHAT IN THE DEPTHS OF--!
CRRNNCH
WHO-- WHO ARE...?
WAIT, I KNOW YOU...
I HAVE HEARD THE STORIES!
YOU ARE THE GHOST OF THE DEAD KING, COME BACK TO PROTECT US!
HEY! WHAT THE DEVIL'S HAPPENING OUT HERE?
PLEASE! YOU ARE THE AQUAMAN!
COME BACK SO I CAN THANK YOU!
THE... WHAT?
"MAGIC."

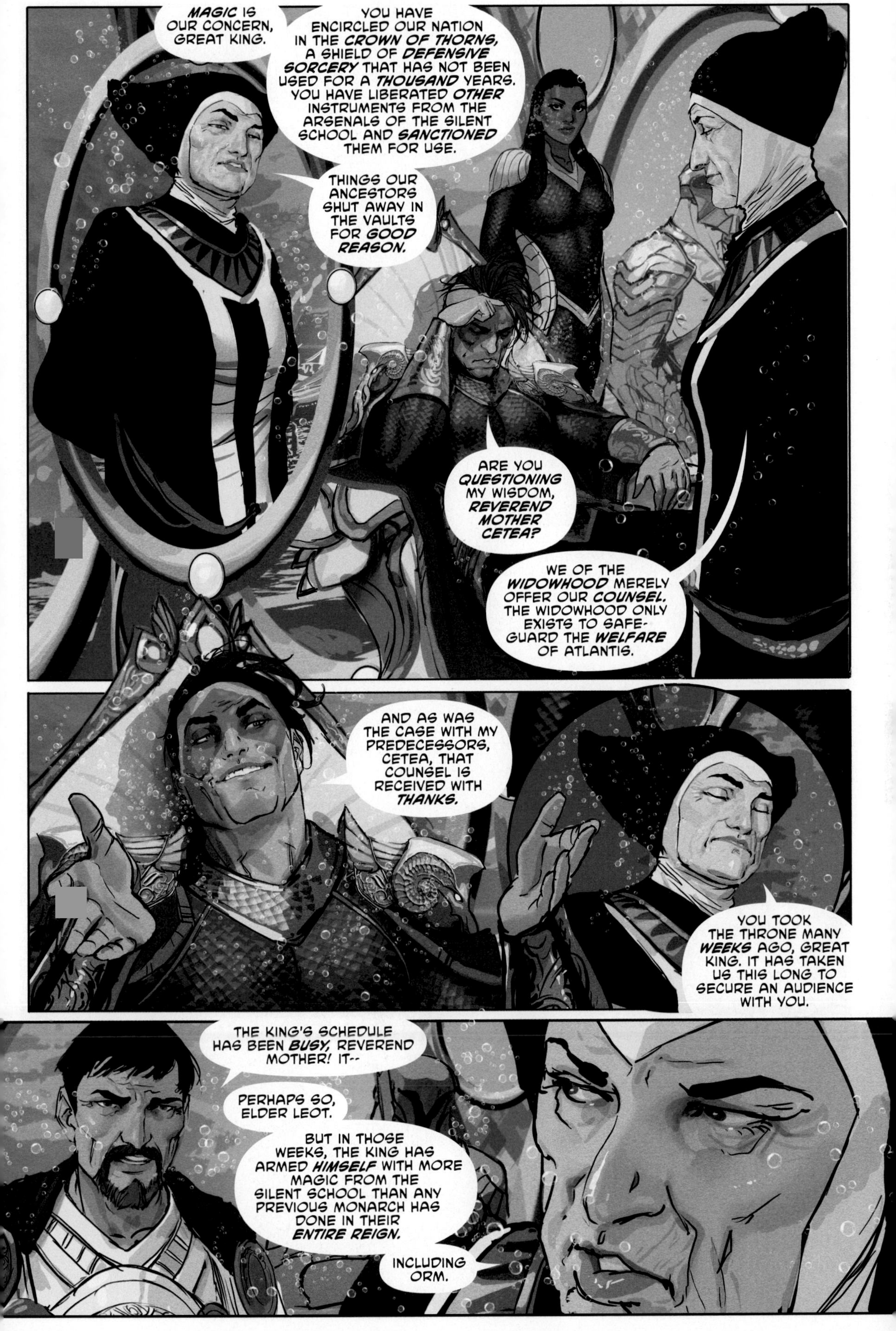
MAGIC IS OUR CONCERN, GREAT KING.
YOU HAVE ENCIRCLED OUR NATION IN THE CROWN OF THORNS, A SHIELD OF DEFENSIVE SORCERY THAT HAS NOT BEEN USED FOR A THOUSAND YEARS. YOU HAVE LIBERATED OTHER INSTRUMENTS FROM THE ARSENALS OF THE SILENT SCHOOL AND SANCTIONED THEM FOR USE.
THINGS OUR ANCESTORS SHUT AWAY IN THE VAULTS FOR GOOD REASON.
ARE YOU QUESTIONING MY WISDOM, REVEREND MOTHER CETEA?
WE OF THE WIDOWHOOD MERELY OFFER OUR COUNSEL. THE WIDOWHOOD ONLY EXISTS TO SAFE-GUARD THE WELFARE OF ATLANTIS.
AND AS WAS THE CASE WITH MY PREDECESSORS, CETEA, THAT COUNSEL IS RECEIVED WITH THANKS.
YOU TOOK THE THRONE MANY WEEKS AGO, GREAT KING. IT HAS TAKEN US THIS LONG TO SECURE AN AUDIENCE WITH YOU.
THE KING'S SCHEDULE HAS BEEN BUSY, REVEREND MOTHER! IT--
PERHAPS SO, ELDER LEOT.
BUT IN THOSE WEEKS, THE KING HAS ARMED HIMSELF WITH MORE MAGIC FROM THE SILENT SCHOOL THAN ANY PREVIOUS MONARCH HAS DONE IN THEIR ENTIRE REIGN.
INCLUDING ORM.

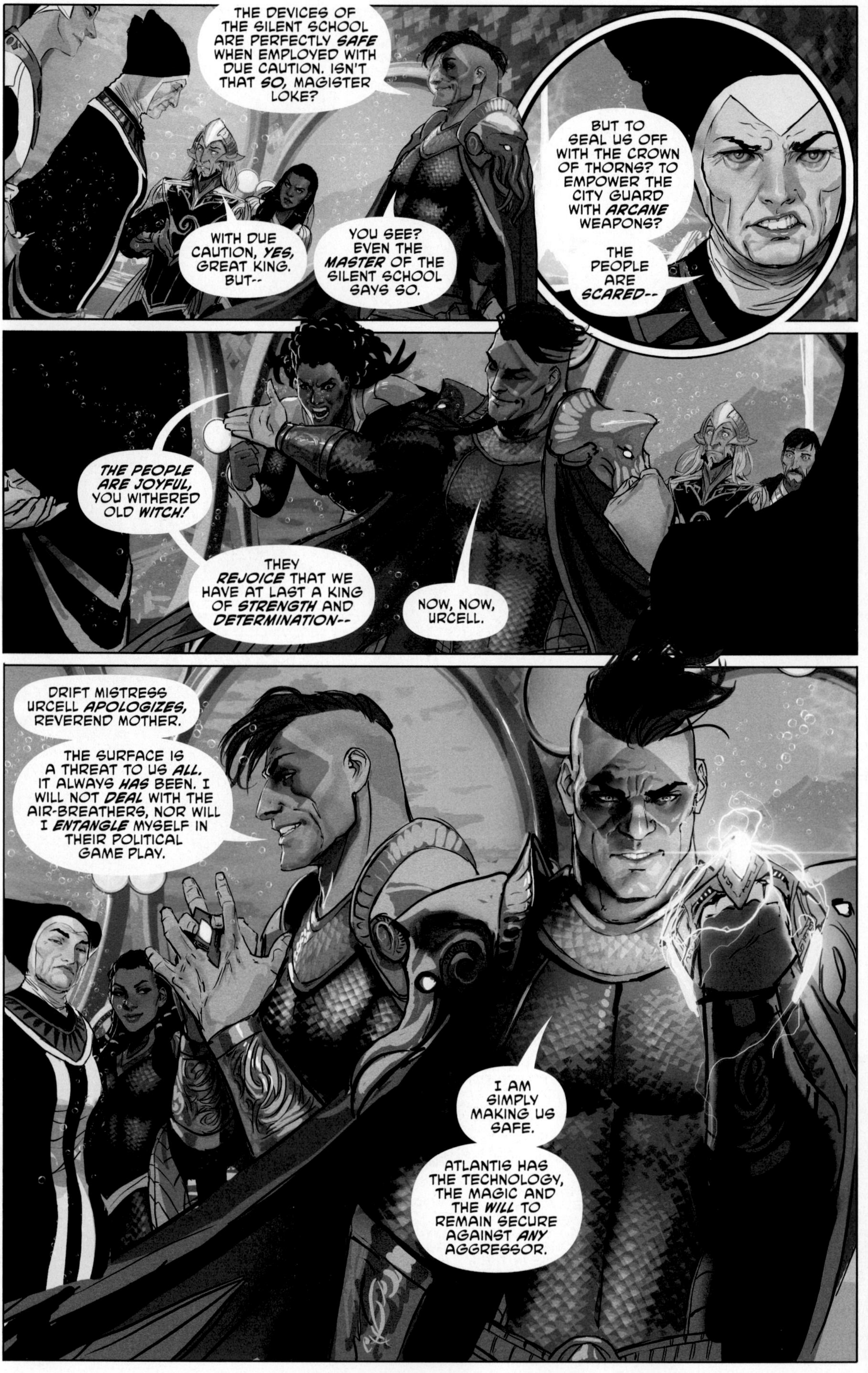
THE DEVICES OF THE SILENT SCHOOL ARE PERFECTLY *SAFE* WHEN EMPLOYED WITH DUE CAUTION. ISN'T THAT *SO*, MAGISTER LOKE?
WITH DUE CAUTION, *YES*, GREAT KING. BUT--
YOU SEE? EVEN THE *MASTER* OF THE SILENT SCHOOL SAYS SO.
BUT TO SEAL US OFF WITH THE CROWN OF THORNS? TO EMPOWER THE CITY GUARD WITH *ARCANE* WEAPONS?
THE PEOPLE ARE *SCARED*--
THE PEOPLE ARE JOYFUL, YOU WITHERED OLD *WITCH!*
THEY *REJOICE* THAT WE HAVE AT LAST A KING OF *STRENGTH* AND *DETERMINATION*--
NOW, NOW, URCELL.
DRIFT MISTRESS URCELL *APOLOGIZES*, REVEREND MOTHER.
THE SURFACE IS A THREAT TO US *ALL*. IT ALWAYS *HAS* BEEN. I WILL NOT *DEAL* WITH THE AIR-BREATHERS, NOR WILL I *ENTANGLE* MYSELF IN THEIR POLITICAL GAME PLAY.
I AM SIMPLY MAKING US SAFE.
ATLANTIS HAS THE TECHNOLOGY, THE MAGIC AND THE *WILL* TO REMAIN SECURE AGAINST *ANY* AGGRESSOR.

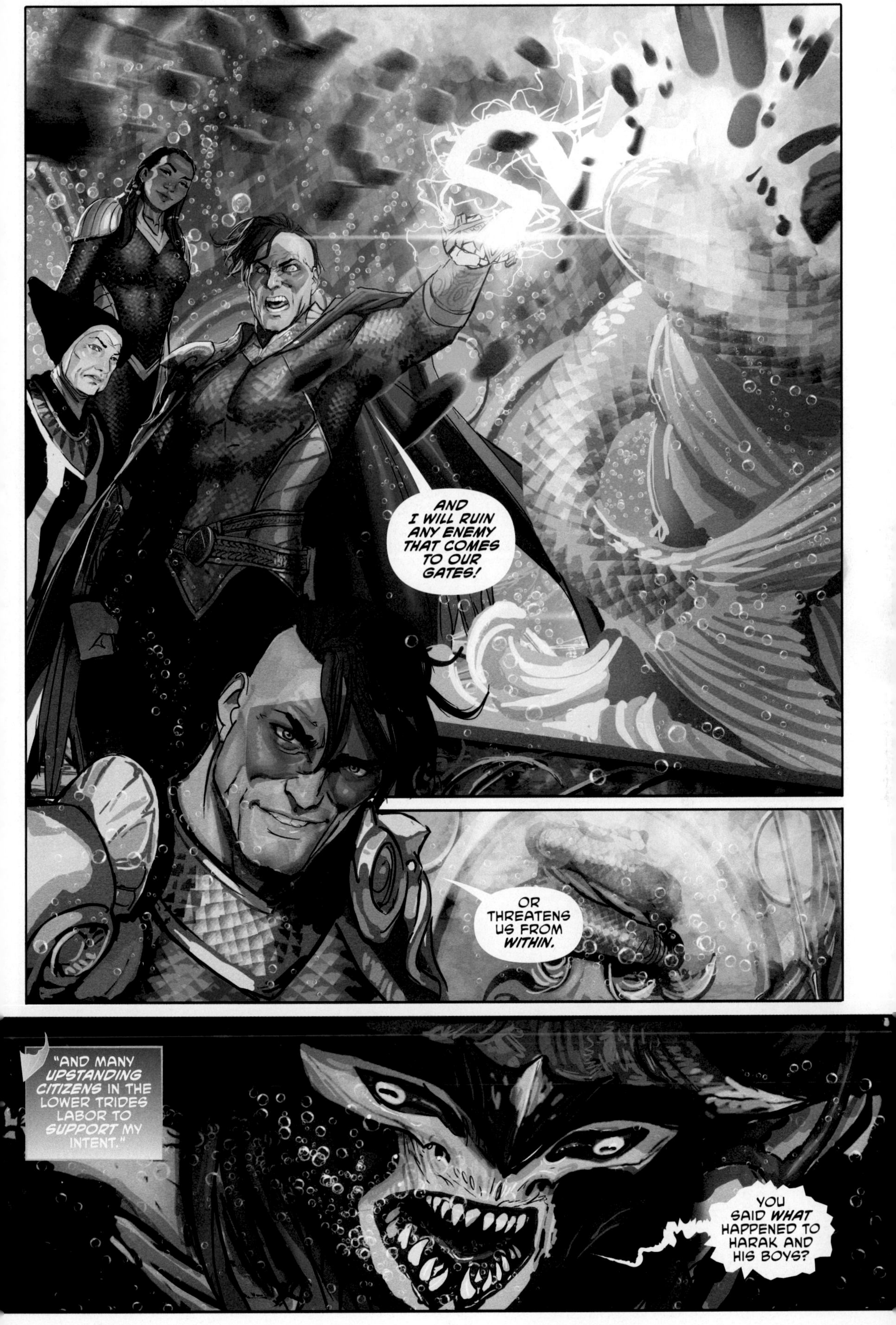
AND I WILL RUIN ANY ENEMY THAT COMES TO OUR GATES!
OR THREATENS US FROM WITHIN.
"AND MANY UPSTANDING CITIZENS IN THE LOWER TRIDES LABOR TO SUPPORT MY INTENT."
YOU SAID WHAT HAPPENED TO HARAK AND HIS BOYS?

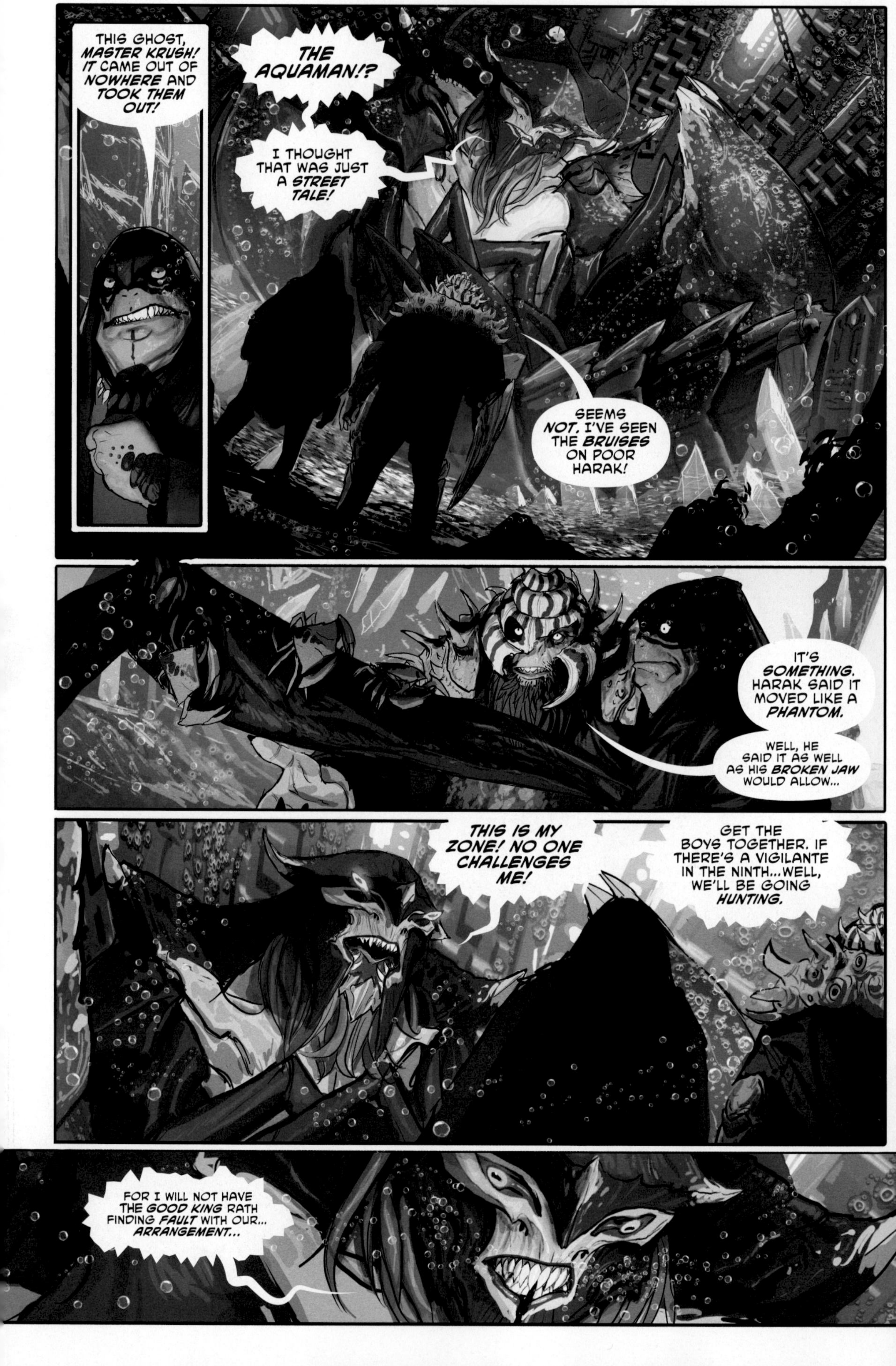
THIS GHOST, MASTER KRUSH! IT CAME OUT OF NOWHERE AND TOOK THEM OUT!
THE AQUAMAN!?
I THOUGHT THAT WAS JUST A STREET TALE!
SEEMS NOT. I'VE SEEN THE BRUISES ON POOR HARAK!
IT'S SOMETHING. HARAK SAID IT MOVED LIKE A PHANTOM.
WELL, HE SAID IT AS WELL AS HIS BROKEN JAW WOULD ALLOW...
THIS IS MY ZONE! NO ONE CHALLENGES ME!
GET THE BOYS TOGETHER. IF THERE'S A VIGILANTE IN THE NINTH...WELL, WE'LL BE GOING HUNTING.
FOR I WILL NOT HAVE THE GOOD KING RATH FINDING FAULT WITH OUR... ARRANGEMENT...

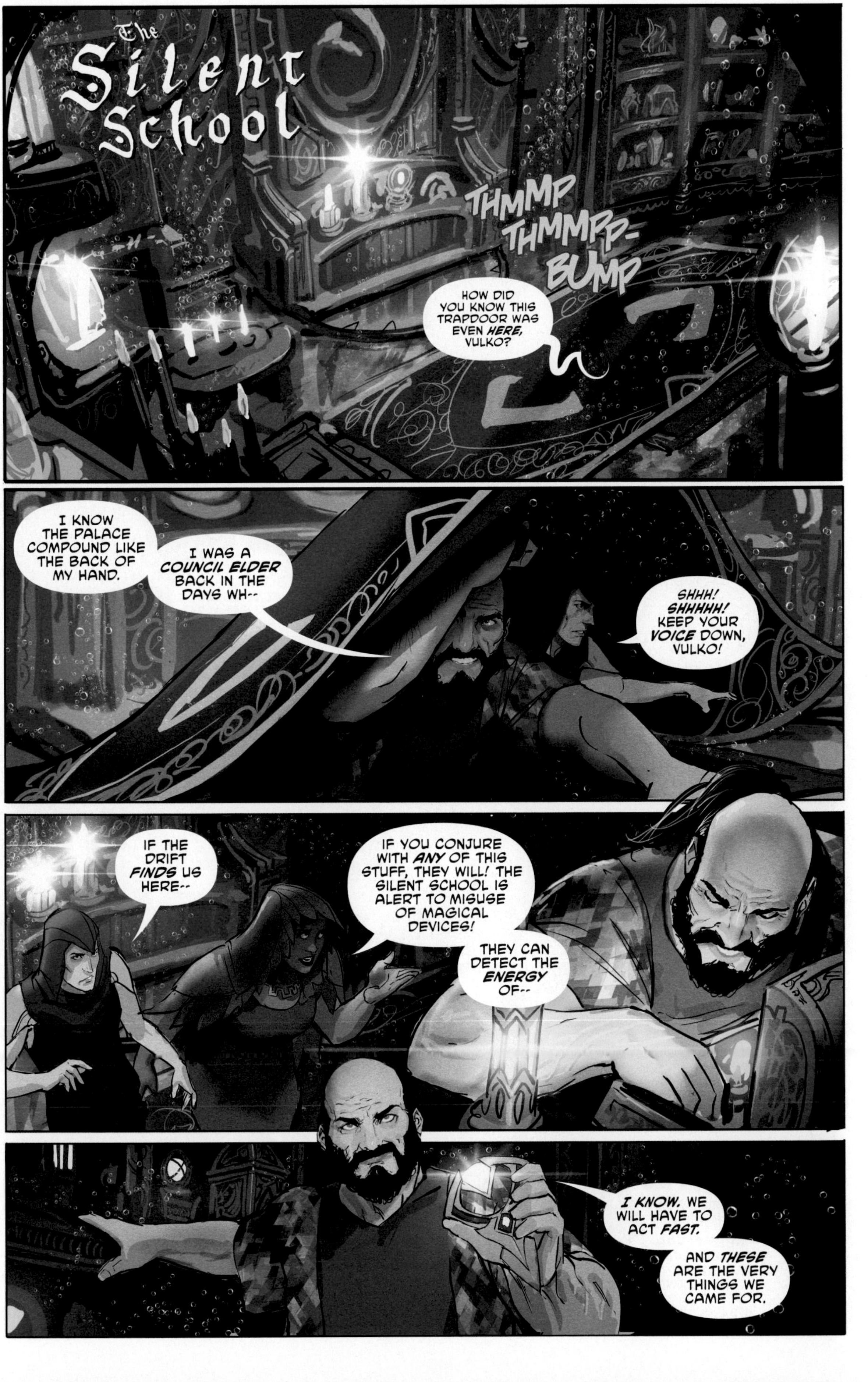
The Silent School
THMMP THMMPP-BUMP
HOW DID YOU KNOW THIS TRAPDOOR WAS EVEN *HERE,* VULKO?
I KNOW THE PALACE COMPOUND LIKE THE BACK OF MY HAND.
I WAS A *COUNCIL ELDER* BACK IN THE DAYS WH--
SHHH! SHHHHH! KEEP YOUR *VOICE* DOWN, VULKO!
IF THE DRIFT *FINDS* US HERE--
IF YOU CONJURE WITH *ANY* OF THIS STUFF, THEY WILL! THE SILENT SCHOOL IS ALERT TO MISUSE OF MAGICAL DEVICES!
THEY CAN DETECT THE *ENERGY* OF--
I KNOW. WE WILL HAVE TO ACT *FAST.*
AND *THESE* ARE THE VERY THINGS WE CAME FOR.

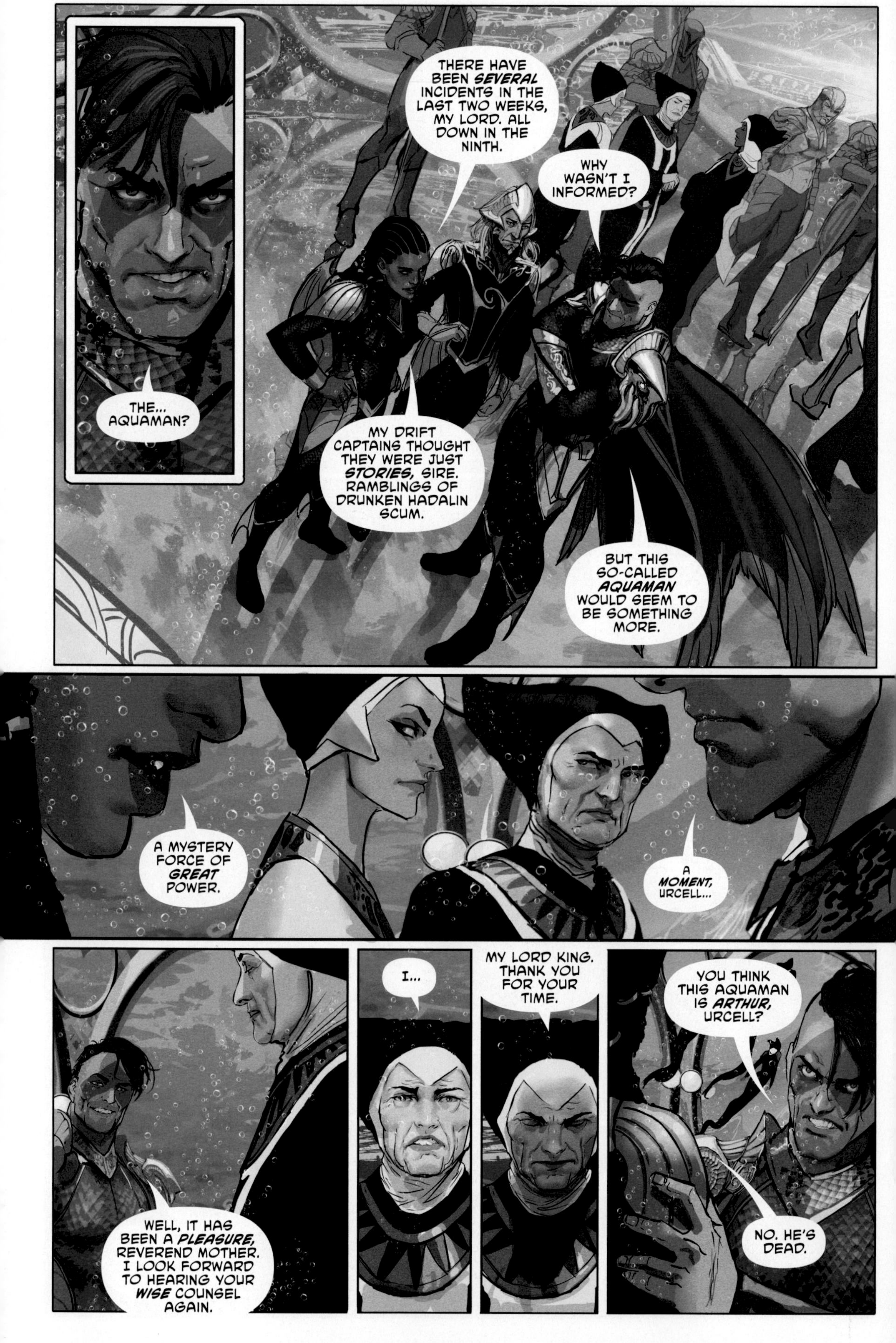
THE... AQUAMAN?
THERE HAVE BEEN SEVERAL INCIDENTS IN THE LAST TWO WEEKS, MY LORD. ALL DOWN IN THE NINTH.
WHY WASN'T I INFORMED?
MY DRIFT CAPTAINS THOUGHT THEY WERE JUST STORIES, SIRE. RAMBLINGS OF DRUNKEN HADALIN SCUM.
BUT THIS SO-CALLED AQUAMAN WOULD SEEM TO BE SOMETHING MORE.
A MYSTERY FORCE OF GREAT POWER.
A MOMENT, URCELL...
WELL, IT HAS BEEN A PLEASURE, REVEREND MOTHER. I LOOK FORWARD TO HEARING YOUR WISE COUNSEL AGAIN.
I...
MY LORD KING. THANK YOU FOR YOUR TIME.
YOU THINK THIS AQUAMAN IS ARTHUR, URCELL?
NO. HE'S DEAD.

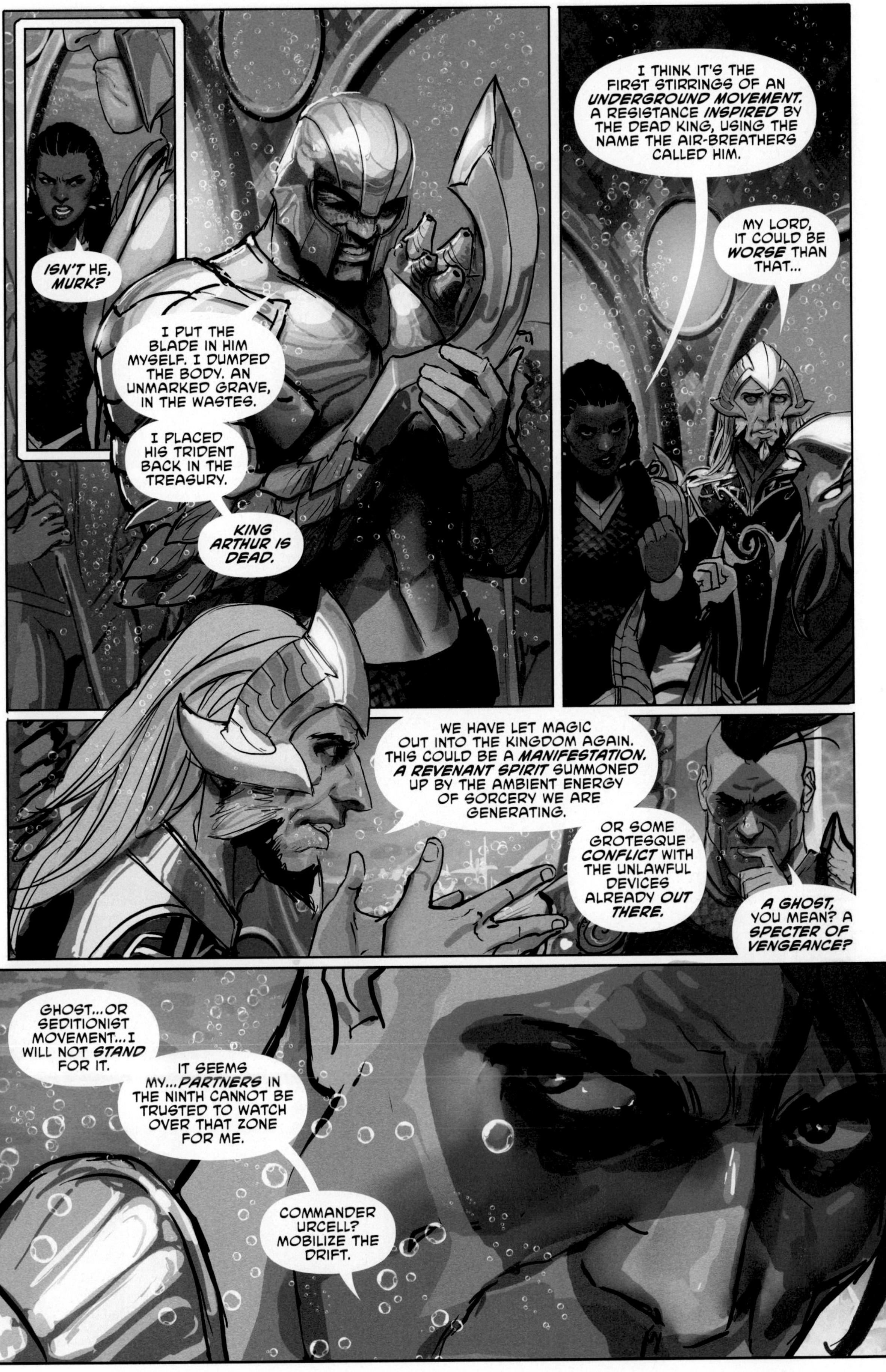

ISN'T HE, MURK?
I PUT THE BLADE IN HIM MYSELF. I DUMPED THE BODY. AN UNMARKED GRAVE, IN THE WASTES.
I PLACED HIS TRIDENT BACK IN THE TREASURY.
KING ARTHUR IS DEAD.
I THINK IT'S THE FIRST STIRRINGS OF AN UNDERGROUND MOVEMENT. A RESISTANCE INSPIRED BY THE DEAD KING, USING THE NAME THE AIR-BREATHERS CALLED HIM.
MY LORD, IT COULD BE WORSE THAN THAT...
WE HAVE LET MAGIC OUT INTO THE KINGDOM AGAIN. THIS COULD BE A MANIFESTATION. A REVENANT SPIRIT SUMMONED UP BY THE AMBIENT ENERGY OF SORCERY WE ARE GENERATING.
OR SOME GROTESQUE CONFLICT WITH THE UNLAWFUL DEVICES ALREADY OUT THERE.
A GHOST, YOU MEAN? A SPECTER OF VENGEANCE?
GHOST...OR SEDITIONIST MOVEMENT...I WILL NOT STAND FOR IT.
IT SEEMS MY...PARTNERS IN THE NINTH CANNOT BE TRUSTED TO WATCH OVER THAT ZONE FOR ME.
COMMANDER URCELL? MOBILIZE THE DRIFT.

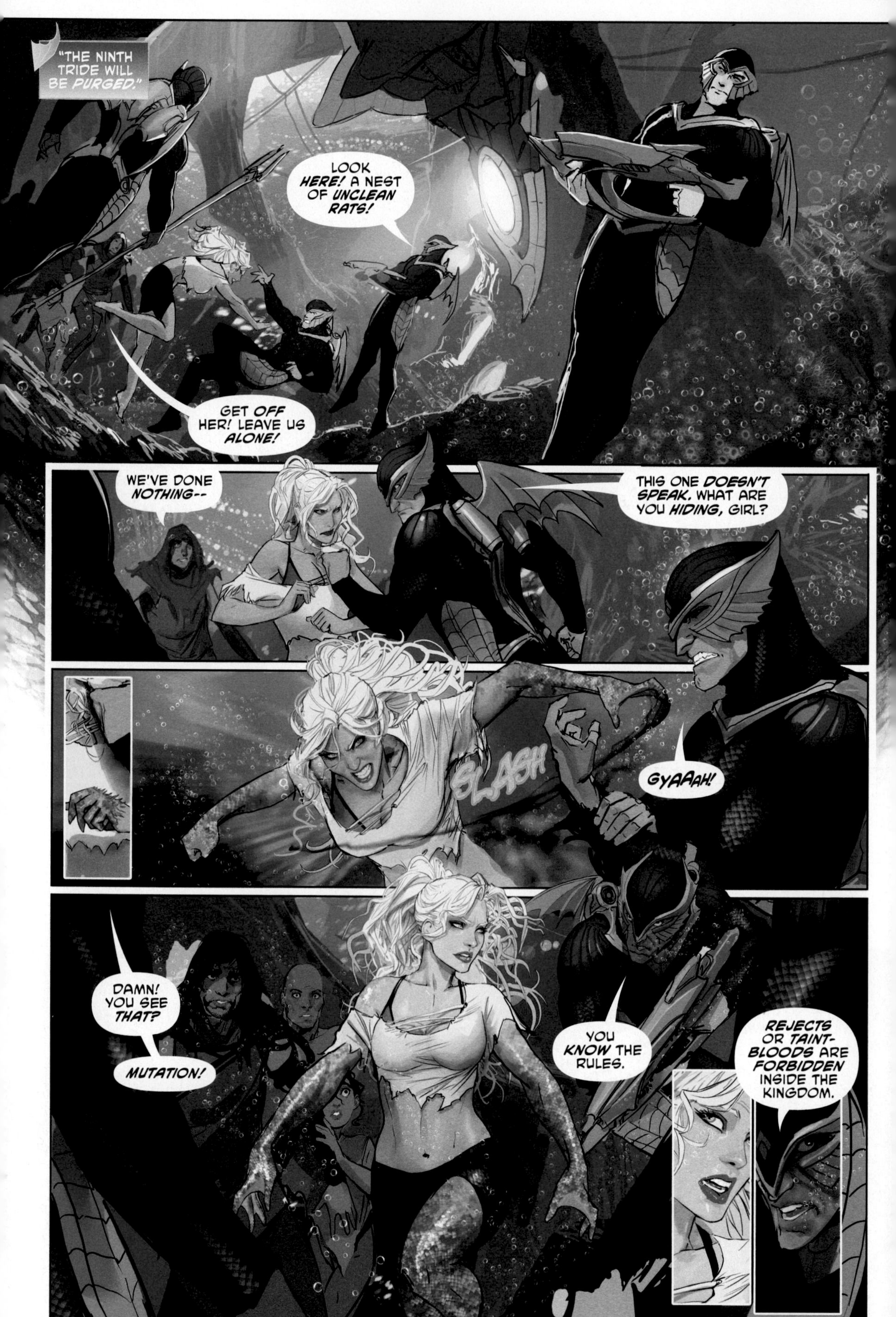
"THE NINTH TRIDE WILL BE PURGED."
LOOK HERE! A NEST OF UNCLEAN RATS!
GET OFF HER! LEAVE US ALONE!
WE'VE DONE NOTHING--
THIS ONE DOESN'T SPEAK. WHAT ARE YOU HIDING, GIRL?
SLASH
GYAAAH!
DAMN! YOU SEE THAT?
MUTATION!
YOU KNOW THE RULES.
REJECTS OR TAINT-BLOODS ARE FORBIDDEN INSIDE THE KINGDOM.

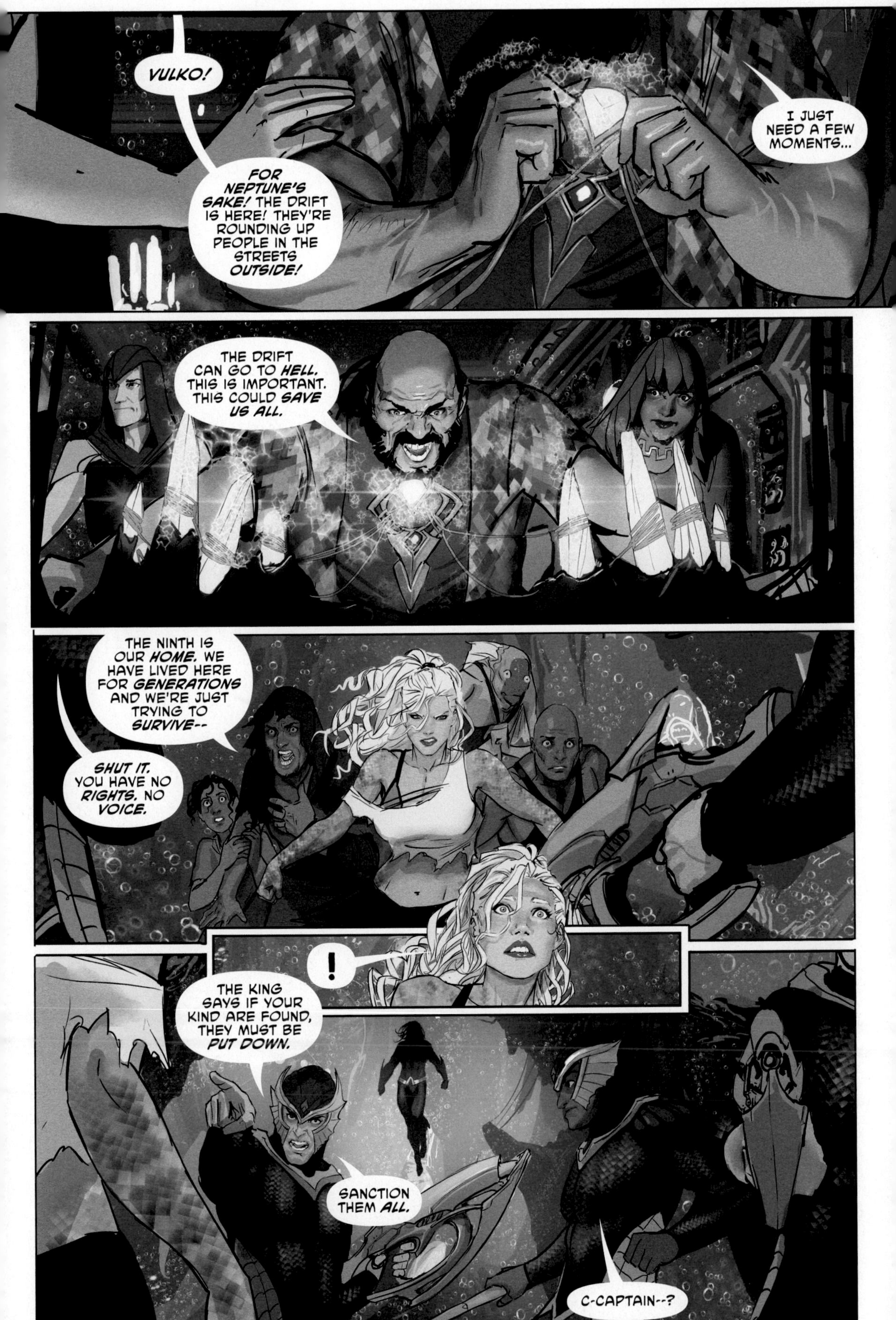
VULKO!
FOR NEPTUNE'S SAKE! THE DRIFT IS HERE! THEY'RE ROUNDING UP PEOPLE IN THE STREETS OUTSIDE!
I JUST NEED A FEW MOMENTS...
THE DRIFT CAN GO TO HELL. THIS IS IMPORTANT. THIS COULD SAVE US ALL.
THE NINTH IS OUR HOME. WE HAVE LIVED HERE FOR GENERATIONS AND WE'RE JUST TRYING TO SURVIVE--
SHUT IT. YOU HAVE NO RIGHTS. NO VOICE.
!
THE KING SAYS IF YOUR KIND ARE FOUND, THEY MUST BE PUT DOWN.
SANCTION THEM ALL.
C-CAPTAIN--?

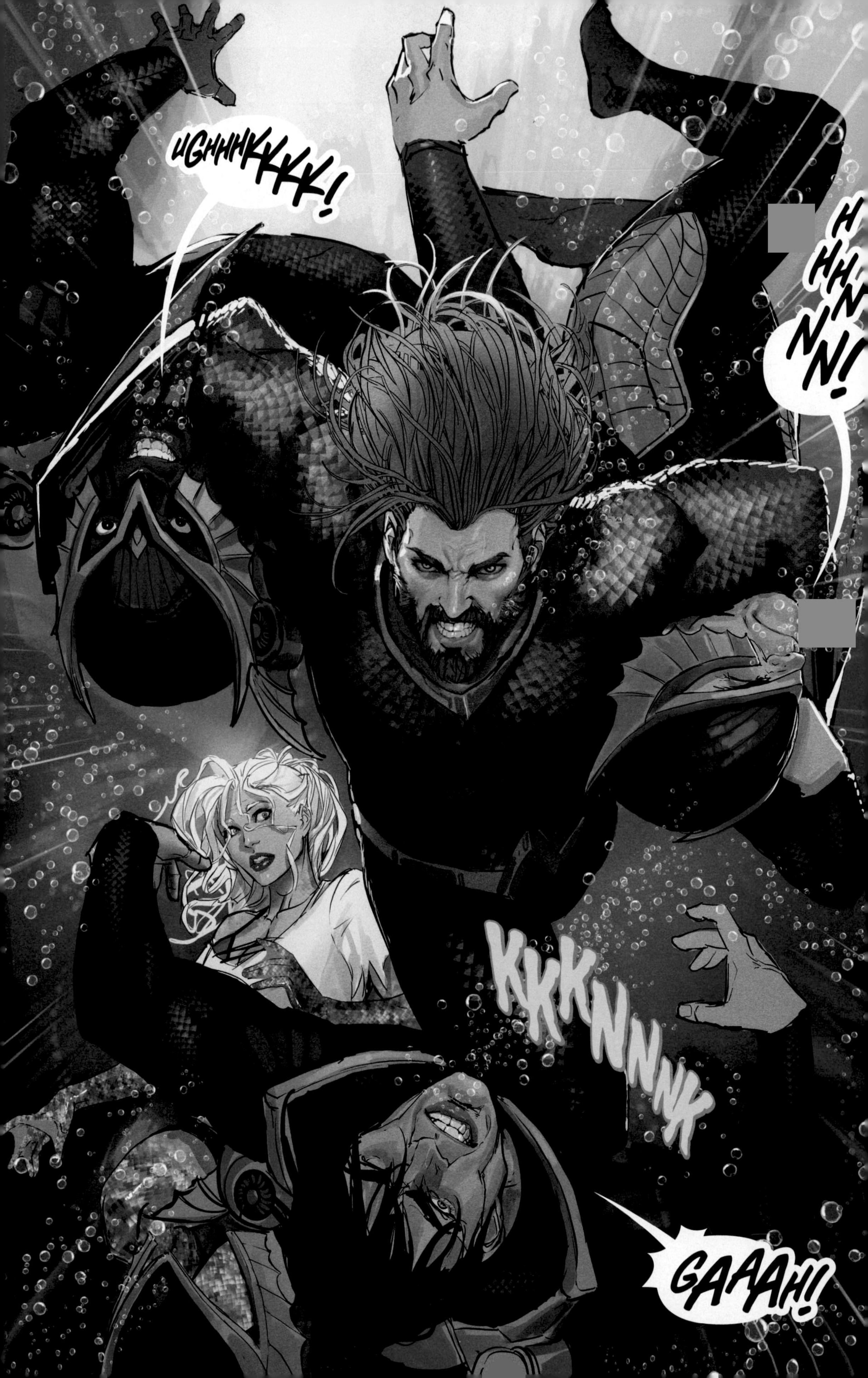
UGHHHKKKK!
HHHNNN!
KKKNNNNK
GAAAH!

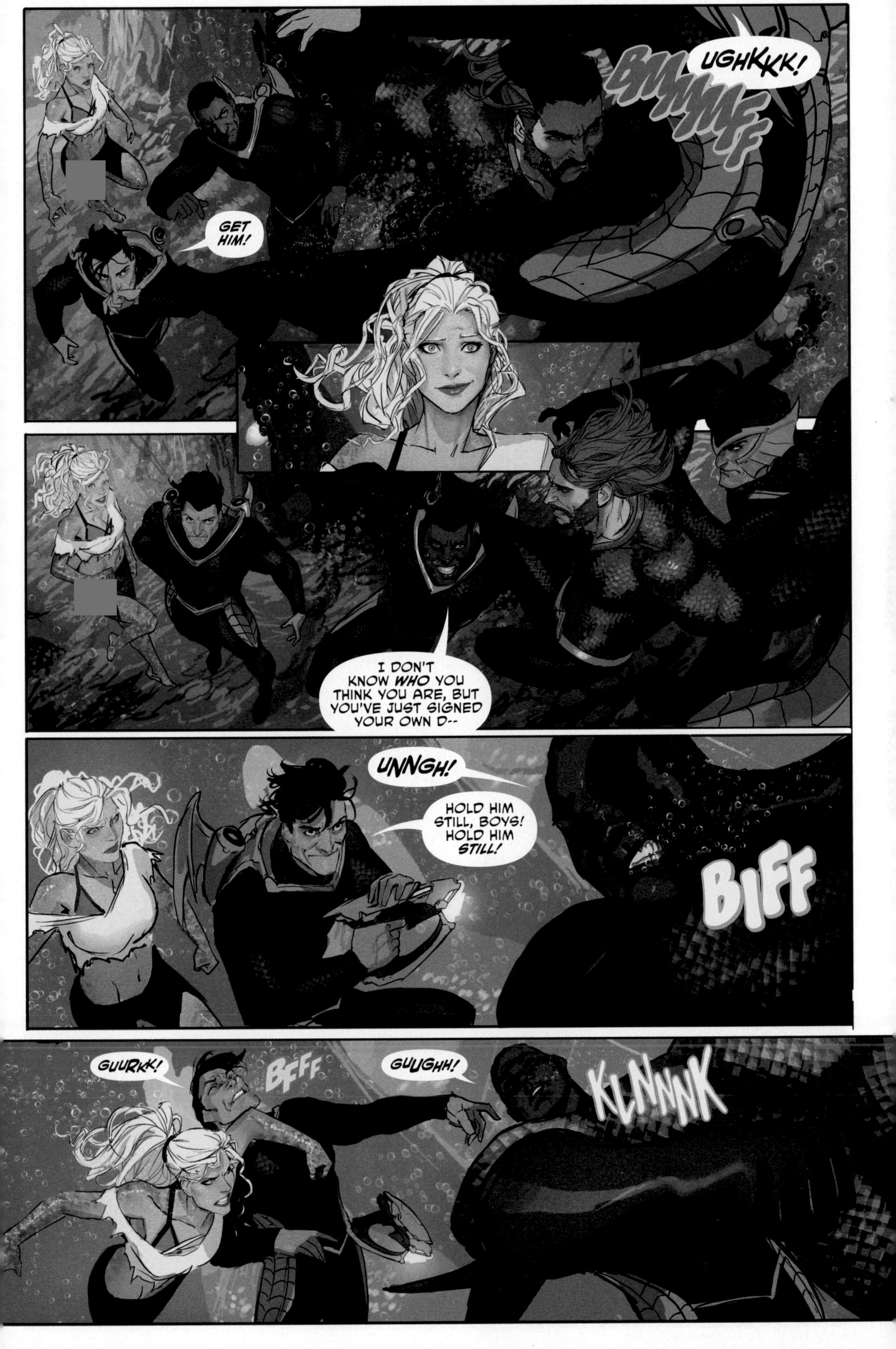
UGHKKK!
BMMMFF
GET HIM!
I DON'T KNOW WHO YOU THINK YOU ARE, BUT YOU'VE JUST SIGNED YOUR OWN D--
UNNGH!
HOLD HIM STILL, BOYS! HOLD HIM STILL!
BIFF
GUURKK!
BFFF
GUUGHH!
KLNNNK

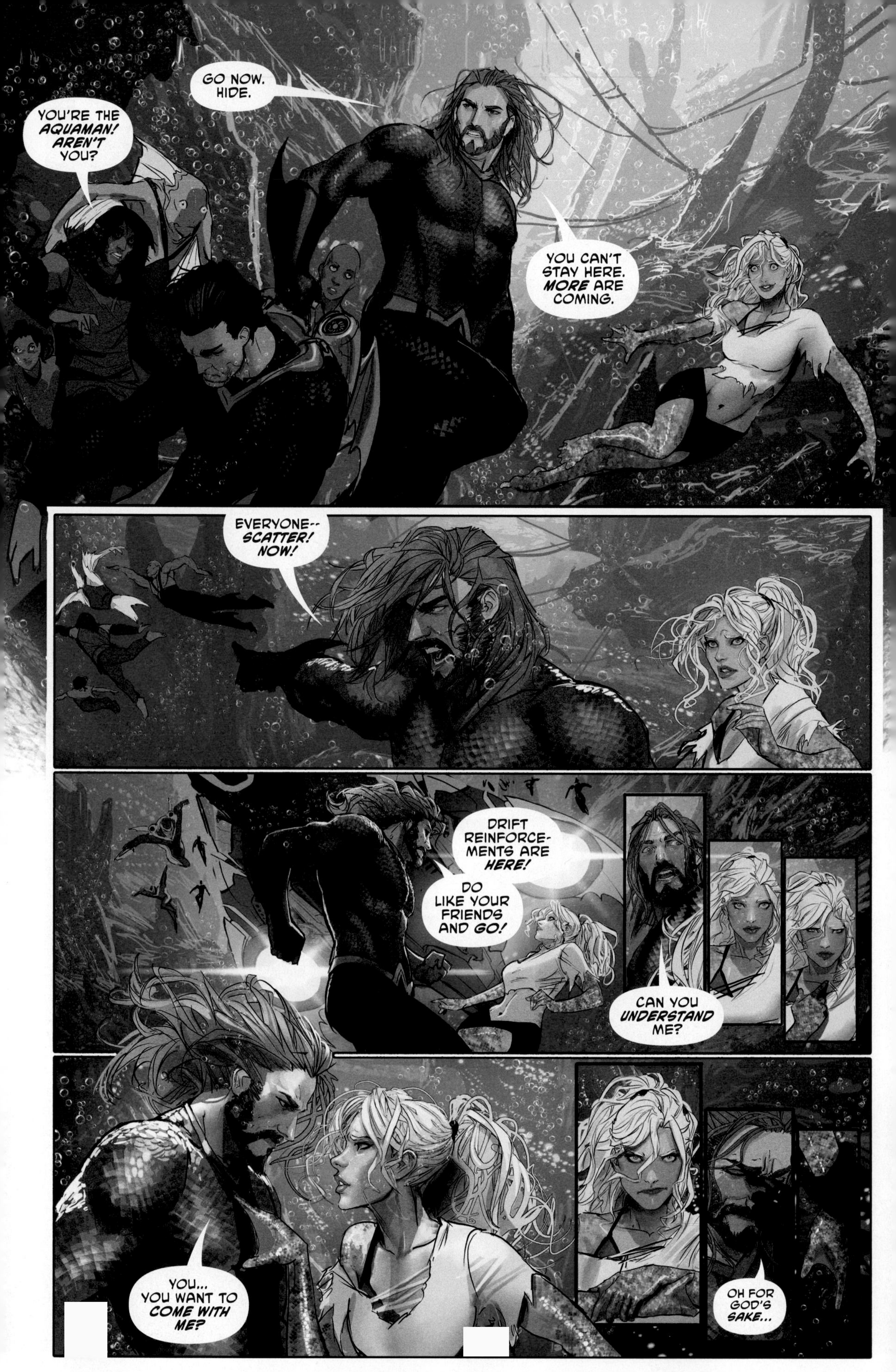
GO NOW. HIDE.
YOU'RE THE AQUAMAN! AREN'T YOU?
YOU CAN'T STAY HERE. MORE ARE COMING.
EVERYONE-- SCATTER! NOW!
DRIFT REINFORCE-MENTS ARE HERE!
DO LIKE YOUR FRIENDS AND GO!
CAN YOU UNDERSTAND ME?
YOU... YOU WANT TO COME WITH ME?
OH FOR GOD'S SAKE...

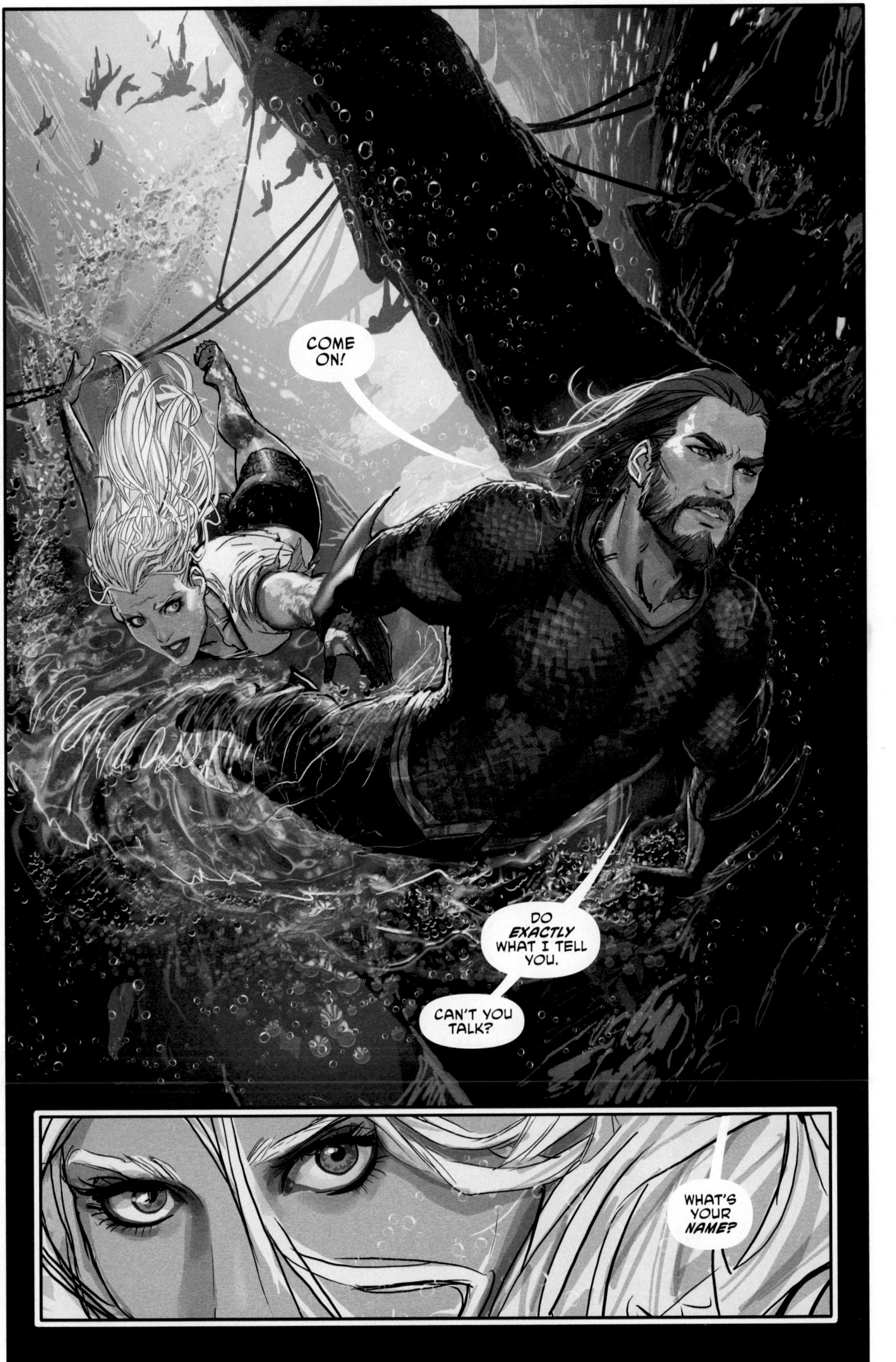
COME ON!
DO *EXACTLY* WHAT I TELL YOU.
CAN'T YOU TALK?
WHAT'S YOUR *NAME?*

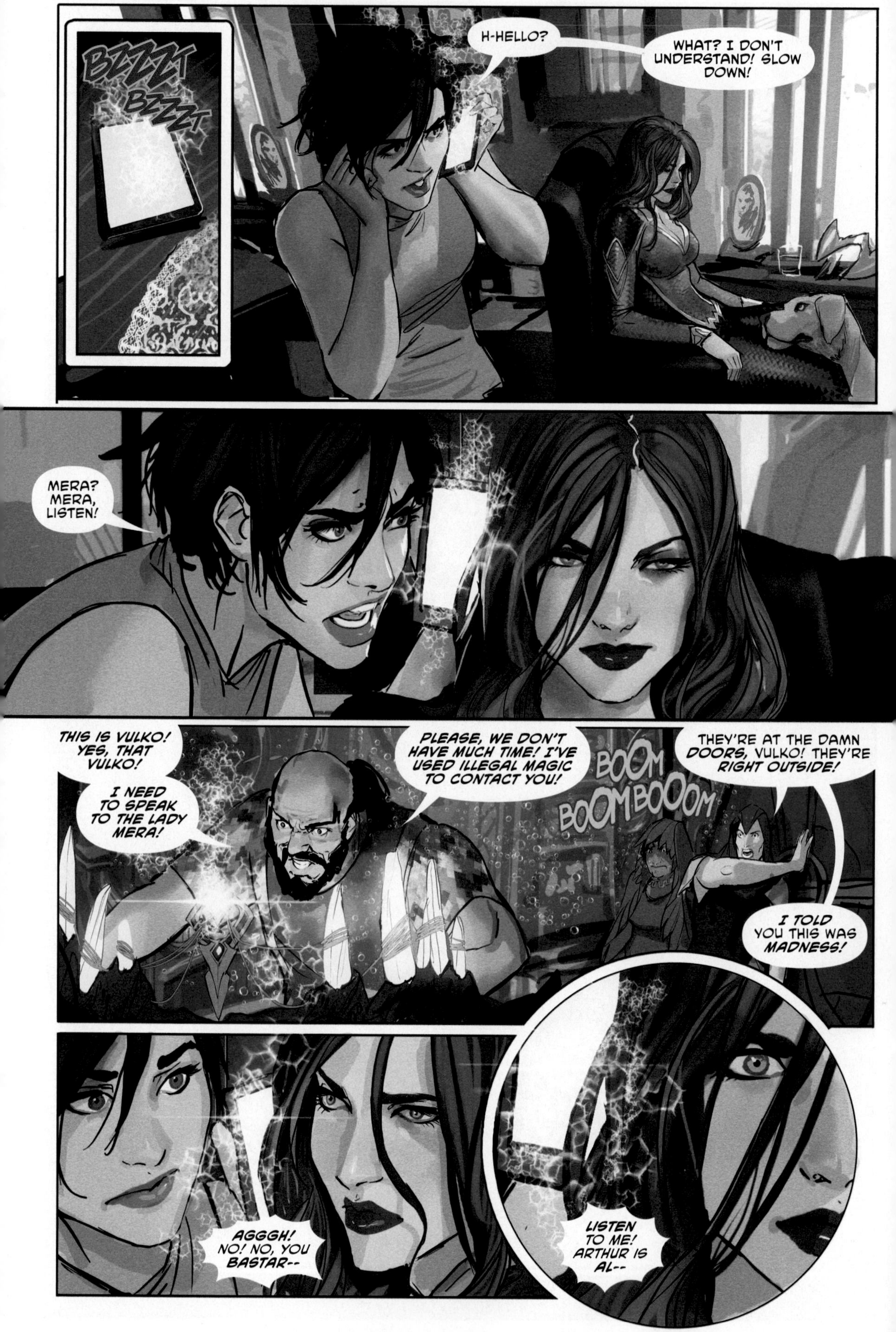
BZZZZT BZZZZT
H-HELLO?
WHAT? I DON'T UNDERSTAND! SLOW DOWN!
MERA? MERA, LISTEN!
THIS IS VULKO! YES, THAT VULKO!
I NEED TO SPEAK TO THE LADY MERA!
PLEASE, WE DON'T HAVE MUCH TIME! I'VE USED ILLEGAL MAGIC TO CONTACT YOU!
BOOM BOOM BOOOM
THEY'RE AT THE DAMN DOORS, VULKO! THEY'RE RIGHT OUTSIDE!
I TOLD YOU THIS WAS MADNESS!
AGGGH! NO! NO, YOU BASTAR--
LISTEN TO ME! ARTHUR IS AL--

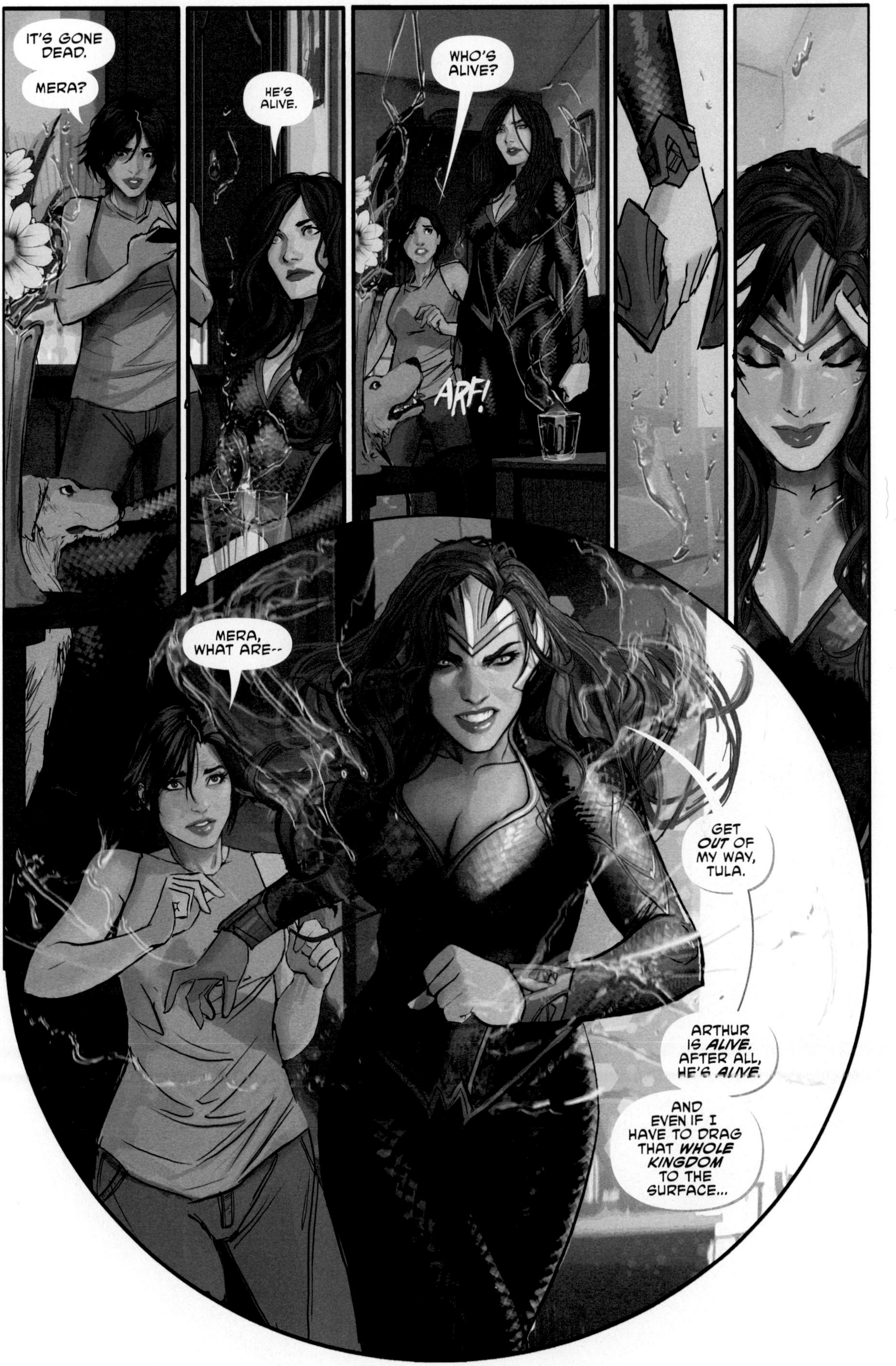
IT'S GONE DEAD.
MERA?
HE'S ALIVE.
WHO'S ALIVE?
ARF!
MERA, WHAT ARE--
GET OUT OF MY WAY, TULA.
ARTHUR IS ALIVE. AFTER ALL, HE'S ALIVE.
AND EVEN IF I HAVE TO DRAG THAT WHOLE KINGDOM TO THE SURFACE...

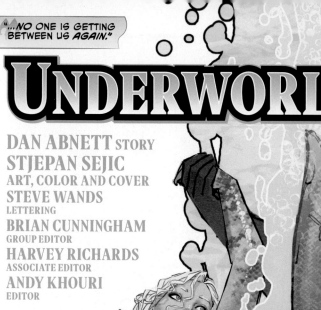

"...NO ONE IS GETTING BETWEEN US *AGAIN.*"

Underworld

DAN ABNETT STORY

STJEPAN SEJIC
ART, COLOR AND COVER

STEVE WANDS
LETTERING

BRIAN CUNNINGHAM
GROUP EDITOR

HARVEY RICHARDS
ASSOCIATE EDITOR

ANDY KHOURI
EDITOR

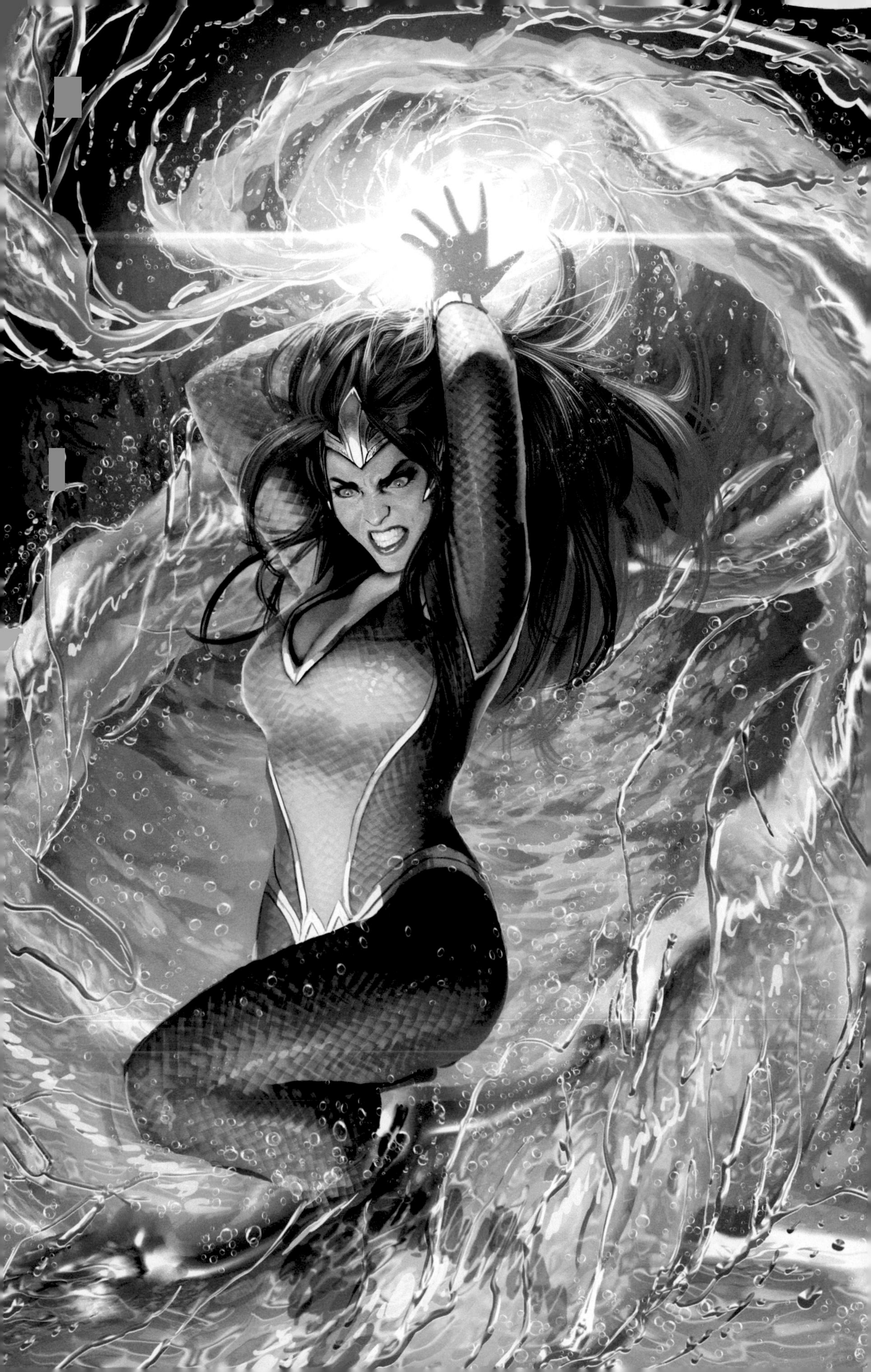

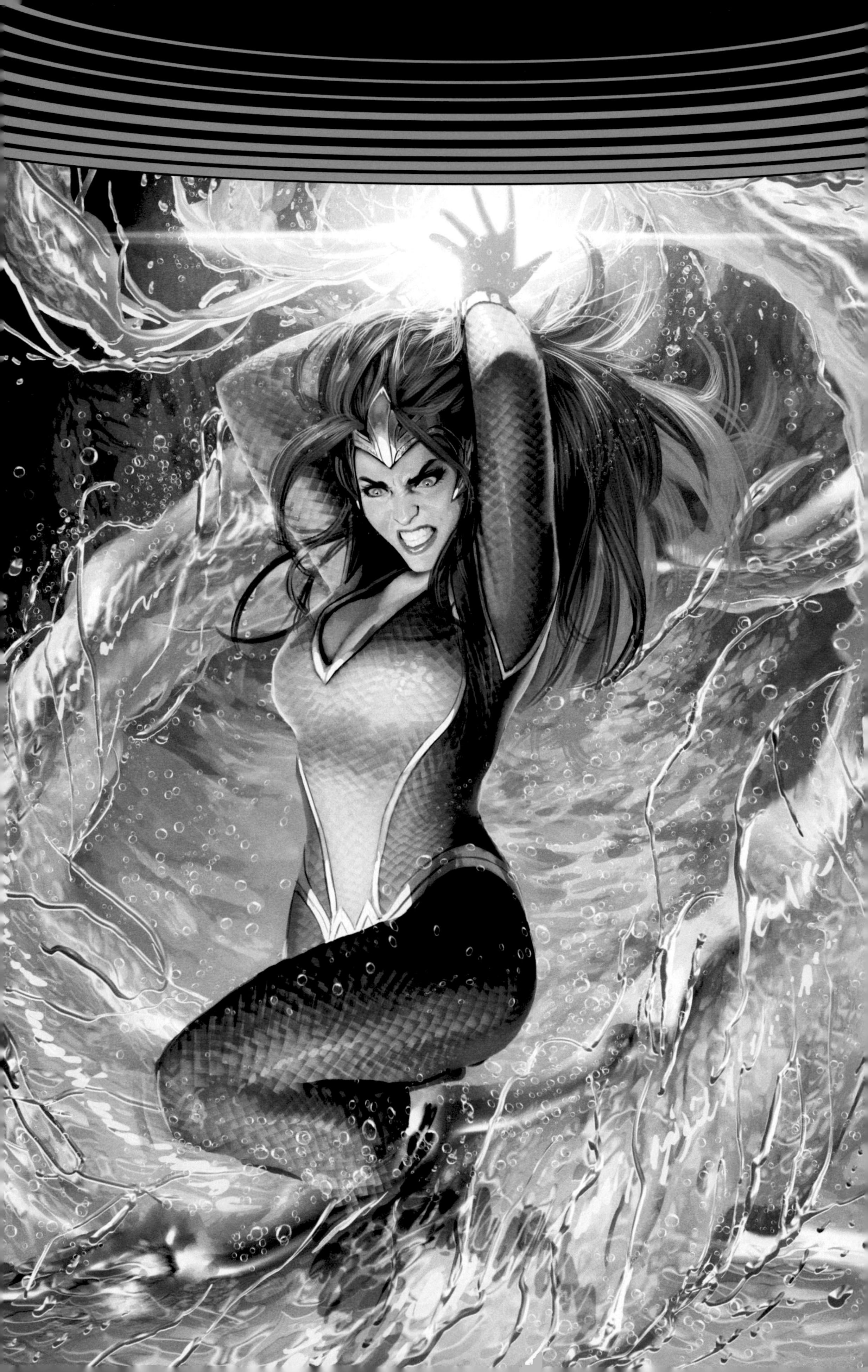

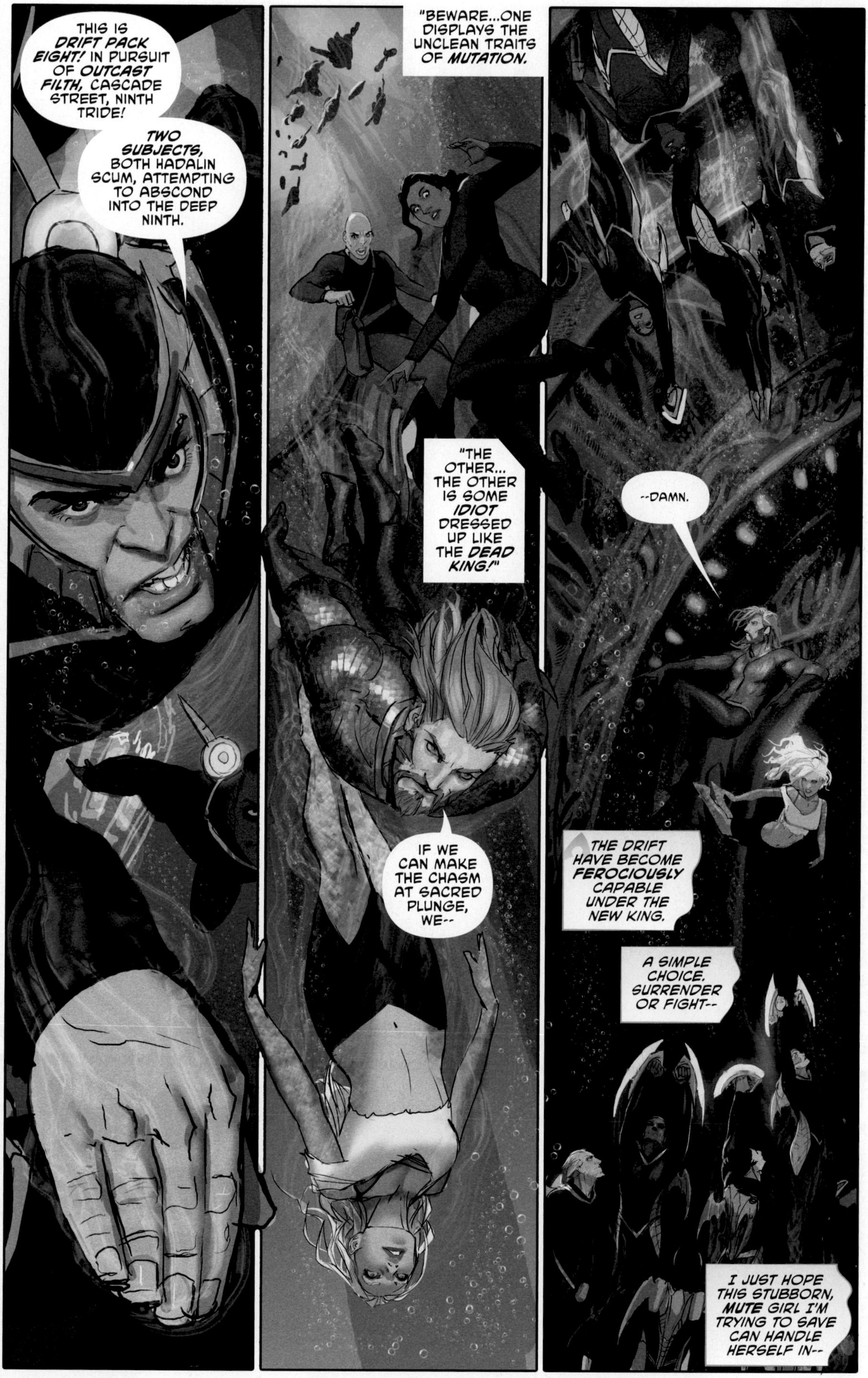
THIS IS DRIFT PACK EIGHT! IN PURSUIT OF OUTCAST FILTH, CASCADE STREET, NINTH TRIDE!
TWO SUBJECTS, BOTH HADALIN SCUM, ATTEMPTING TO ABSCOND INTO THE DEEP NINTH.
"BEWARE...ONE DISPLAYS THE UNCLEAN TRAITS OF MUTATION.
"THE OTHER... THE OTHER IS SOME IDIOT DRESSED UP LIKE THE DEAD KING!"
IF WE CAN MAKE THE CHASM AT SACRED PLUNGE, WE--
--DAMN.
THE DRIFT HAVE BECOME FEROCIOUSLY CAPABLE UNDER THE NEW KING.
A SIMPLE CHOICE. SURRENDER OR FIGHT--
I JUST HOPE THIS STUBBORN, MUTE GIRL I'M TRYING TO SAVE CAN HANDLE HERSELF IN--

OUTSIDERS
SEEMS SHE CAN.
DAN ABNETT STORY
STJEPAN SEJIC
ART, COLOR AND COVER
STEVE WANDS
LETTERING
BRIAN CUNNINGHAM
GROUP EDITOR
HARVEY RICHARDS
ASSOCIATE EDITOR
ANDY KHOURI
EDITOR

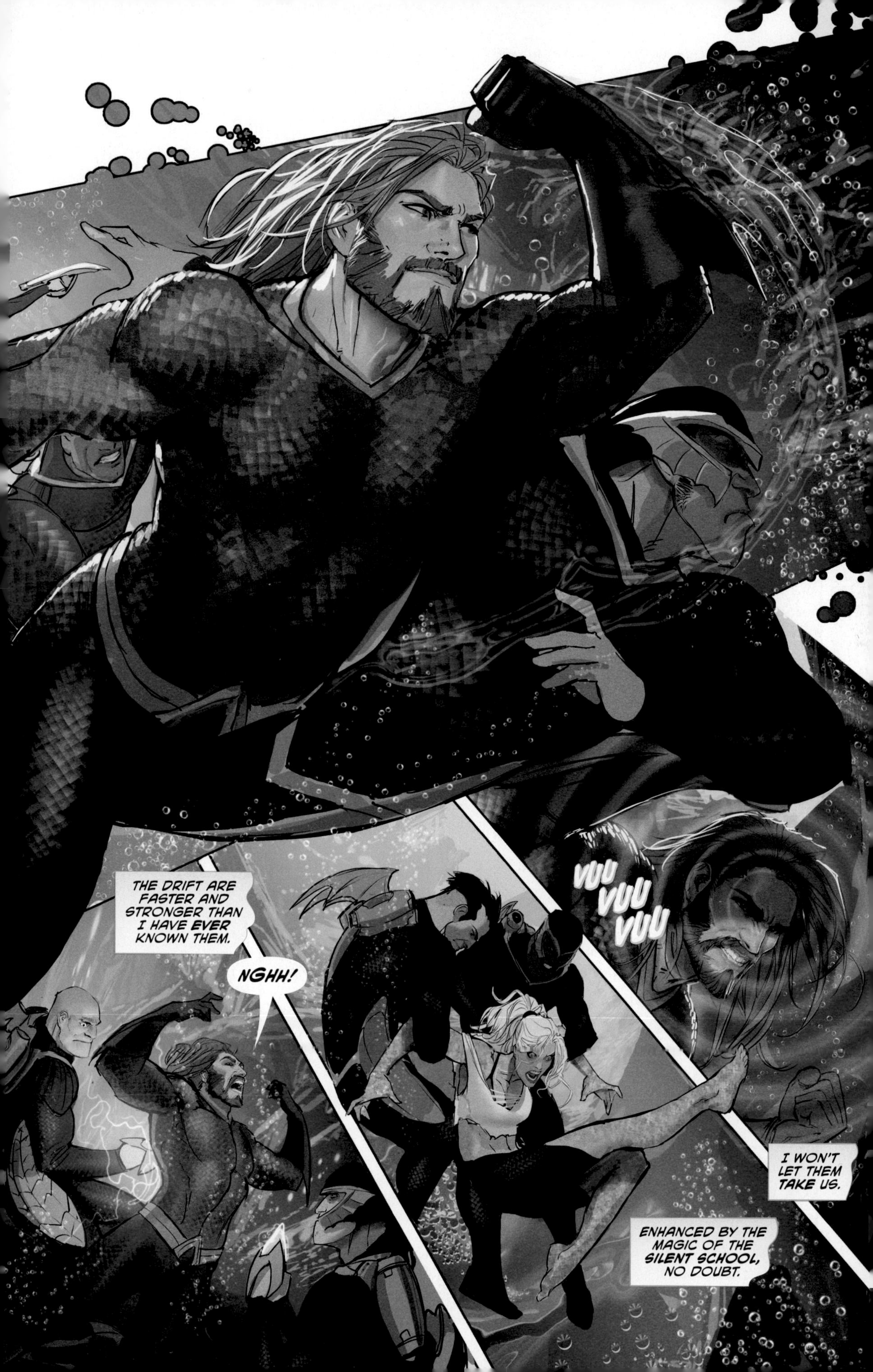
THE DRIFT ARE FASTER AND STRONGER THAN I HAVE EVER KNOWN THEM.
NGHH!
VUU VUU VUU
I WON'T LET THEM TAKE US.
ENHANCED BY THE MAGIC OF THE SILENT SCHOOL, NO DOUBT.

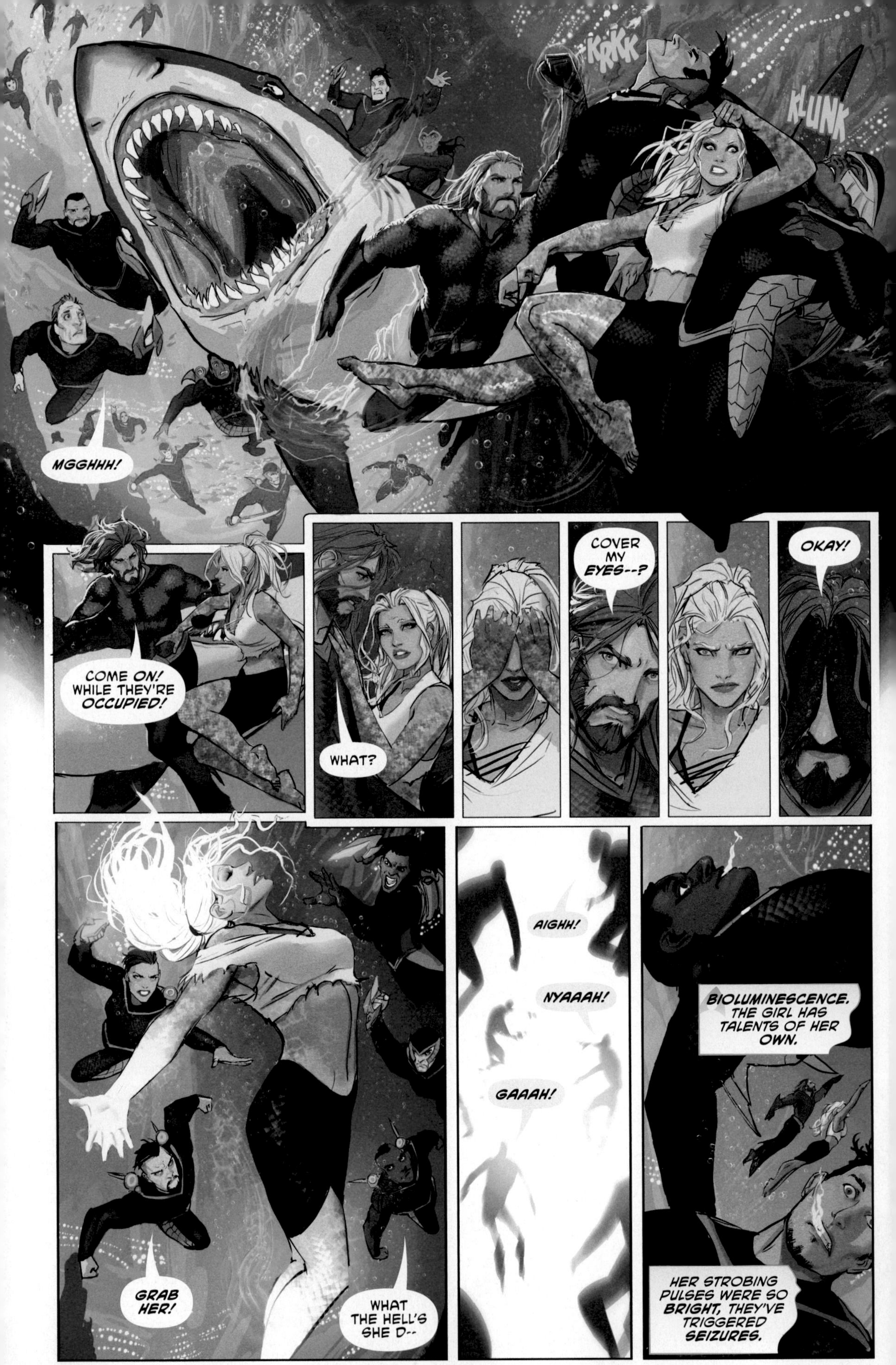
KRKK
KLUNK
MGGHHH!
COME ON! WHILE THEY'RE OCCUPIED!
WHAT?
COVER MY EYES--?
OKAY!
GRAB HER!
WHAT THE HELL'S SHE D--
AIGHH!
NYAAAH!
GAAAH!
BIOLUMINESCENCE. THE GIRL HAS TALENTS OF HER OWN.
HER STROBING PULSES WERE SO BRIGHT, THEY'VE TRIGGERED SEIZURES.

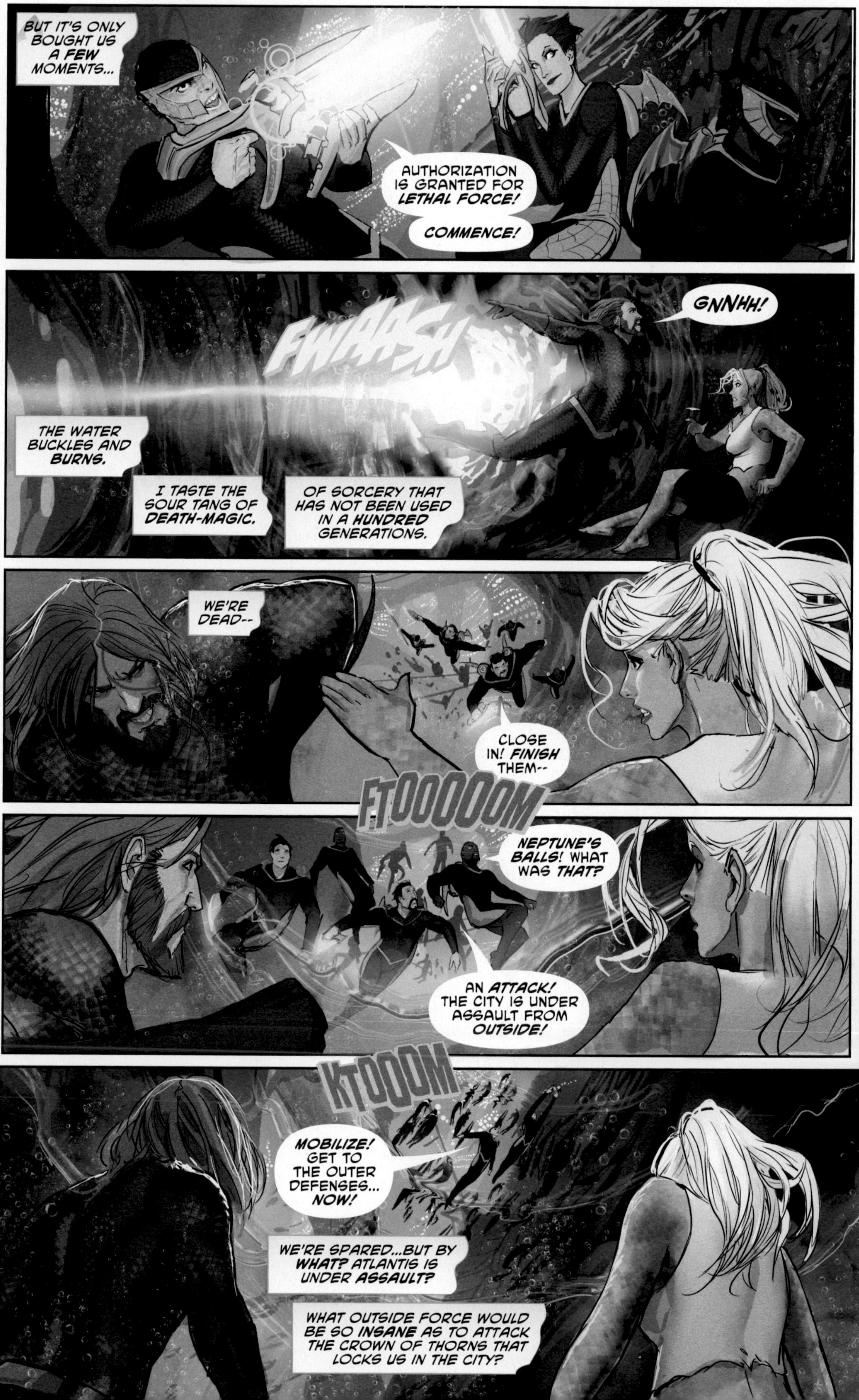

BUT IT'S ONLY BOUGHT US A FEW MOMENTS...
AUTHORIZATION IS GRANTED FOR LETHAL FORCE!
COMMENCE!
FWAASH
GNNHH!
THE WATER BUCKLES AND BURNS.
I TASTE THE SOUR TANG OF DEATH-MAGIC.
OF SORCERY THAT HAS NOT BEEN USED IN A HUNDRED GENERATIONS.
WE'RE DEAD--
CLOSE IN! FINISH THEM--
FTOOOOOM
NEPTUNE'S BALLS! WHAT WAS THAT?
AN ATTACK! THE CITY IS UNDER ASSAULT FROM OUTSIDE!
KTOOOM
MOBILIZE! GET TO THE OUTER DEFENSES... NOW!
WE'RE SPARED...BUT BY WHAT? ATLANTIS IS UNDER ASSAULT?
WHAT OUTSIDE FORCE WOULD BE SO INSANE AS TO ATTACK THE CROWN OF THORNS THAT LOCKS US IN THE CITY?

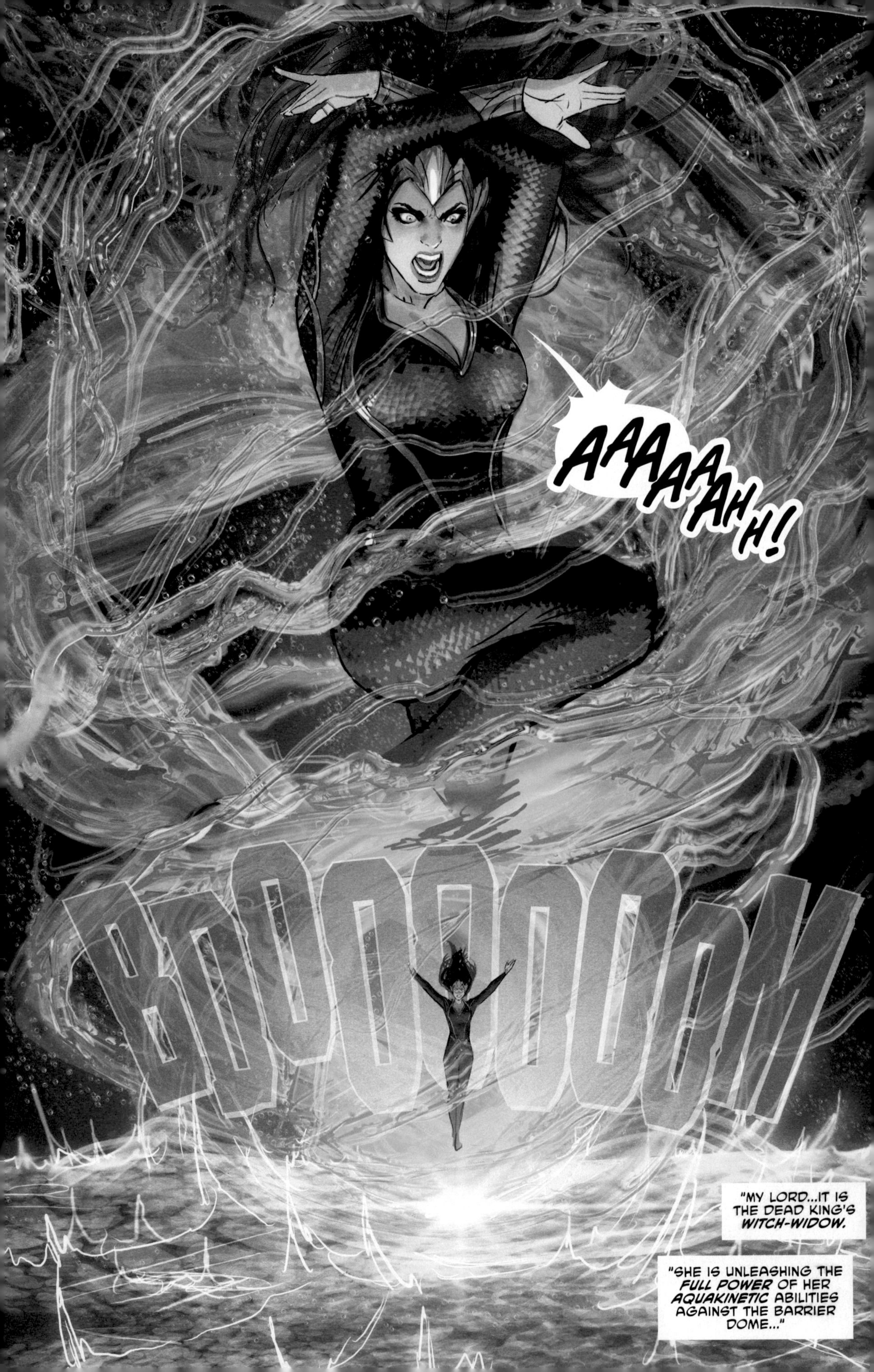
AAAAAAHH!
BOOOOOM
"MY LORD...IT IS THE DEAD KING'S WITCH-WIDOW.
"SHE IS UNLEASHING THE FULL POWER OF HER AQUAKINETIC ABILITIES AGAINST THE BARRIER DOME..."

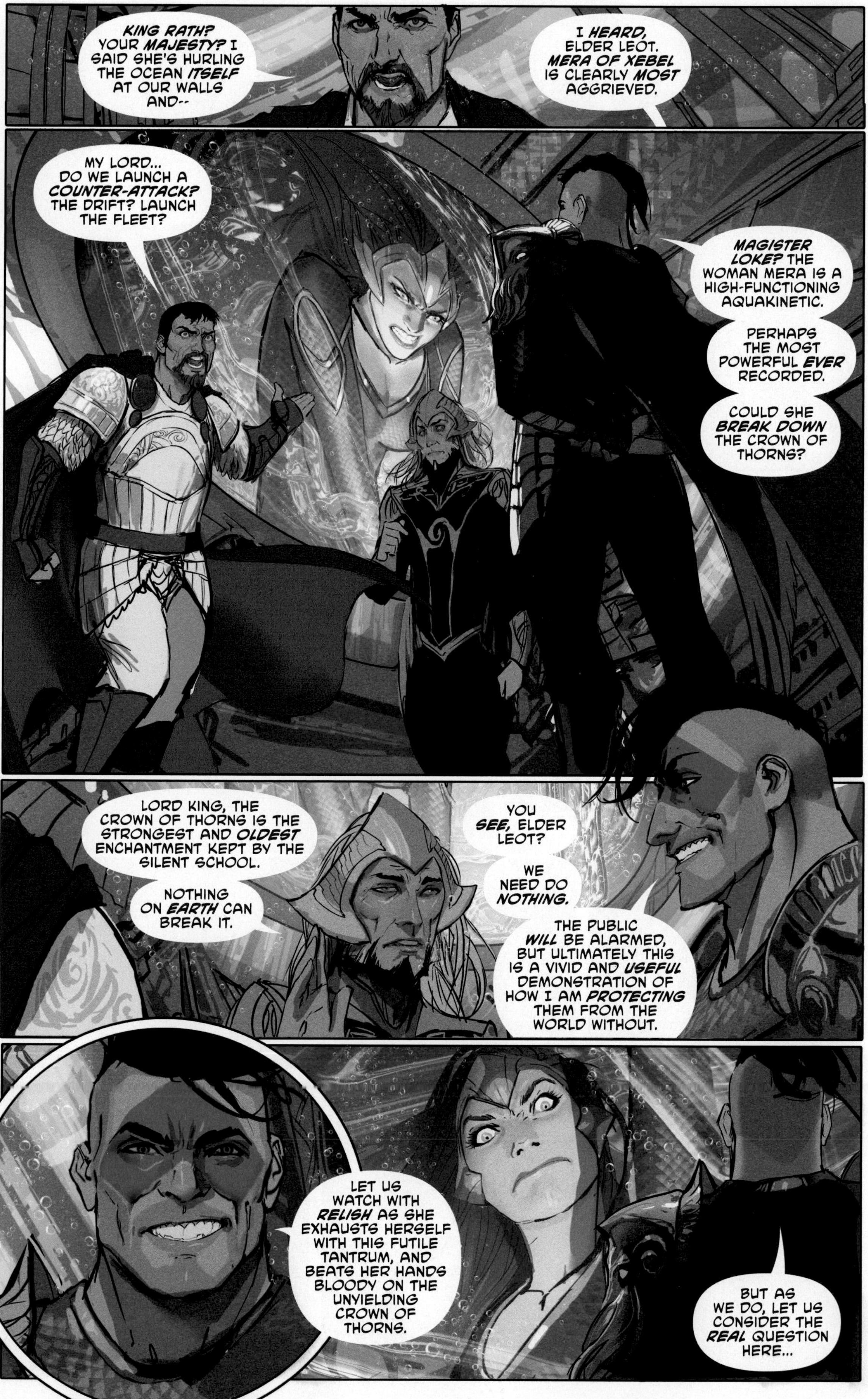
KING RATH? YOUR MAJESTY? I SAID SHE'S HURLING THE OCEAN ITSELF AT OUR WALLS AND--
I HEARD, ELDER LEOT. MERA OF XEBEL IS CLEARLY MOST AGGRIEVED.
MY LORD... DO WE LAUNCH A COUNTER-ATTACK? THE DRIFT? LAUNCH THE FLEET?
MAGISTER LOKE? THE WOMAN MERA IS A HIGH-FUNCTIONING AQUAKINETIC.
PERHAPS THE MOST POWERFUL EVER RECORDED.
COULD SHE BREAK DOWN THE CROWN OF THORNS?
LORD KING, THE CROWN OF THORNS IS THE STRONGEST AND OLDEST ENCHANTMENT KEPT BY THE SILENT SCHOOL.
NOTHING ON EARTH CAN BREAK IT.
YOU SEE, ELDER LEOT?
WE NEED DO NOTHING.
THE PUBLIC WILL BE ALARMED, BUT ULTIMATELY THIS IS A VIVID AND USEFUL DEMONSTRATION OF HOW I AM PROTECTING THEM FROM THE WORLD WITHOUT.
LET US WATCH WITH RELISH AS SHE EXHAUSTS HERSELF WITH THIS FUTILE TANTRUM, AND BEATS HER HANDS BLOODY ON THE UNYIELDING CROWN OF THORNS.
BUT AS WE DO, LET US CONSIDER THE REAL QUESTION HERE...

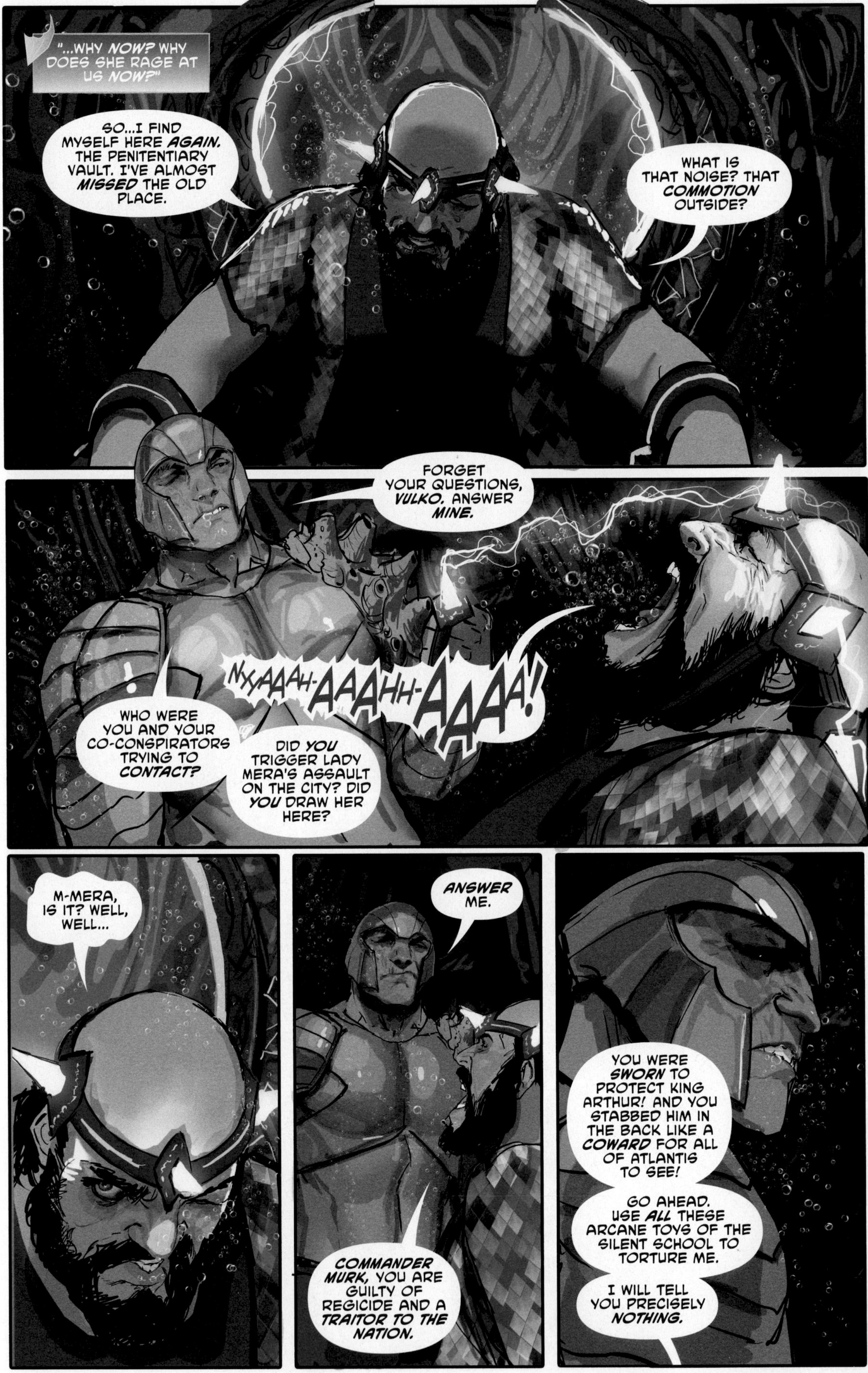
"...WHY NOW? WHY DOES SHE RAGE AT US NOW?"
SO...I FIND MYSELF HERE AGAIN. THE PENITENTIARY VAULT. I'VE ALMOST MISSED THE OLD PLACE.
WHAT IS THAT NOISE? THAT COMMOTION OUTSIDE?
FORGET YOUR QUESTIONS, VULKO. ANSWER MINE.
NYYAAAH-AAAHH-AAAA!
WHO WERE YOU AND YOUR CO-CONSPIRATORS TRYING TO CONTACT?
DID YOU TRIGGER LADY MERA'S ASSAULT ON THE CITY? DID YOU DRAW HER HERE?
M-MERA, IS IT? WELL, WELL...
ANSWER ME.
COMMANDER MURK, YOU ARE GUILTY OF REGICIDE AND A TRAITOR TO THE NATION.
YOU WERE SWORN TO PROTECT KING ARTHUR! AND YOU STABBED HIM IN THE BACK LIKE A COWARD FOR ALL OF ATLANTIS TO SEE!
GO AHEAD. USE ALL THESE ARCANE TOYS OF THE SILENT SCHOOL TO TORTURE ME.
I WILL TELL YOU PRECISELY NOTHING.

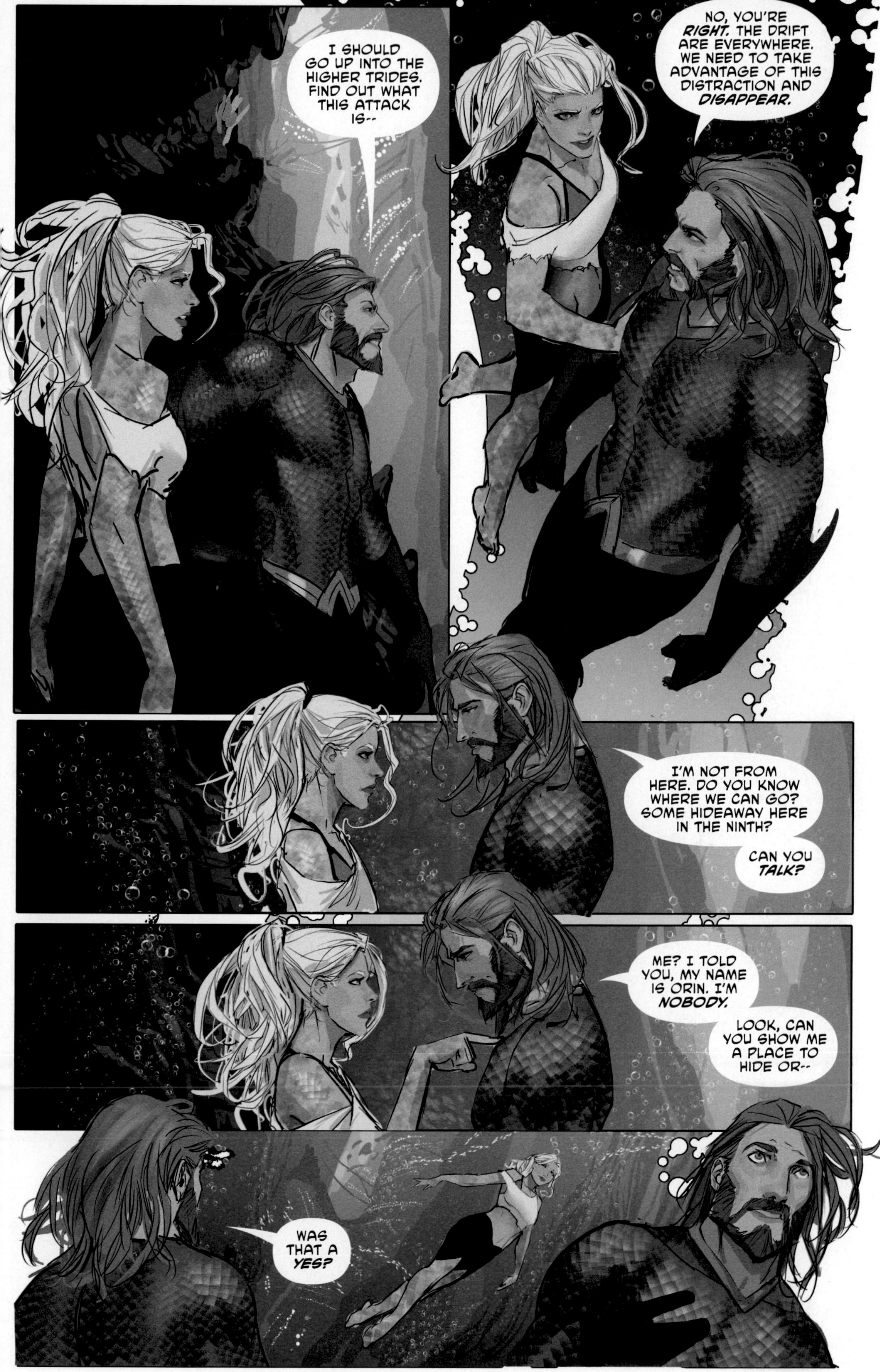
I SHOULD GO UP INTO THE HIGHER TRIDES. FIND OUT WHAT THIS ATTACK IS--
NO, YOU'RE *RIGHT.* THE DRIFT ARE EVERYWHERE. WE NEED TO TAKE ADVANTAGE OF THIS DISTRACTION AND *DISAPPEAR.*
I'M NOT FROM HERE. DO YOU KNOW WHERE WE CAN GO? SOME HIDEAWAY HERE IN THE NINTH?
CAN YOU *TALK?*
ME? I TOLD YOU, MY NAME IS ORIN. I'M *NOBODY.*
LOOK, CAN YOU SHOW ME A PLACE TO HIDE OR--
WAS THAT A *YES?*

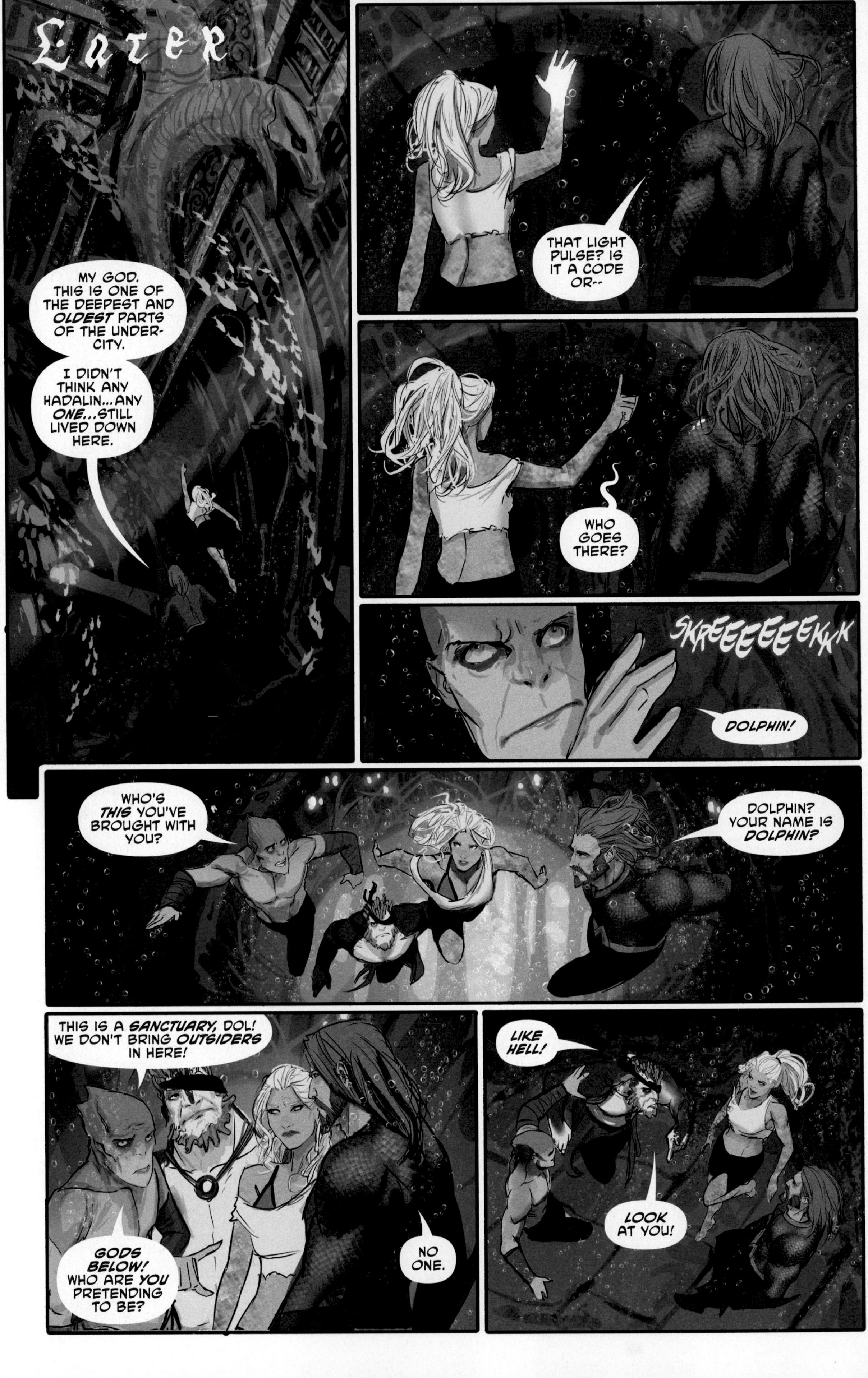
Later
MY GOD. THIS IS ONE OF THE DEEPEST AND OLDEST PARTS OF THE UNDER-CITY.
I DIDN'T THINK ANY HADALIN...ANY ONE...STILL LIVED DOWN HERE.
THAT LIGHT PULSE? IS IT A CODE OR--
WHO GOES THERE?
SKREEEEEEEKKK
DOLPHIN!
WHO'S THIS YOU'VE BROUGHT WITH YOU?
DOLPHIN? YOUR NAME IS DOLPHIN?
THIS IS A SANCTUARY, DOL! WE DON'T BRING OUTSIDERS IN HERE!
GODS BELOW! WHO ARE YOU PRETENDING TO BE?
NO ONE.
LIKE HELL!
LOOK AT YOU!

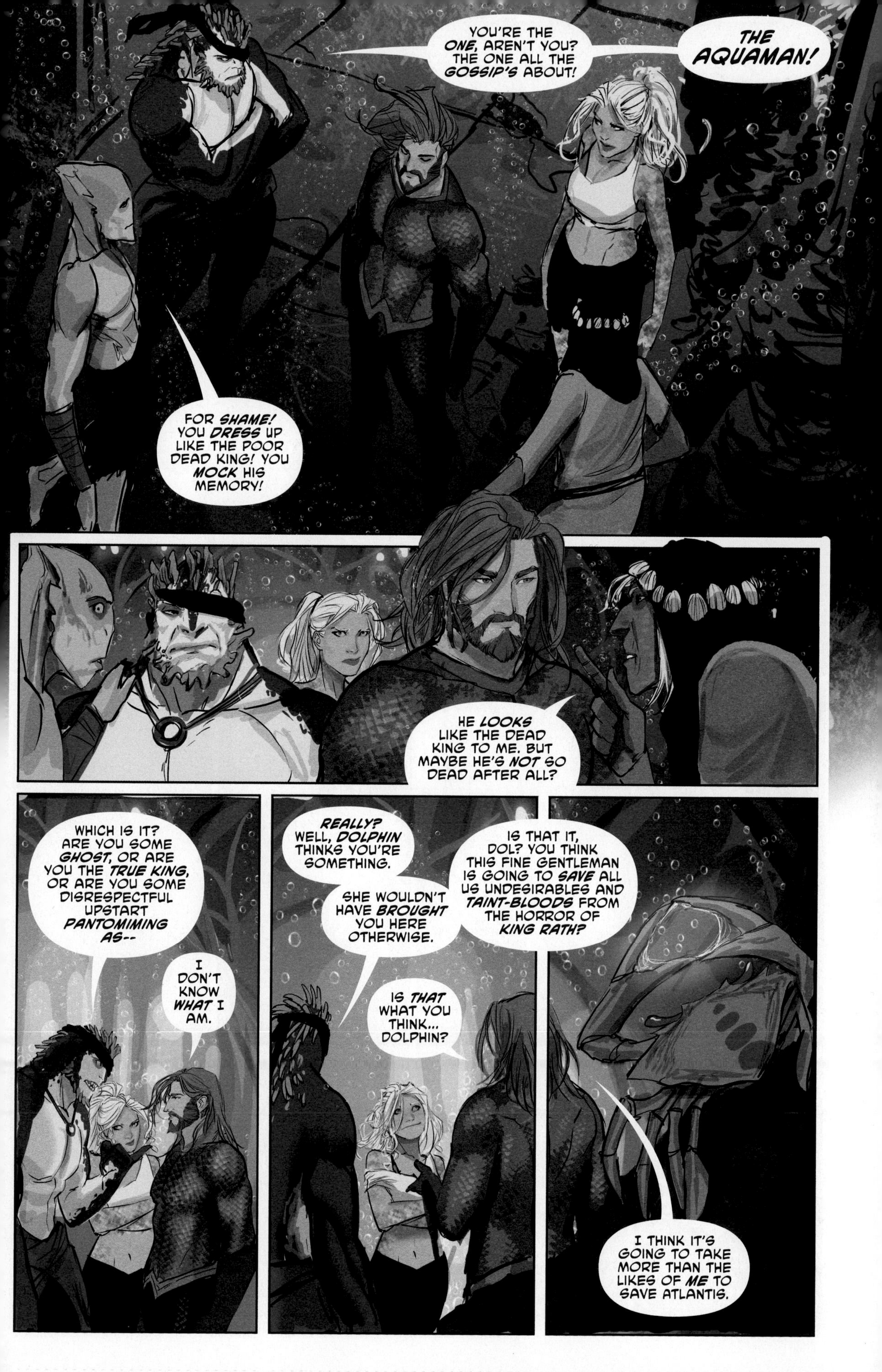
YOU'RE THE ONE, AREN'T YOU? THE ONE ALL THE GOSSIP'S ABOUT!
THE AQUAMAN!
FOR SHAME! YOU DRESS UP LIKE THE POOR DEAD KING! YOU MOCK HIS MEMORY!
HE LOOKS LIKE THE DEAD KING TO ME. BUT MAYBE HE'S NOT SO DEAD AFTER ALL?
WHICH IS IT? ARE YOU SOME GHOST, OR ARE YOU THE TRUE KING, OR ARE YOU SOME DISRESPECTFUL UPSTART PANTOMIMING AS--
I DON'T KNOW WHAT I AM.
REALLY? WELL, DOLPHIN THINKS YOU'RE SOMETHING.
SHE WOULDN'T HAVE BROUGHT YOU HERE OTHERWISE.
IS THAT WHAT YOU THINK... DOLPHIN?
IS THAT IT, DOL? YOU THINK THIS FINE GENTLEMAN IS GOING TO SAVE ALL US UNDESIRABLES AND TAINT-BLOODS FROM THE HORROR OF KING RATH?
I THINK IT'S GOING TO TAKE MORE THAN THE LIKES OF ME TO SAVE ATLANTIS.

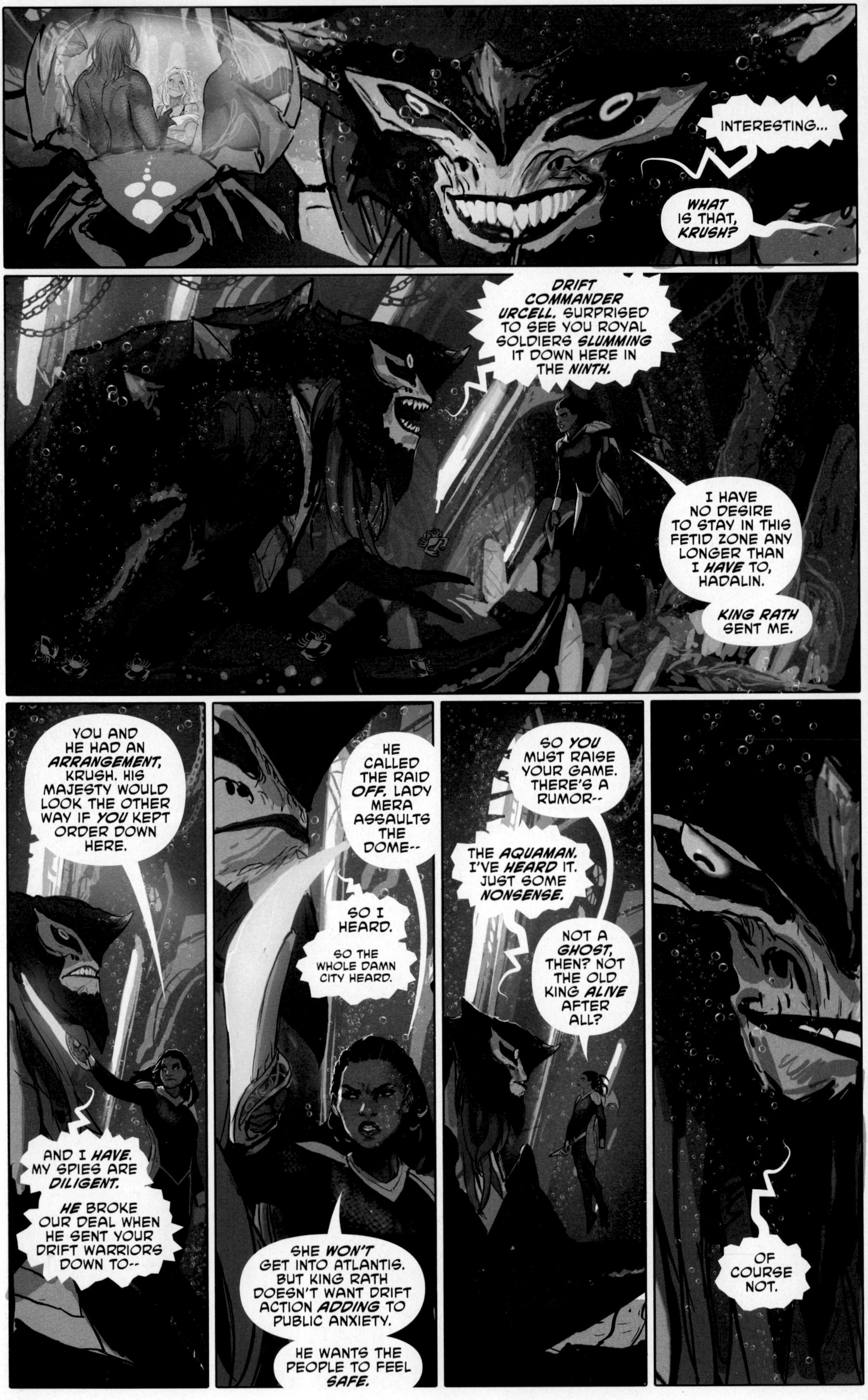
INTERESTING...
WHAT IS THAT, KRUSH?
DRIFT COMMANDER URCELL. SURPRISED TO SEE YOU ROYAL SOLDIERS SLUMMING IT DOWN HERE IN THE NINTH.
I HAVE NO DESIRE TO STAY IN THIS FETID ZONE ANY LONGER THAN I HAVE TO, HADALIN.
KING RATH SENT ME.
YOU AND HE HAD AN ARRANGEMENT, KRUSH. HIS MAJESTY WOULD LOOK THE OTHER WAY IF YOU KEPT ORDER DOWN HERE.
AND I HAVE. MY SPIES ARE DILIGENT.
HE BROKE OUR DEAL WHEN HE SENT YOUR DRIFT WARRIORS DOWN TO--
HE CALLED THE RAID OFF. LADY MERA ASSAULTS THE DOME--
SO I HEARD.
SO THE WHOLE DAMN CITY HEARD.
SHE WON'T GET INTO ATLANTIS. BUT KING RATH DOESN'T WANT DRIFT ACTION ADDING TO PUBLIC ANXIETY.
HE WANTS THE PEOPLE TO FEEL SAFE.
SO YOU MUST RAISE YOUR GAME. THERE'S A RUMOR--
THE AQUAMAN. I'VE HEARD IT. JUST SOME NONSENSE.
NOT A GHOST, THEN? NOT THE OLD KING ALIVE AFTER ALL?
OF COURSE NOT.

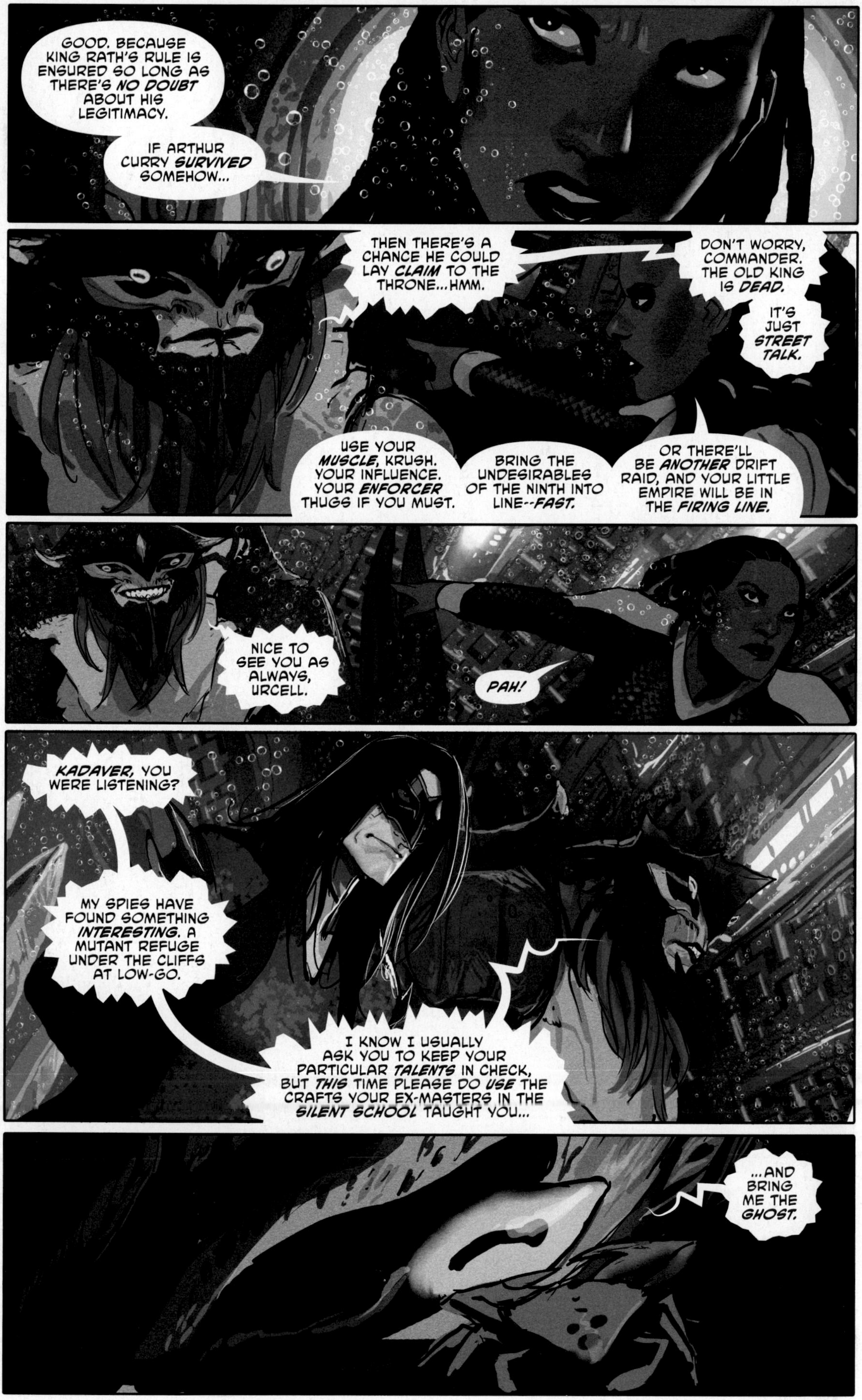
GOOD. BECAUSE KING RATH'S RULE IS ENSURED SO LONG AS THERE'S NO DOUBT ABOUT HIS LEGITIMACY.
IF ARTHUR CURRY SURVIVED SOMEHOW...
THEN THERE'S A CHANCE HE COULD LAY CLAIM TO THE THRONE...HMM.
DON'T WORRY, COMMANDER. THE OLD KING IS DEAD.
IT'S JUST STREET TALK.
USE YOUR MUSCLE, KRUSH. YOUR INFLUENCE. YOUR ENFORCER THUGS IF YOU MUST.
BRING THE UNDESIRABLES OF THE NINTH INTO LINE--FAST.
OR THERE'LL BE ANOTHER DRIFT RAID, AND YOUR LITTLE EMPIRE WILL BE IN THE FIRING LINE.
NICE TO SEE YOU AS ALWAYS, URCELL.
PAH!
KADAVER, YOU WERE LISTENING?
MY SPIES HAVE FOUND SOMETHING INTERESTING. A MUTANT REFUGE UNDER THE CLIFFS AT LOW-GO.
I KNOW I USUALLY ASK YOU TO KEEP YOUR PARTICULAR TALENTS IN CHECK, BUT THIS TIME PLEASE DO USE THE CRAFTS YOUR EX-MASTERS IN THE SILENT SCHOOL TAUGHT YOU...
...AND BRING ME THE GHOST.

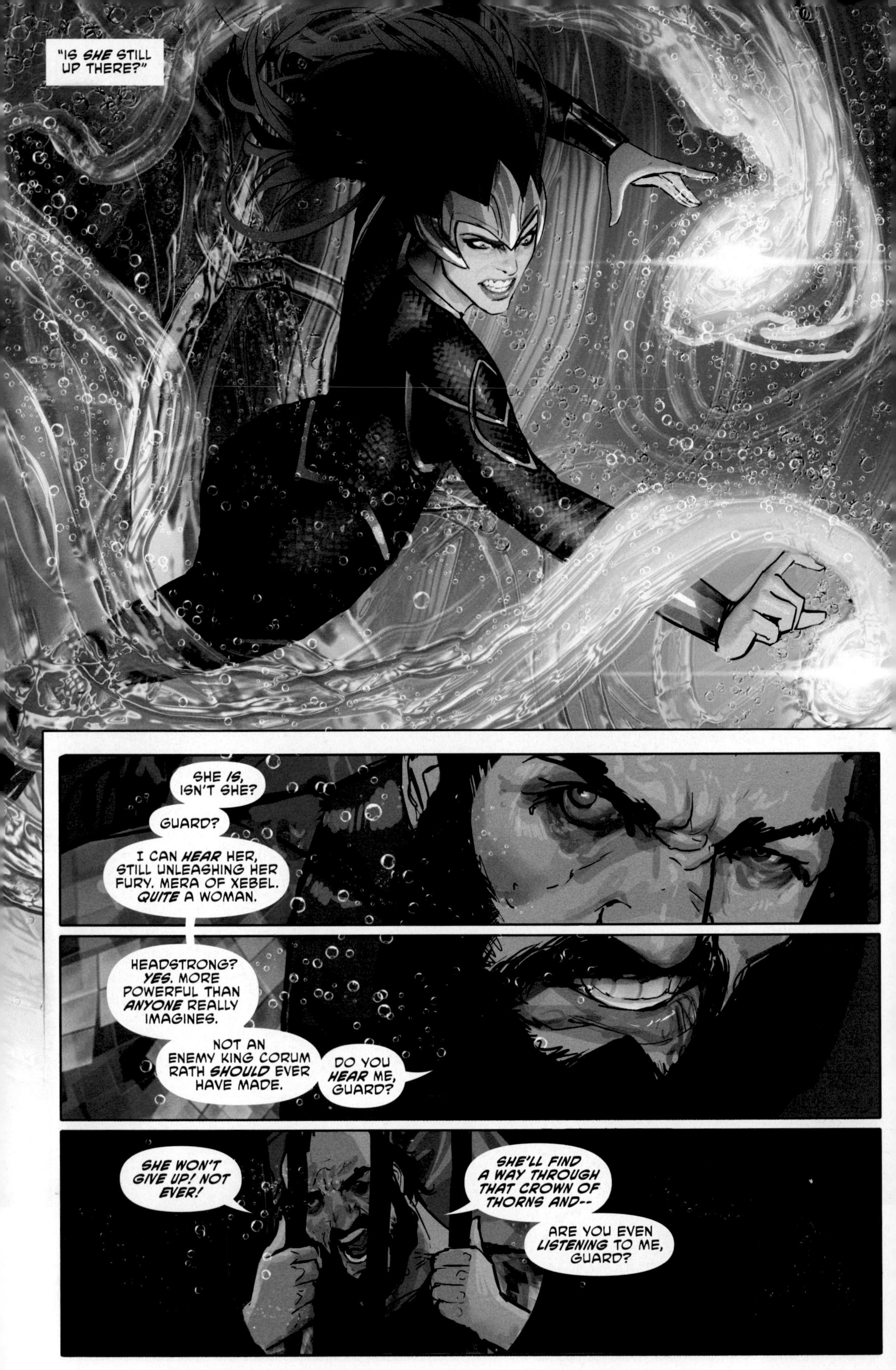
"IS SHE STILL UP THERE?"
SHE IS, ISN'T SHE?
GUARD?
I CAN HEAR HER, STILL UNLEASHING HER FURY. MERA OF XEBEL. QUITE A WOMAN.
HEADSTRONG? YES. MORE POWERFUL THAN ANYONE REALLY IMAGINES.
NOT AN ENEMY KING CORUM RATH SHOULD EVER HAVE MADE.
DO YOU HEAR ME, GUARD?
SHE WON'T GIVE UP! NOT EVER!
SHE'LL FIND A WAY THROUGH THAT CROWN OF THORNS AND--
ARE YOU EVEN LISTENING TO ME, GUARD?

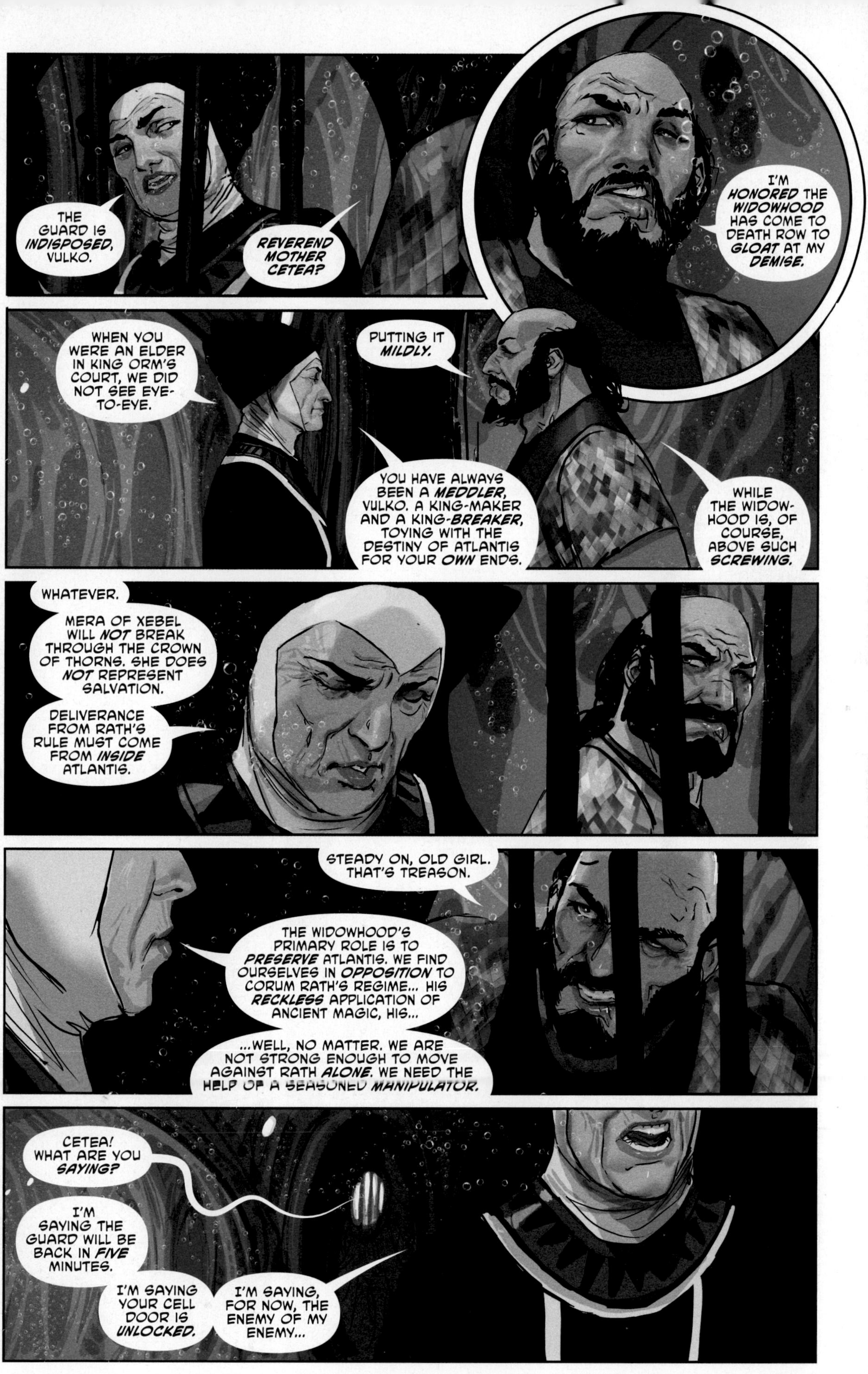
THE GUARD IS *INDISPOSED,* VULKO.
REVEREND MOTHER CETEA?
I'M *HONORED* THE *WIDOWHOOD* HAS COME TO DEATH ROW TO *GLOAT* AT MY *DEMISE.*
WHEN YOU WERE AN ELDER IN KING ORM'S COURT, WE DID NOT SEE EYE-TO-EYE.
PUTTING IT *MILDLY.*
YOU HAVE ALWAYS BEEN A *MEDDLER,* VULKO. A KING-MAKER AND A KING-*BREAKER,* TOYING WITH THE DESTINY OF ATLANTIS FOR YOUR *OWN* ENDS.
WHILE THE WIDOWHOOD IS, OF COURSE, ABOVE SUCH *SCREWING.*
WHATEVER.
MERA OF XEBEL WILL *NOT* BREAK THROUGH THE CROWN OF THORNS. SHE DOES *NOT* REPRESENT SALVATION.
DELIVERANCE FROM RATH'S RULE MUST COME FROM *INSIDE* ATLANTIS.
STEADY ON, OLD GIRL. THAT'S TREASON.
THE WIDOWHOOD'S PRIMARY ROLE IS TO *PRESERVE* ATLANTIS. WE FIND OURSELVES IN *OPPOSITION* TO CORUM RATH'S REGIME... HIS *RECKLESS* APPLICATION OF ANCIENT MAGIC, HIS...
...WELL, NO MATTER. WE ARE NOT STRONG ENOUGH TO MOVE AGAINST RATH *ALONE.* WE NEED THE HELP OF A SEASONED *MANIPULATOR.*
CETEA! WHAT ARE YOU *SAYING?*
I'M SAYING THE GUARD WILL BE BACK IN *FIVE* MINUTES.
I'M SAYING YOUR CELL DOOR IS *UNLOCKED.*
I'M SAYING, FOR NOW, THE ENEMY OF MY ENEMY...

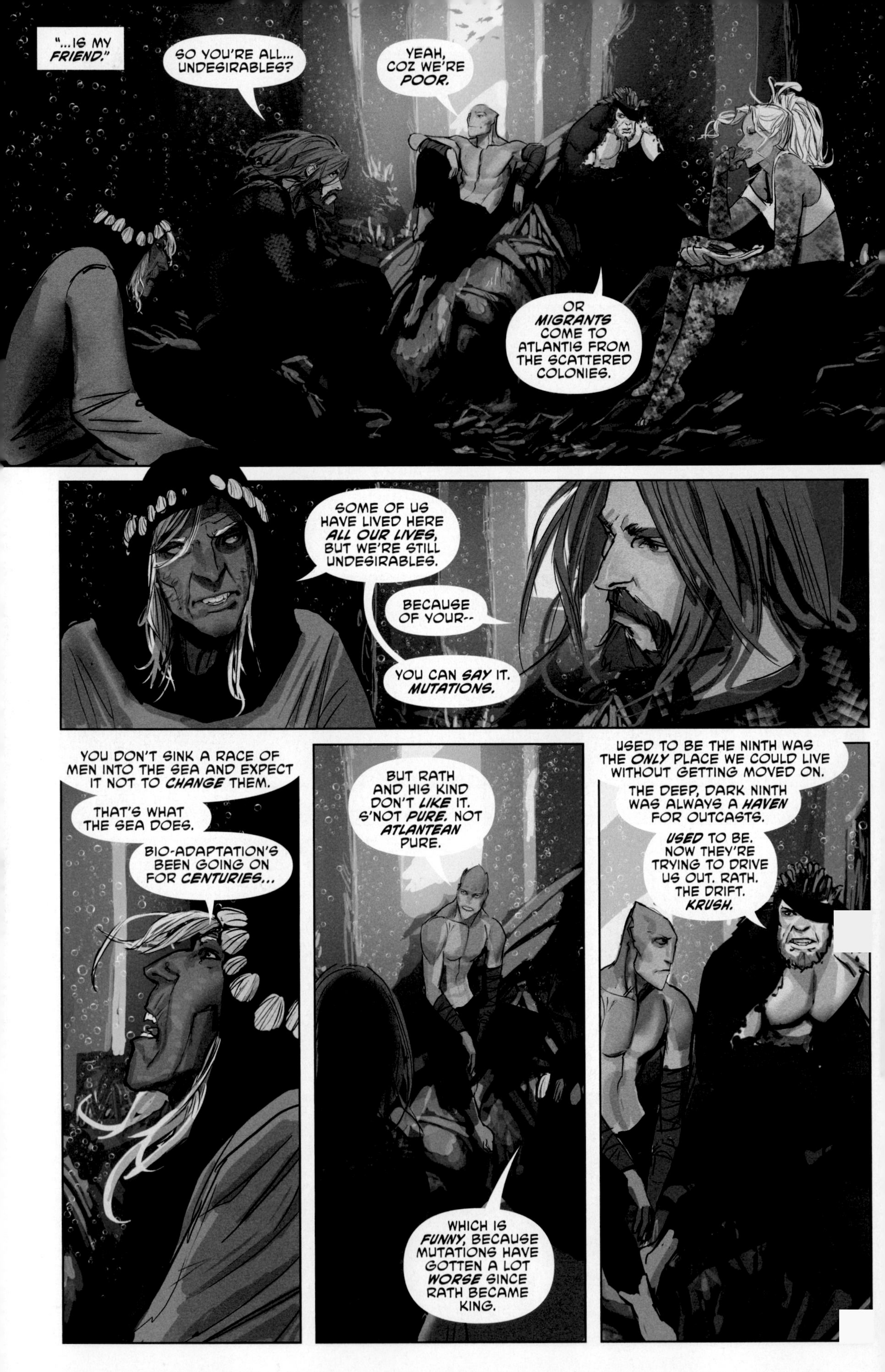
"...IS MY FRIEND."
SO YOU'RE ALL... UNDESIRABLES?
YEAH, COZ WE'RE POOR.
OR MIGRANTS COME TO ATLANTIS FROM THE SCATTERED COLONIES.
SOME OF US HAVE LIVED HERE ALL OUR LIVES, BUT WE'RE STILL UNDESIRABLES.
BECAUSE OF YOUR--
YOU CAN SAY IT. MUTATIONS.
YOU DON'T SINK A RACE OF MEN INTO THE SEA AND EXPECT IT NOT TO CHANGE THEM.
THAT'S WHAT THE SEA DOES.
BIO-ADAPTATION'S BEEN GOING ON FOR CENTURIES...
BUT RATH AND HIS KIND DON'T LIKE IT. S'NOT PURE. NOT ATLANTEAN PURE.
WHICH IS FUNNY, BECAUSE MUTATIONS HAVE GOTTEN A LOT WORSE SINCE RATH BECAME KING.
USED TO BE THE NINTH WAS THE ONLY PLACE WE COULD LIVE WITHOUT GETTING MOVED ON.
THE DEEP, DARK NINTH WAS ALWAYS A HAVEN FOR OUTCASTS.
USED TO BE. NOW THEY'RE TRYING TO DRIVE US OUT. RATH. THE DRIFT. KRUSH.

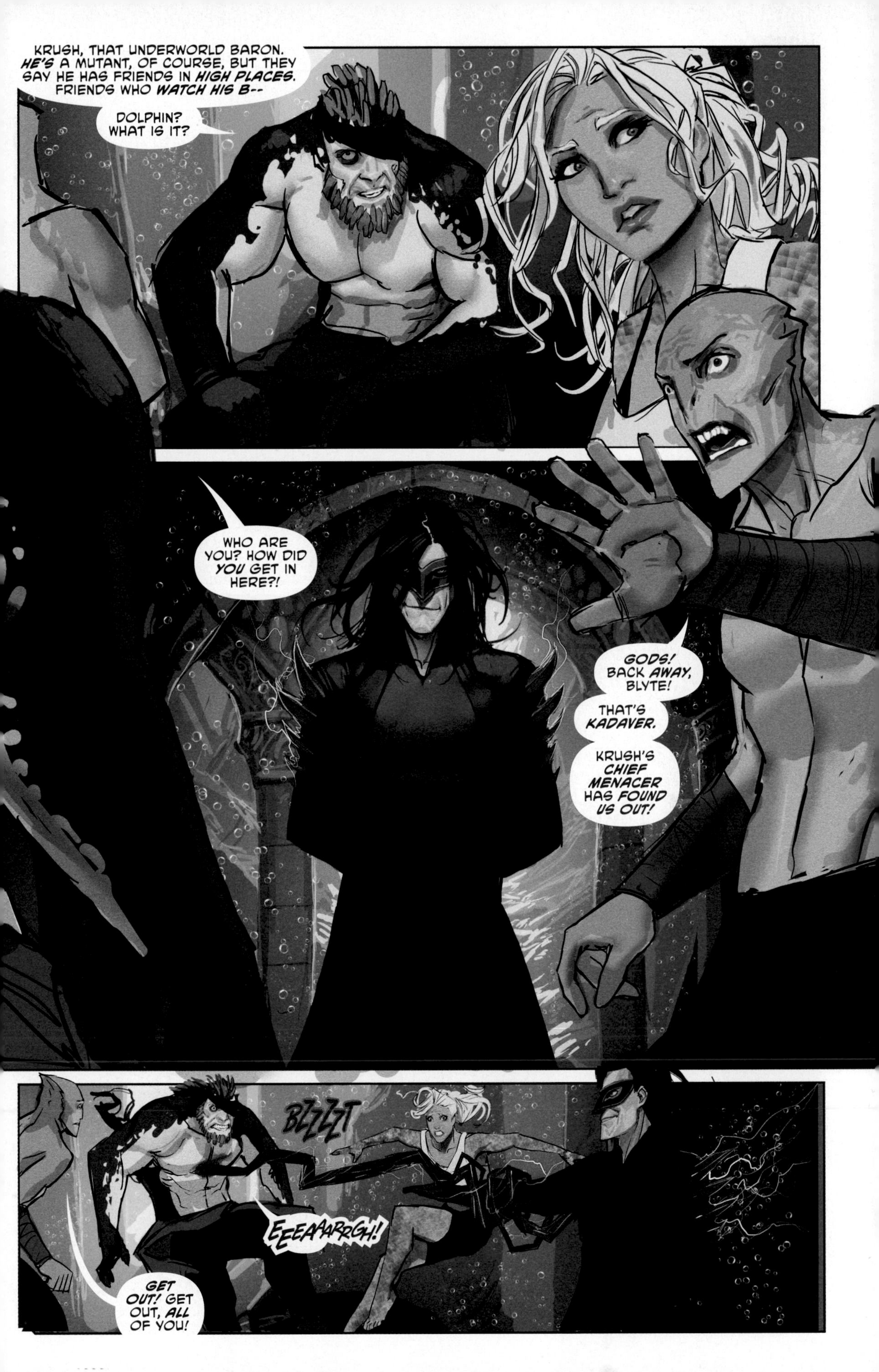

KRUSH, THAT UNDERWORLD BARON. HE'S A MUTANT, OF COURSE, BUT THEY SAY HE HAS FRIENDS IN HIGH PLACES. FRIENDS WHO WATCH HIS B--
DOLPHIN? WHAT IS IT?
WHO ARE YOU? HOW DID YOU GET IN HERE?!
GODS! BACK AWAY, BLYTE!
THAT'S KADAVER.
KRUSH'S CHIEF MENACER HAS FOUND US OUT!
BZZZZT
EEEAAARRGH!
GET OUT! GET OUT, ALL OF YOU!

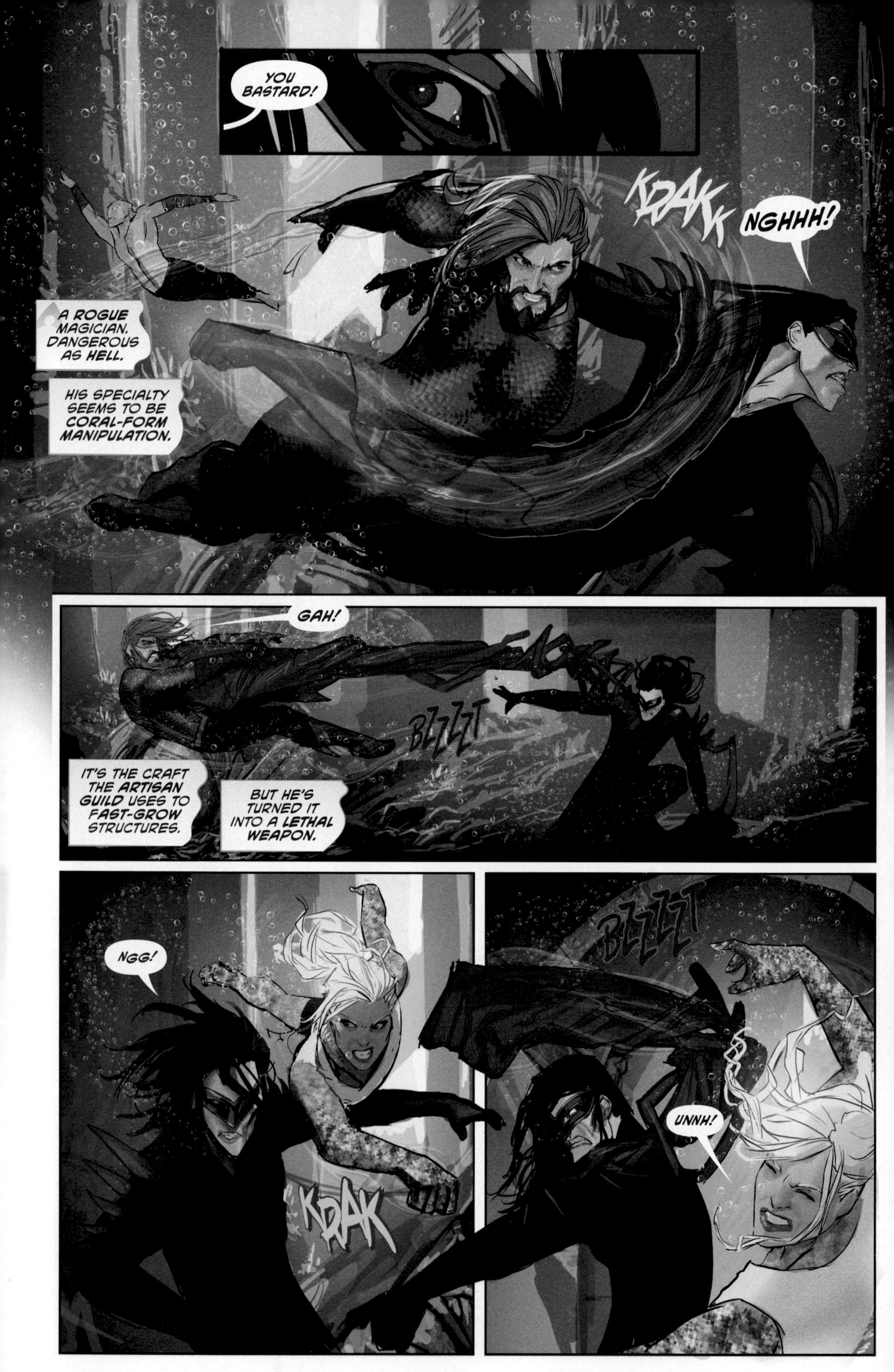
YOU BASTARD!
KDAKK
NGHHH!
A ROGUE MAGICIAN. DANGEROUS AS HELL.
HIS SPECIALTY SEEMS TO BE CORAL-FORM MANIPULATION.
GAH!
BZZZT
IT'S THE CRAFT THE ARTISAN GUILD USES TO FAST-GROW STRUCTURES.
BUT HE'S TURNED IT INTO A LETHAL WEAPON.
NGG!
KDAK
BZZZZT
UNNH!

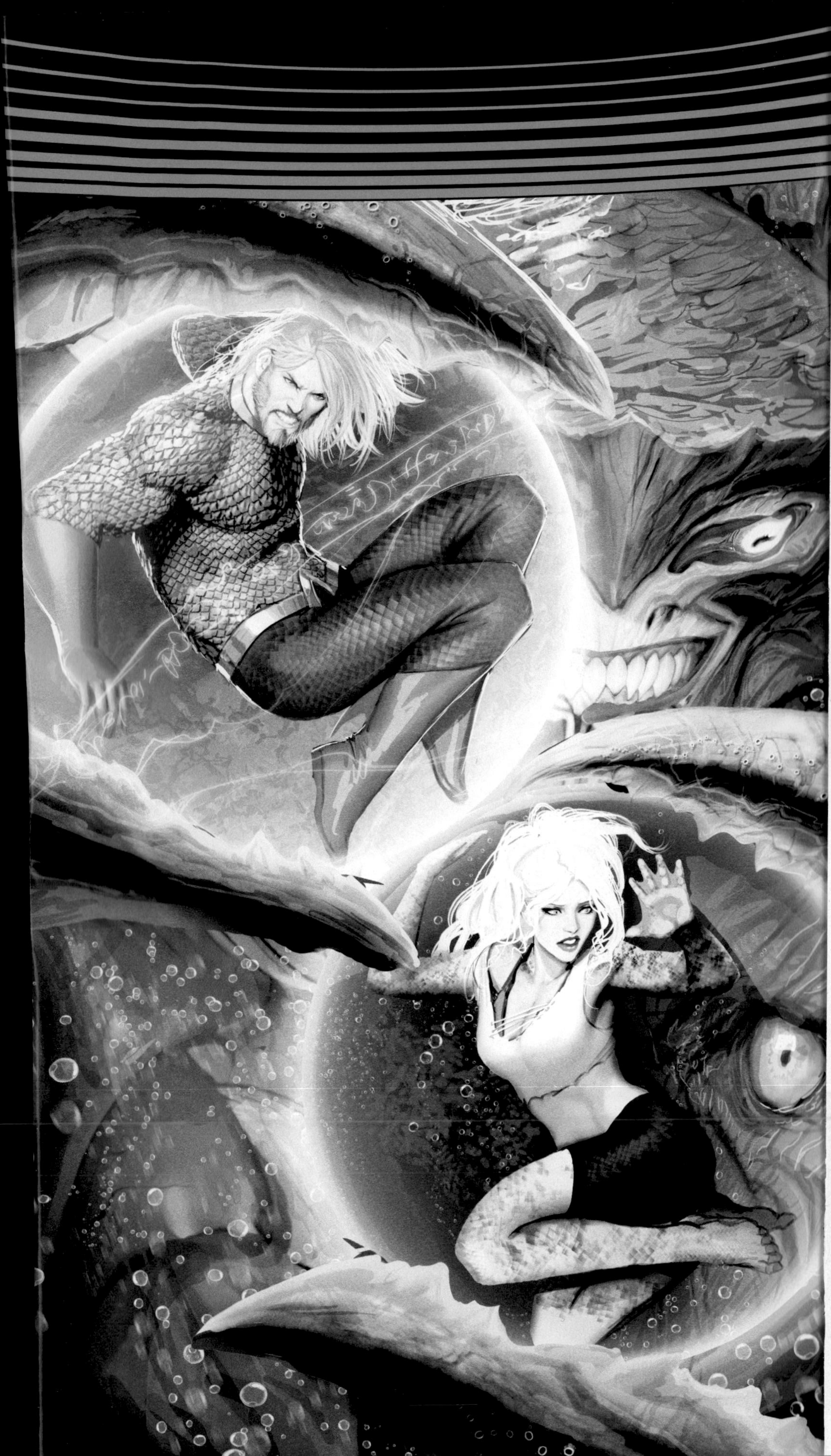

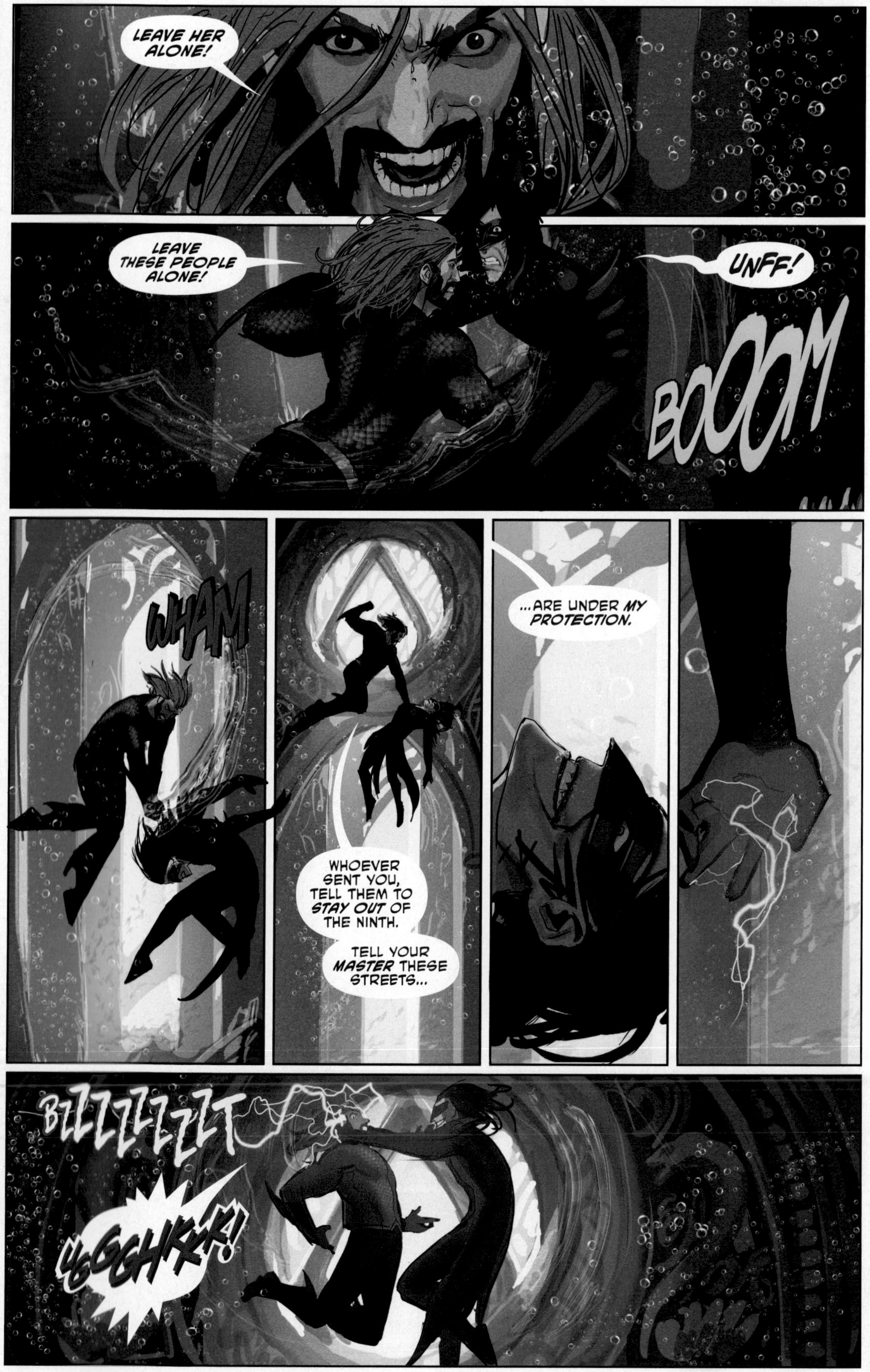
LEAVE HER ALONE!
LEAVE THESE PEOPLE ALONE!
UNFF!
BOOOM
WHAM
WHOEVER SENT YOU, TELL THEM TO STAY OUT OF THE NINTH.
TELL YOUR MASTER THESE STREETS...
...ARE UNDER MY PROTECTION.
BZZZZZZZZT
UGGGHKKK!

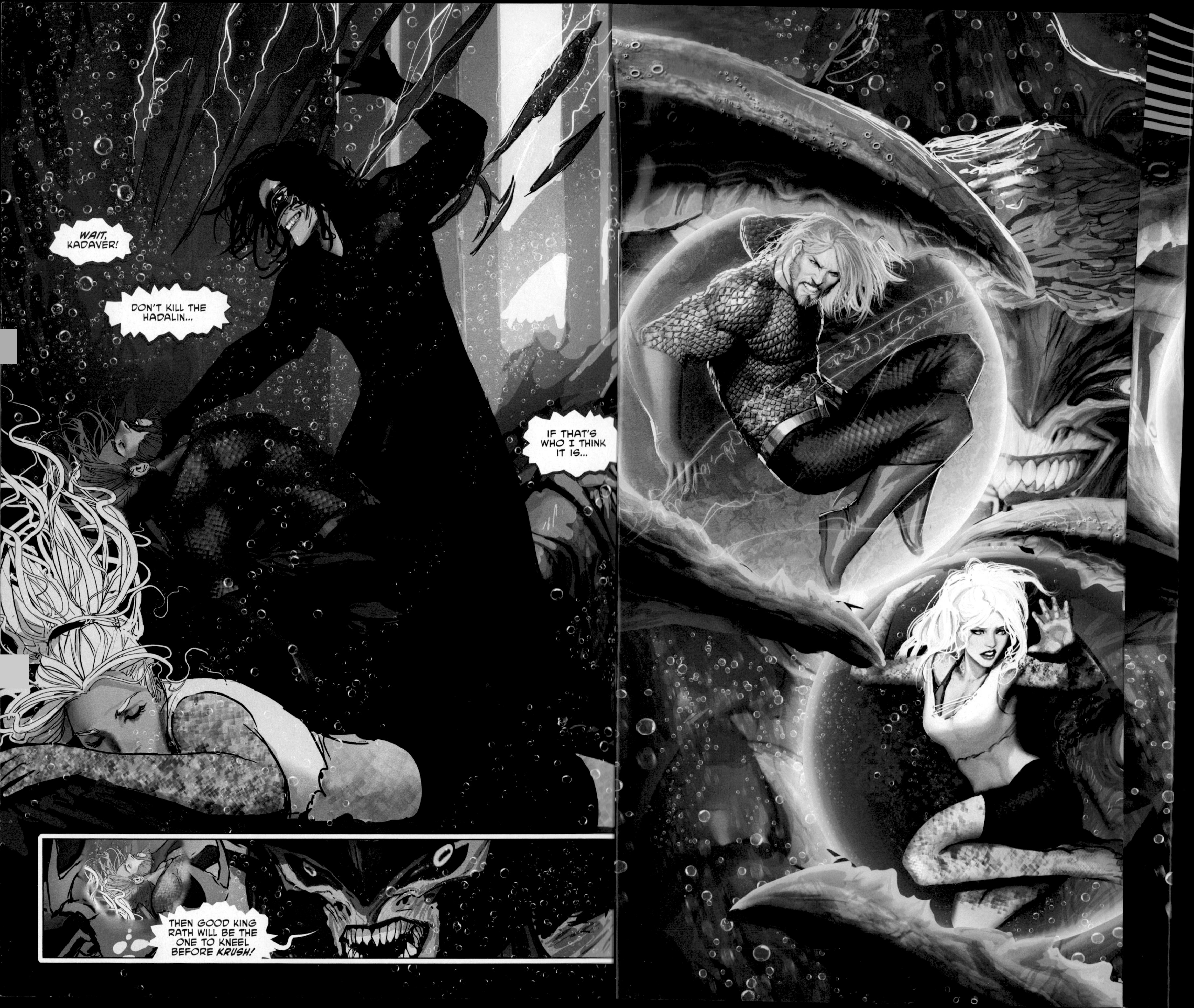
WAIT, KADAVER!
DON'T KILL THE HADALIN...
IF THAT'S WHO I THINK IT IS...
THEN GOOD KING RATH WILL BE THE ONE TO KNEEL BEFORE KRUSH!

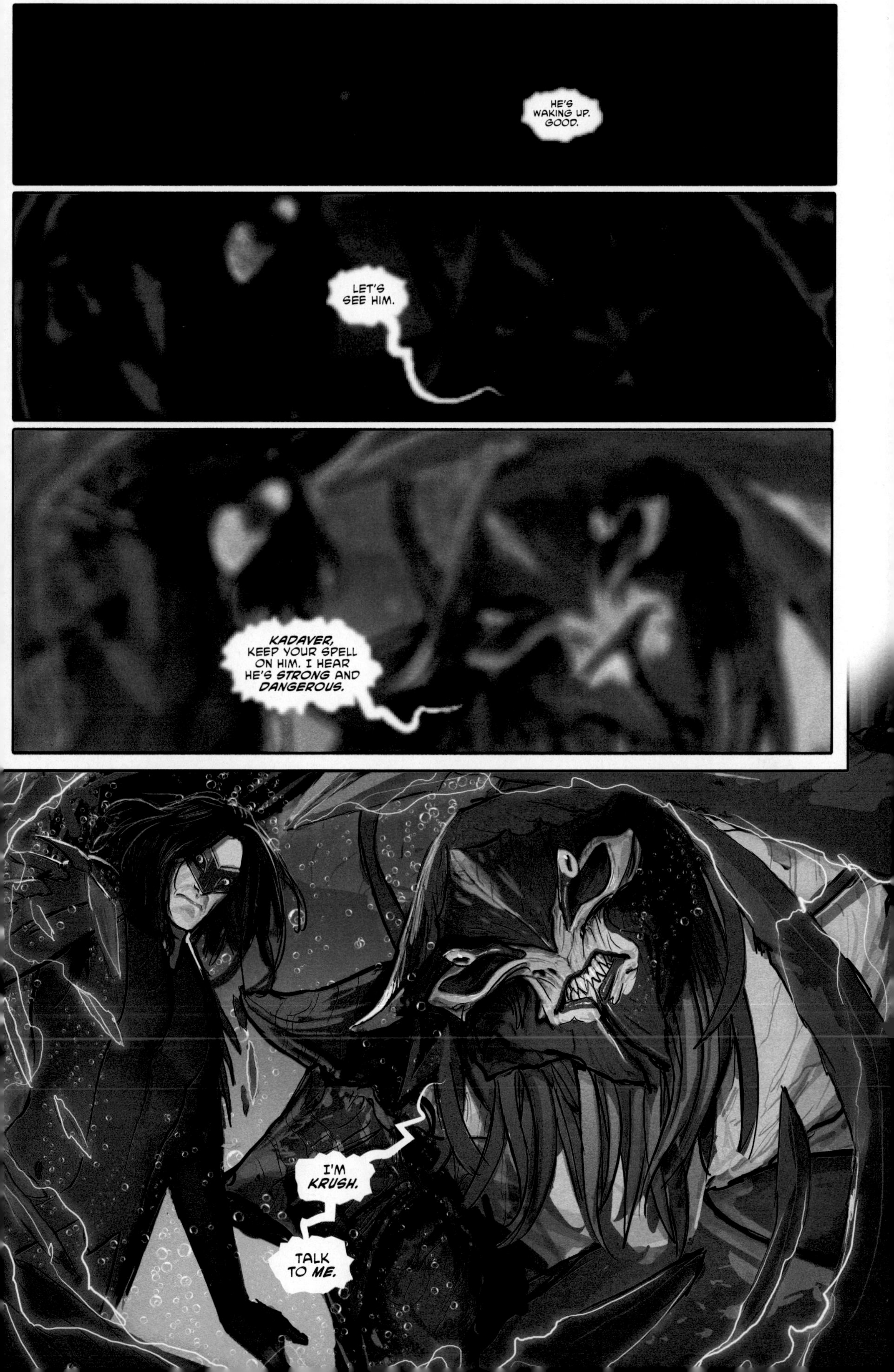
HE'S WAKING UP. GOOD.
LET'S SEE HIM.
KADAVER, KEEP YOUR SPELL ON HIM. I HEAR HE'S STRONG AND DANGEROUS.
I'M KRUSH.
TALK TO ME.

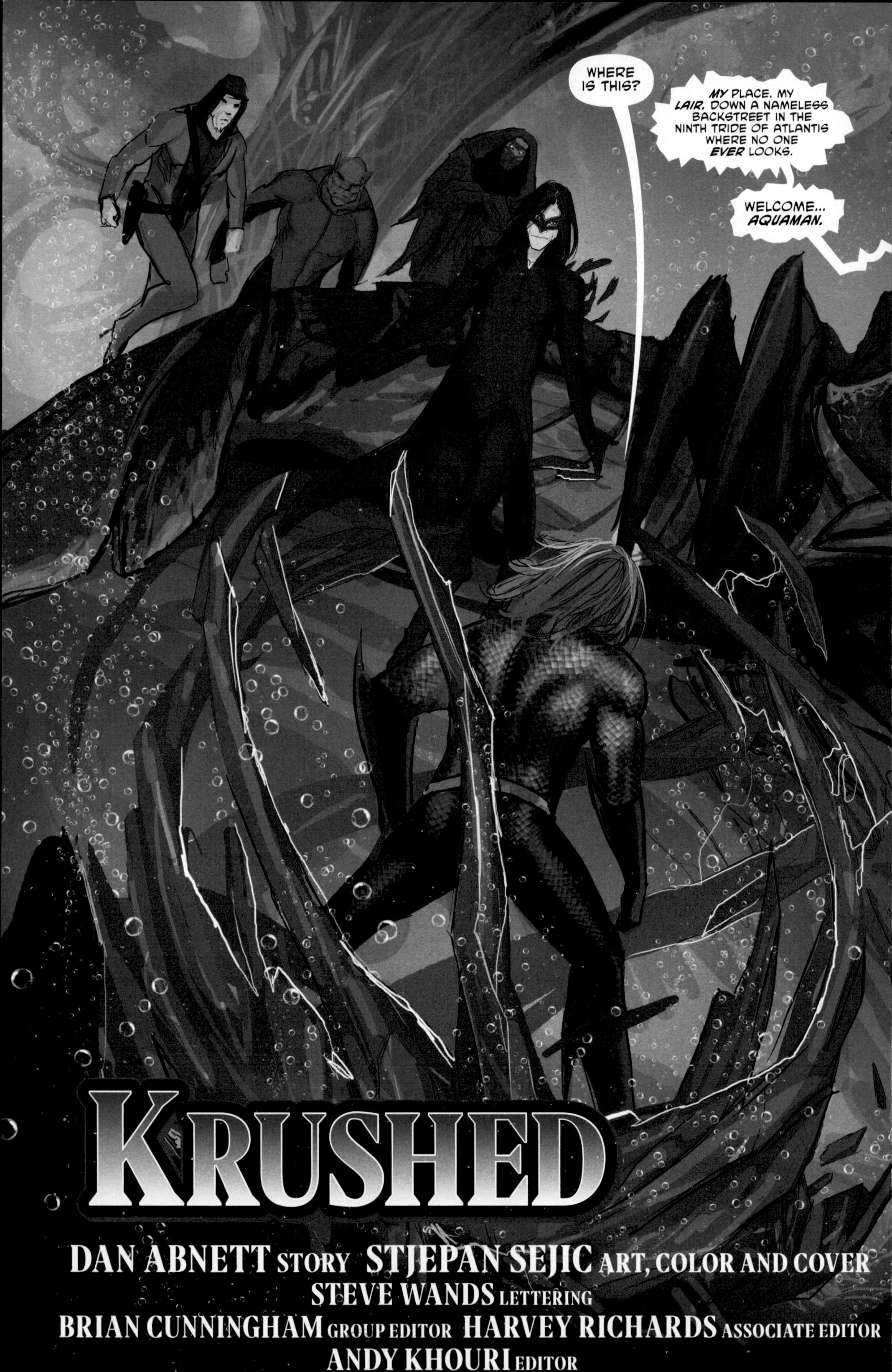
WHERE IS THIS?
MY PLACE. MY LAIR. DOWN A NAMELESS BACKSTREET IN THE NINTH TRIDE OF ATLANTIS WHERE NO ONE EVER LOOKS.
WELCOME... AQUAMAN.
KRUSHED
DAN ABNETT STORY STJEPAN SEJIC ART, COLOR AND COVER
STEVE WANDS LETTERING
BRIAN CUNNINGHAM GROUP EDITOR HARVEY RICHARDS ASSOCIATE EDITOR
ANDY KHOURI EDITOR

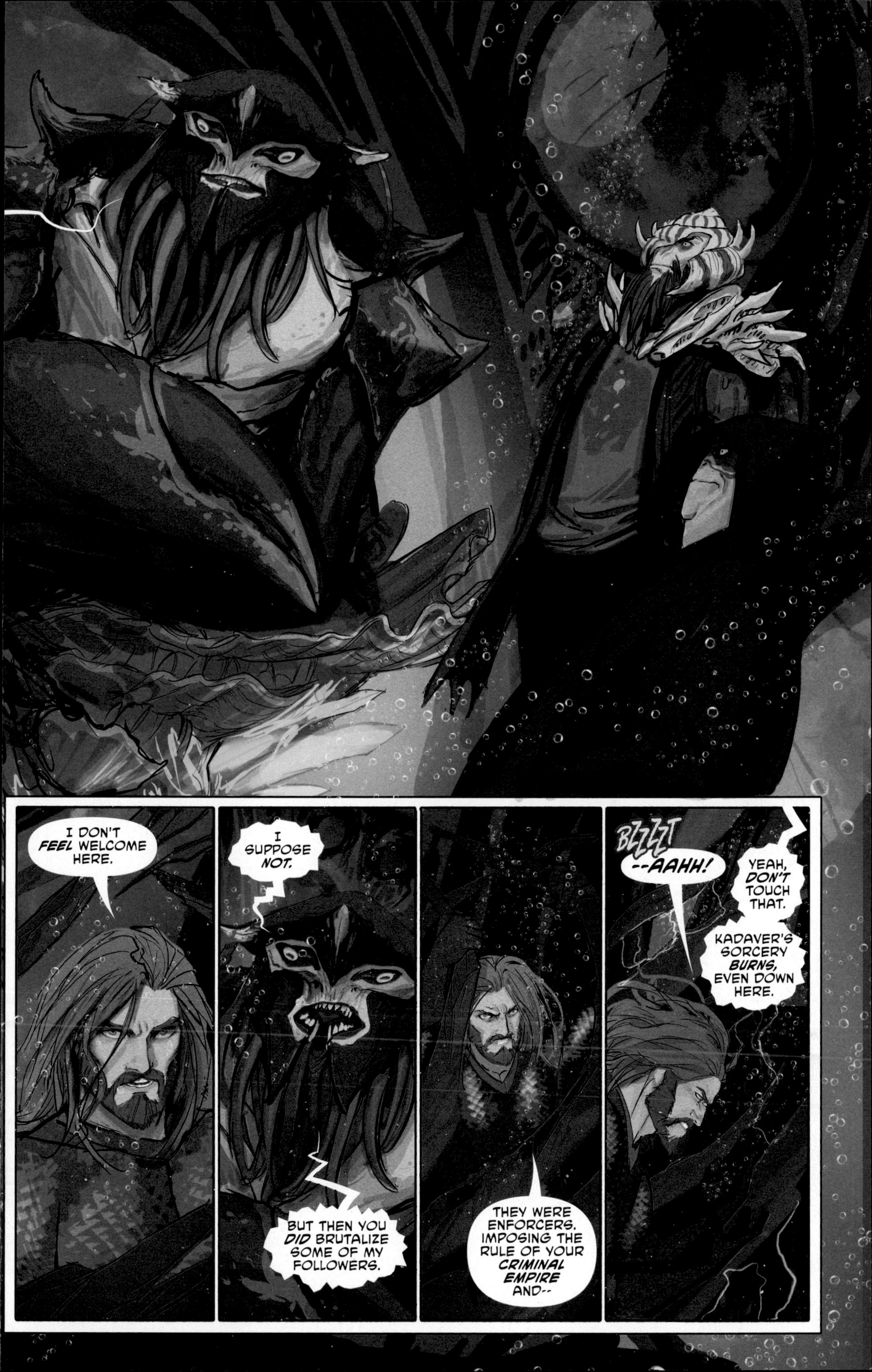
I DON'T FEEL WELCOME HERE.
I SUPPOSE NOT.
BUT THEN YOU DID BRUTALIZE SOME OF MY FOLLOWERS.
THEY WERE ENFORCERS. IMPOSING THE RULE OF YOUR CRIMINAL EMPIRE AND--
BZZZZT
--AAHH!
YEAH, DON'T TOUCH THAT.
KADAVER'S SORCERY BURNS, EVEN DOWN HERE.

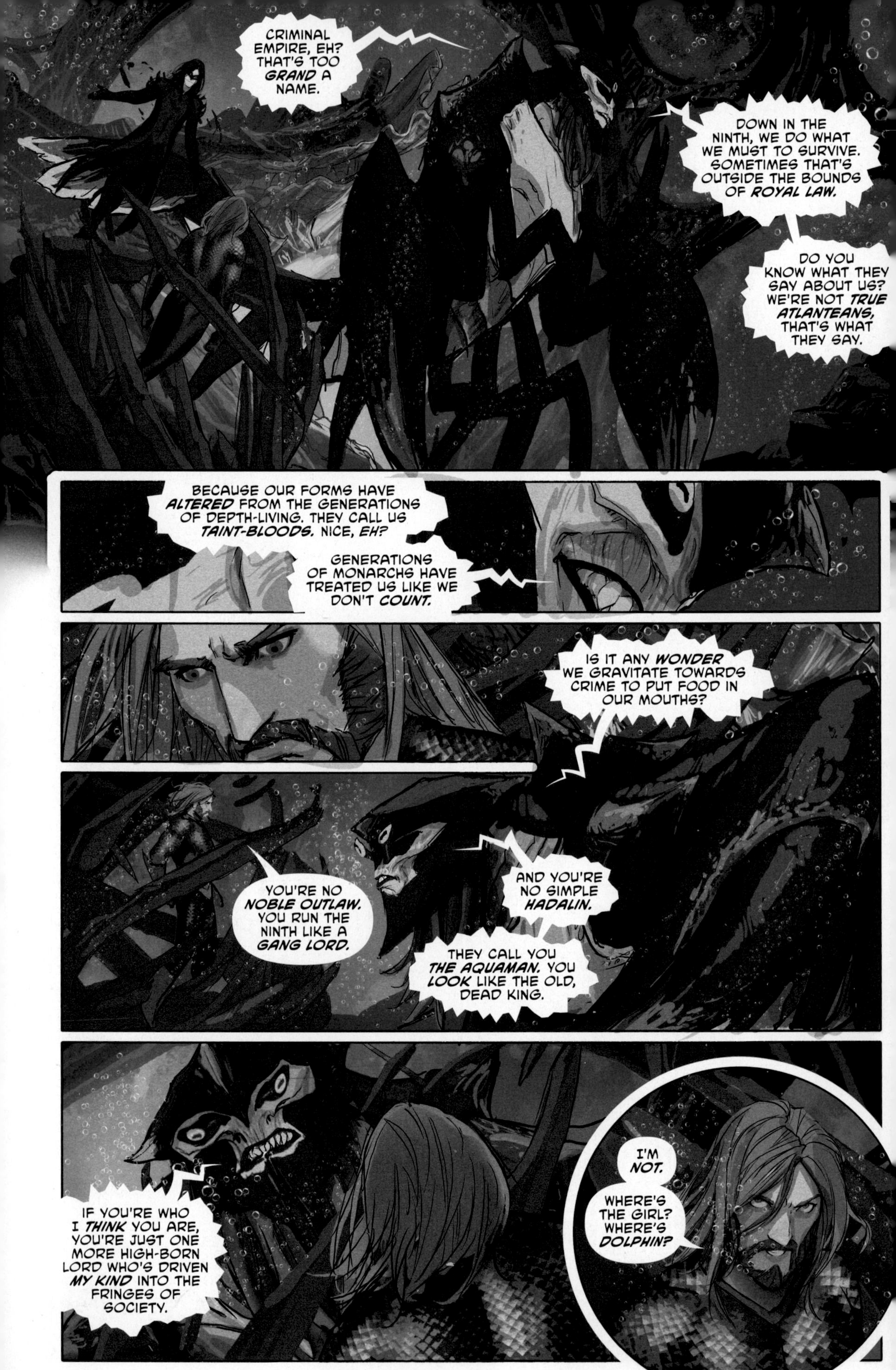
CRIMINAL EMPIRE, EH? THAT'S TOO GRAND A NAME.
DOWN IN THE NINTH, WE DO WHAT WE MUST TO SURVIVE. SOMETIMES THAT'S OUTSIDE THE BOUNDS OF ROYAL LAW.
DO YOU KNOW WHAT THEY SAY ABOUT US? WE'RE NOT TRUE ATLANTEANS, THAT'S WHAT THEY SAY.
BECAUSE OUR FORMS HAVE ALTERED FROM THE GENERATIONS OF DEPTH-LIVING. THEY CALL US TAINT-BLOODS. NICE, EH?
GENERATIONS OF MONARCHS HAVE TREATED US LIKE WE DON'T COUNT.
IS IT ANY WONDER WE GRAVITATE TOWARDS CRIME TO PUT FOOD IN OUR MOUTHS?
YOU'RE NO NOBLE OUTLAW. YOU RUN THE NINTH LIKE A GANG LORD.
AND YOU'RE NO SIMPLE HADALIN.
THEY CALL YOU THE AQUAMAN. YOU LOOK LIKE THE OLD, DEAD KING.
IF YOU'RE WHO I THINK YOU ARE, YOU'RE JUST ONE MORE HIGH-BORN LORD WHO'S DRIVEN MY KIND INTO THE FRINGES OF SOCIETY.
I'M NOT.
WHERE'S THE GIRL? WHERE'S DOLPHIN?

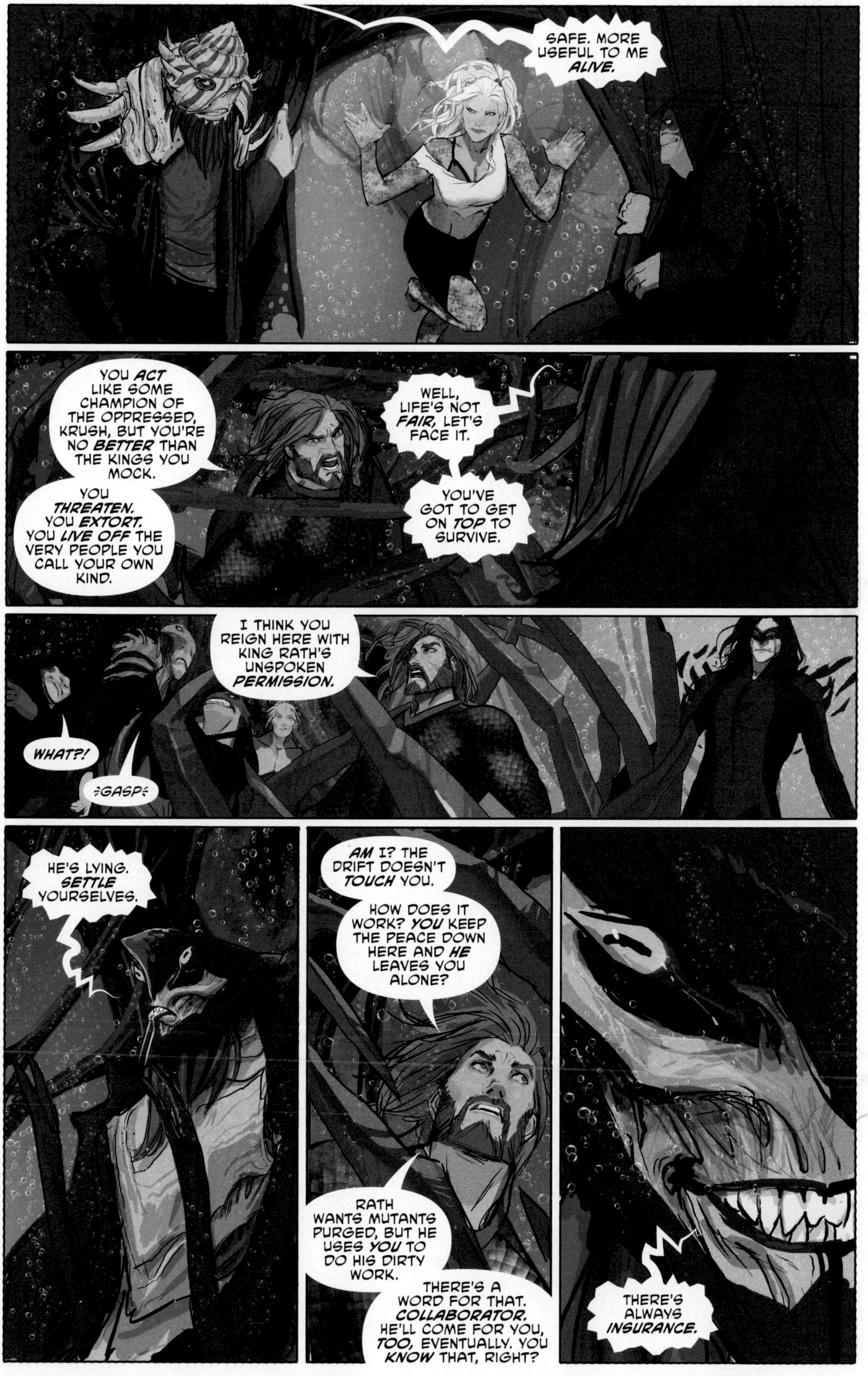
SAFE. MORE USEFUL TO ME ALIVE.
YOU ACT LIKE SOME CHAMPION OF THE OPPRESSED, KRUSH, BUT YOU'RE NO BETTER THAN THE KINGS YOU MOCK.
YOU THREATEN. YOU EXTORT. YOU LIVE OFF THE VERY PEOPLE YOU CALL YOUR OWN KIND.
WELL, LIFE'S NOT FAIR, LET'S FACE IT.
YOU'VE GOT TO GET ON TOP TO SURVIVE.
I THINK YOU REIGN HERE WITH KING RATH'S UNSPOKEN PERMISSION.
WHAT?!
GASP
HE'S LYING. SETTLE YOURSELVES.
AM I? THE DRIFT DOESN'T TOUCH YOU.
HOW DOES IT WORK? YOU KEEP THE PEACE DOWN HERE AND HE LEAVES YOU ALONE?
RATH WANTS MUTANTS PURGED, BUT HE USES YOU TO DO HIS DIRTY WORK.
THERE'S A WORD FOR THAT. COLLABORATOR. HE'LL COME FOR YOU, TOO, EVENTUALLY. YOU KNOW THAT, RIGHT?
THERE'S ALWAYS INSURANCE.

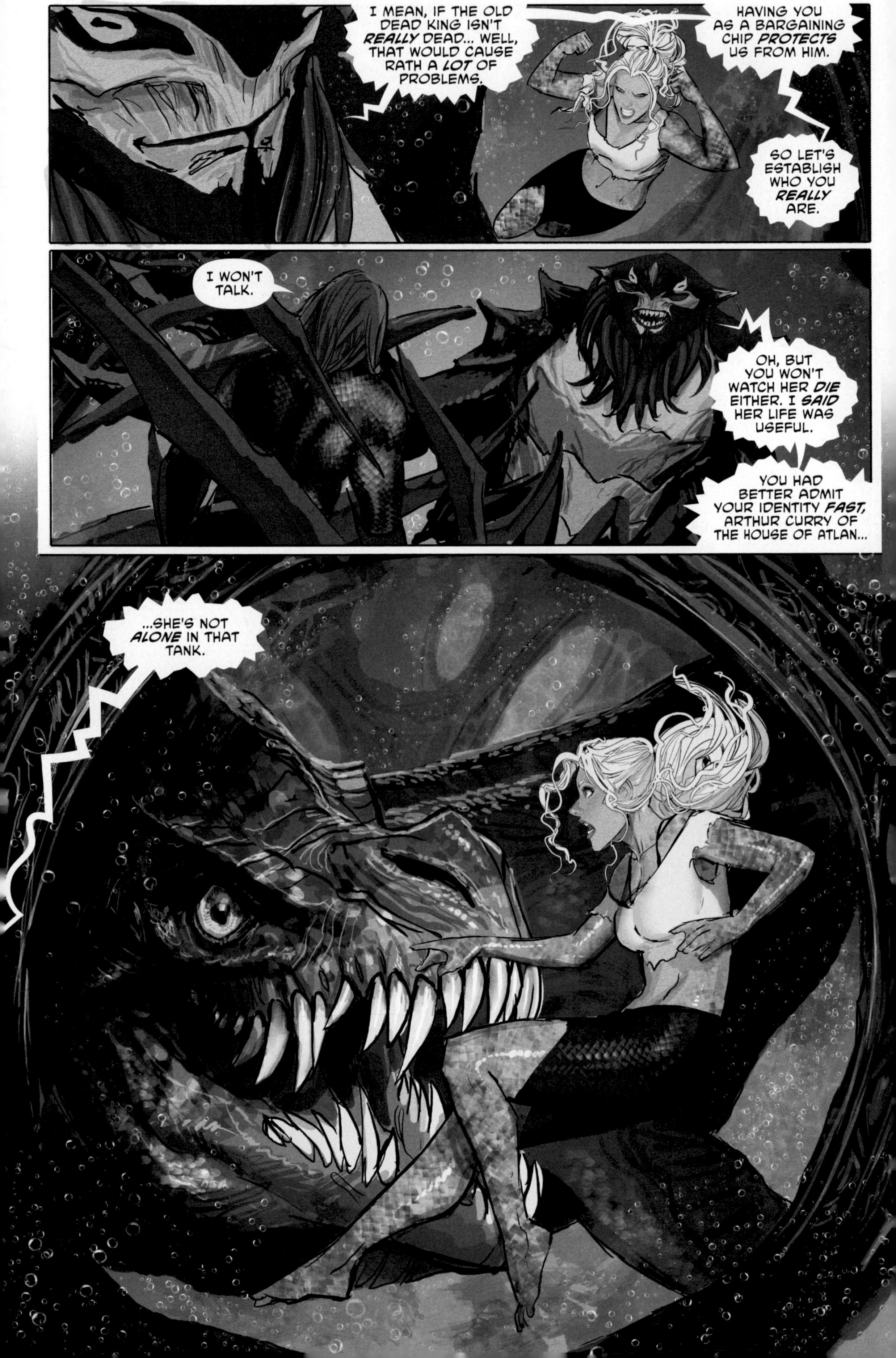
I MEAN, IF THE OLD DEAD KING ISN'T *REALLY* DEAD... WELL, THAT WOULD CAUSE RATH A *LOT* OF PROBLEMS.
HAVING YOU AS A BARGAINING CHIP *PROTECTS* US FROM HIM.
SO LET'S ESTABLISH WHO YOU *REALLY* ARE.
I WON'T TALK.
OH, BUT YOU WON'T WATCH HER *DIE* EITHER. I *SAID* HER LIFE WAS USEFUL.
YOU HAD BETTER ADMIT YOUR IDENTITY *FAST*, ARTHUR CURRY OF THE HOUSE OF ATLAN...
...SHE'S NOT *ALONE* IN THAT TANK.

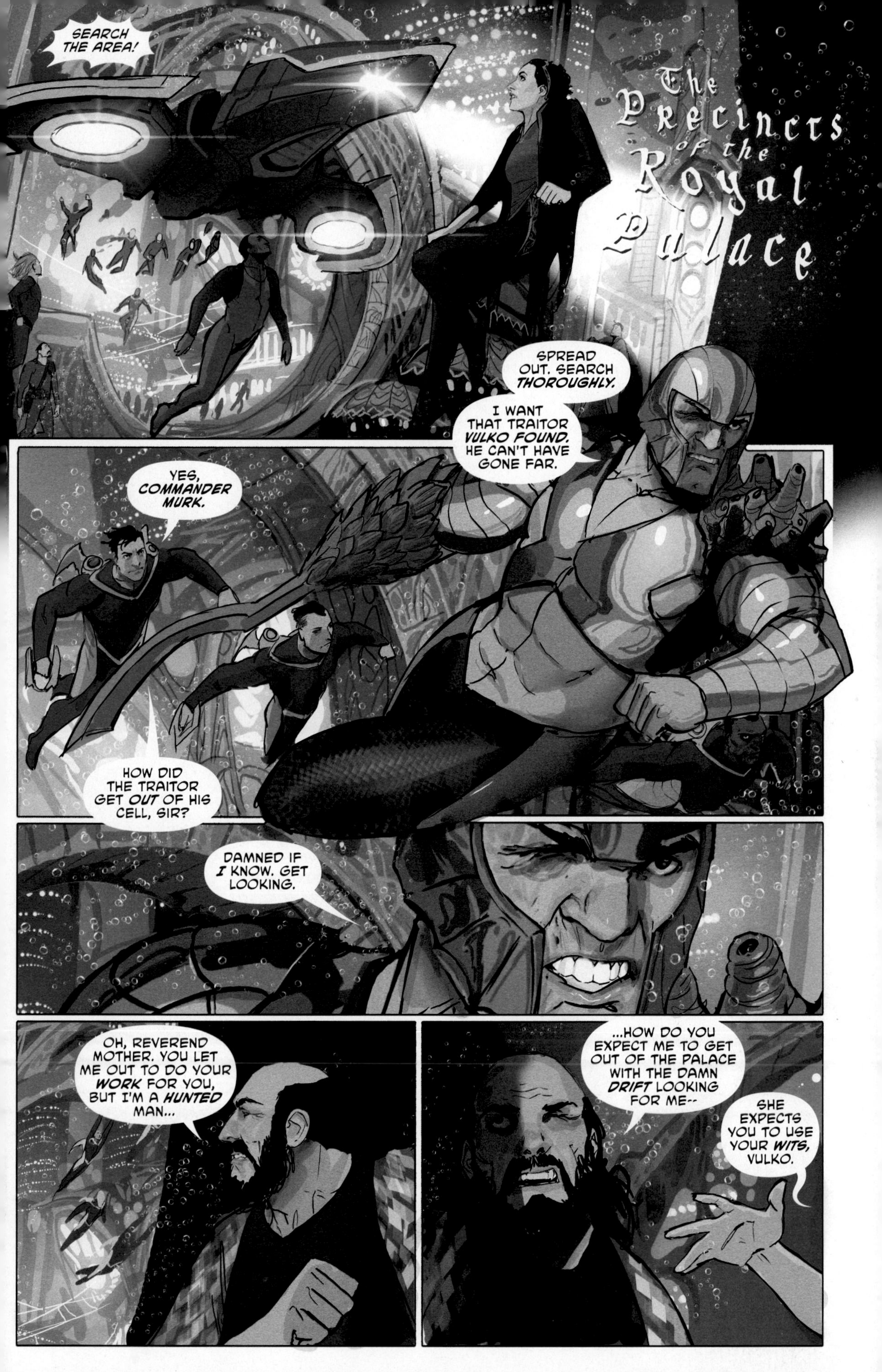
SEARCH THE AREA!
The Precincts of the Royal Palace
SPREAD OUT. SEARCH THOROUGHLY.
I WANT THAT TRAITOR VULKO FOUND. HE CAN'T HAVE GONE FAR.
YES, COMMANDER MURK.
HOW DID THE TRAITOR GET OUT OF HIS CELL, SIR?
DAMNED IF I KNOW. GET LOOKING.
OH, REVEREND MOTHER. YOU LET ME OUT TO DO YOUR WORK FOR YOU, BUT I'M A HUNTED MAN...
...HOW DO YOU EXPECT ME TO GET OUT OF THE PALACE WITH THE DAMN DRIFT LOOKING FOR ME--
SHE EXPECTS YOU TO USE YOUR WITS, VULKO.

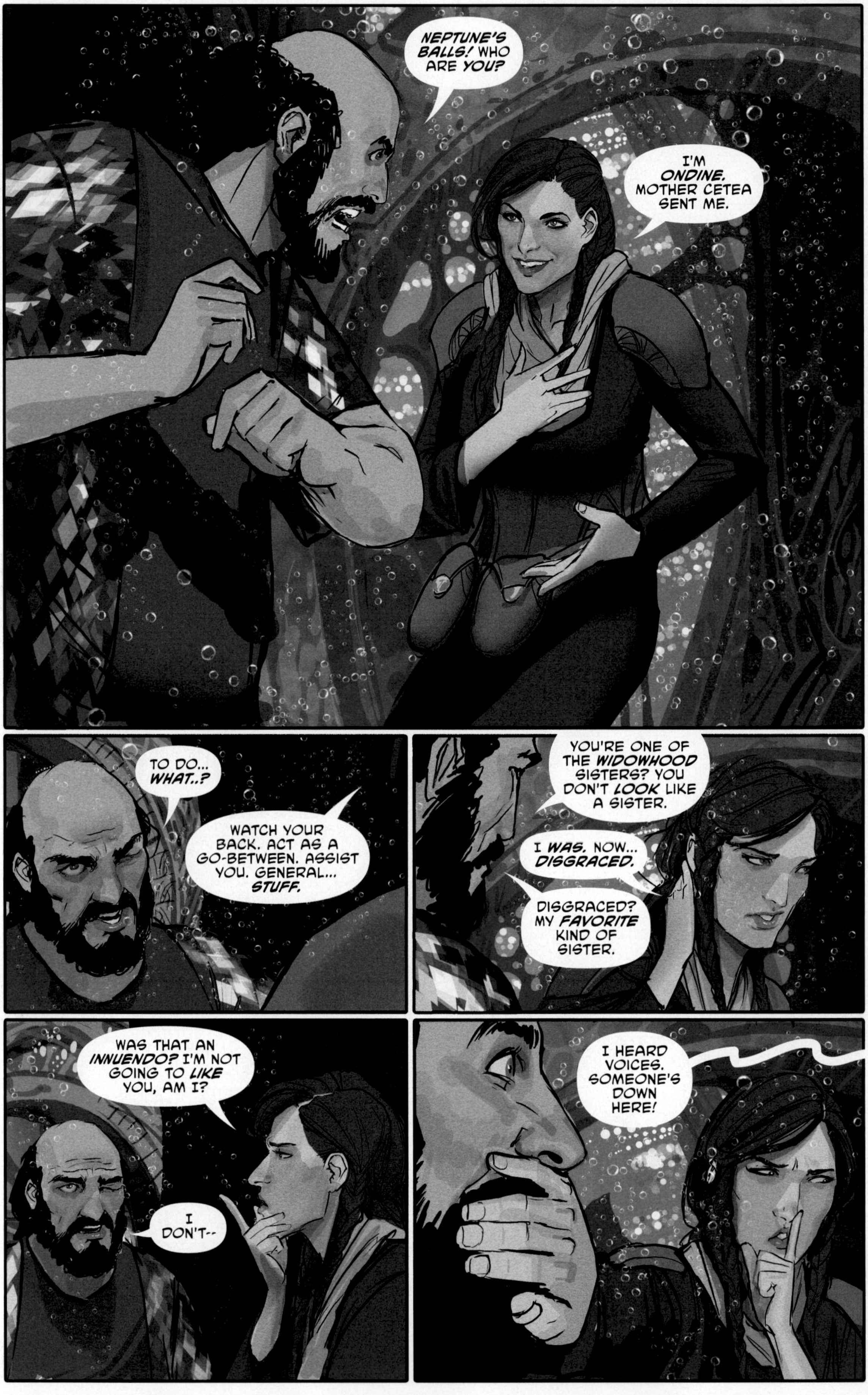
NEPTUNE'S BALLS! WHO ARE YOU?
I'M ONDINE. MOTHER CETEA SENT ME.
TO DO... WHAT..?
WATCH YOUR BACK. ACT AS A GO-BETWEEN. ASSIST YOU. GENERAL... STUFF.
YOU'RE ONE OF THE WIDOWHOOD SISTERS? YOU DON'T LOOK LIKE A SISTER.
I WAS. NOW... DISGRACED.
DISGRACED? MY FAVORITE KIND OF SISTER.
WAS THAT AN INNUENDO? I'M NOT GOING TO LIKE YOU, AM I?
I DON'T--
I HEARD VOICES. SOMEONE'S DOWN HERE!

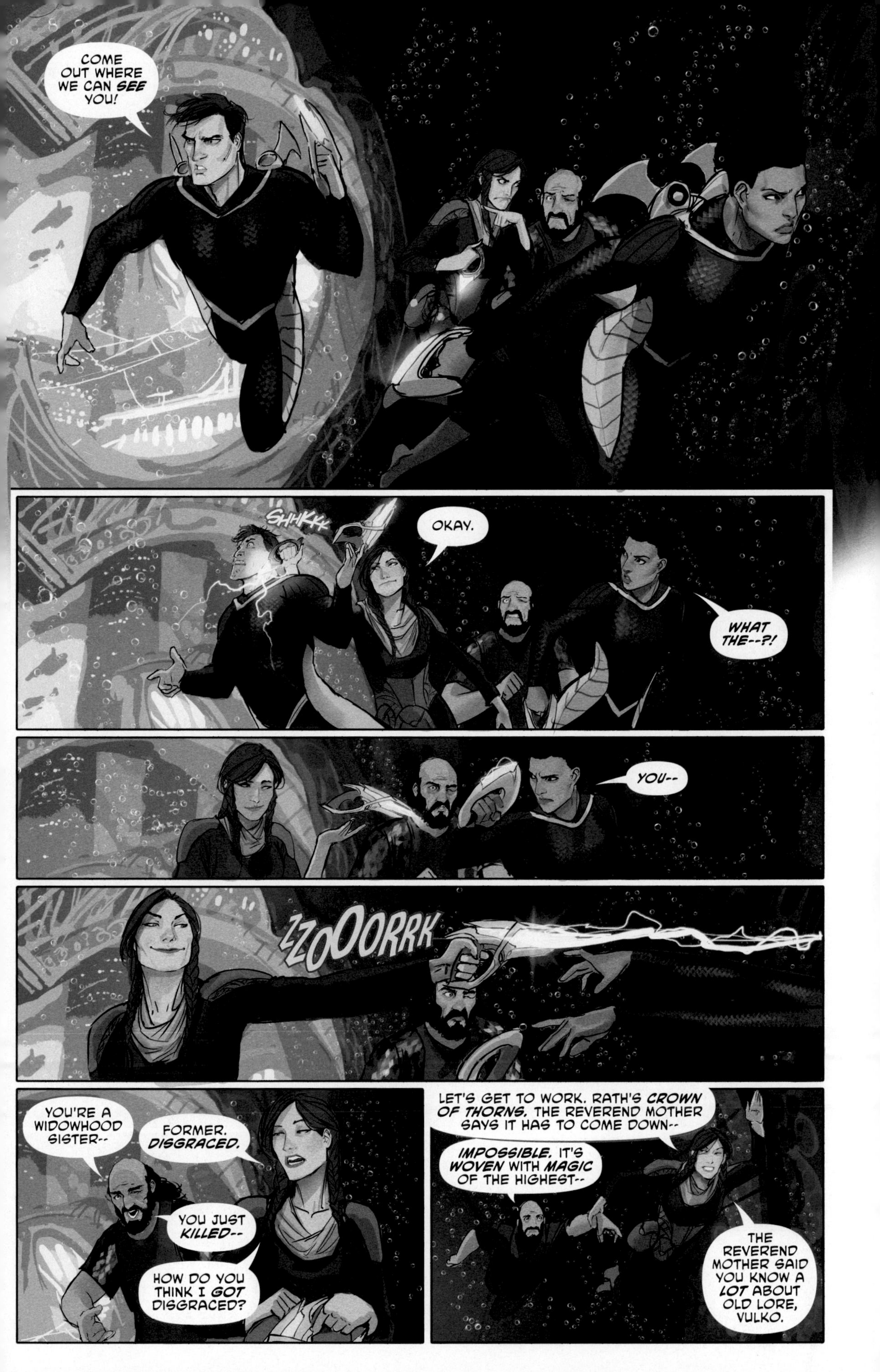
COME OUT WHERE WE CAN *SEE* YOU!
SHHKKK
OKAY.
WHAT THE--?!
YOU--
ZZOOORRRK
YOU'RE A WIDOWHOOD SISTER--
FORMER. *DISGRACED.*
YOU JUST *KILLED--*
HOW DO YOU THINK I *GOT* DISGRACED?
LET'S GET TO WORK. RATH'S *CROWN OF THORNS.* THE REVEREND MOTHER SAYS IT HAS TO COME DOWN--
IMPOSSIBLE. IT'S *WOVEN* WITH *MAGIC* OF THE HIGHEST--
THE REVEREND MOTHER SAID YOU KNOW A *LOT* ABOUT OLD LORE, VULKO.

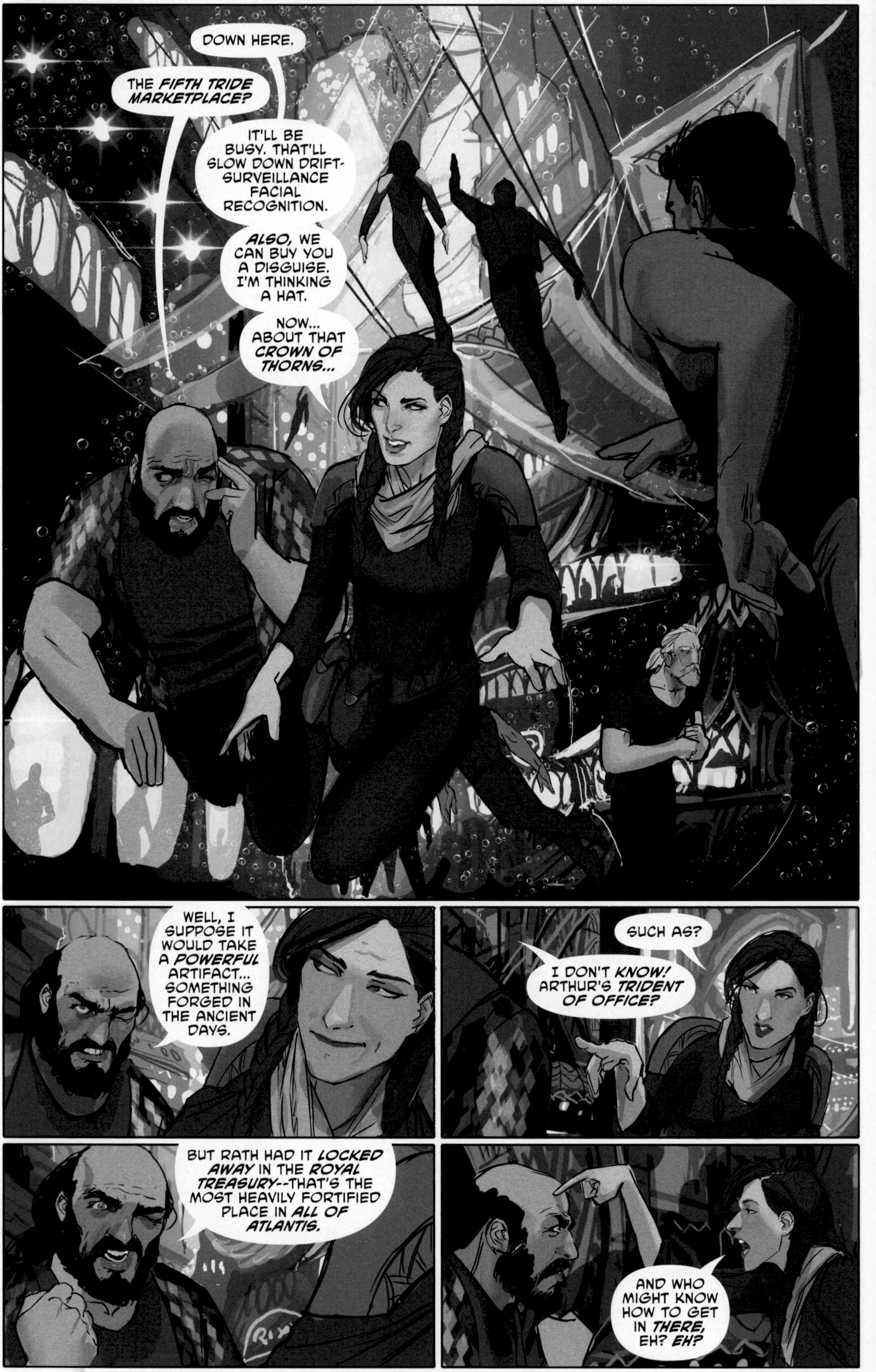
DOWN HERE.
THE FIFTH TRIDE MARKETPLACE?
IT'LL BE BUSY. THAT'LL SLOW DOWN DRIFT-SURVEILLANCE FACIAL RECOGNITION.
ALSO, WE CAN BUY YOU A DISGUISE. I'M THINKING A HAT.
NOW... ABOUT THAT CROWN OF THORNS...
WELL, I SUPPOSE IT WOULD TAKE A POWERFUL ARTIFACT... SOMETHING FORGED IN THE ANCIENT DAYS.
SUCH AS?
I DON'T KNOW! ARTHUR'S TRIDENT OF OFFICE?
BUT RATH HAD IT LOCKED AWAY IN THE ROYAL TREASURY--THAT'S THE MOST HEAVILY FORTIFIED PLACE IN ALL OF ATLANTIS.
AND WHO MIGHT KNOW HOW TO GET IN THERE, EH? EH?

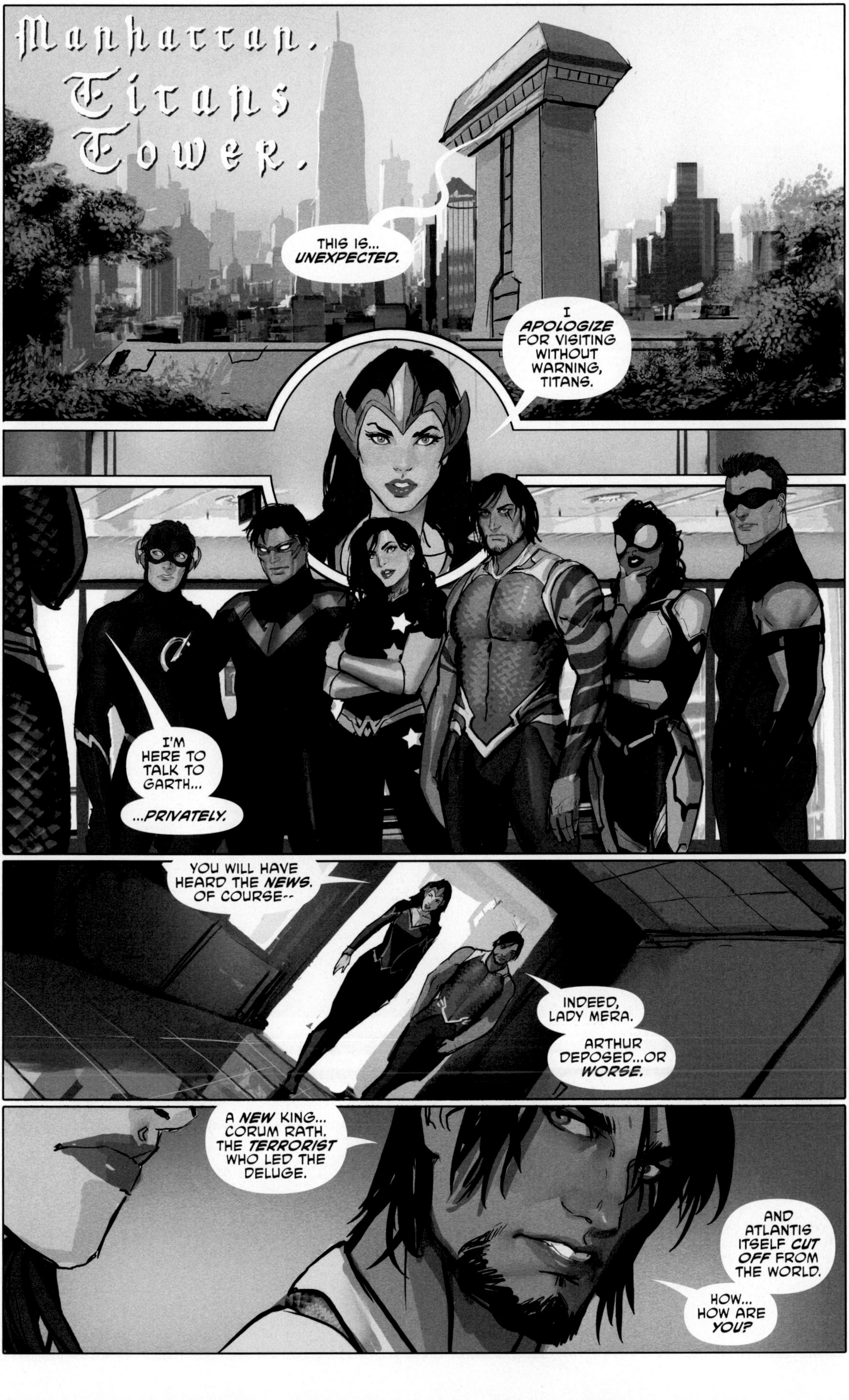
Manhattan.
Titans Tower.
THIS IS... UNEXPECTED.
I APOLOGIZE FOR VISITING WITHOUT WARNING, TITANS.
I'M HERE TO TALK TO GARTH...
...PRIVATELY.
YOU WILL HAVE HEARD THE NEWS, OF COURSE--
INDEED, LADY MERA.
ARTHUR DEPOSED...OR WORSE.
A NEW KING... CORUM RATH. THE TERRORIST WHO LED THE DELUGE.
AND ATLANTIS ITSELF CUT OFF FROM THE WORLD.
HOW... HOW ARE YOU?

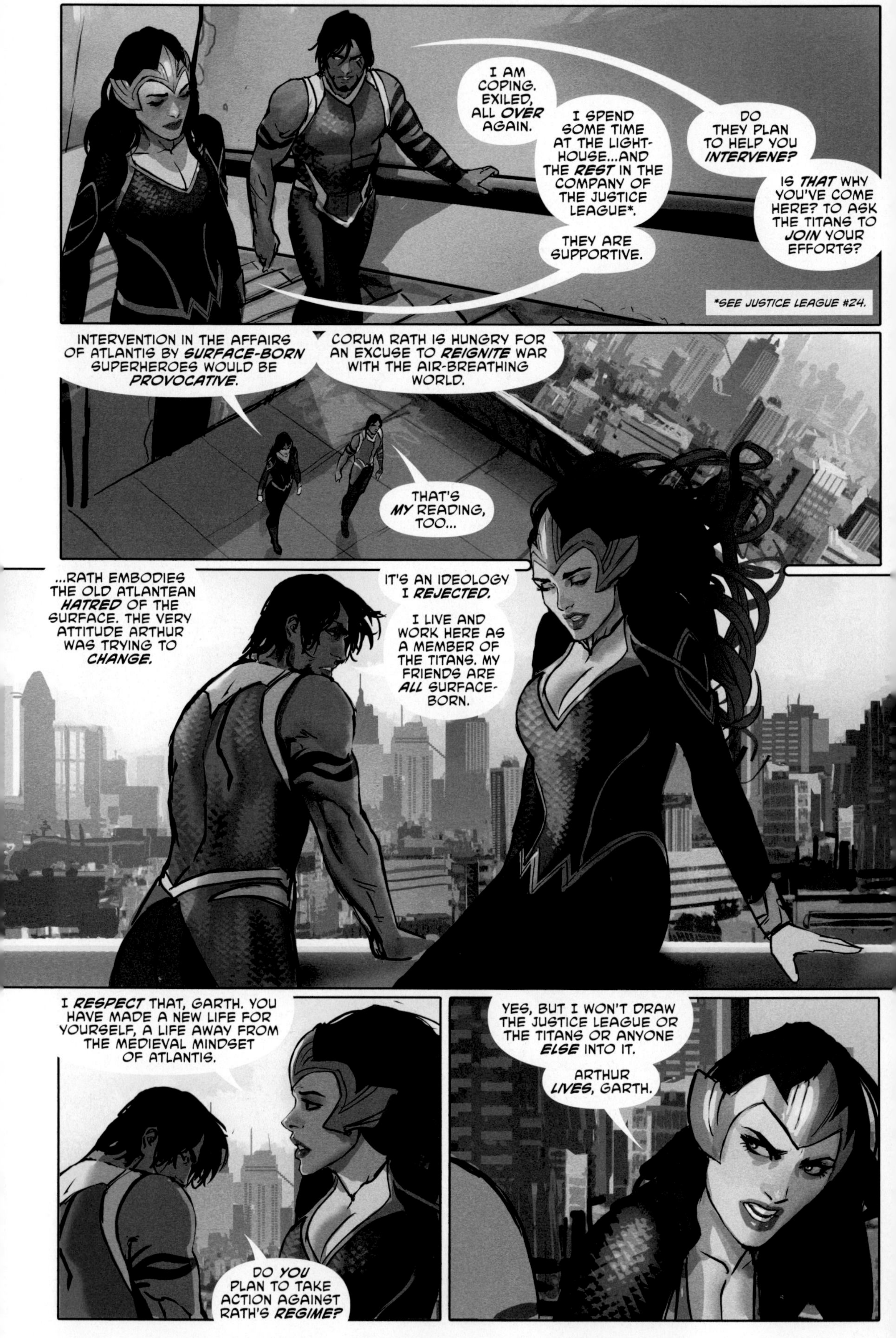
I AM COPING. EXILED, ALL OVER AGAIN.
I SPEND SOME TIME AT THE LIGHT-HOUSE...AND THE REST IN THE COMPANY OF THE JUSTICE LEAGUE*.
THEY ARE SUPPORTIVE.
DO THEY PLAN TO HELP YOU INTERVENE?
IS THAT WHY YOU'VE COME HERE? TO ASK THE TITANS TO JOIN YOUR EFFORTS?
*SEE JUSTICE LEAGUE #24.
INTERVENTION IN THE AFFAIRS OF ATLANTIS BY SURFACE-BORN SUPERHEROES WOULD BE PROVOCATIVE.
CORUM RATH IS HUNGRY FOR AN EXCUSE TO REIGNITE WAR WITH THE AIR-BREATHING WORLD.
THAT'S MY READING, TOO...
...RATH EMBODIES THE OLD ATLANTEAN HATRED OF THE SURFACE. THE VERY ATTITUDE ARTHUR WAS TRYING TO CHANGE.
IT'S AN IDEOLOGY I REJECTED.
I LIVE AND WORK HERE AS A MEMBER OF THE TITANS. MY FRIENDS ARE ALL SURFACE-BORN.
I RESPECT THAT, GARTH. YOU HAVE MADE A NEW LIFE FOR YOURSELF, A LIFE AWAY FROM THE MEDIEVAL MINDSET OF ATLANTIS.
DO YOU PLAN TO TAKE ACTION AGAINST RATH'S REGIME?
YES, BUT I WON'T DRAW THE JUSTICE LEAGUE OR THE TITANS OR ANYONE ELSE INTO IT.
ARTHUR LIVES, GARTH.

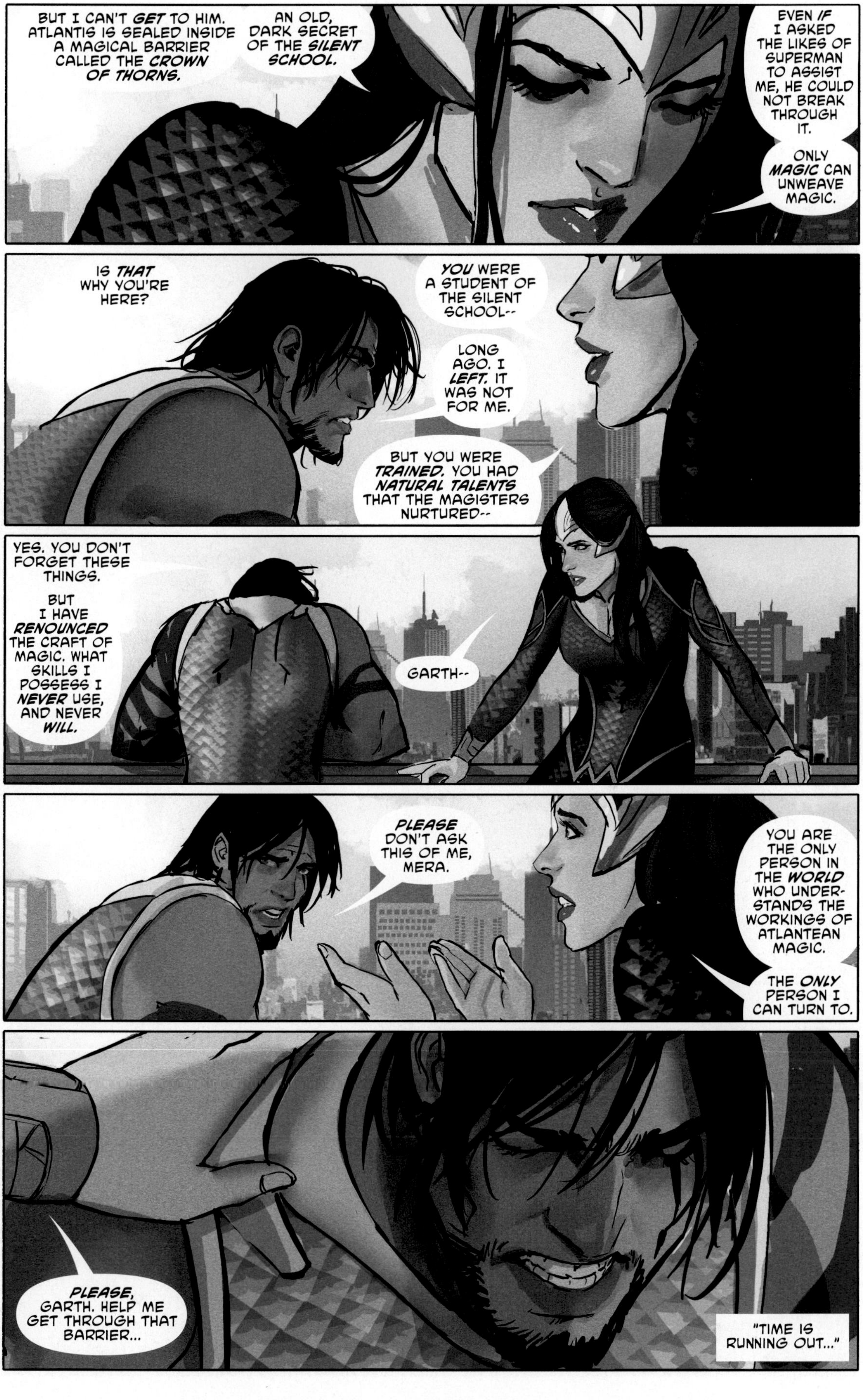
BUT I CAN'T GET TO HIM. ATLANTIS IS SEALED INSIDE A MAGICAL BARRIER CALLED THE CROWN OF THORNS.
AN OLD, DARK SECRET OF THE SILENT SCHOOL.
EVEN IF I ASKED THE LIKES OF SUPERMAN TO ASSIST ME, HE COULD NOT BREAK THROUGH IT.
ONLY MAGIC CAN UNWEAVE MAGIC.
IS THAT WHY YOU'RE HERE?
YOU WERE A STUDENT OF THE SILENT SCHOOL--
LONG AGO. I LEFT. IT WAS NOT FOR ME.
BUT YOU WERE TRAINED. YOU HAD NATURAL TALENTS THAT THE MAGISTERS NURTURED--
YES. YOU DON'T FORGET THESE THINGS.
BUT I HAVE RENOUNCED THE CRAFT OF MAGIC. WHAT SKILLS I POSSESS I NEVER USE, AND NEVER WILL.
GARTH--
PLEASE DON'T ASK THIS OF ME, MERA.
YOU ARE THE ONLY PERSON IN THE WORLD WHO UNDERSTANDS THE WORKINGS OF ATLANTEAN MAGIC.
THE ONLY PERSON I CAN TURN TO.
PLEASE, GARTH. HELP ME GET THROUGH THAT BARRIER...
"TIME IS RUNNING OUT..."

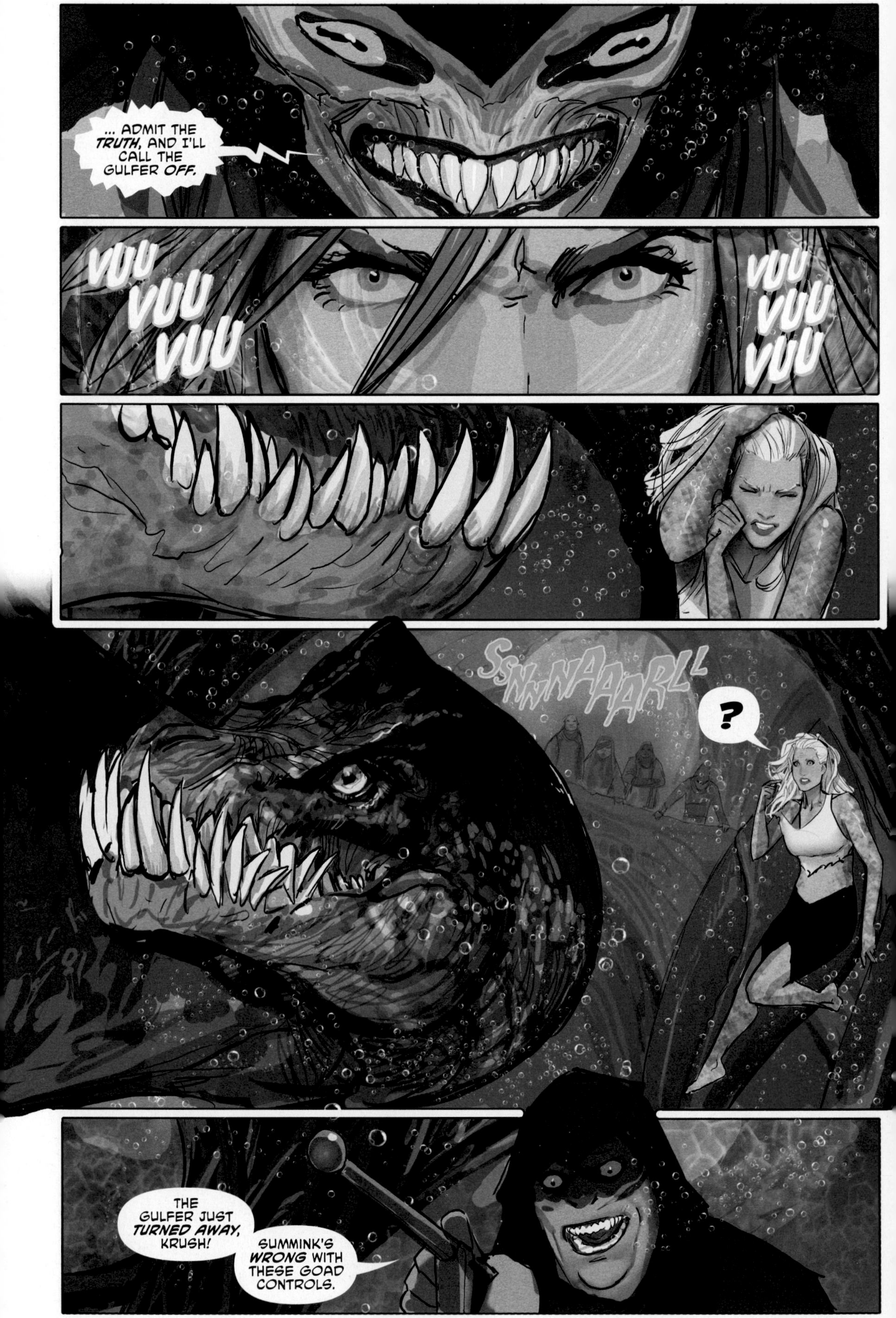
... ADMIT THE TRUTH, AND I'LL CALL THE GULFER OFF.
VUU VUU VUU
VUU VUU VUU
SSNNNAAARLL
?
THE GULFER JUST TURNED AWAY, KRUSH!
SUMMINK'S WRONG WITH THESE GOAD CONTROLS.

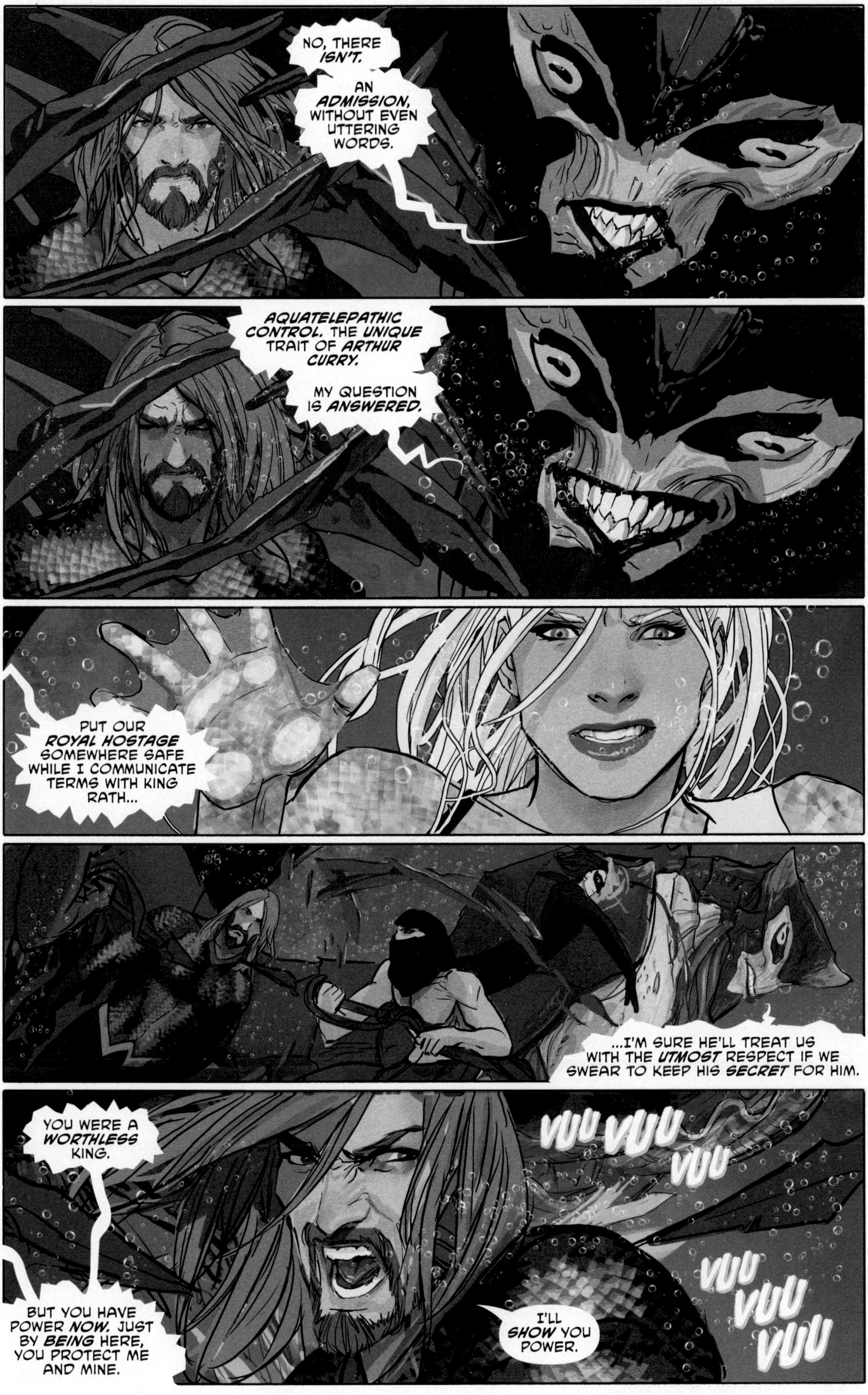
NO, THERE ISN'T.
AN ADMISSION, WITHOUT EVEN UTTERING WORDS.
AQUATELEPATHIC CONTROL. THE UNIQUE TRAIT OF ARTHUR CURRY.
MY QUESTION IS ANSWERED.
PUT OUR ROYAL HOSTAGE SOMEWHERE SAFE WHILE I COMMUNICATE TERMS WITH KING RATH...
...I'M SURE HE'LL TREAT US WITH THE UTMOST RESPECT IF WE SWEAR TO KEEP HIS SECRET FOR HIM.
YOU WERE A WORTHLESS KING.
VUU VUU VUU
BUT YOU HAVE POWER NOW. JUST BY BEING HERE, YOU PROTECT ME AND MINE.
I'LL SHOW YOU POWER.
VUU VUU VUU

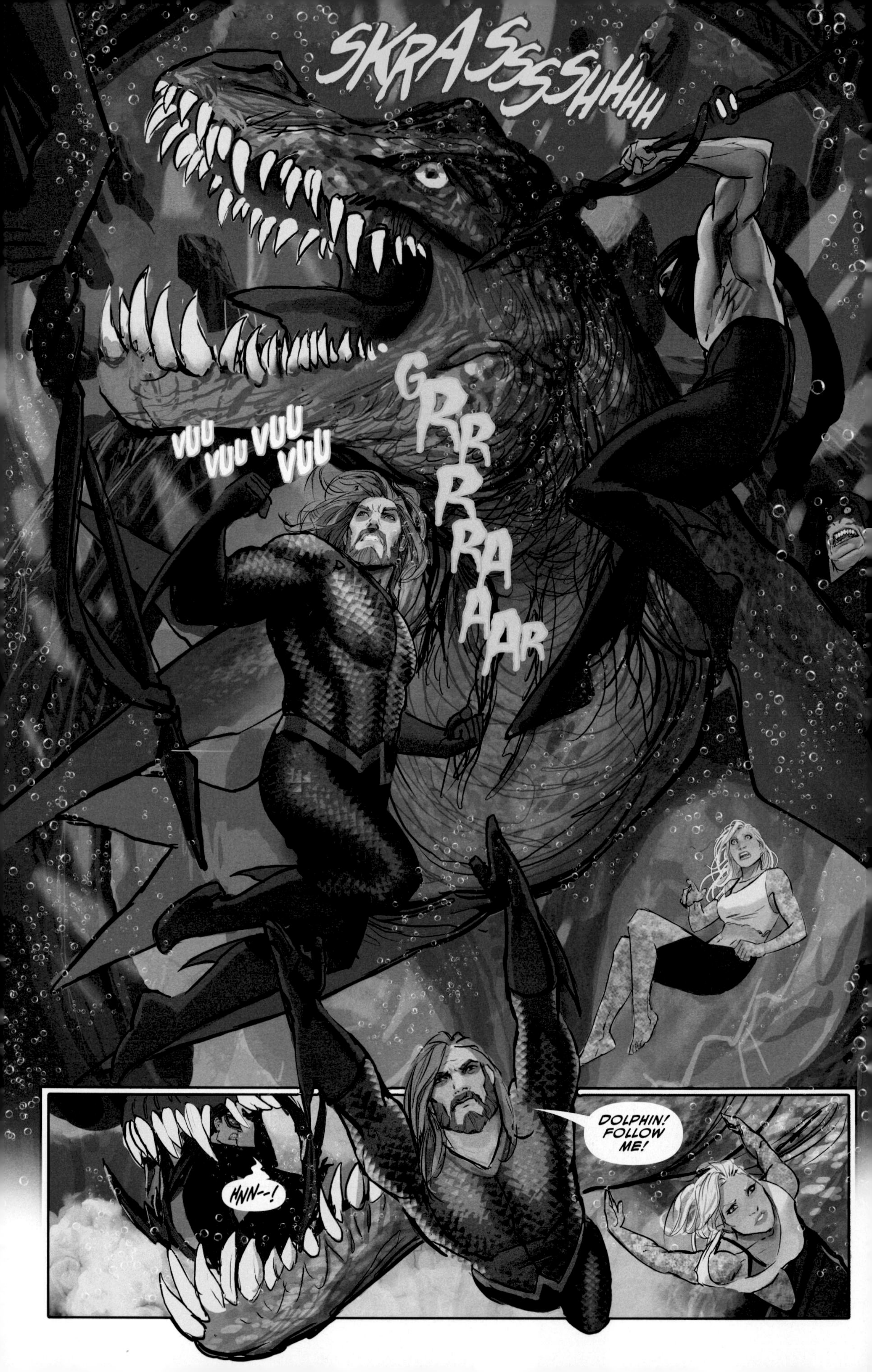
SKRASSSSHHHH
VUU VUU VUU VUU
GRRRRAAAR
DOLPHIN! FOLLOW ME!
HNN--!

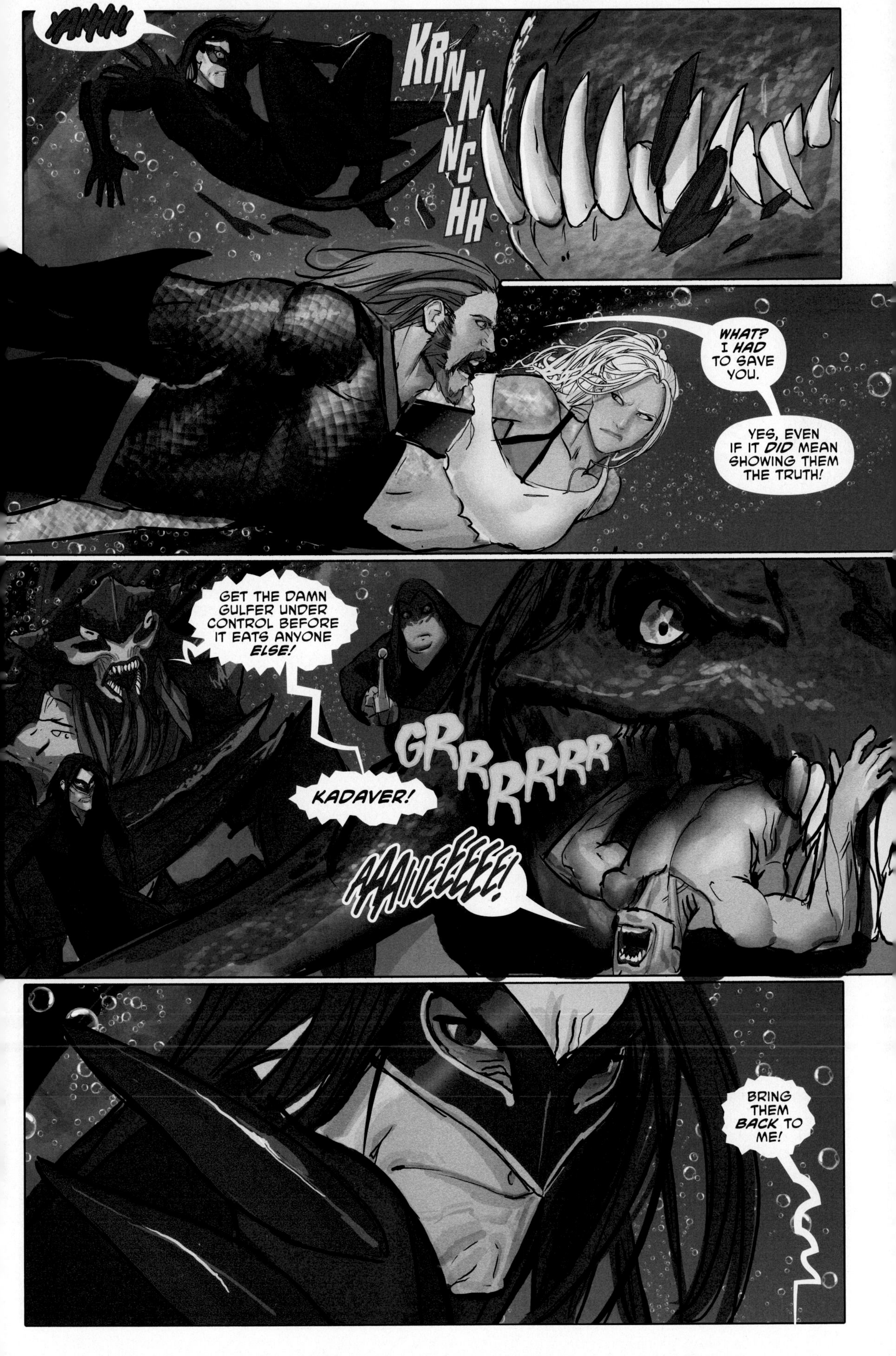
YAHHH!
KRNNNCHH
WHAT? I HAD TO SAVE YOU.
YES, EVEN IF IT DID MEAN SHOWING THEM THE TRUTH!
GET THE DAMN GULFER UNDER CONTROL BEFORE IT EATS ANYONE ELSE!
KADAVER!
GRRRRRRR
AAAIIEEEEE!
BRING THEM BACK TO ME!

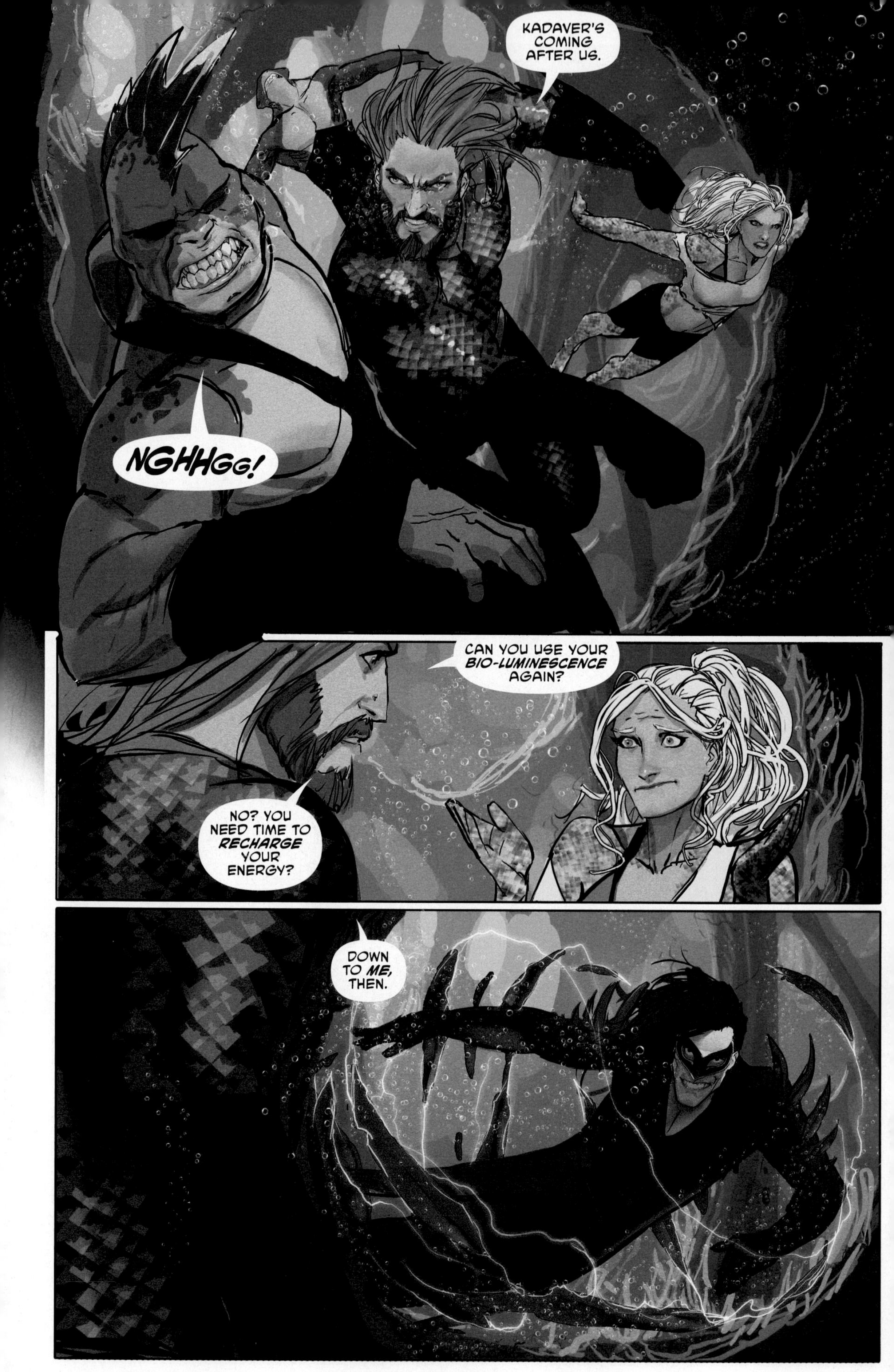
KADAVER'S COMING AFTER US.
NGHHGG!
CAN YOU USE YOUR BIO-LUMINESCENCE AGAIN?
NO? YOU NEED TIME TO RECHARGE YOUR ENERGY?
DOWN TO ME, THEN.

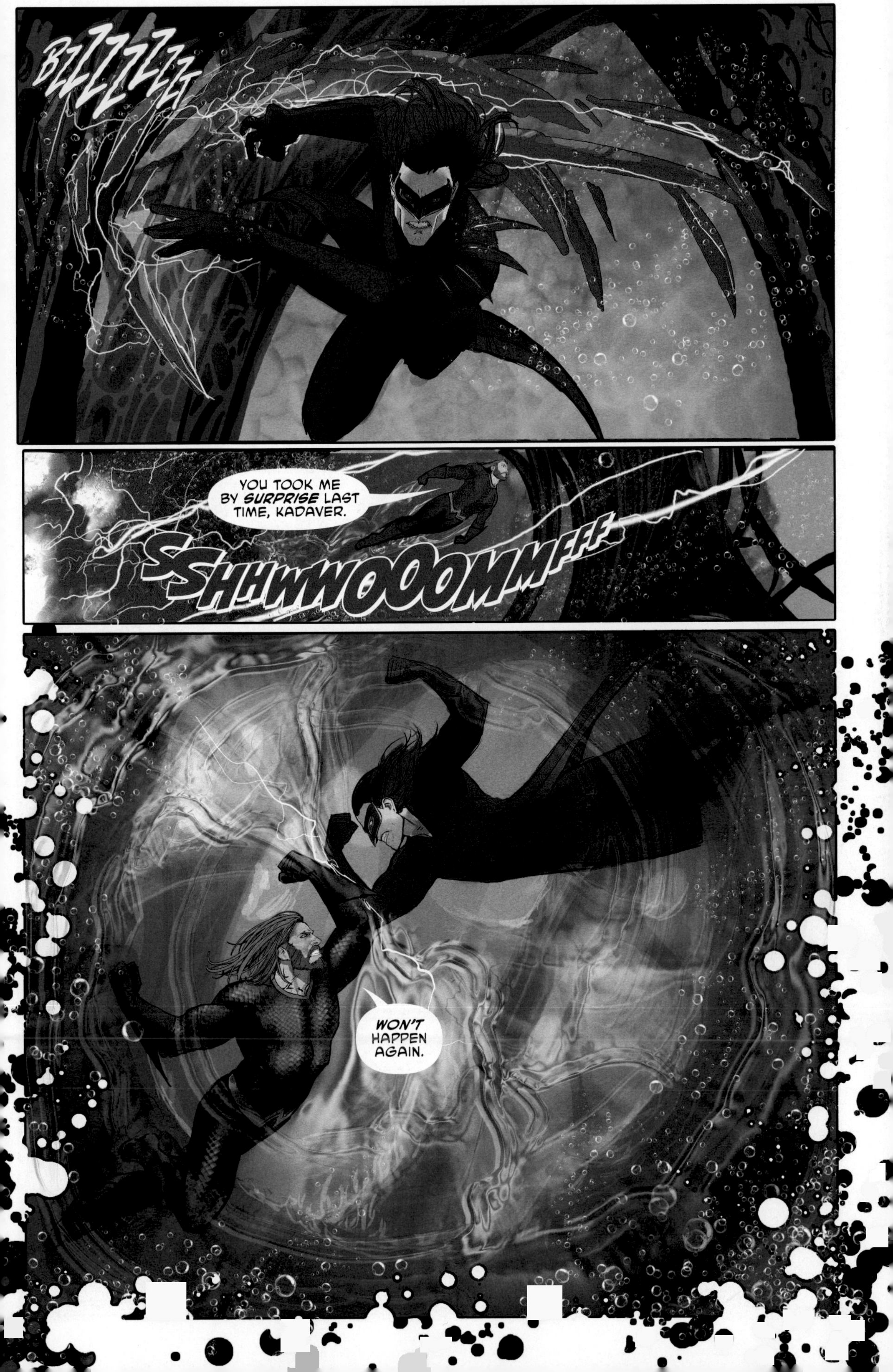
BZZZZZZZT
YOU TOOK ME BY SURPRISE LAST TIME, KADAVER.
SSHHWWOOOOMMFFF
WON'T HAPPEN AGAIN.

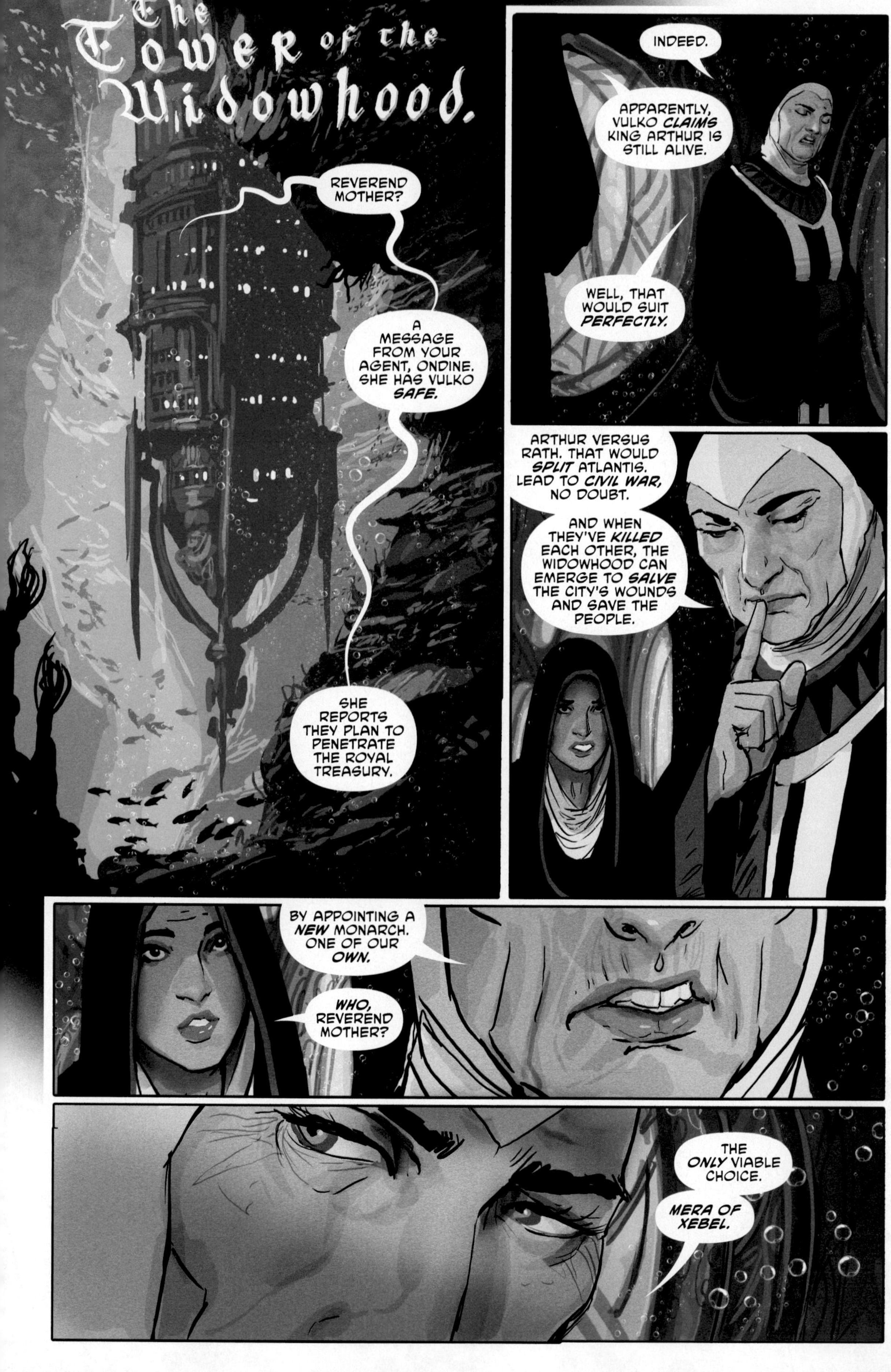
The Tower of the Widowhood.
REVEREND MOTHER?
A MESSAGE FROM YOUR AGENT, ONDINE. SHE HAS VULKO SAFE.
SHE REPORTS THEY PLAN TO PENETRATE THE ROYAL TREASURY.
INDEED.
APPARENTLY, VULKO CLAIMS KING ARTHUR IS STILL ALIVE.
WELL, THAT WOULD SUIT PERFECTLY.
ARTHUR VERSUS RATH. THAT WOULD SPLIT ATLANTIS. LEAD TO CIVIL WAR, NO DOUBT.
AND WHEN THEY'VE KILLED EACH OTHER, THE WIDOWHOOD CAN EMERGE TO SALVE THE CITY'S WOUNDS AND SAVE THE PEOPLE.
BY APPOINTING A NEW MONARCH. ONE OF OUR OWN.
WHO, REVEREND MOTHER?
THE ONLY VIABLE CHOICE.
MERA OF XEBEL.

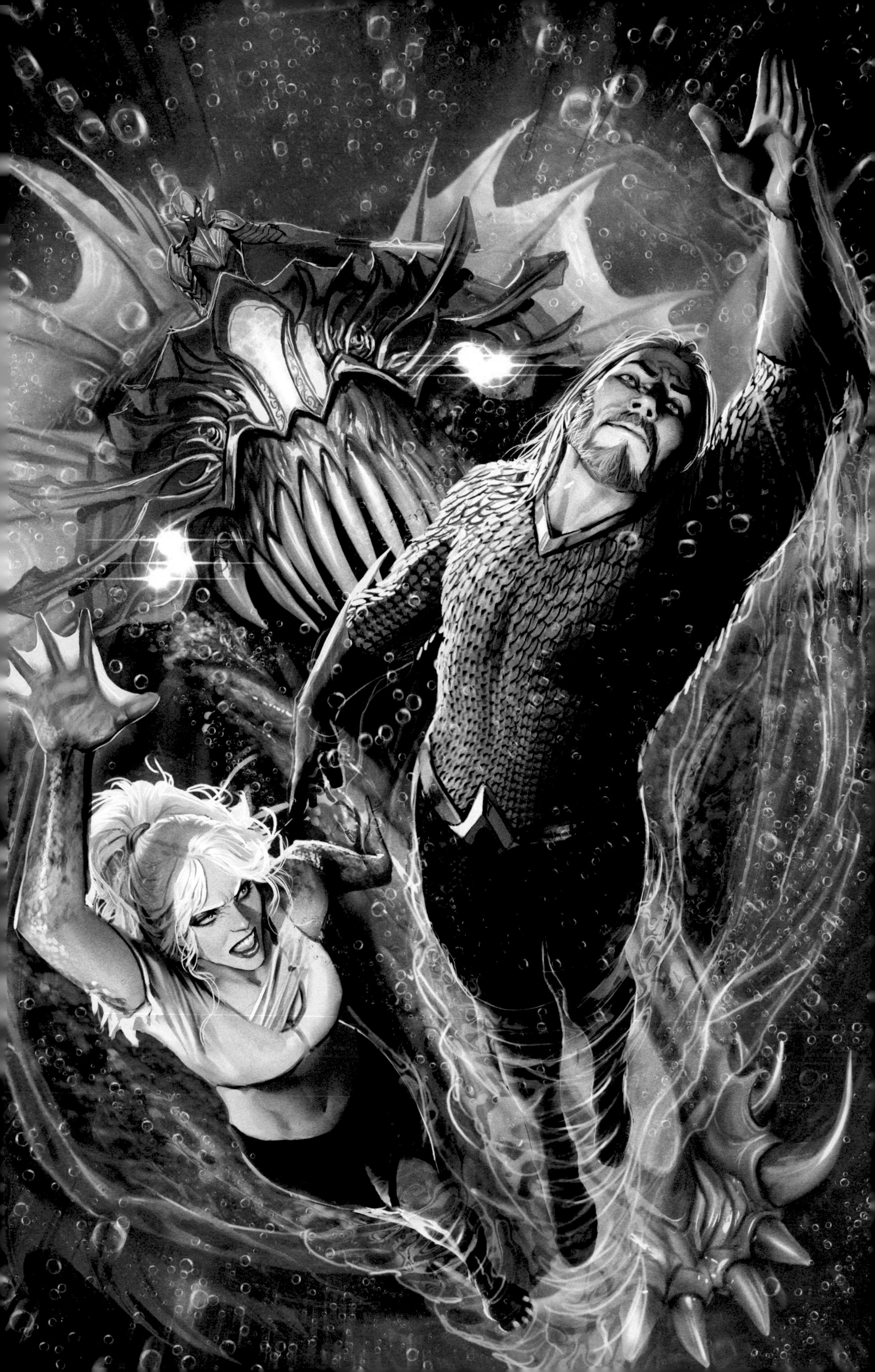

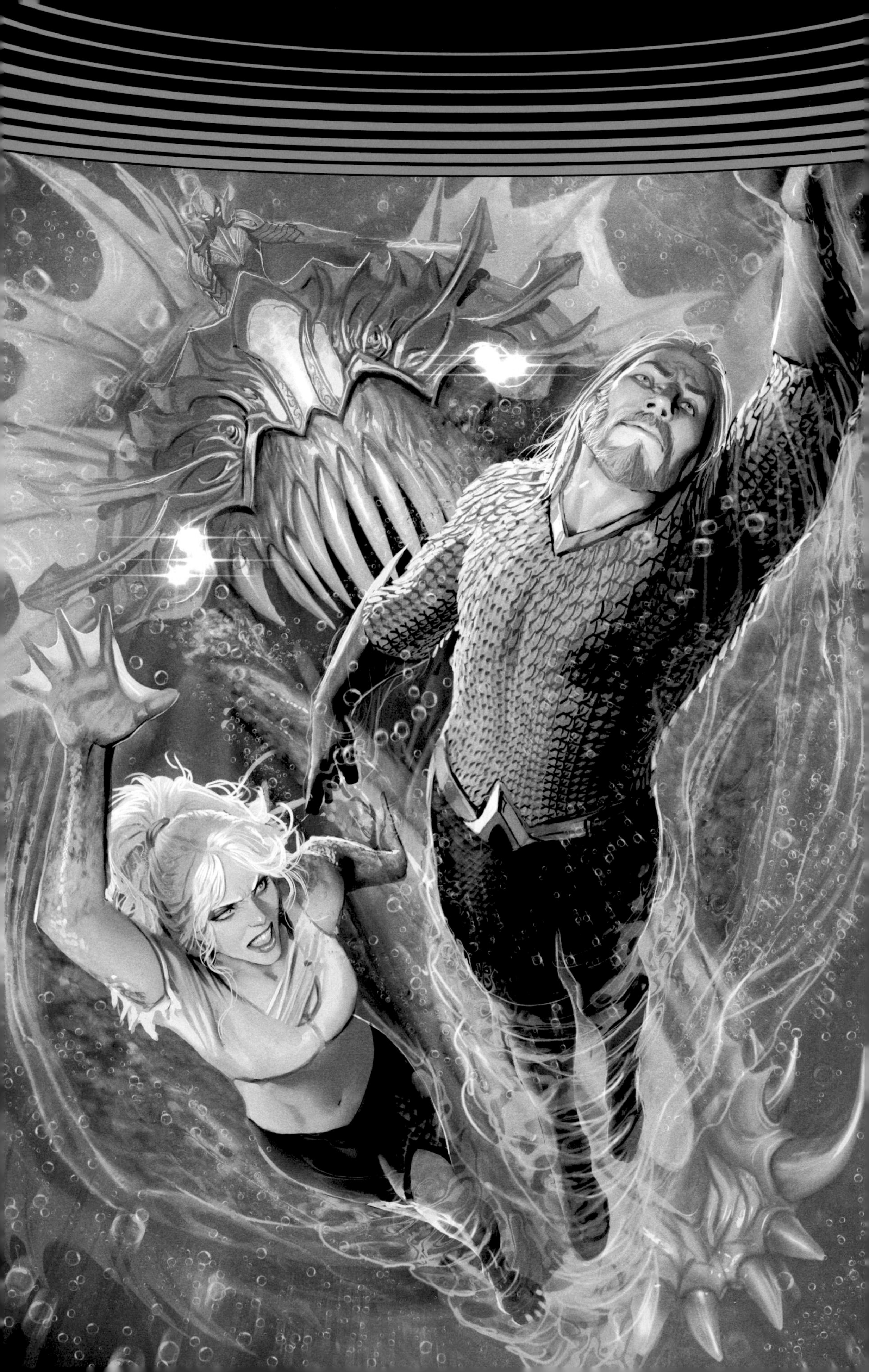

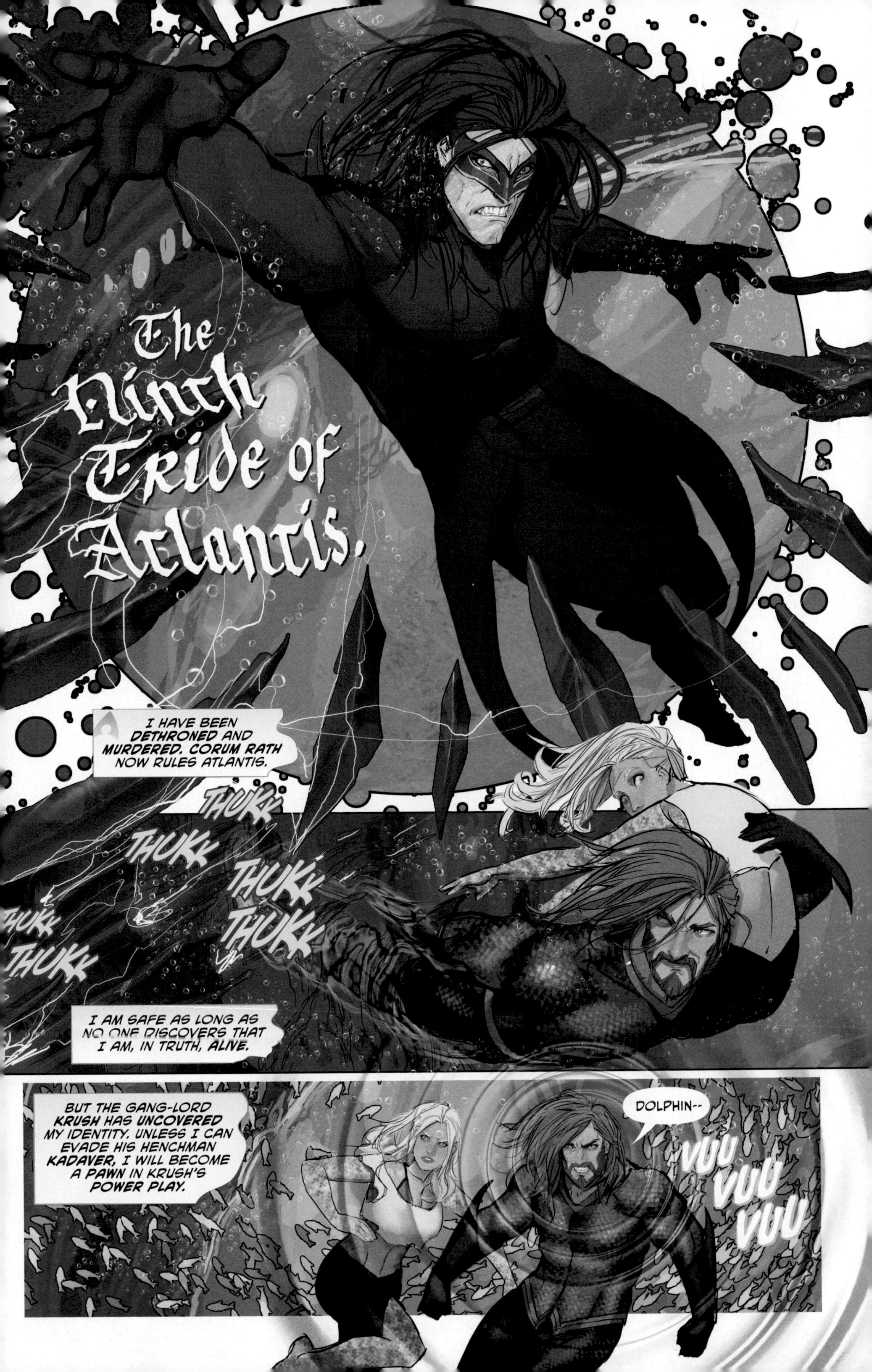
The Ninth Tride of Atlantis.
I HAVE BEEN DETHRONED AND MURDERED. CORUM RATH NOW RULES ATLANTIS.
THUKK
THUKK
THUKK
THUKK
THUKK
THUKK
I AM SAFE AS LONG AS NO ONE DISCOVERS THAT I AM, IN TRUTH, ALIVE.
BUT THE GANG-LORD KRUSH HAS UNCOVERED MY IDENTITY. UNLESS I CAN EVADE HIS HENCHMAN KADAVER, I WILL BECOME A PAWN IN KRUSH'S POWER PLAY.
DOLPHIN--
VUU VUU VUU

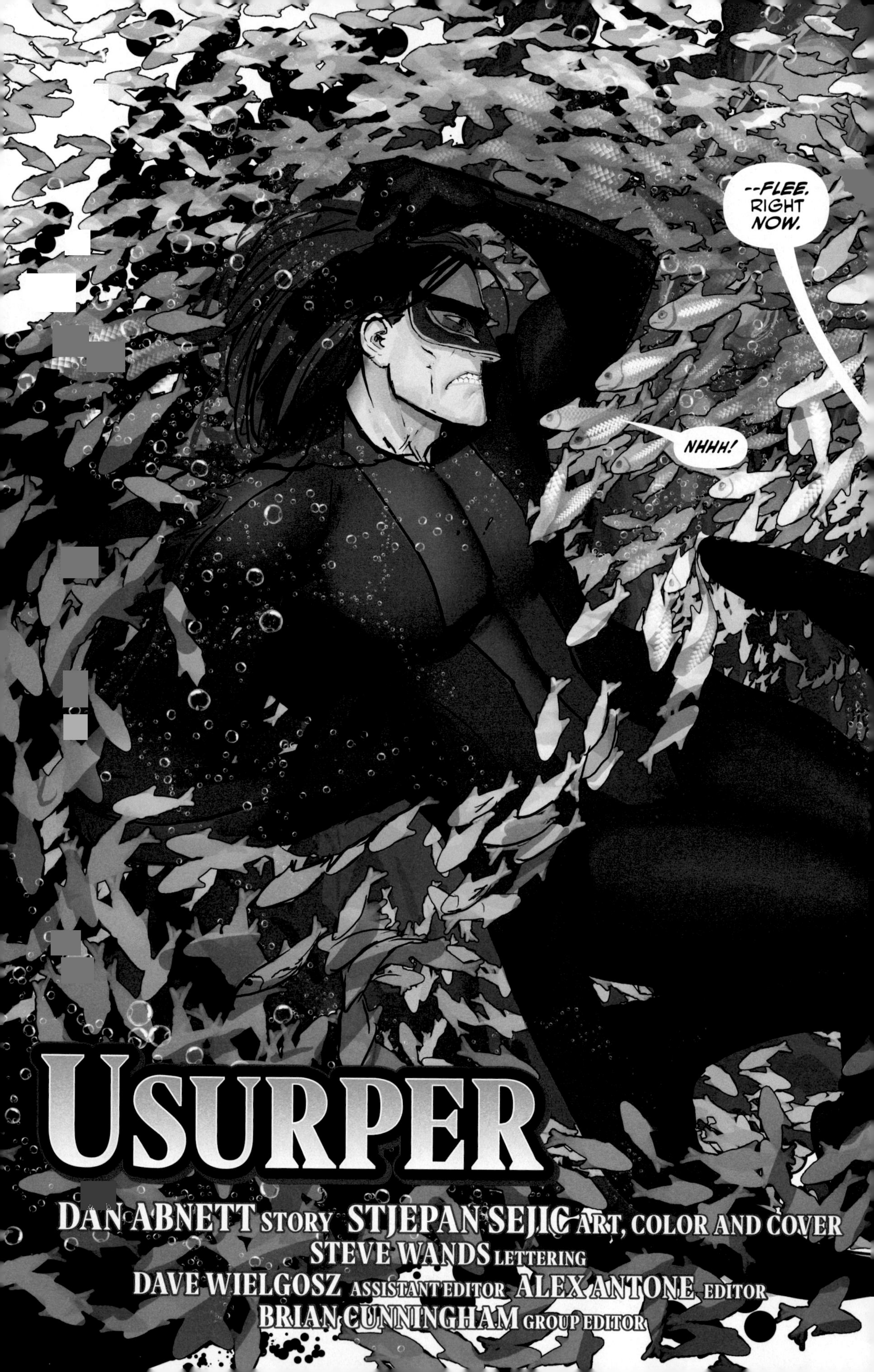
--FLEE. RIGHT NOW.
NHHH!
USURPER
DAN ABNETT STORY STJEPAN SEJIC ART, COLOR AND COVER
STEVE WANDS LETTERING
DAVE WIELGOSZ ASSISTANT EDITOR ALEX ANTONE EDITOR
BRIAN CUNNINGHAM GROUP EDITOR

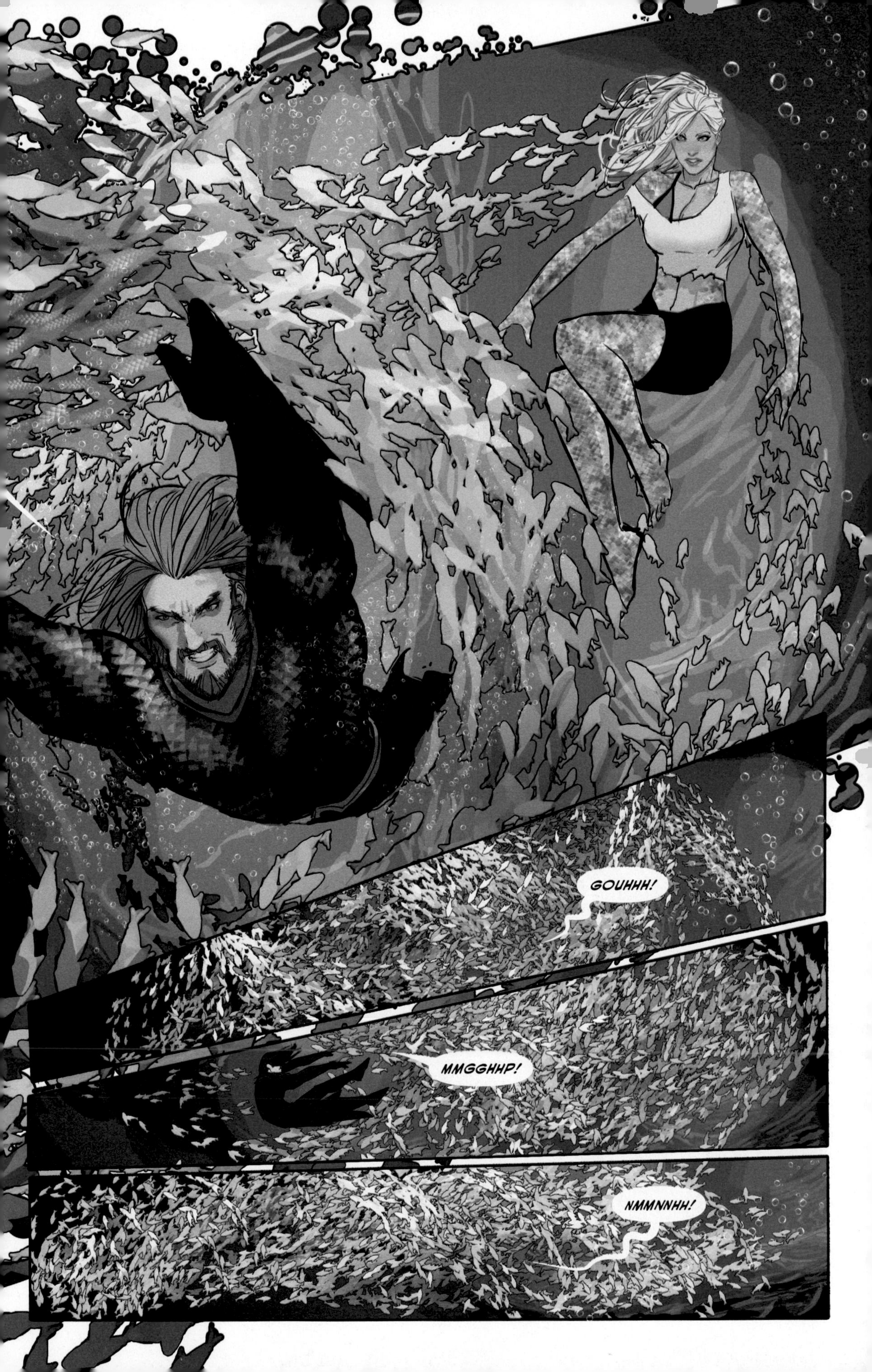
GOUHHH!
MMGGHHP!
NMMNNHH!

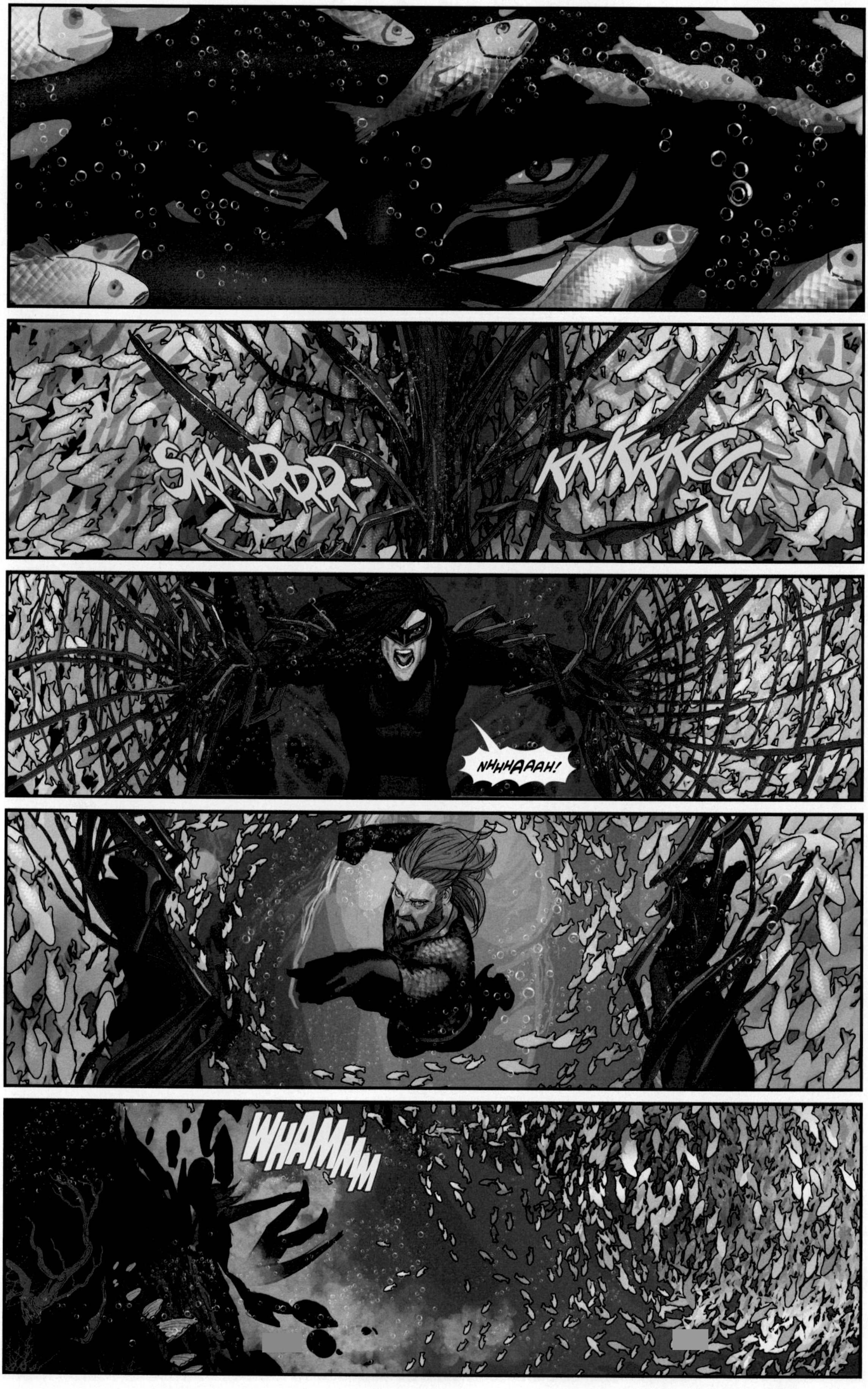
SKKKDDD-
KKKKKCCH
NHHHAAAH!
WHAMMM

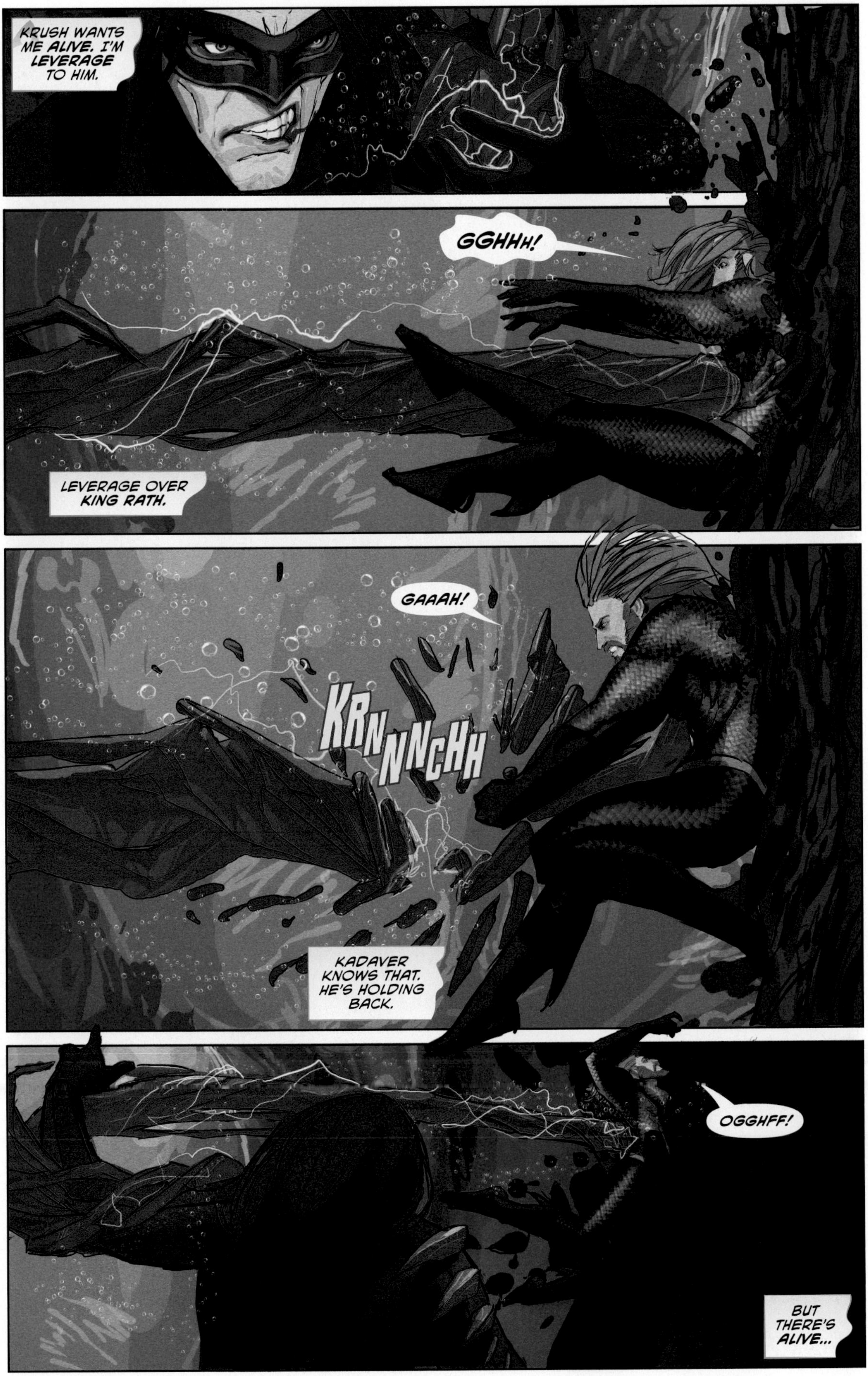
KRUSH WANTS ME ALIVE. I'M LEVERAGE TO HIM.
GGHHH!
LEVERAGE OVER KING RATH.
GAAAH!
KRNNNCHH
KADAVER KNOWS THAT. HE'S HOLDING BACK.
OGGHFF!
BUT THERE'S ALIVE...

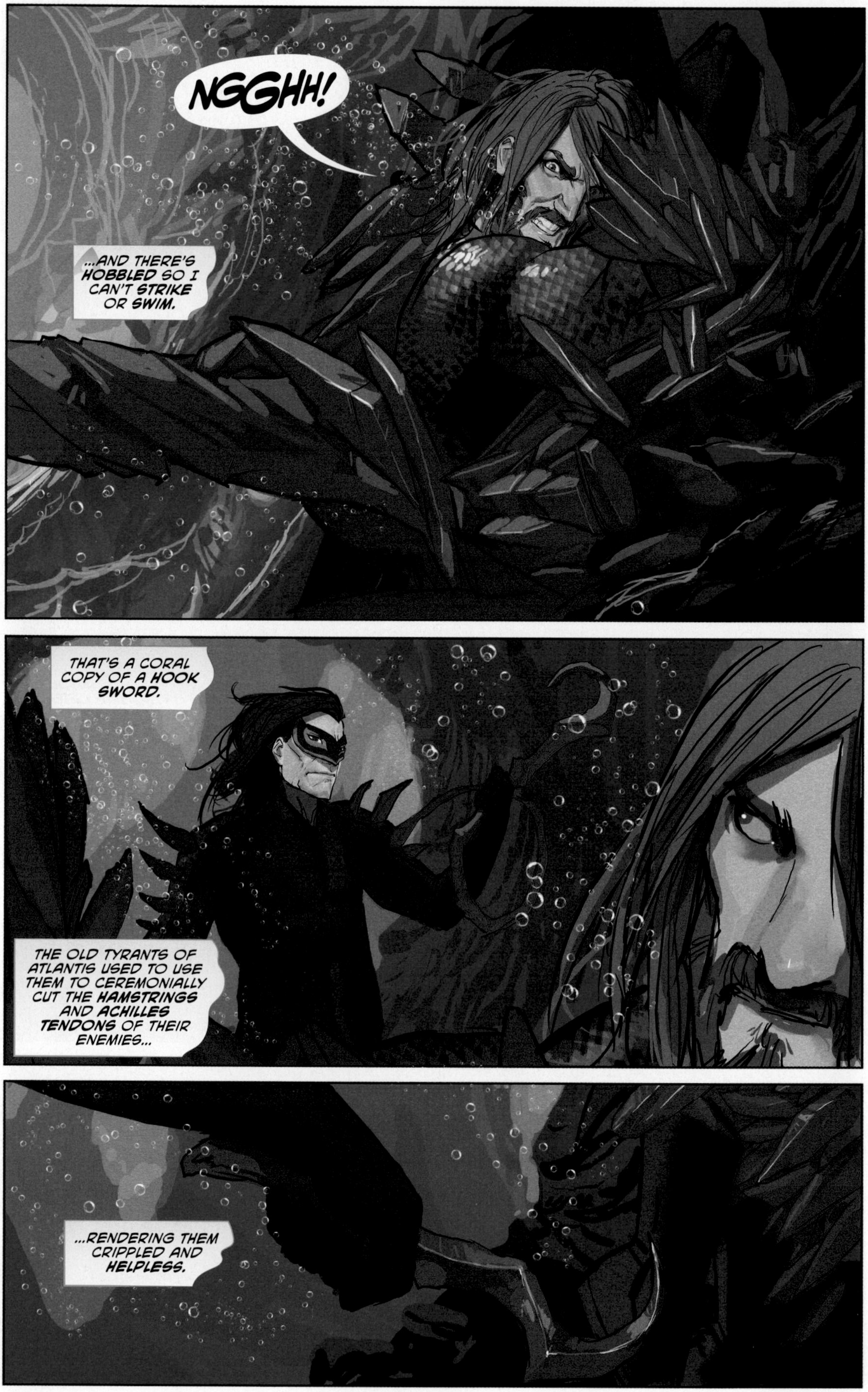
NGGHH!
...AND THERE'S HOBBLED SO I CAN'T STRIKE OR SWIM.
THAT'S A CORAL COPY OF A HOOK SWORD.
THE OLD TYRANTS OF ATLANTIS USED TO USE THEM TO CEREMONIALLY CUT THE HAMSTRINGS AND ACHILLES TENDONS OF THEIR ENEMIES...
...RENDERING THEM CRIPPLED AND HELPLESS.

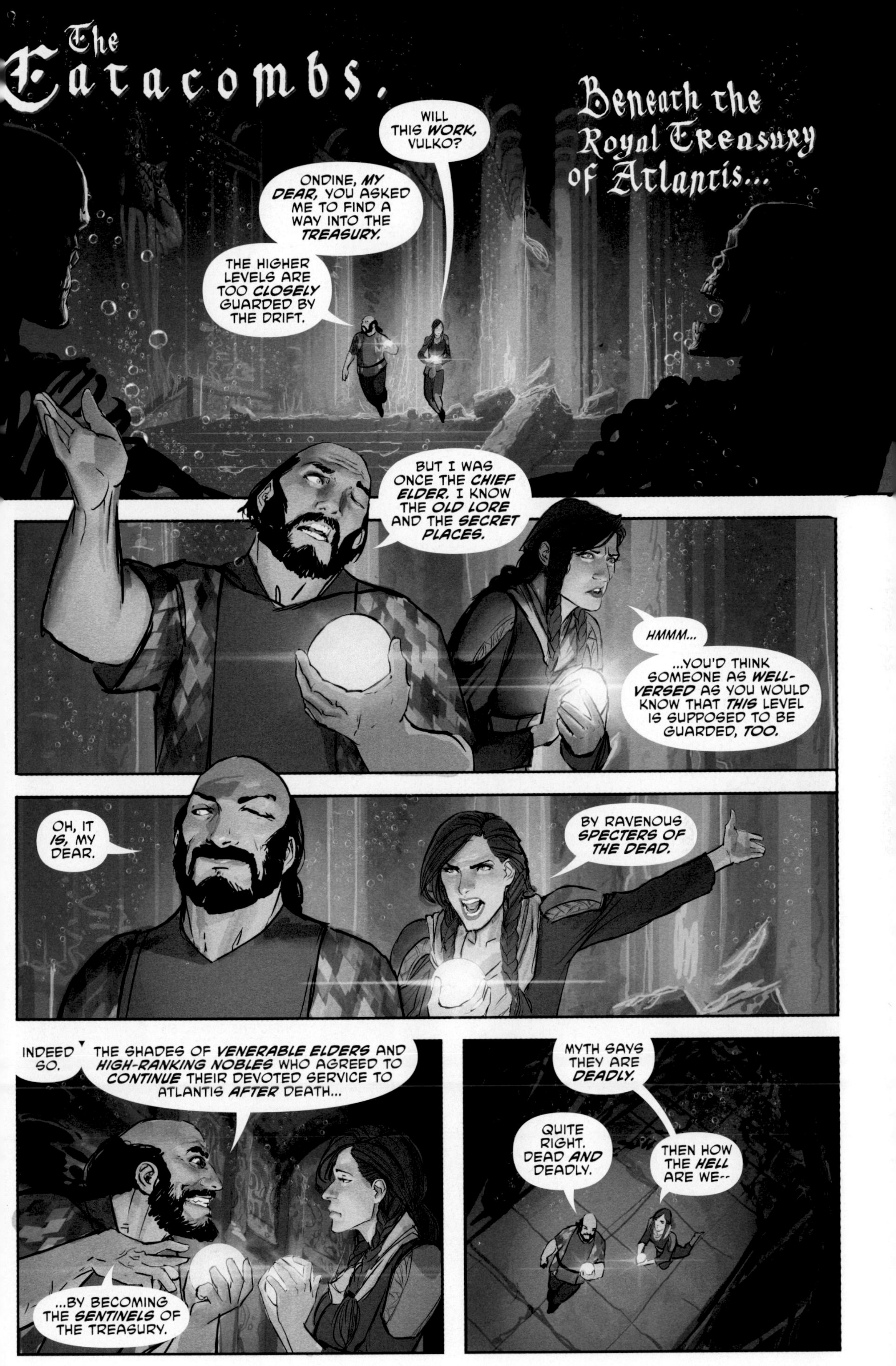
The Catacombs.
Beneath the Royal Treasury of Atlantis...
WILL THIS WORK, VULKO?
ONDINE, MY DEAR, YOU ASKED ME TO FIND A WAY INTO THE TREASURY.
THE HIGHER LEVELS ARE TOO CLOSELY GUARDED BY THE DRIFT.
BUT I WAS ONCE THE CHIEF ELDER. I KNOW THE OLD LORE AND THE SECRET PLACES.
HMMM...
...YOU'D THINK SOMEONE AS WELL-VERSED AS YOU WOULD KNOW THAT THIS LEVEL IS SUPPOSED TO BE GUARDED, TOO.
OH, IT IS, MY DEAR.
BY RAVENOUS SPECTERS OF THE DEAD.
INDEED SO.
THE SHADES OF VENERABLE ELDERS AND HIGH-RANKING NOBLES WHO AGREED TO CONTINUE THEIR DEVOTED SERVICE TO ATLANTIS AFTER DEATH...
...BY BECOMING THE SENTINELS OF THE TREASURY.
MYTH SAYS THEY ARE DEADLY.
QUITE RIGHT. DEAD AND DEADLY.
THEN HOW THE HELL ARE WE--

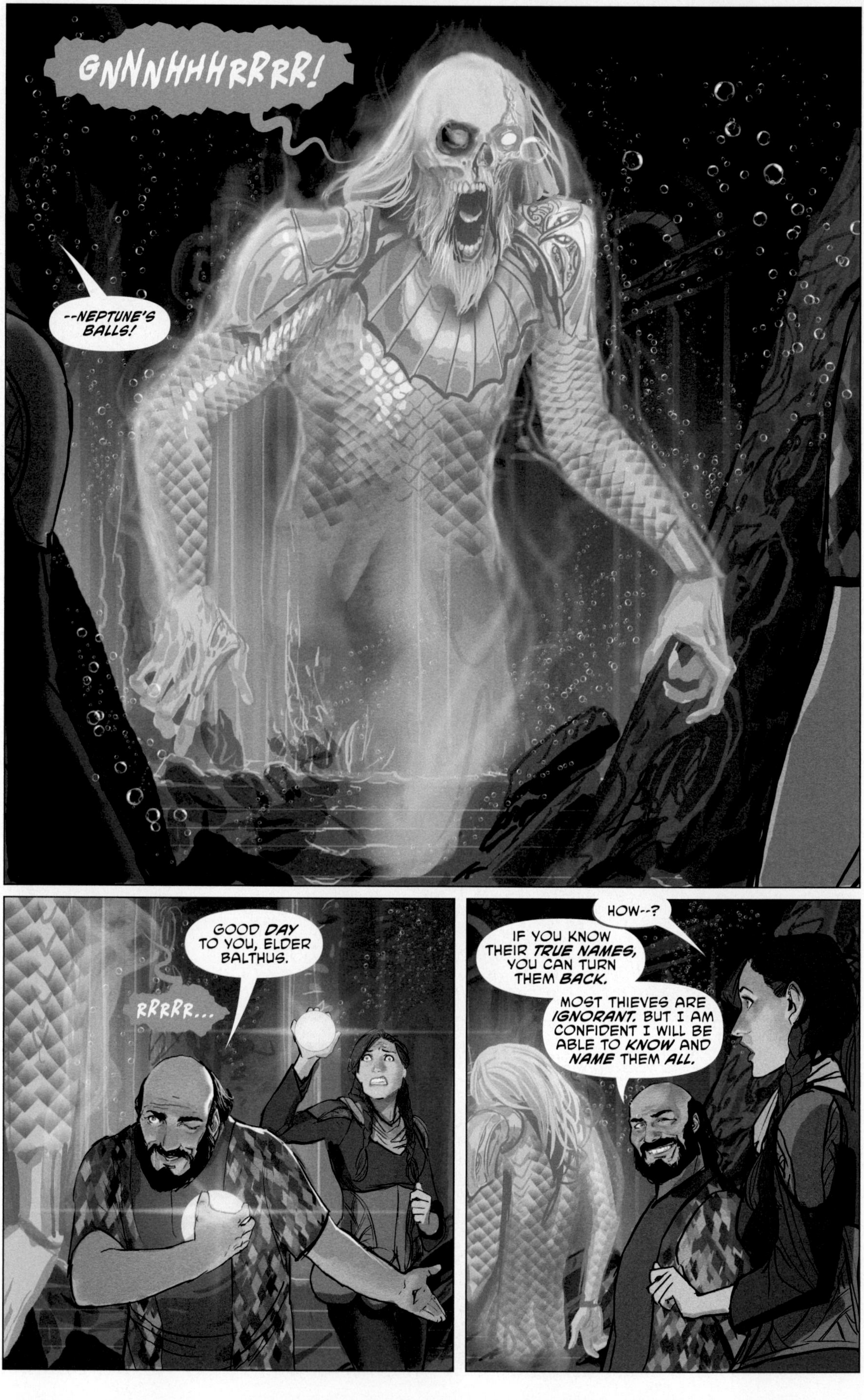
GNNNHHHRRRR!
--NEPTUNE'S BALLS!
GOOD DAY TO YOU, ELDER BALTHUS.
RRRRR...
HOW--?
IF YOU KNOW THEIR TRUE NAMES, YOU CAN TURN THEM BACK.
MOST THIEVES ARE IGNORANT. BUT I AM CONFIDENT I WILL BE ABLE TO KNOW AND NAME THEM ALL.

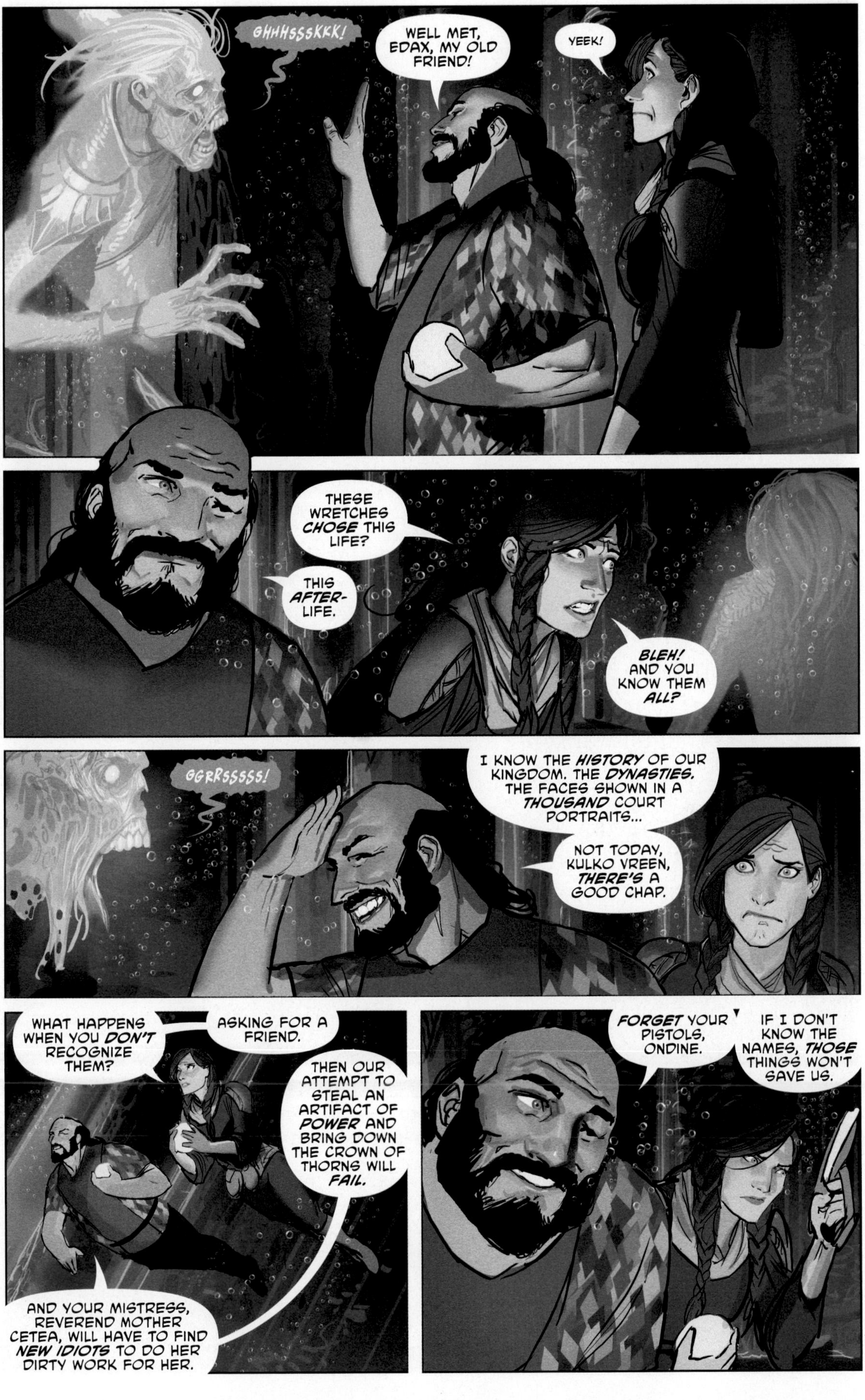
GHHHSSSKKK!
WELL MET, EDAX, MY OLD FRIEND!
YEEK!
THESE WRETCHES *CHOSE* THIS LIFE?
THIS *AFTER-* LIFE.
BLEH! AND YOU KNOW THEM *ALL?*
GGRRSSSSS!
I KNOW THE *HISTORY* OF OUR KINGDOM. THE *DYNASTIES.* THE FACES SHOWN IN A *THOUSAND* COURT PORTRAITS...
NOT TODAY, KULKO VREEN, *THERE'S* A GOOD CHAP.
WHAT HAPPENS WHEN YOU *DON'T* RECOGNIZE THEM?
ASKING FOR A FRIEND.
THEN OUR ATTEMPT TO STEAL AN ARTIFACT OF *POWER* AND BRING DOWN THE CROWN OF THORNS WILL *FAIL.*
AND YOUR MISTRESS, REVEREND MOTHER CETEA, WILL HAVE TO FIND *NEW IDIOTS* TO DO HER DIRTY WORK FOR HER.
FORGET YOUR PISTOLS, ONDINE.
IF I DON'T KNOW THE NAMES, *THOSE* THINGS WON'T SAVE US.

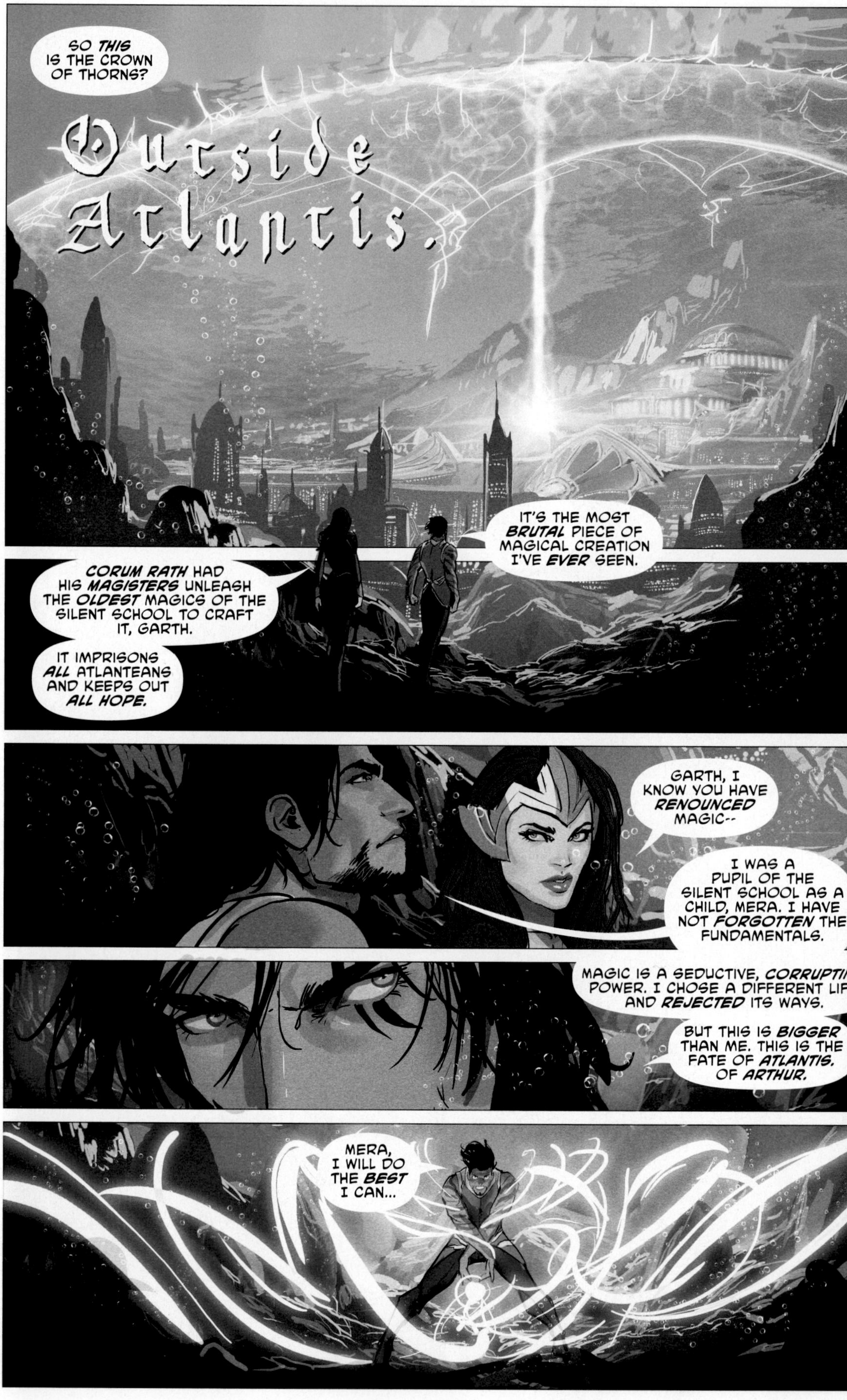
SO THIS IS THE CROWN OF THORNS?
Outside Atlantis.
IT'S THE MOST BRUTAL PIECE OF MAGICAL CREATION I'VE EVER SEEN.
CORUM RATH HAD HIS MAGISTERS UNLEASH THE OLDEST MAGICS OF THE SILENT SCHOOL TO CRAFT IT, GARTH.
IT IMPRISONS ALL ATLANTEANS AND KEEPS OUT ALL HOPE.
GARTH, I KNOW YOU HAVE RENOUNCED MAGIC--
I WAS A PUPIL OF THE SILENT SCHOOL AS A CHILD, MERA. I HAVE NOT FORGOTTEN THE FUNDAMENTALS.
MAGIC IS A SEDUCTIVE, CORRUPTING POWER. I CHOSE A DIFFERENT LIFE AND REJECTED ITS WAYS.
BUT THIS IS BIGGER THAN ME. THIS IS THE FATE OF ATLANTIS. OF ARTHUR.
MERA, I WILL DO THE BEST I CAN...

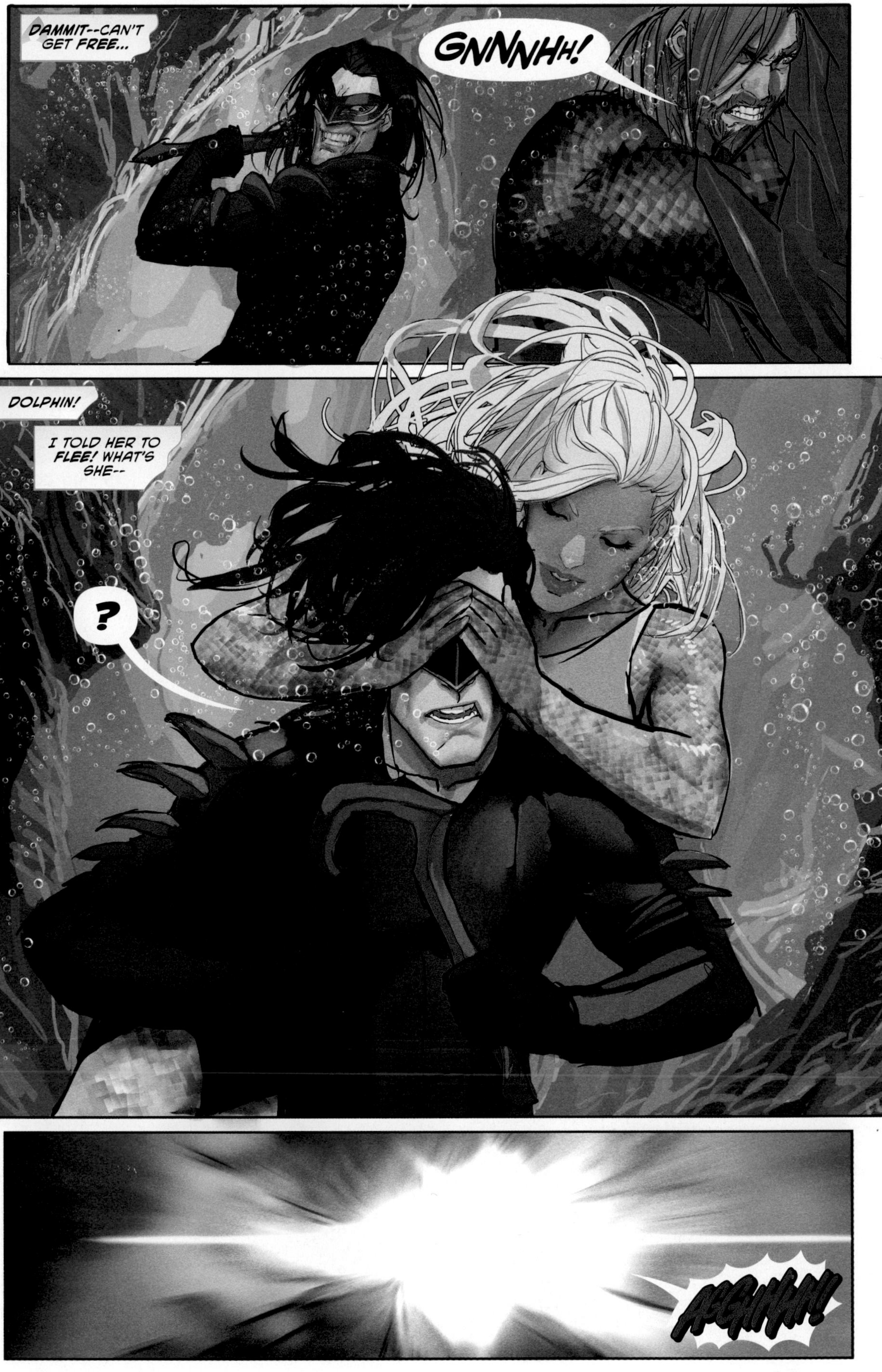
DAMMIT--CAN'T GET FREE...
GNNNHH!
DOLPHIN!
I TOLD HER TO FLEE! WHAT'S SHE--
?
AGHHH!

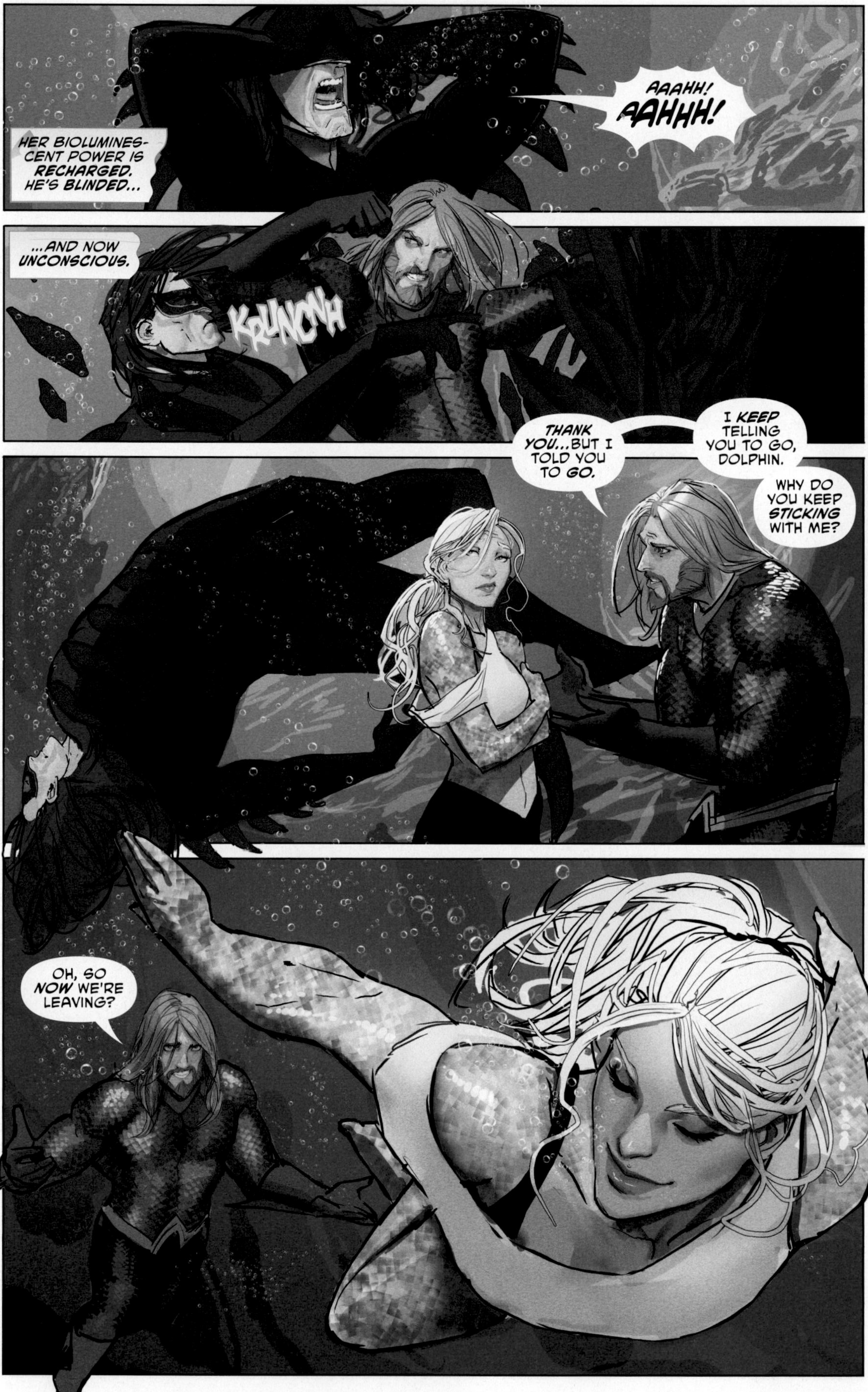
HER BIOLUMINESCENT POWER IS RECHARGED. HE'S BLINDED...
AAAHH! AAHHH!
...AND NOW UNCONSCIOUS.
KRUNCNH
THANK YOU...BUT I TOLD YOU TO GO.
I KEEP TELLING YOU TO GO, DOLPHIN.
WHY DO YOU KEEP STICKING WITH ME?
OH, SO NOW WE'RE LEAVING?

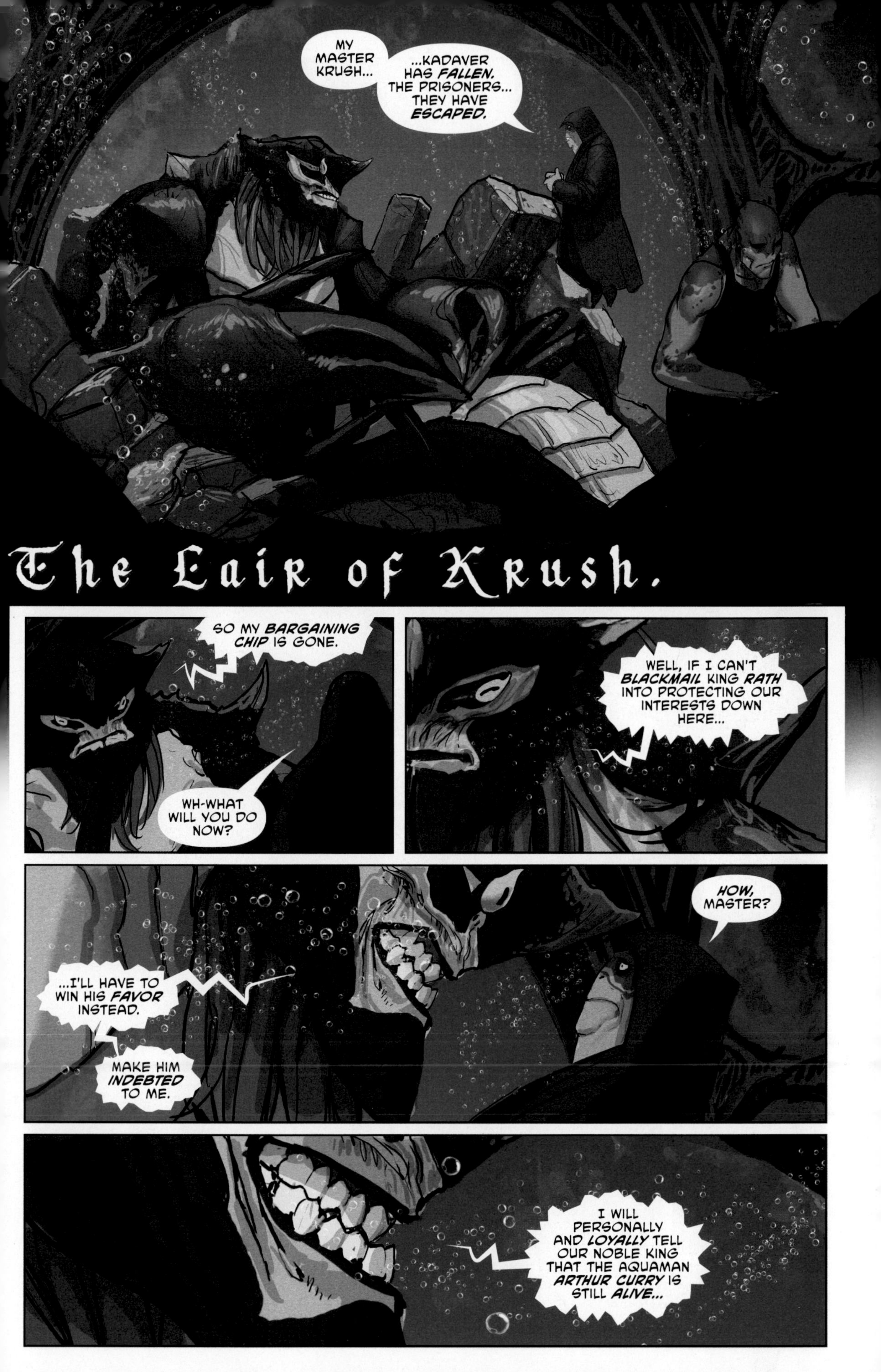
MY MASTER KRUSH...
...KADAVER HAS FALLEN. THE PRISONERS... THEY HAVE ESCAPED.
The Lair of Krush.
SO MY BARGAINING CHIP IS GONE.
WH-WHAT WILL YOU DO NOW?
WELL, IF I CAN'T BLACKMAIL KING RATH INTO PROTECTING OUR INTERESTS DOWN HERE...
...I'LL HAVE TO WIN HIS FAVOR INSTEAD.
MAKE HIM INDEBTED TO ME.
HOW, MASTER?
I WILL PERSONALLY AND LOYALLY TELL OUR NOBLE KING THAT THE AQUAMAN ARTHUR CURRY IS STILL ALIVE...

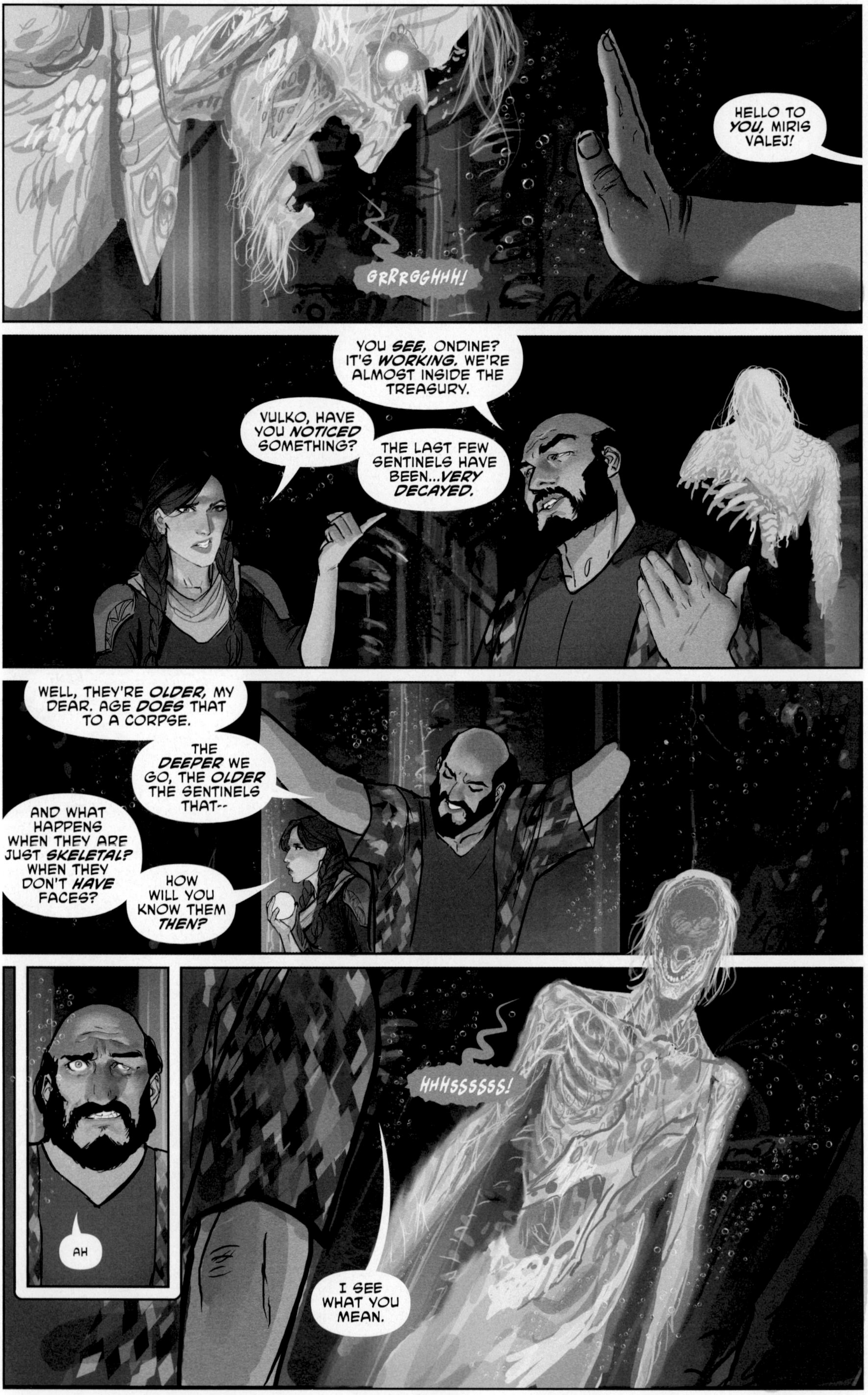
HELLO TO YOU, MIRIS VALEJ!
GRRRGGHHH!
YOU SEE, ONDINE? IT'S WORKING. WE'RE ALMOST INSIDE THE TREASURY.
VULKO, HAVE YOU NOTICED SOMETHING?
THE LAST FEW SENTINELS HAVE BEEN...VERY DECAYED.
WELL, THEY'RE OLDER, MY DEAR. AGE DOES THAT TO A CORPSE.
THE DEEPER WE GO, THE OLDER THE SENTINELS THAT--
AND WHAT HAPPENS WHEN THEY ARE JUST SKELETAL? WHEN THEY DON'T HAVE FACES?
HOW WILL YOU KNOW THEM THEN?
HHHSSSSSS!
AH
I SEE WHAT YOU MEAN.

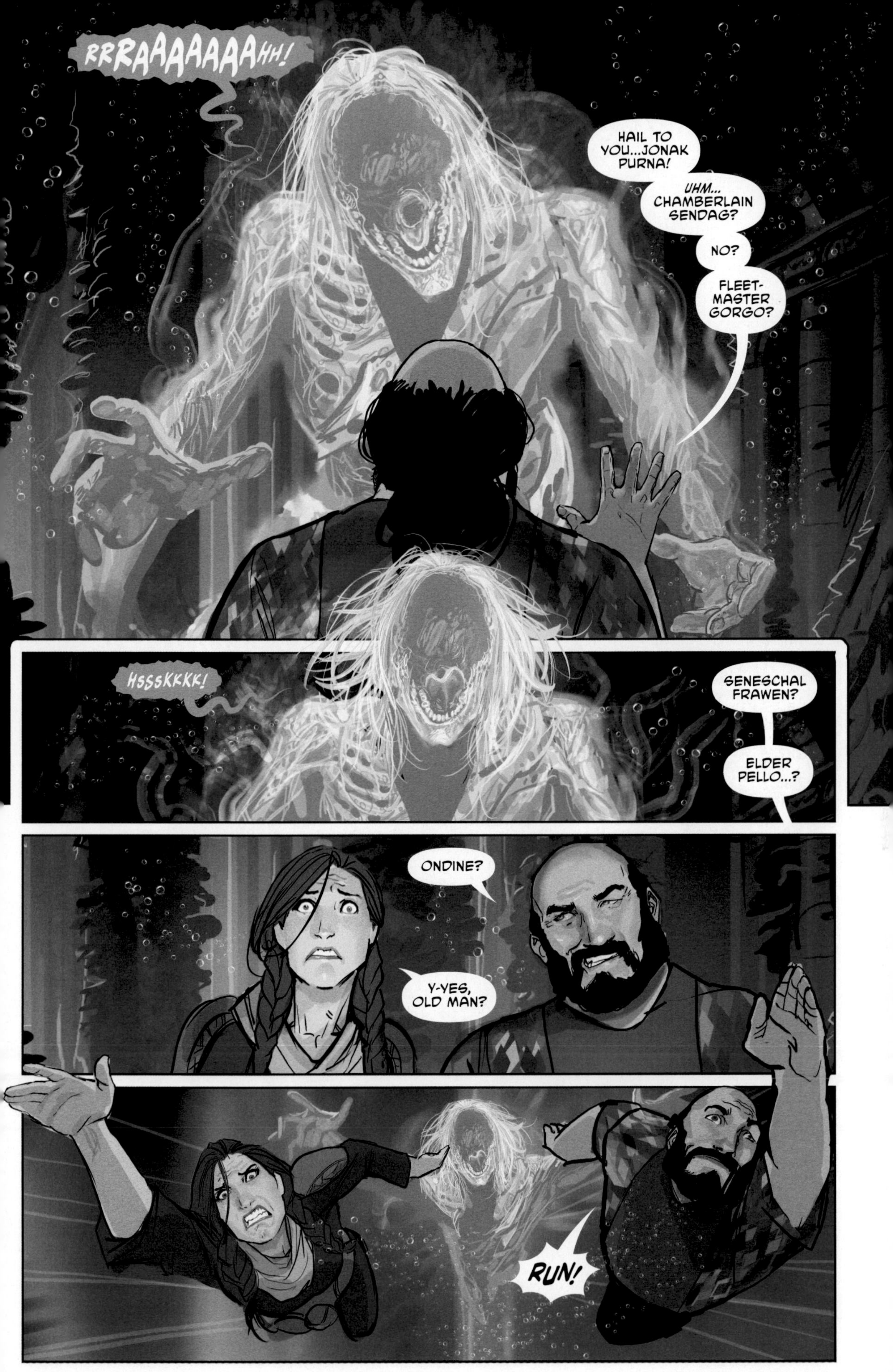
RRRAAAAAAAHH!
HAIL TO YOU...JONAK PURNA!
UHM... CHAMBERLAIN SENDAG?
NO?
FLEET-MASTER GORGO?
HSSSKKKK!
SENESCHAL FRAWEN?
ELDER PELLO...?
ONDINE?
Y-YES, OLD MAN?
RUN!

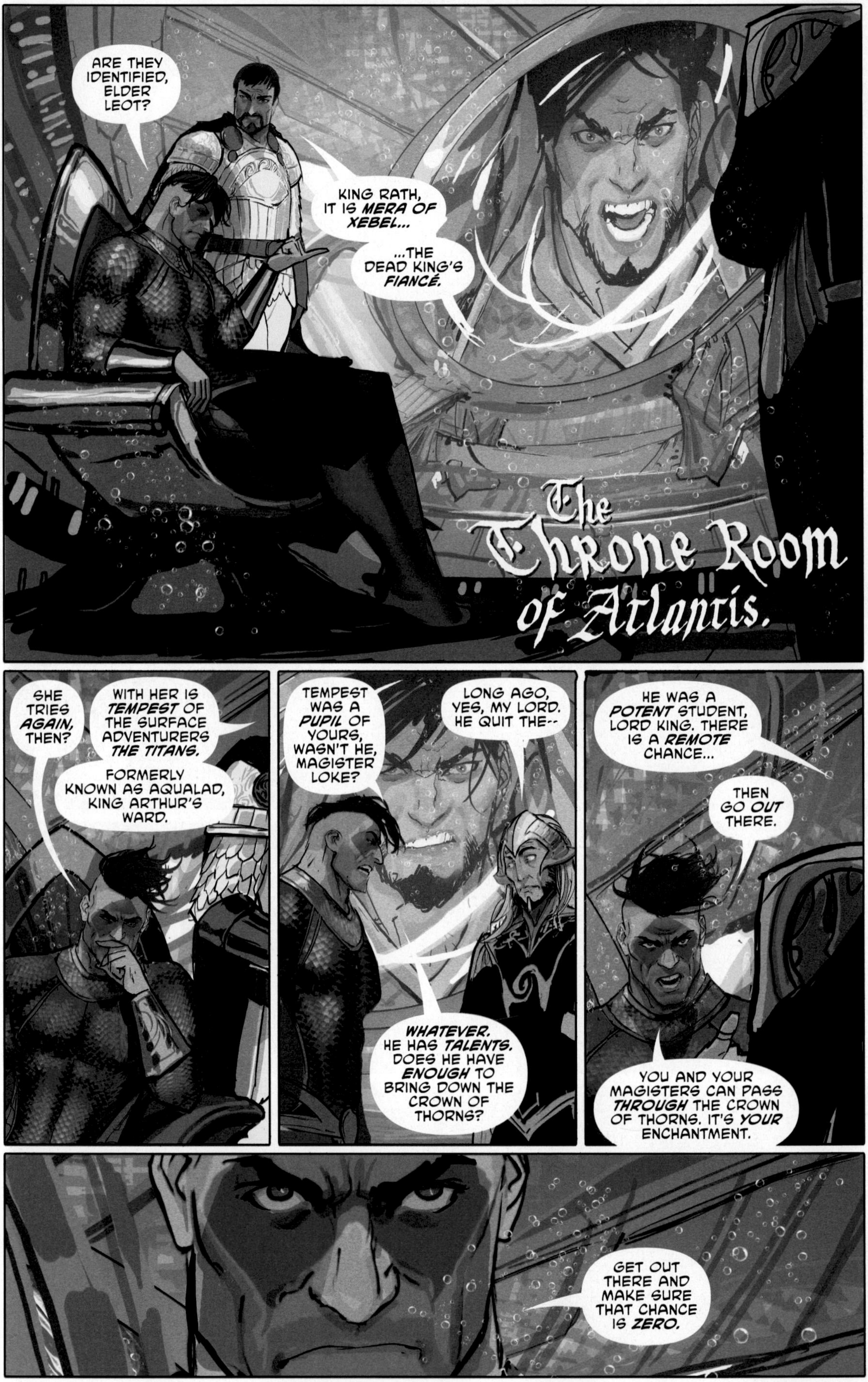

ARE THEY IDENTIFIED, ELDER LEOT?
KING RATH, IT IS MERA OF XEBEL...
...THE DEAD KING'S FIANCÉ.
The Throne Room of Atlantis.
SHE TRIES AGAIN, THEN?
WITH HER IS TEMPEST OF THE SURFACE ADVENTURERS THE TITANS.
FORMERLY KNOWN AS AQUALAD, KING ARTHUR'S WARD.
TEMPEST WAS A PUPIL OF YOURS, WASN'T HE, MAGISTER LOKE?
LONG AGO, YES, MY LORD. HE QUIT THE--
WHATEVER. HE HAS TALENTS. DOES HE HAVE ENOUGH TO BRING DOWN THE CROWN OF THORNS?
HE WAS A POTENT STUDENT, LORD KING. THERE IS A REMOTE CHANCE...
THEN GO OUT THERE.
YOU AND YOUR MAGISTERS CAN PASS THROUGH THE CROWN OF THORNS. IT'S YOUR ENCHANTMENT.
GET OUT THERE AND MAKE SURE THAT CHANCE IS ZERO.

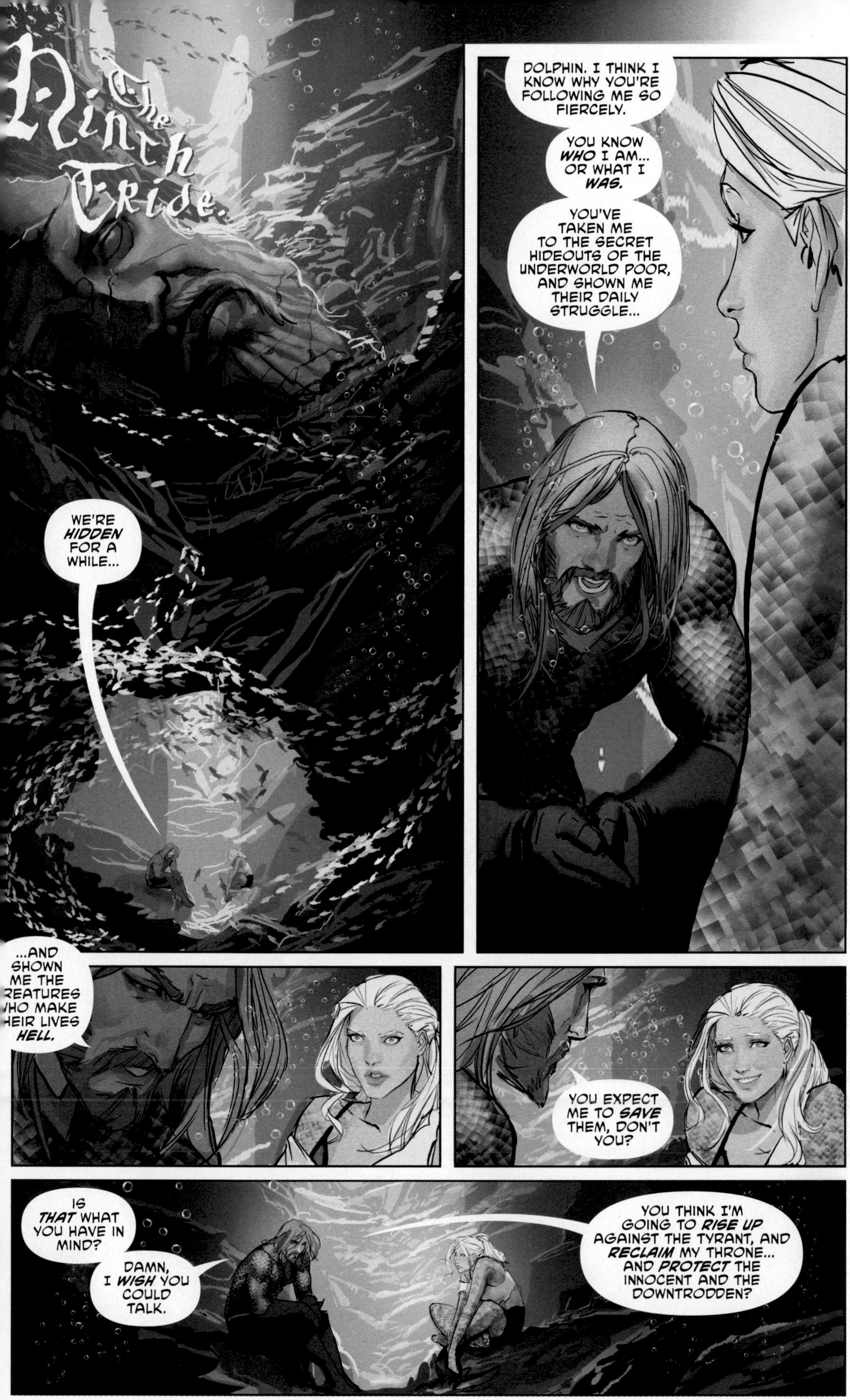
The Ninth Tride.
WE'RE HIDDEN FOR A WHILE...
DOLPHIN. I THINK I KNOW WHY YOU'RE FOLLOWING ME SO FIERCELY.
YOU KNOW WHO I AM... OR WHAT I WAS.
YOU'VE TAKEN ME TO THE SECRET HIDEOUTS OF THE UNDERWORLD POOR, AND SHOWN ME THEIR DAILY STRUGGLE...
...AND SHOWN ME THE REATURES HO MAKE HEIR LIVES HELL.
YOU EXPECT ME TO SAVE THEM, DON'T YOU?
IS THAT WHAT YOU HAVE IN MIND?
DAMN, I WISH YOU COULD TALK.
YOU THINK I'M GOING TO RISE UP AGAINST THE TYRANT, AND RECLAIM MY THRONE... AND PROTECT THE INNOCENT AND THE DOWNTRODDEN?

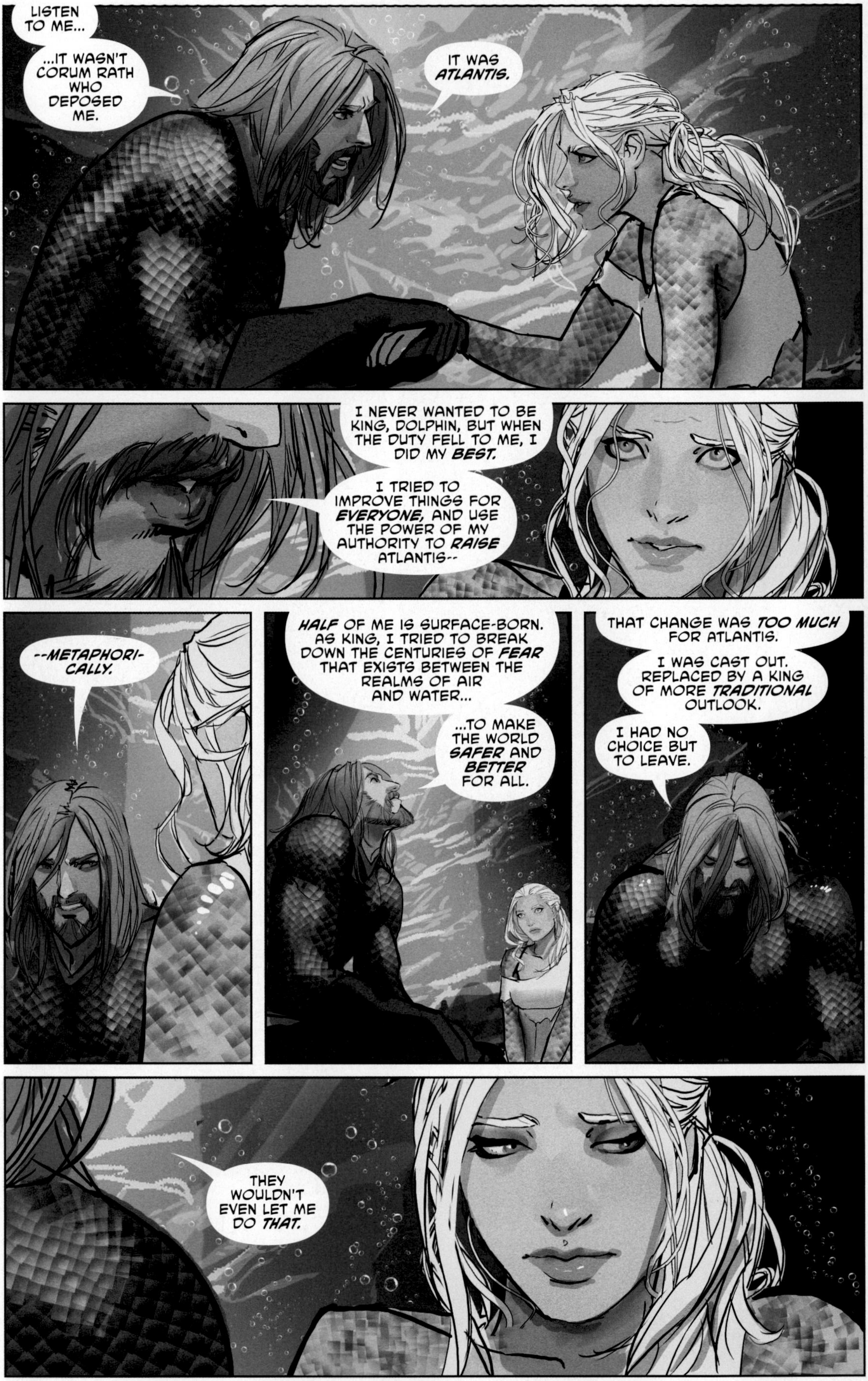
LISTEN TO ME...
...IT WASN'T CORUM RATH WHO DEPOSED ME.
IT WAS *ATLANTIS.*
I NEVER WANTED TO BE KING, DOLPHIN, BUT WHEN THE DUTY FELL TO ME, I DID MY *BEST.*
I TRIED TO IMPROVE THINGS FOR *EVERYONE,* AND USE THE POWER OF MY AUTHORITY TO *RAISE* ATLANTIS--
--*METAPHORICALLY.*
HALF OF ME IS SURFACE-BORN. AS KING, I TRIED TO BREAK DOWN THE CENTURIES OF *FEAR* THAT EXISTS BETWEEN THE REALMS OF AIR AND WATER...
...TO MAKE THE WORLD *SAFER* AND *BETTER* FOR ALL.
THAT CHANGE WAS *TOO MUCH* FOR ATLANTIS.
I WAS CAST OUT. REPLACED BY A KING OF MORE *TRADITIONAL* OUTLOOK.
I HAD NO CHOICE BUT TO LEAVE.
THEY WOULDN'T EVEN LET ME DO *THAT.*

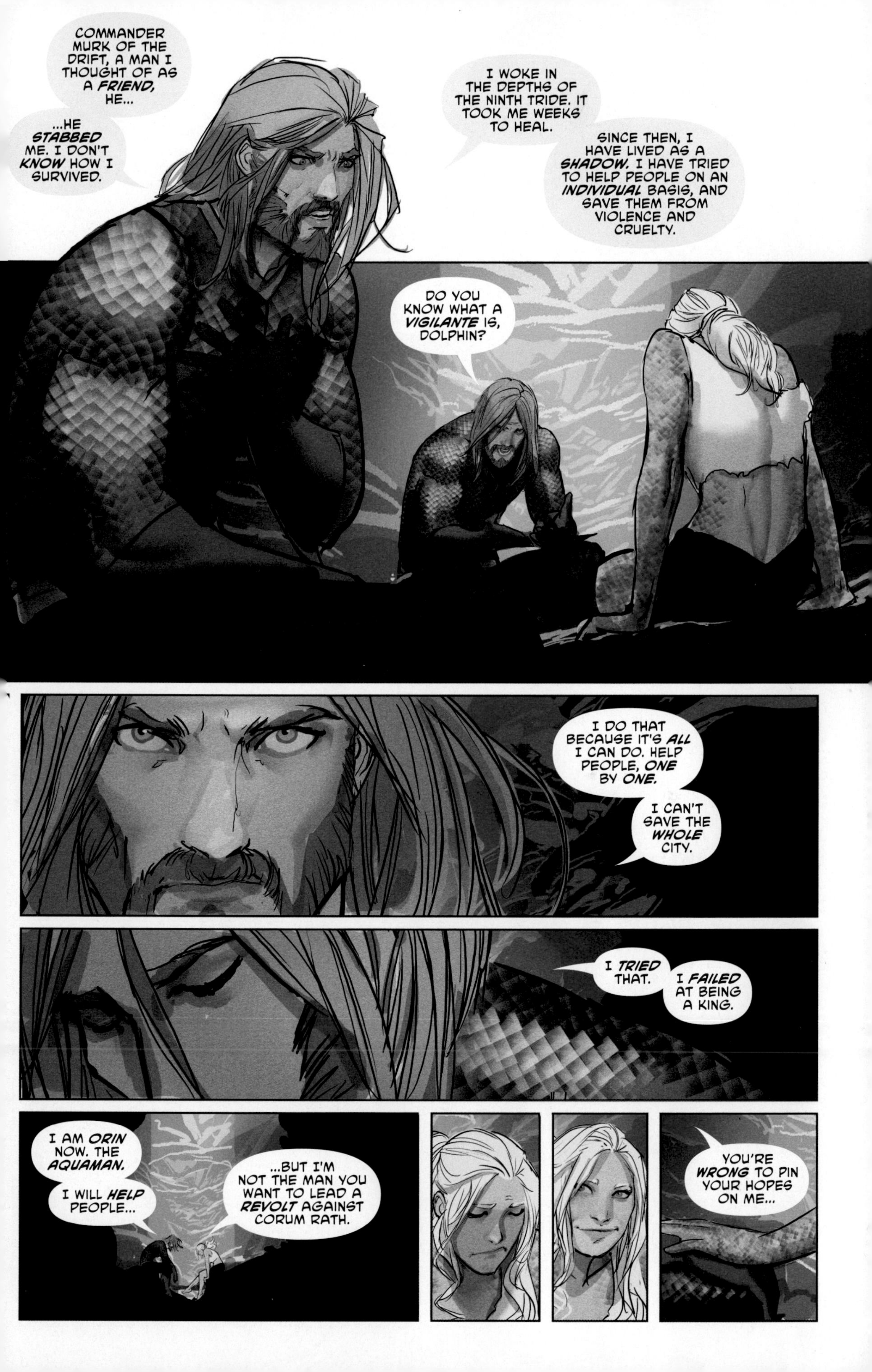
COMMANDER MURK OF THE DRIFT, A MAN I THOUGHT OF AS A *FRIEND,* HE...
...HE *STABBED* ME. I DON'T *KNOW* HOW I SURVIVED.
I WOKE IN THE DEPTHS OF THE NINTH TRIDE. IT TOOK ME WEEKS TO HEAL.
SINCE THEN, I HAVE LIVED AS A *SHADOW.* I HAVE TRIED TO HELP PEOPLE ON AN *INDIVIDUAL* BASIS, AND SAVE THEM FROM VIOLENCE AND CRUELTY.
DO YOU KNOW WHAT A *VIGILANTE* IS, DOLPHIN?
I DO THAT BECAUSE IT'S *ALL* I CAN DO. HELP PEOPLE, *ONE* BY *ONE.*
I CAN'T SAVE THE *WHOLE* CITY.
I *TRIED* THAT.
I *FAILED* AT BEING A KING.
I AM *ORIN* NOW. THE *AQUAMAN.*
I WILL *HELP* PEOPLE...
...BUT I'M NOT THE MAN YOU WANT TO LEAD A *REVOLT* AGAINST CORUM RATH.
YOU'RE *WRONG* TO PIN YOUR HOPES ON ME...

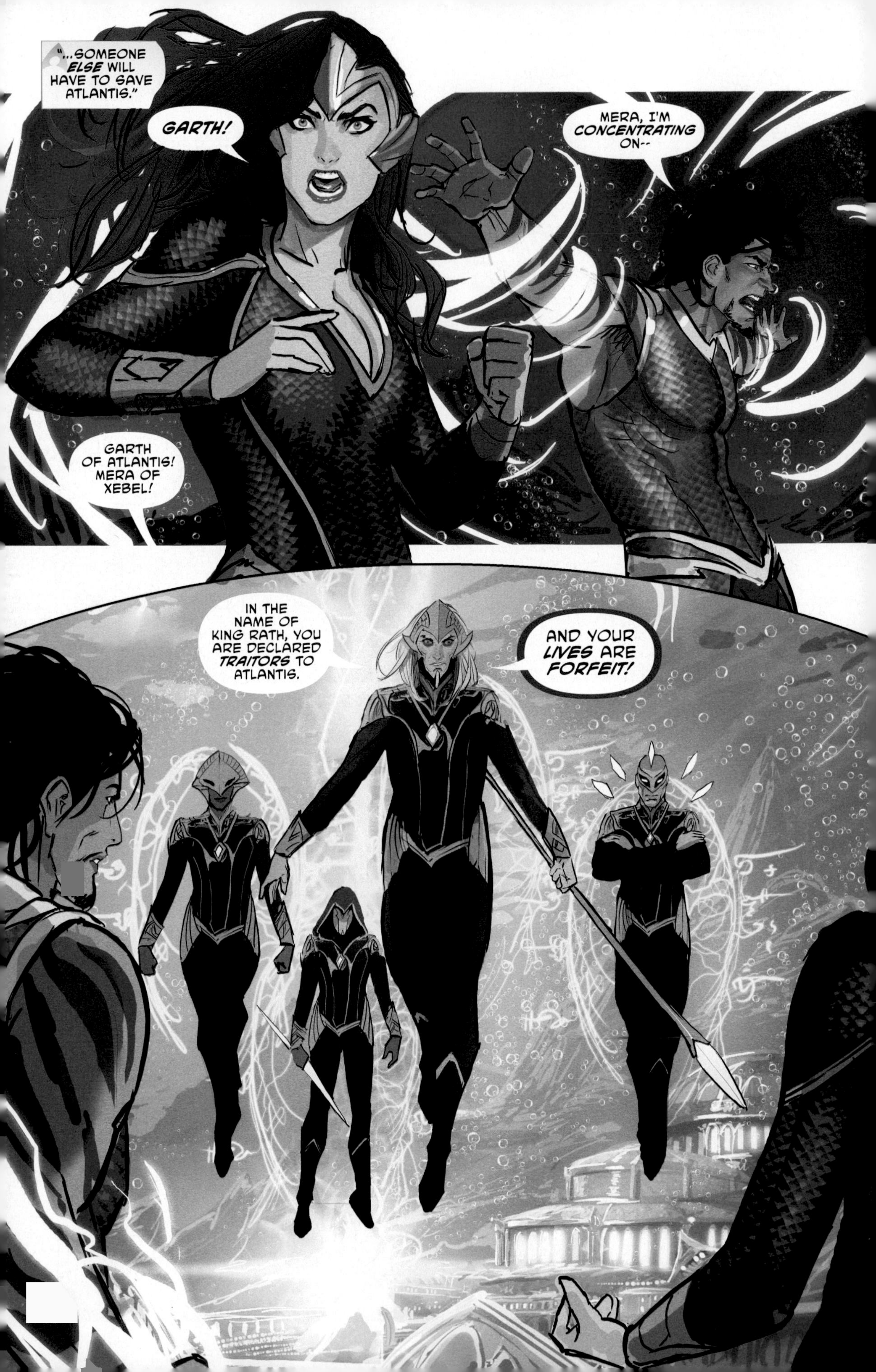
"...SOMEONE ELSE WILL HAVE TO SAVE ATLANTIS."
GARTH!
MERA, I'M CONCENTRATING ON--
GARTH OF ATLANTIS! MERA OF XEBEL!
IN THE NAME OF KING RATH, YOU ARE DECLARED TRAITORS TO ATLANTIS.
AND YOUR LIVES ARE FORFEIT!

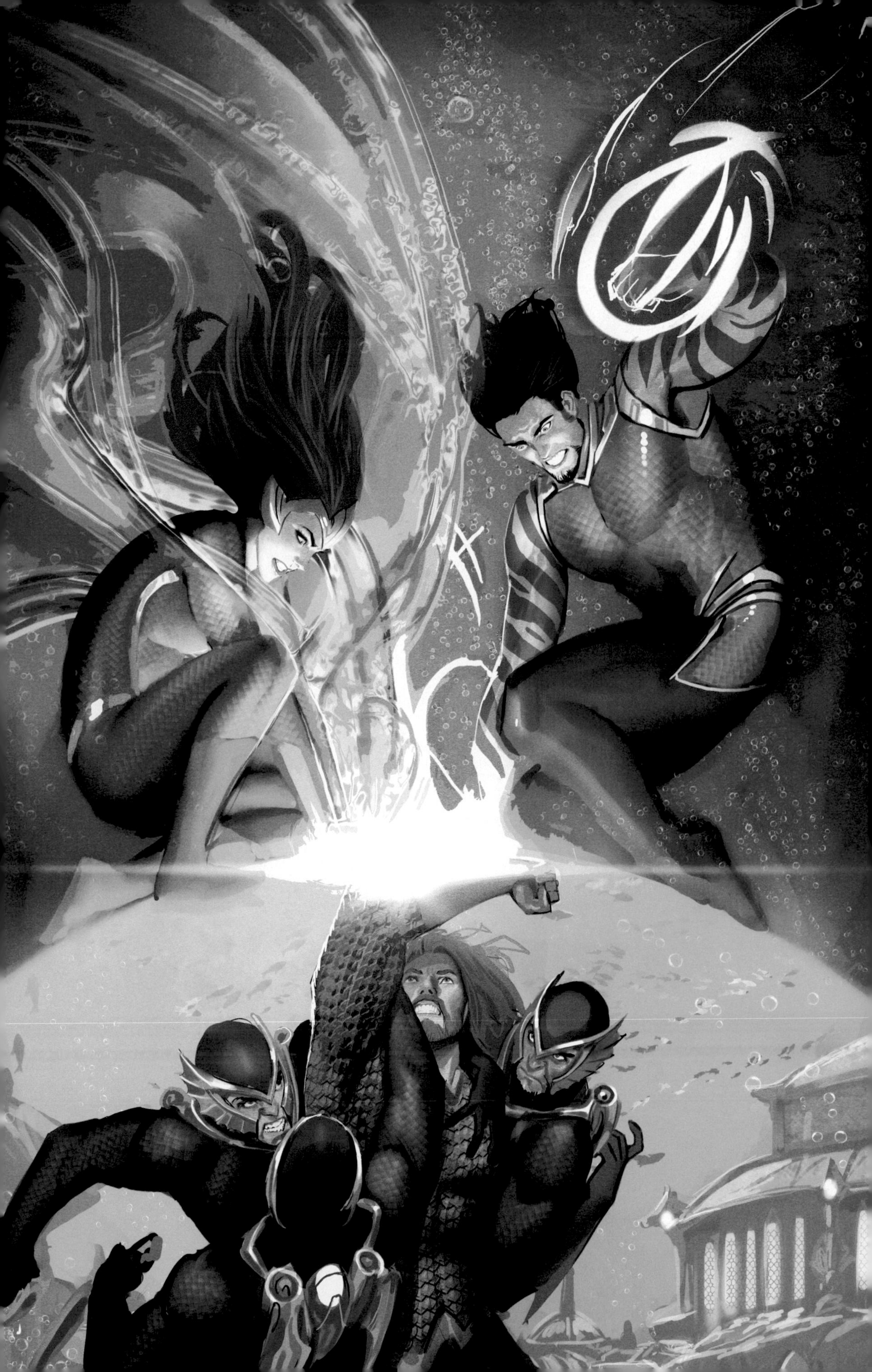

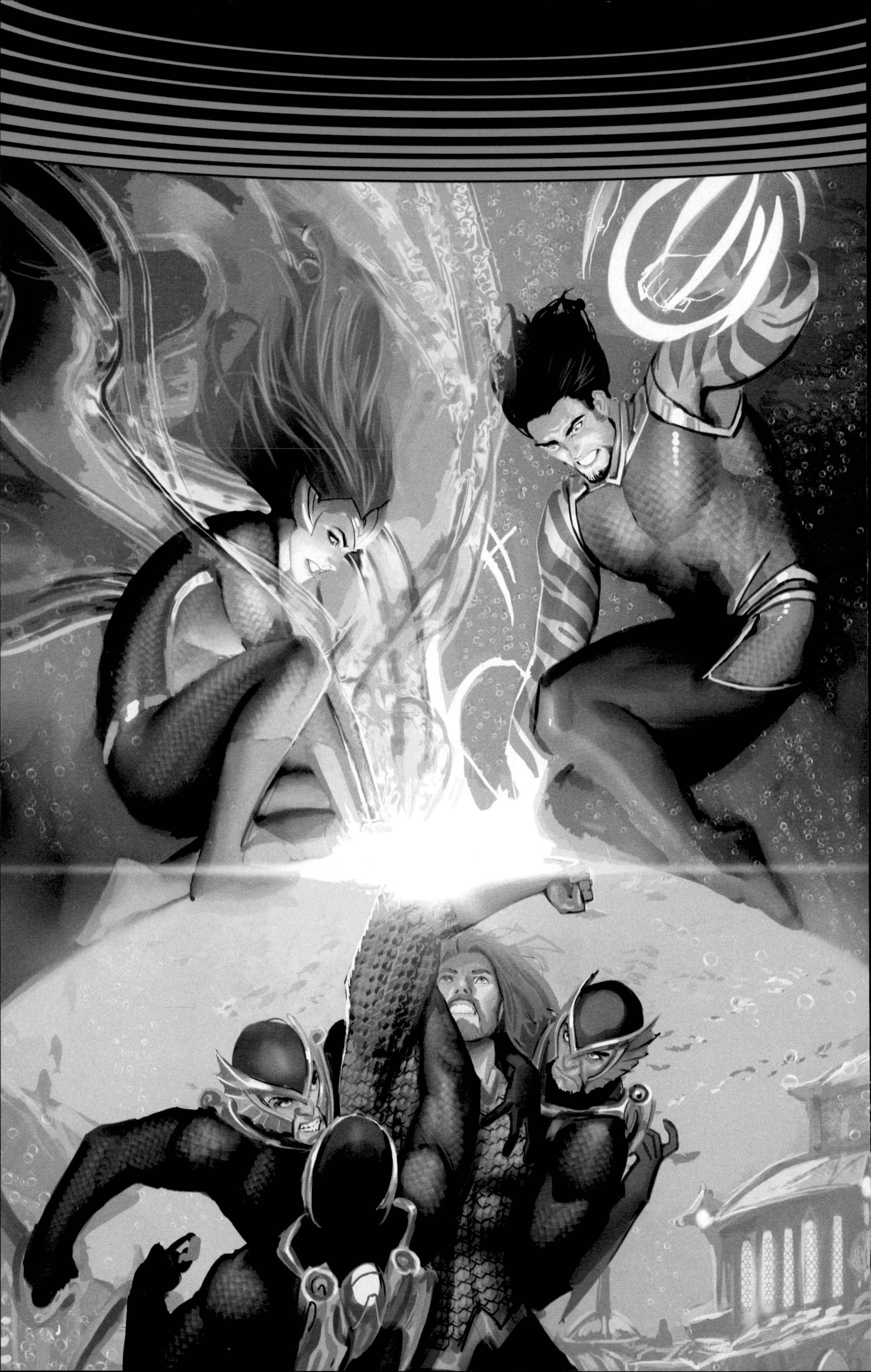

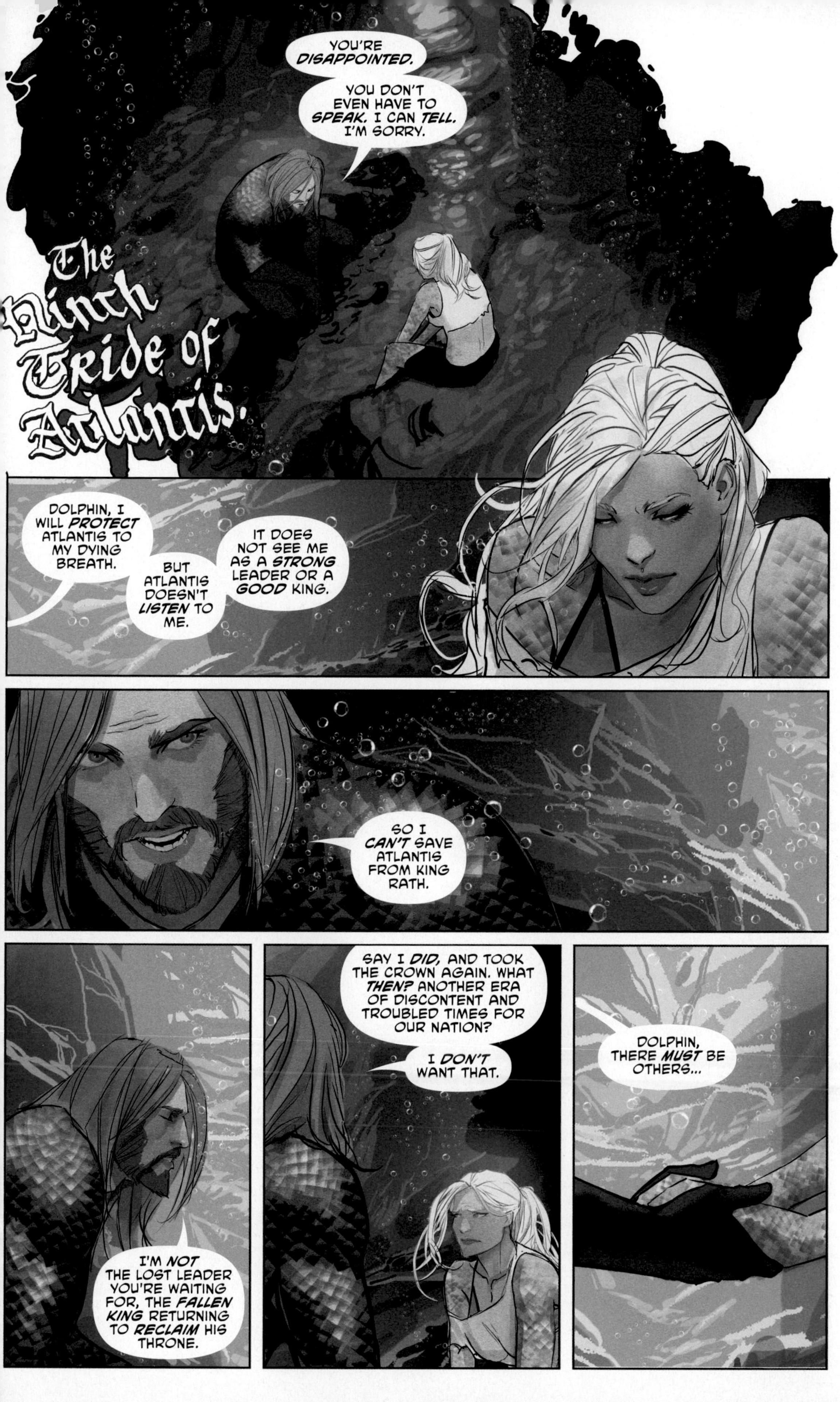
YOU'RE DISAPPOINTED.
YOU DON'T EVEN HAVE TO SPEAK. I CAN TELL. I'M SORRY.
The Ninth Tride of Atlantis.
DOLPHIN, I WILL PROTECT ATLANTIS TO MY DYING BREATH.
BUT ATLANTIS DOESN'T LISTEN TO ME.
IT DOES NOT SEE ME AS A STRONG LEADER OR A GOOD KING.
SO I CAN'T SAVE ATLANTIS FROM KING RATH.
I'M NOT THE LOST LEADER YOU'RE WAITING FOR, THE FALLEN KING RETURNING TO RECLAIM HIS THRONE.
SAY I DID, AND TOOK THE CROWN AGAIN. WHAT THEN? ANOTHER ERA OF DISCONTENT AND TROUBLED TIMES FOR OUR NATION?
I DON'T WANT THAT.
DOLPHIN, THERE MUST BE OTHERS...

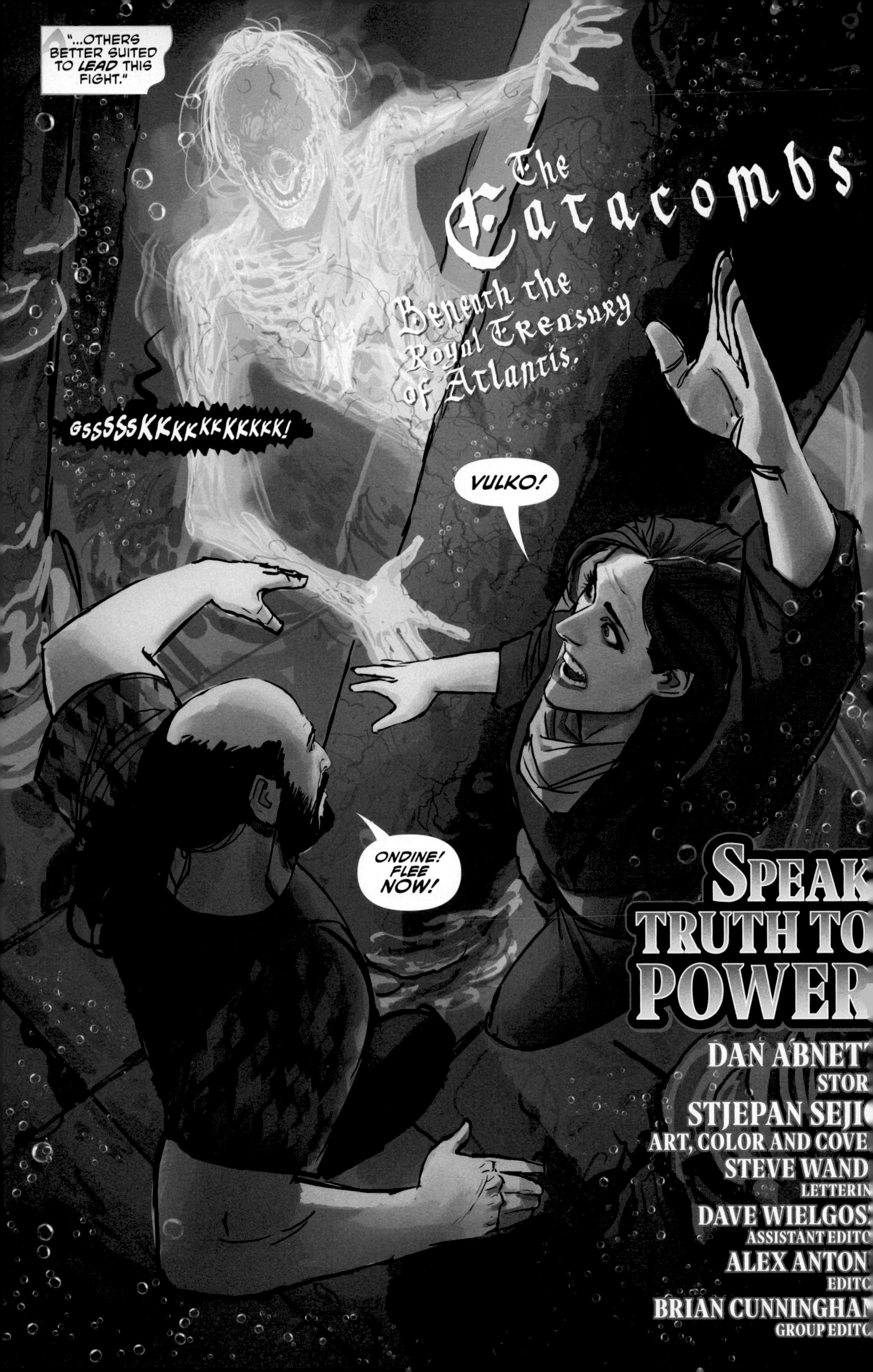
"...OTHERS BETTER SUITED TO LEAD THIS FIGHT."
The Catacombs
Beneath the Royal Treasury of Atlantis.
GSSSSSKKKKKKKKKK!
VULKO!
ONDINE! FLEE NOW!
SPEAK TRUTH TO POWER
DAN ABNETT STORY
STJEPAN SEJIC ART, COLOR AND COVER
STEVE WANDS LETTERING
DAVE WIELGOSZ ASSISTANT EDITOR
ALEX ANTONE EDITOR
BRIAN CUNNINGHAM GROUP EDITOR

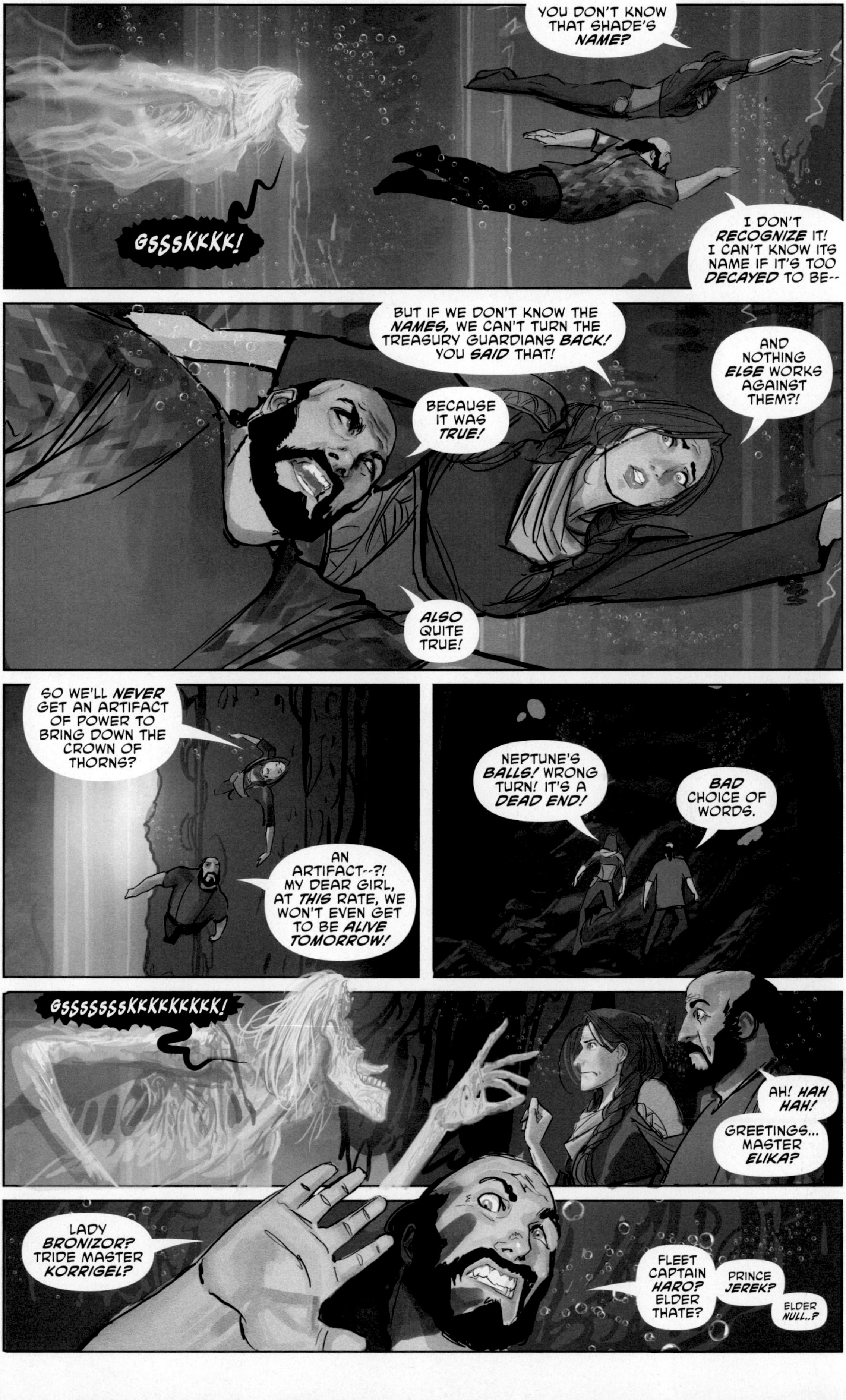

YOU DON'T KNOW THAT SHADE'S NAME?
GSSSKKKK!
I DON'T RECOGNIZE IT! I CAN'T KNOW ITS NAME IF IT'S TOO DECAYED TO BE--
BUT IF WE DON'T KNOW THE NAMES, WE CAN'T TURN THE TREASURY GUARDIANS BACK! YOU SAID THAT!
BECAUSE IT WAS TRUE!
AND NOTHING ELSE WORKS AGAINST THEM?!
ALSO QUITE TRUE!
SO WE'LL NEVER GET AN ARTIFACT OF POWER TO BRING DOWN THE CROWN OF THORNS?
AN ARTIFACT--?! MY DEAR GIRL, AT THIS RATE, WE WON'T EVEN GET TO BE ALIVE TOMORROW!
NEPTUNE'S BALLS! WRONG TURN! IT'S A DEAD END!
BAD CHOICE OF WORDS.
GSSSSSSSKKKKKKKK!
AH! HAH HAH!
GREETINGS... MASTER ELIKA?
LADY BRONIZOR? TRIDE MASTER KORRIGEL?
FLEET CAPTAIN HARO? ELDER THATE?
PRINCE JEREK?
ELDER NULL..?

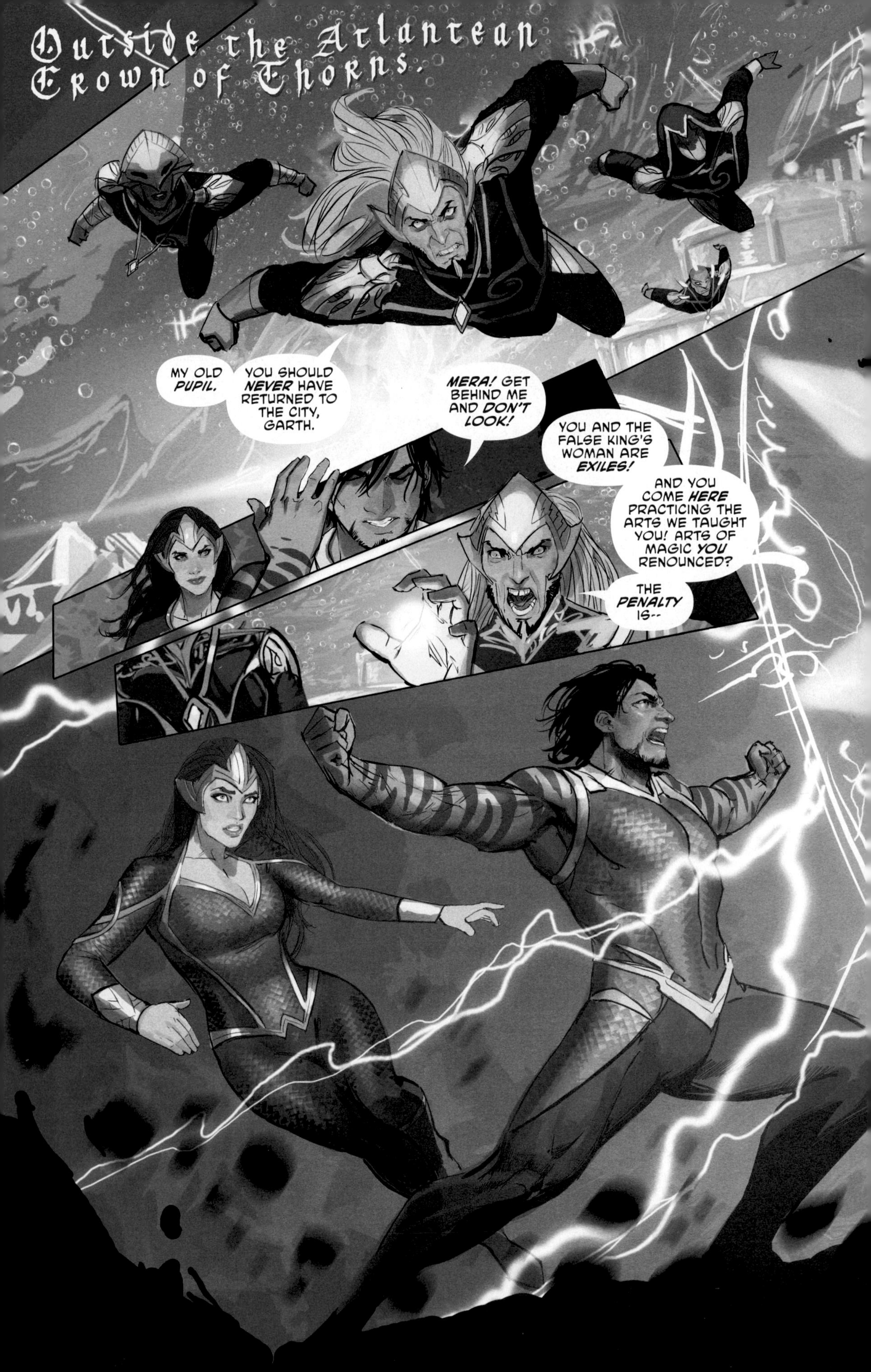
Outside the Atlantean Crown of Thorns.
MY OLD PUPIL.
YOU SHOULD NEVER HAVE RETURNED TO THE CITY, GARTH.
MERA! GET BEHIND ME AND DON'T LOOK!
YOU AND THE FALSE KING'S WOMAN ARE EXILES!
AND YOU COME HERE PRACTICING THE ARTS WE TAUGHT YOU! ARTS OF MAGIC YOU RENOUNCED?
THE PENALTY IS--

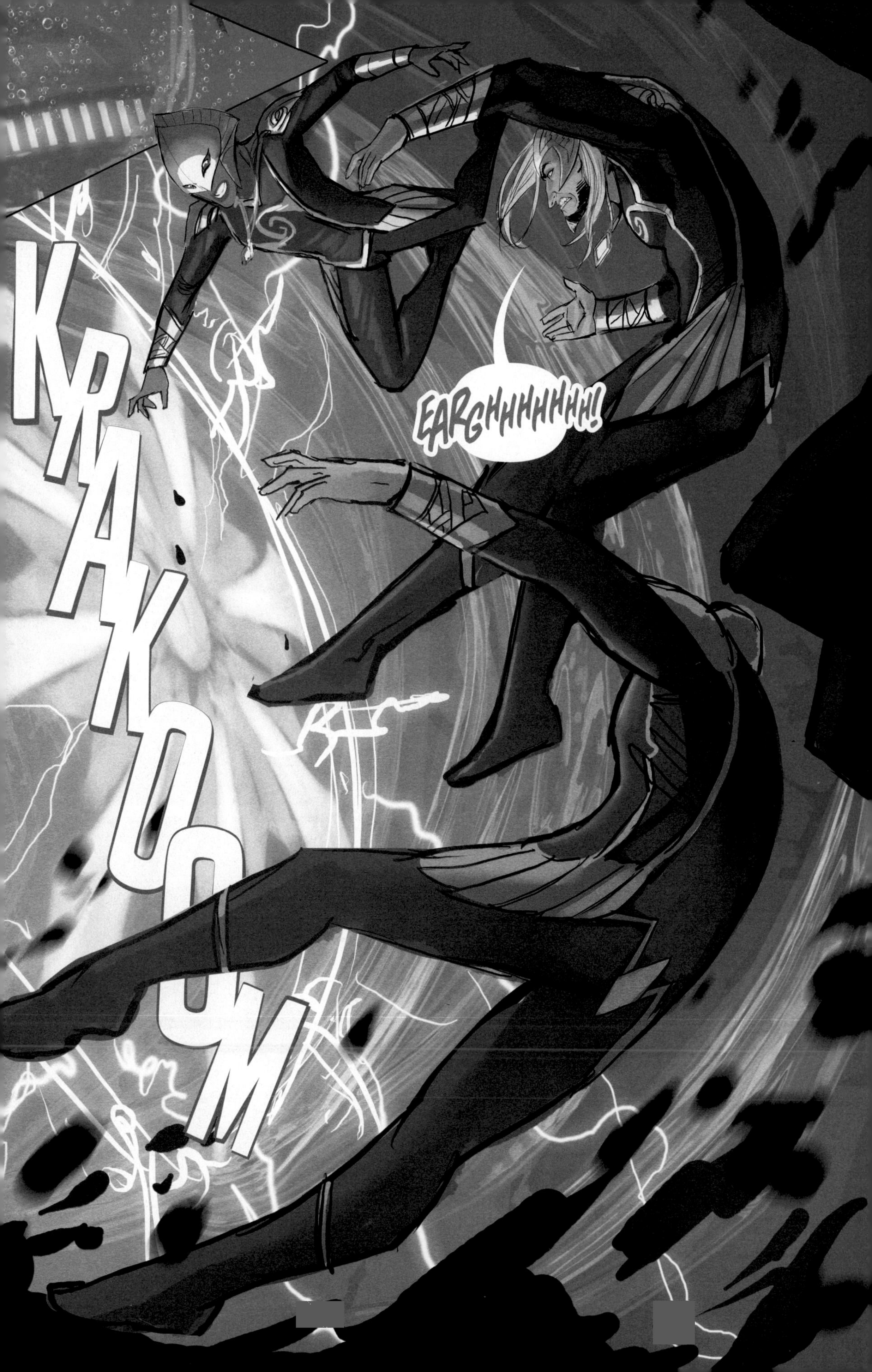
KRAKOOM
EARGHHHHHHH!

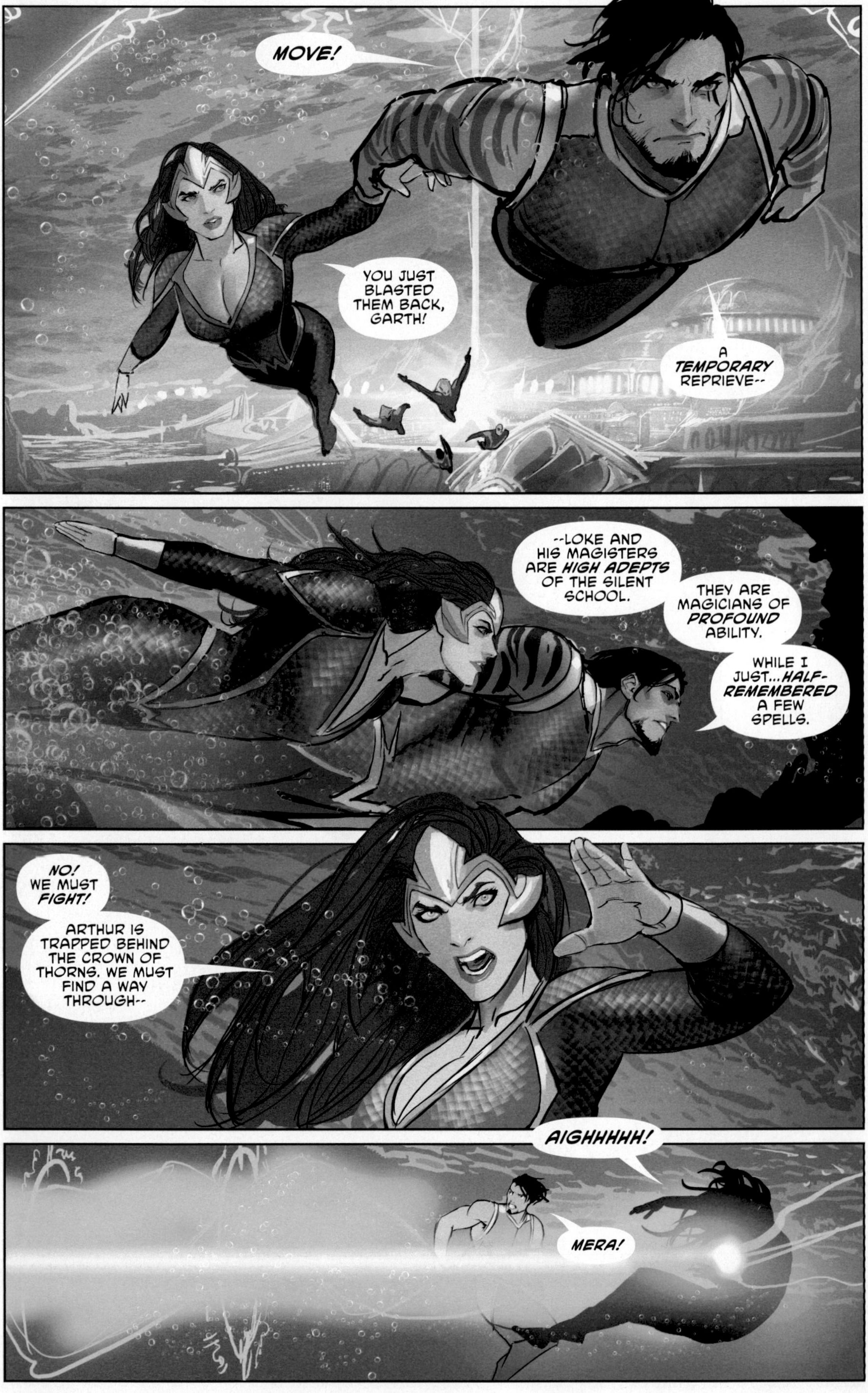
MOVE!
YOU JUST BLASTED THEM BACK, GARTH!
A TEMPORARY REPRIEVE--
--LOKE AND HIS MAGISTERS ARE HIGH ADEPTS OF THE SILENT SCHOOL.
THEY ARE MAGICIANS OF PROFOUND ABILITY.
WHILE I JUST...HALF-REMEMBERED A FEW SPELLS.
NO! WE MUST FIGHT!
ARTHUR IS TRAPPED BEHIND THE CROWN OF THORNS. WE MUST FIND A WAY THROUGH--
AIGHHHHH!
MERA!

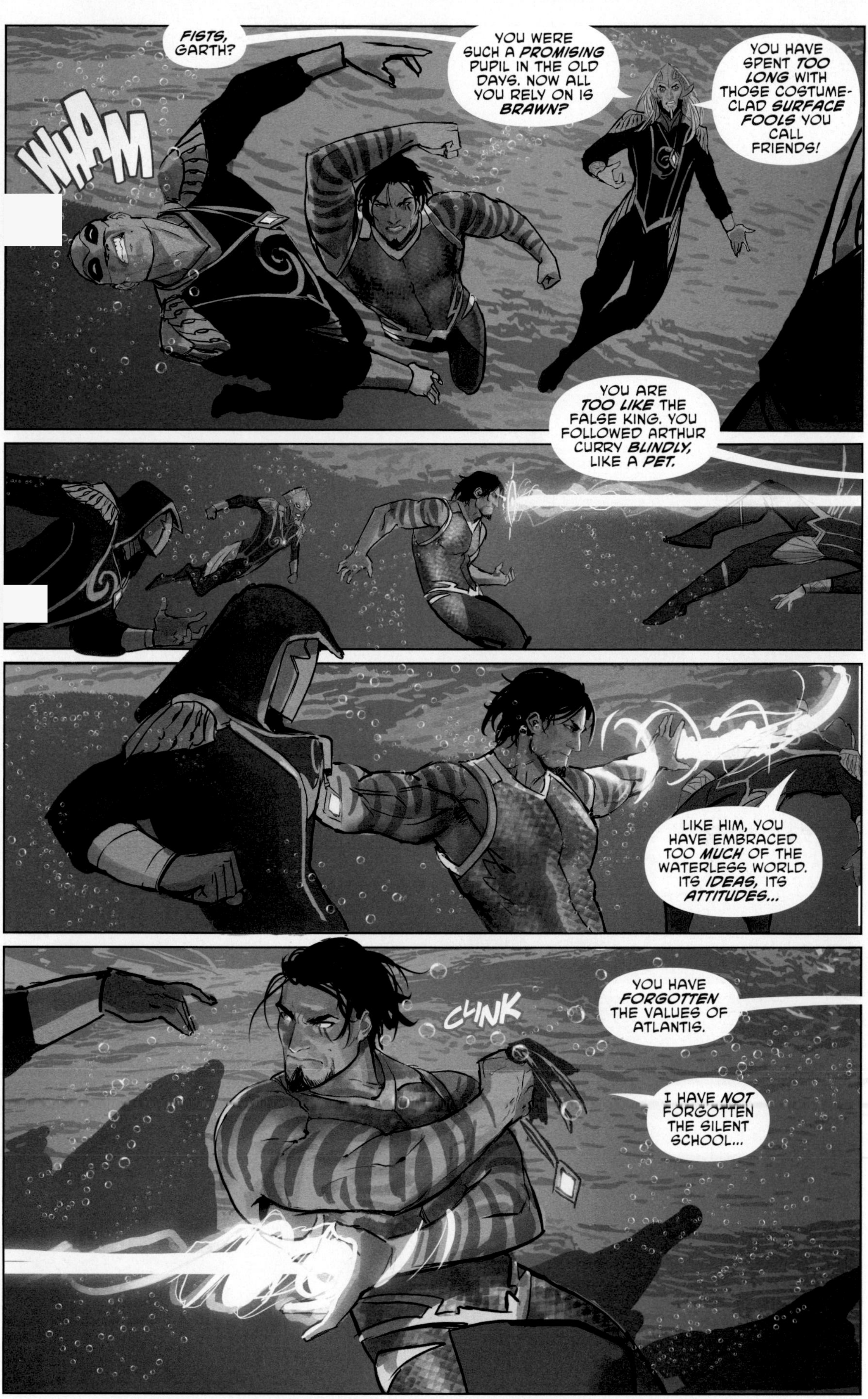
FISTS, GARTH?
YOU WERE SUCH A PROMISING PUPIL IN THE OLD DAYS. NOW ALL YOU RELY ON IS BRAWN?
YOU HAVE SPENT TOO LONG WITH THOSE COSTUME-CLAD SURFACE FOOLS YOU CALL FRIENDS!
WHAM
YOU ARE TOO LIKE THE FALSE KING. YOU FOLLOWED ARTHUR CURRY BLINDLY, LIKE A PET.
LIKE HIM, YOU HAVE EMBRACED TOO MUCH OF THE WATERLESS WORLD. ITS IDEAS, ITS ATTITUDES...
YOU HAVE FORGOTTEN THE VALUES OF ATLANTIS.
CLINK
I HAVE NOT FORGOTTEN THE SILENT SCHOOL...

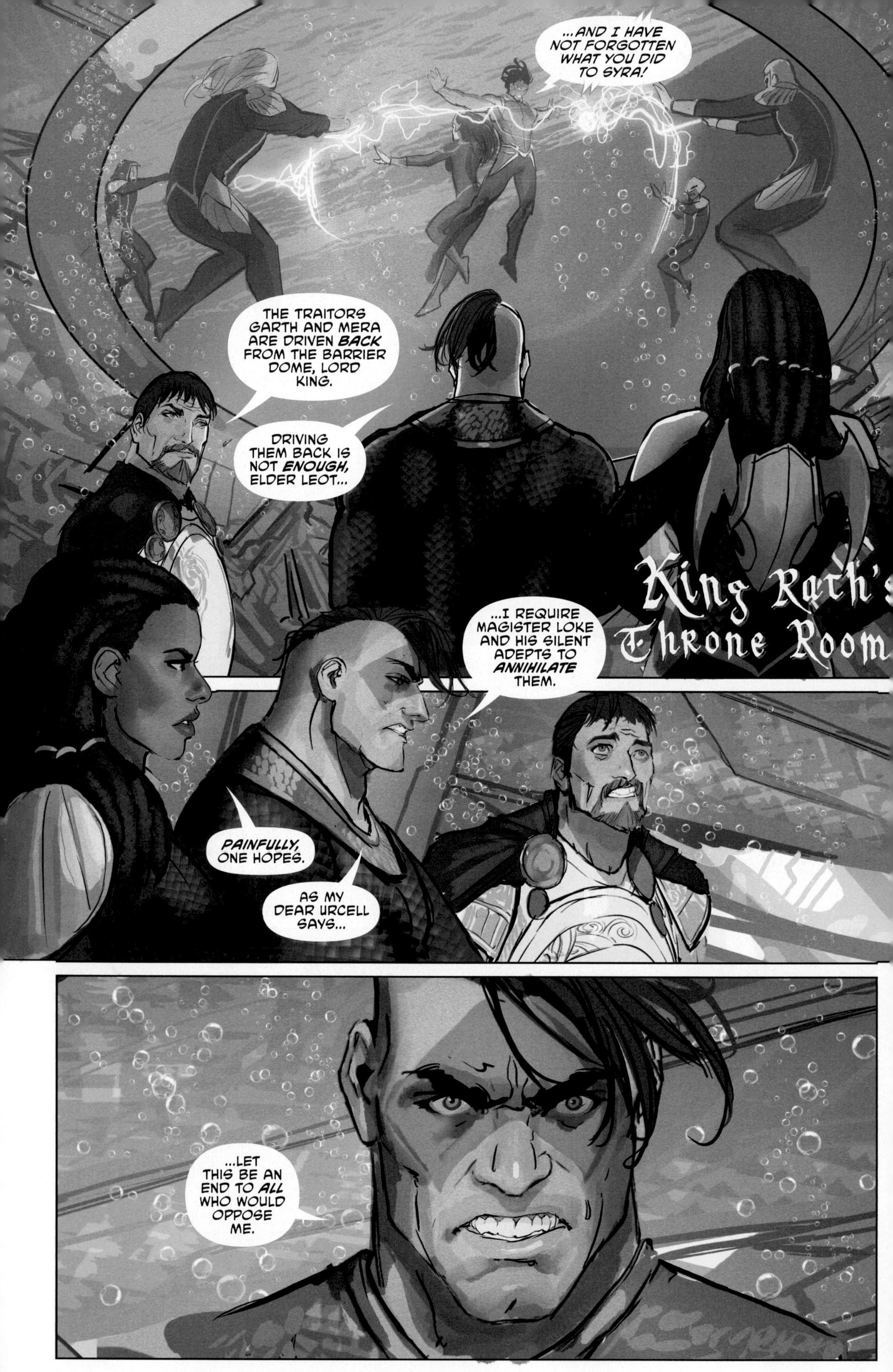
...AND I HAVE NOT FORGOTTEN WHAT YOU DID TO SYRA!
THE TRAITORS GARTH AND MERA ARE DRIVEN BACK FROM THE BARRIER DOME, LORD KING.
DRIVING THEM BACK IS NOT ENOUGH, ELDER LEOT...
King Rath's Throne Room
...I REQUIRE MAGISTER LOKE AND HIS SILENT ADEPTS TO ANNIHILATE THEM.
PAINFULLY, ONE HOPES.
AS MY DEAR URCELL SAYS...
...LET THIS BE AN END TO ALL WHO WOULD OPPOSE ME.

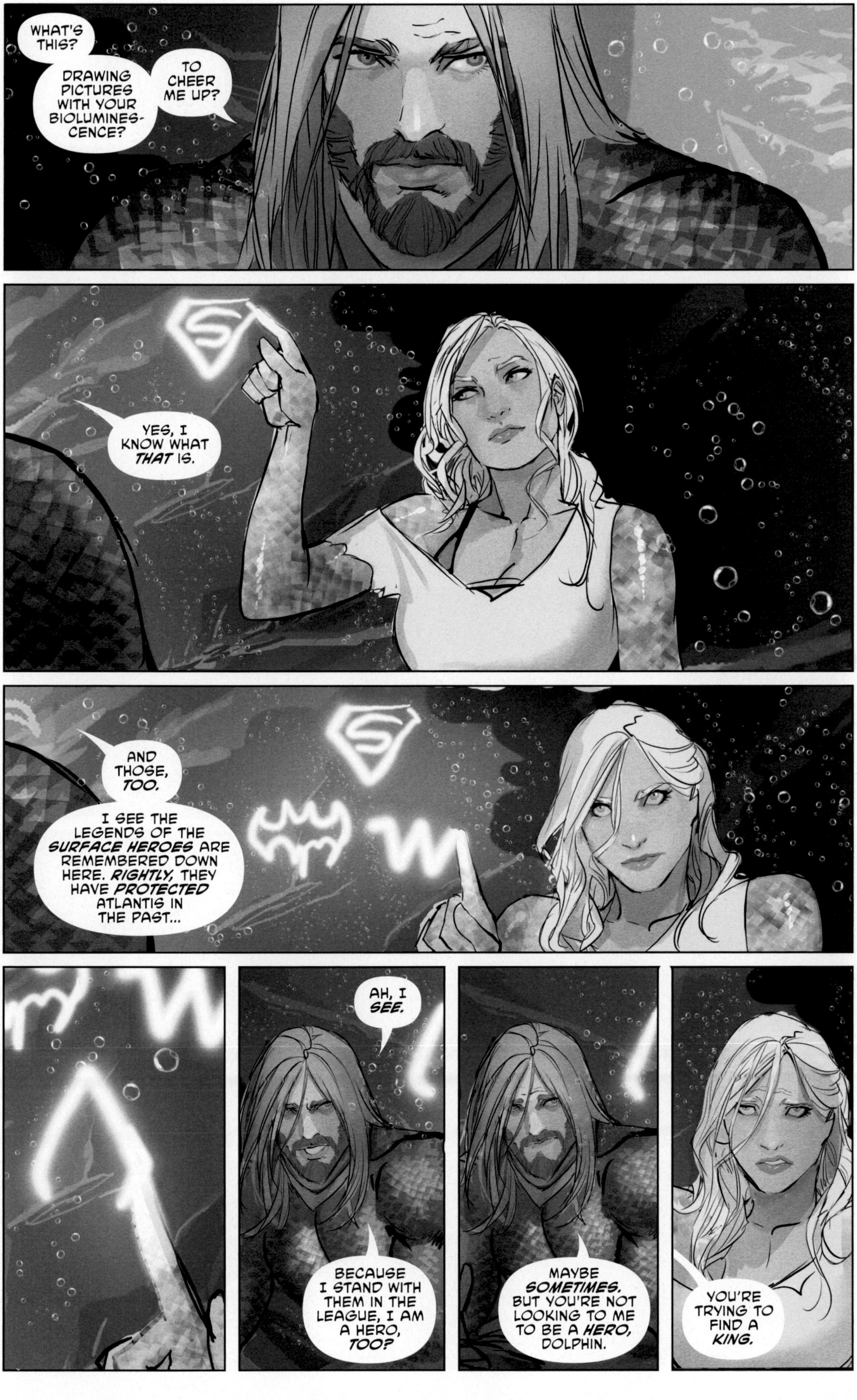
WHAT'S THIS?
DRAWING PICTURES WITH YOUR BIOLUMINESCENCE?
TO CHEER ME UP?
YES, I KNOW WHAT THAT IS.
AND THOSE, TOO.
I SEE THE LEGENDS OF THE SURFACE HEROES ARE REMEMBERED DOWN HERE. RIGHTLY, THEY HAVE PROTECTED ATLANTIS IN THE PAST...
AH, I SEE.
BECAUSE I STAND WITH THEM IN THE LEAGUE, I AM A HERO, TOO?
MAYBE SOMETIMES. BUT YOU'RE NOT LOOKING TO ME TO BE A HERO, DOLPHIN.
YOU'RE TRYING TO FIND A KING.

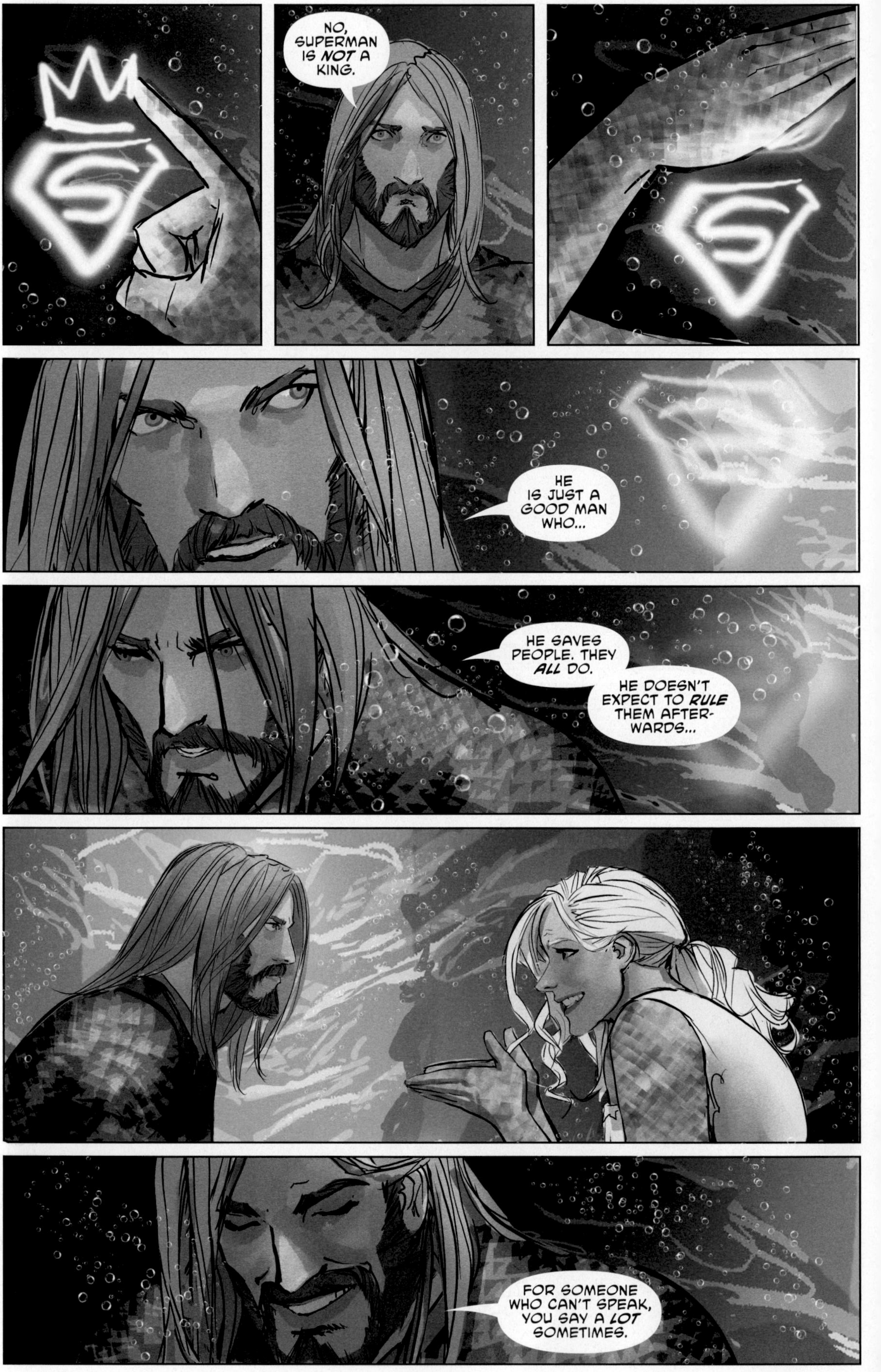
NO, SUPERMAN IS NOT A KING.
HE IS JUST A GOOD MAN WHO...
HE SAVES PEOPLE. THEY ALL DO.
HE DOESN'T EXPECT TO RULE THEM AFTER-WARDS...
FOR SOMEONE WHO CAN'T SPEAK, YOU SAY A LOT SOMETIMES.

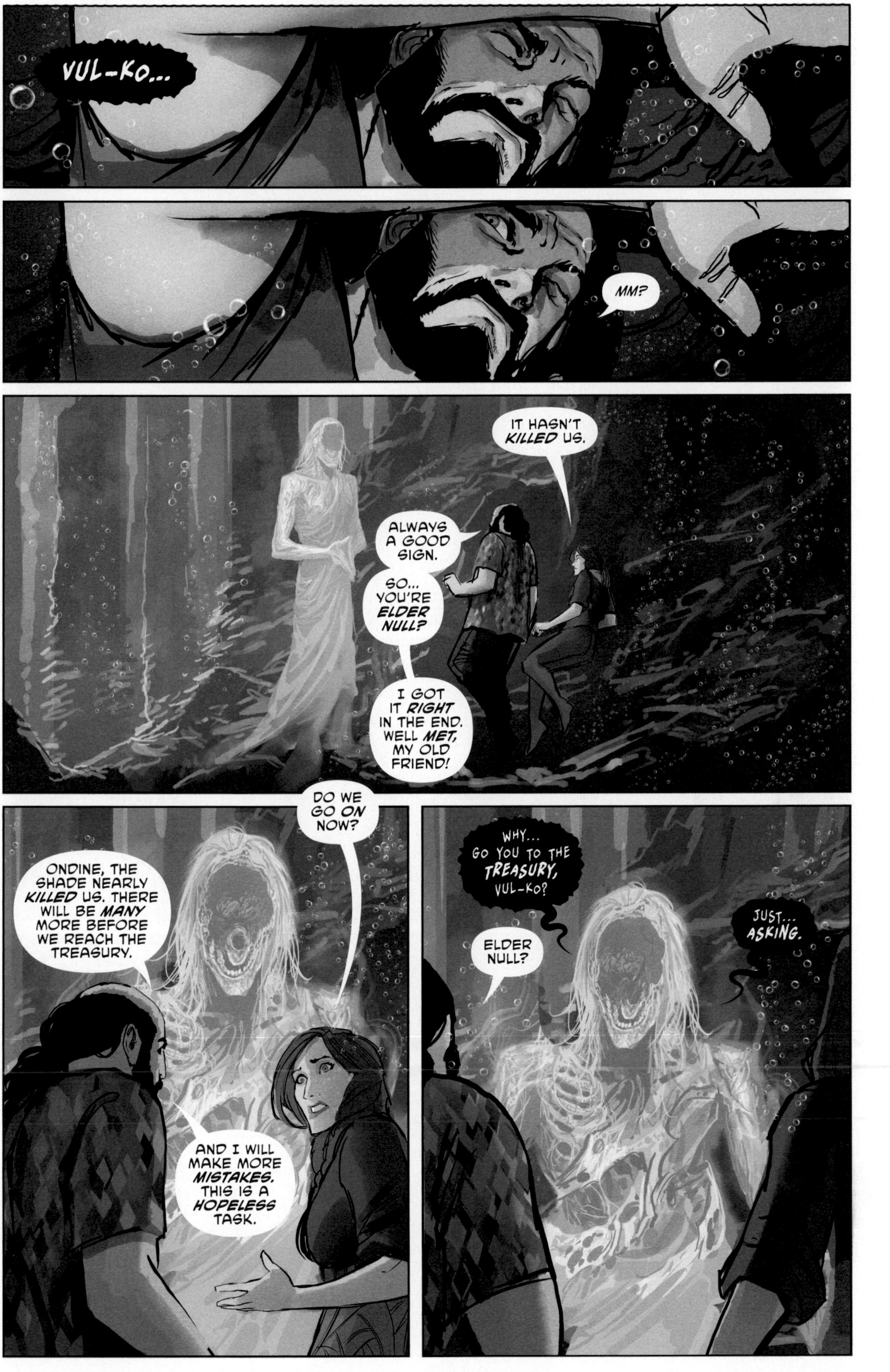
VUL-KO...
MM?
IT HASN'T KILLED US.
ALWAYS A GOOD SIGN.
SO... YOU'RE ELDER NULL?
I GOT IT RIGHT IN THE END. WELL MET, MY OLD FRIEND!
DO WE GO ON NOW?
ONDINE, THE SHADE NEARLY KILLED US. THERE WILL BE MANY MORE BEFORE WE REACH THE TREASURY.
AND I WILL MAKE MORE MISTAKES. THIS IS A HOPELESS TASK.
WHY... GO YOU TO THE TREASURY, VUL-KO?
ELDER NULL?
JUST... ASKING.

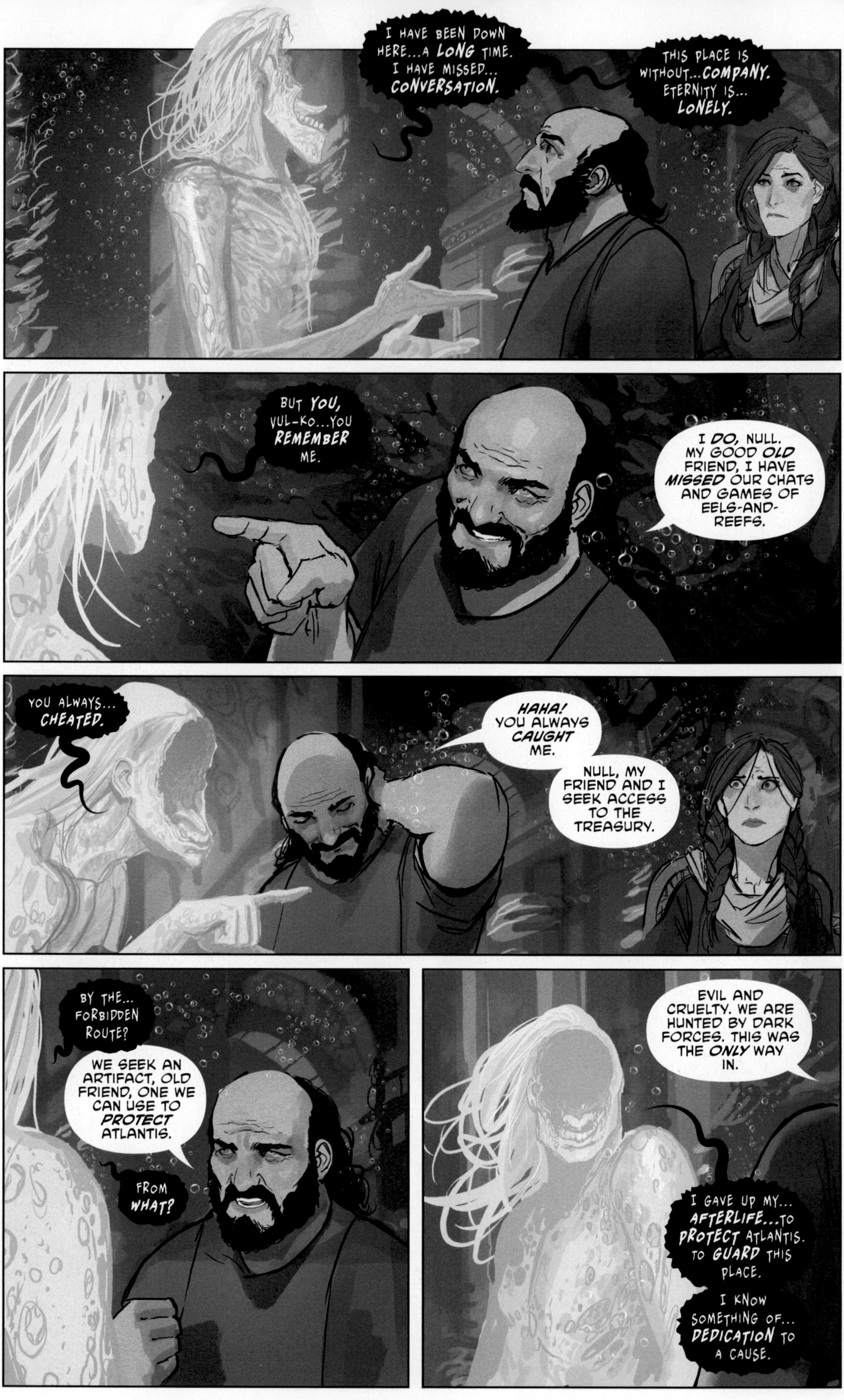
I HAVE BEEN DOWN HERE...A LONG TIME. I HAVE MISSED... CONVERSATION.
THIS PLACE IS WITHOUT...COMPANY. ETERNITY IS... LONELY.
BUT YOU, VUL-KO...YOU REMEMBER ME.
I DO, NULL. MY GOOD OLD FRIEND, I HAVE MISSED OUR CHATS AND GAMES OF EELS-AND-REEFS.
YOU ALWAYS... CHEATED.
HAHA! YOU ALWAYS CAUGHT ME.
NULL, MY FRIEND AND I SEEK ACCESS TO THE TREASURY.
BY THE... FORBIDDEN ROUTE?
WE SEEK AN ARTIFACT, OLD FRIEND, ONE WE CAN USE TO PROTECT ATLANTIS.
FROM WHAT?
EVIL AND CRUELTY. WE ARE HUNTED BY DARK FORCES. THIS WAS THE ONLY WAY IN.
I GAVE UP MY... AFTERLIFE...TO PROTECT ATLANTIS. TO GUARD THIS PLACE.
I KNOW SOMETHING OF... DEDICATION TO A CAUSE.

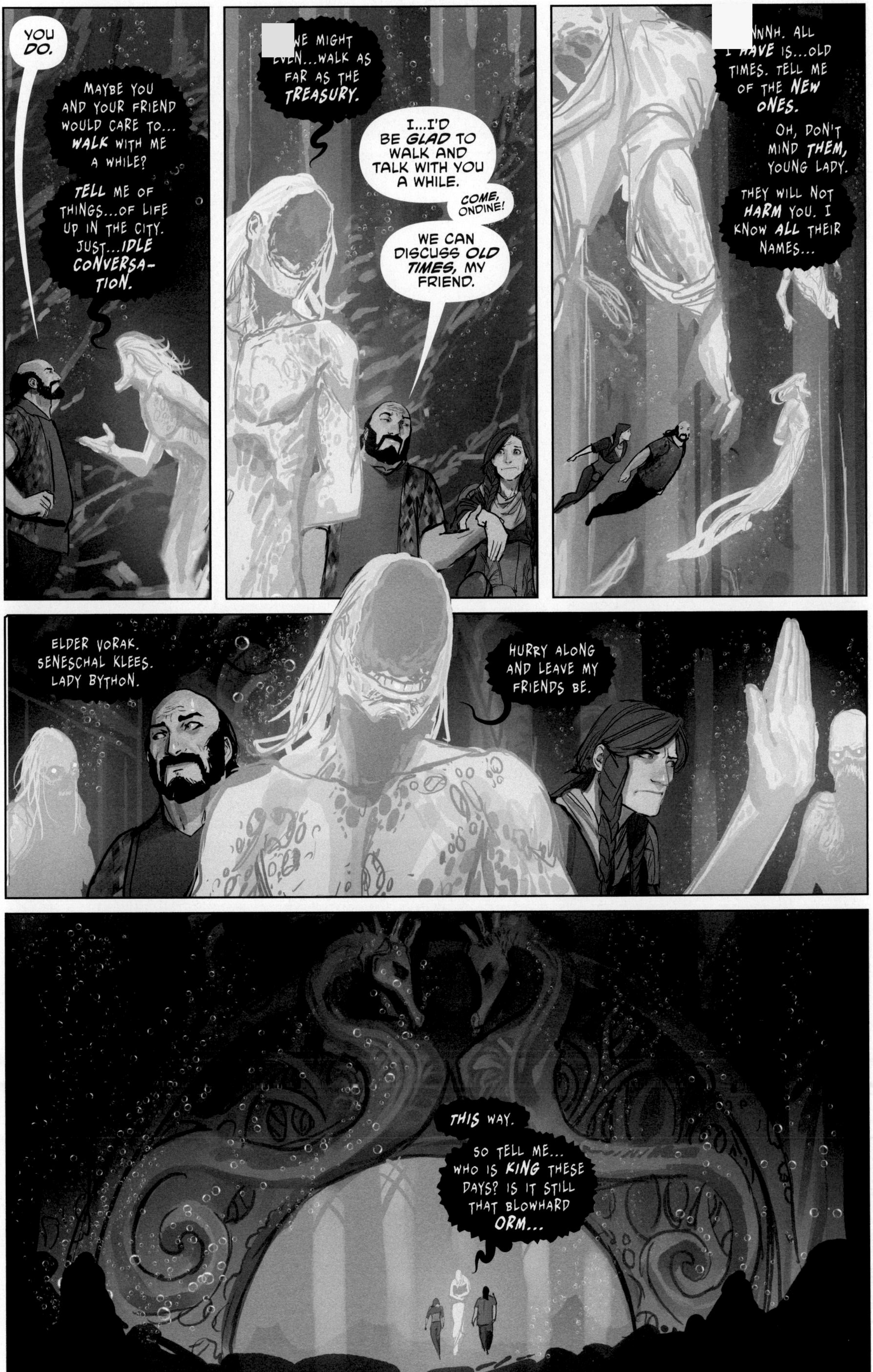
YOU DO.
MAYBE YOU AND YOUR FRIEND WOULD CARE TO... WALK WITH ME A WHILE?
TELL ME OF THINGS...OF LIFE UP IN THE CITY. JUST...IDLE CONVERSATION.
WE MIGHT EVEN...WALK AS FAR AS THE TREASURY.
I...I'D BE GLAD TO WALK AND TALK WITH YOU A WHILE.
COME, ONDINE!
WE CAN DISCUSS OLD TIMES, MY FRIEND.
NNH. ALL I HAVE IS...OLD TIMES. TELL ME OF THE NEW ONES.
OH, DON'T MIND THEM, YOUNG LADY.
THEY WILL NOT HARM YOU. I KNOW ALL THEIR NAMES...
ELDER VORAK. SENESCHAL KLEES. LADY BYTHON.
HURRY ALONG AND LEAVE MY FRIENDS BE.
THIS WAY.
SO TELL ME... WHO IS KING THESE DAYS? IS IT STILL THAT BLOWHARD ORM...

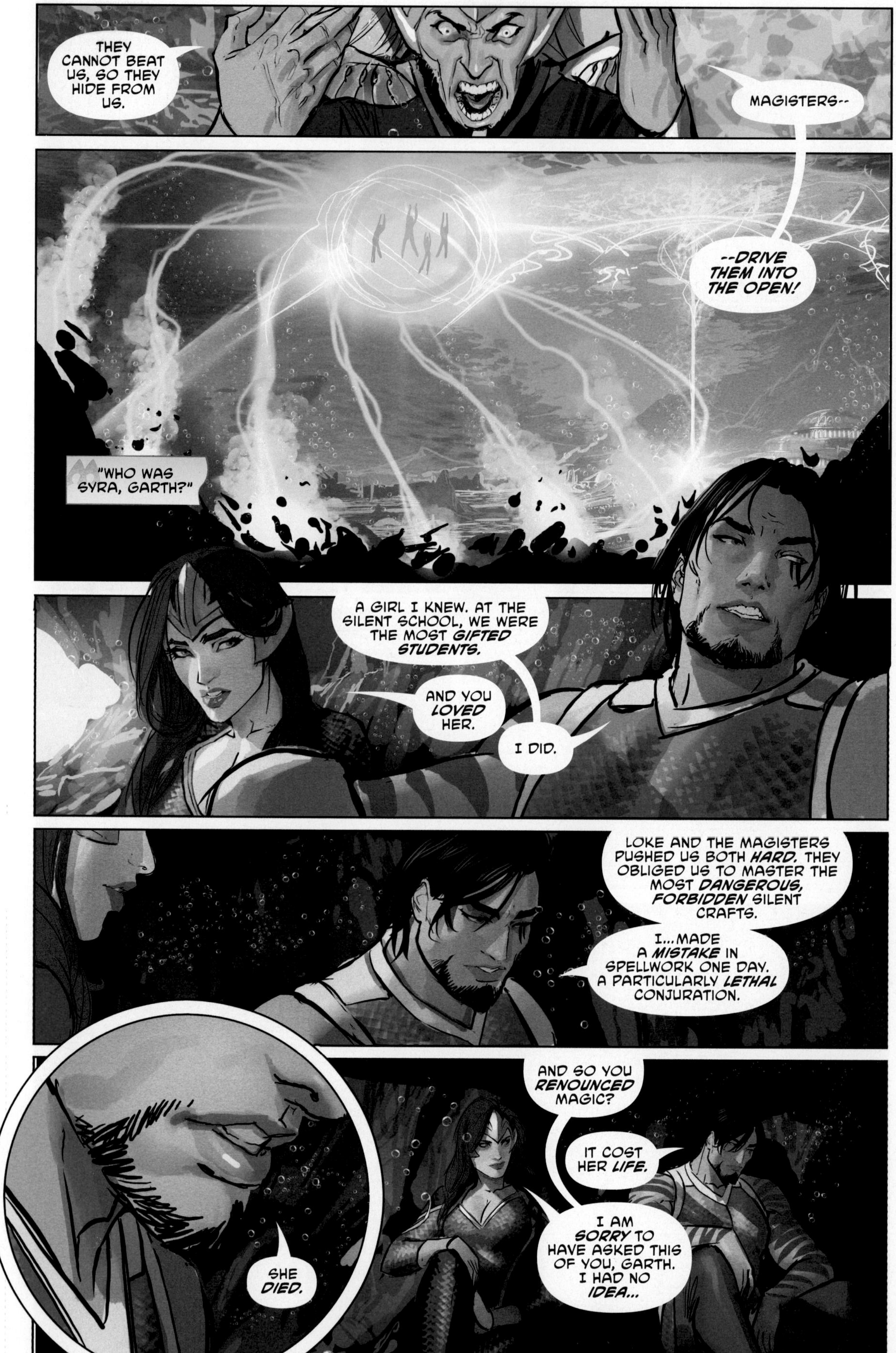

THEY CANNOT BEAT US, SO THEY HIDE FROM US.
MAGISTERS--
--DRIVE THEM INTO THE OPEN!
"WHO WAS SYRA, GARTH?"
A GIRL I KNEW. AT THE SILENT SCHOOL, WE WERE THE MOST GIFTED STUDENTS.
AND YOU LOVED HER.
I DID.
LOKE AND THE MAGISTERS PUSHED US BOTH HARD. THEY OBLIGED US TO MASTER THE MOST DANGEROUS, FORBIDDEN SILENT CRAFTS.
I...MADE A MISTAKE IN SPELLWORK ONE DAY. A PARTICULARLY LETHAL CONJURATION.
SHE DIED.
AND SO YOU RENOUNCED MAGIC?
IT COST HER LIFE.
I AM SORRY TO HAVE ASKED THIS OF YOU, GARTH. I HAD NO IDEA...

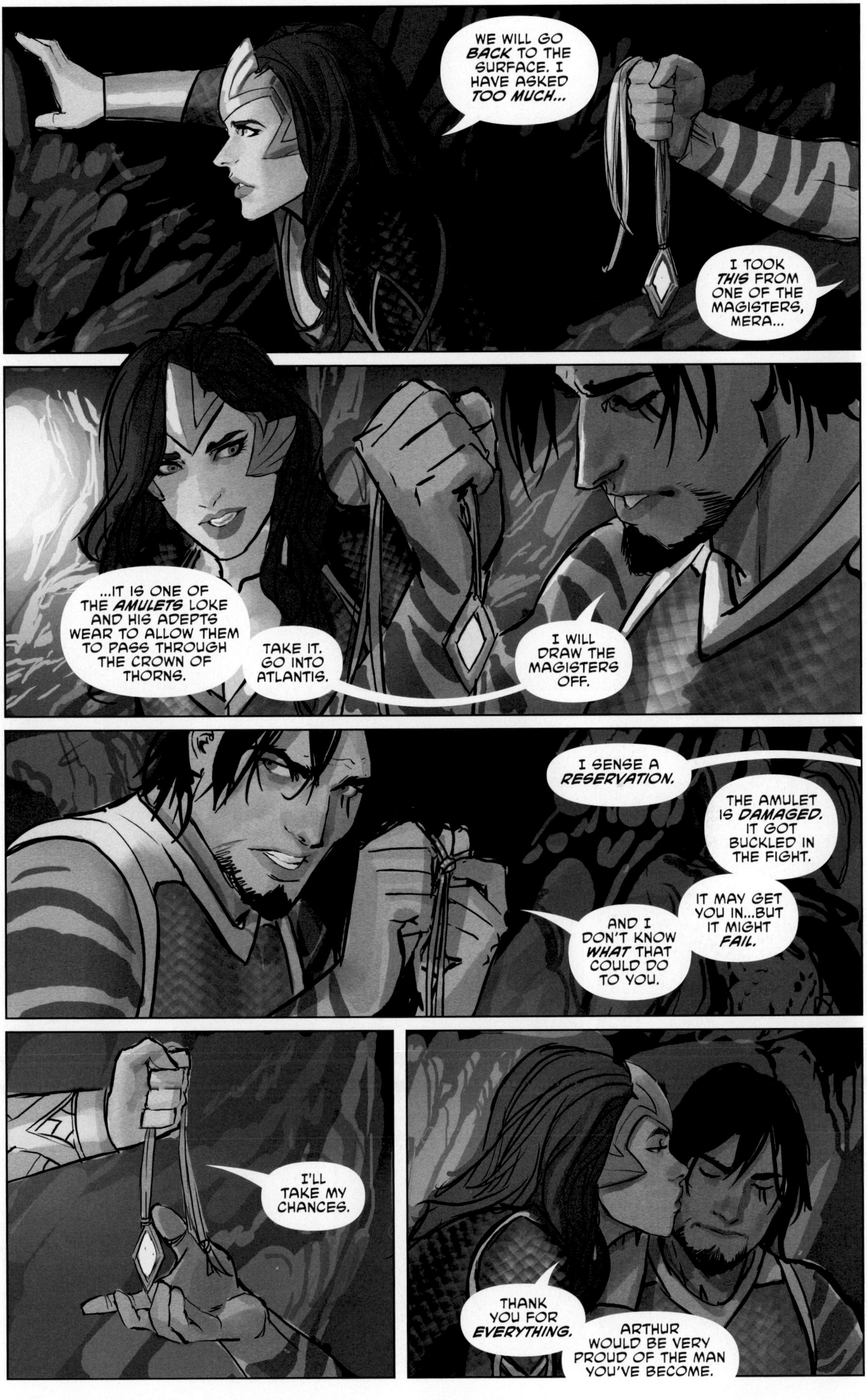
WE WILL GO BACK TO THE SURFACE. I HAVE ASKED TOO MUCH...
I TOOK THIS FROM ONE OF THE MAGISTERS, MERA...
...IT IS ONE OF THE AMULETS LOKE AND HIS ADEPTS WEAR TO ALLOW THEM TO PASS THROUGH THE CROWN OF THORNS.
TAKE IT. GO INTO ATLANTIS.
I WILL DRAW THE MAGISTERS OFF.
I SENSE A RESERVATION.
THE AMULET IS DAMAGED. IT GOT BUCKLED IN THE FIGHT.
IT MAY GET YOU IN...BUT IT MIGHT FAIL.
AND I DON'T KNOW WHAT THAT COULD DO TO YOU.
I'LL TAKE MY CHANCES.
THANK YOU FOR EVERYTHING.
ARTHUR WOULD BE VERY PROUD OF THE MAN YOU'VE BECOME.

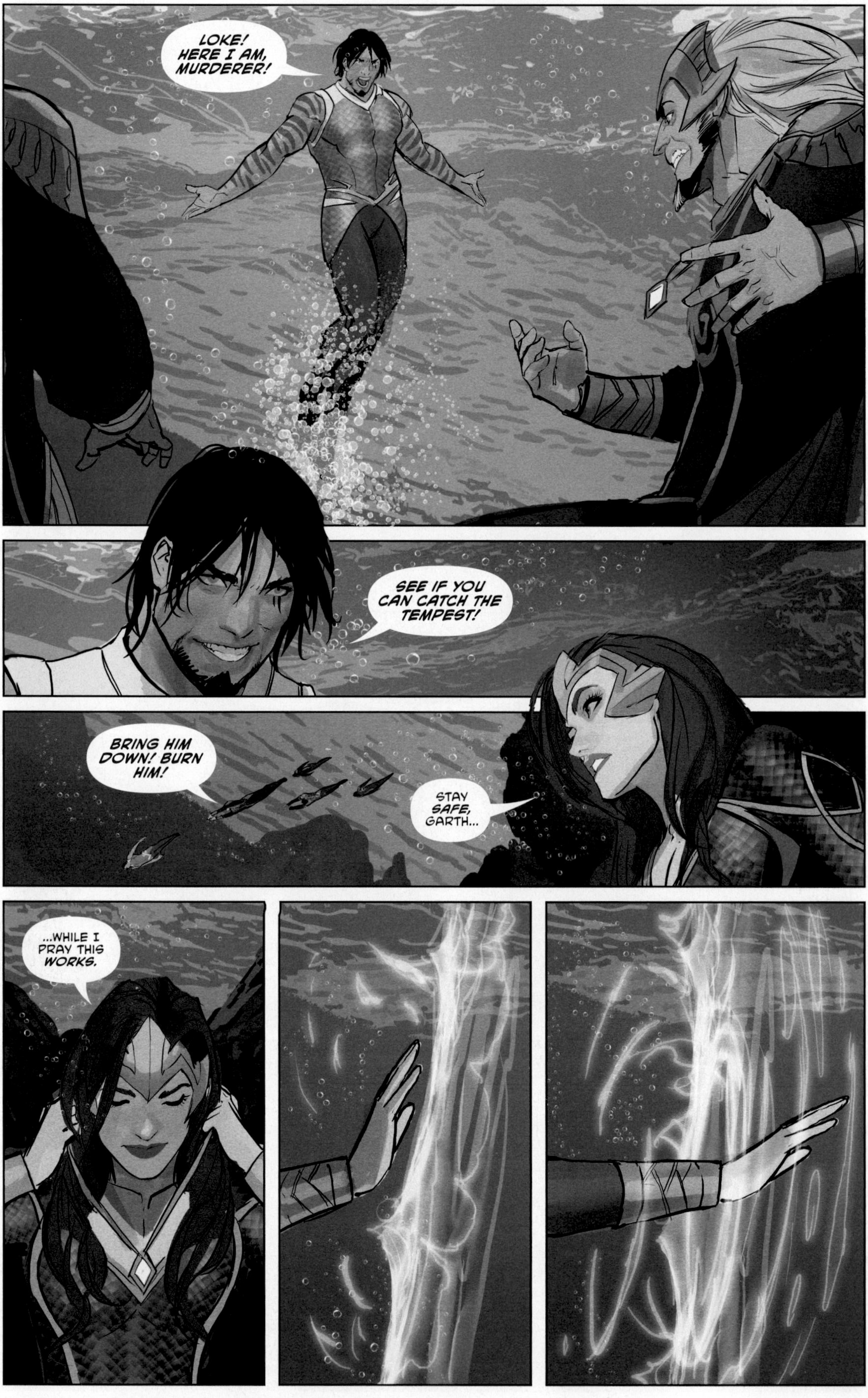
LOKE! HERE I AM, MURDERER!
SEE IF YOU CAN CATCH THE TEMPEST!
BRING HIM DOWN! BURN HIM!
STAY SAFE, GARTH...
...WHILE I PRAY THIS WORKS.

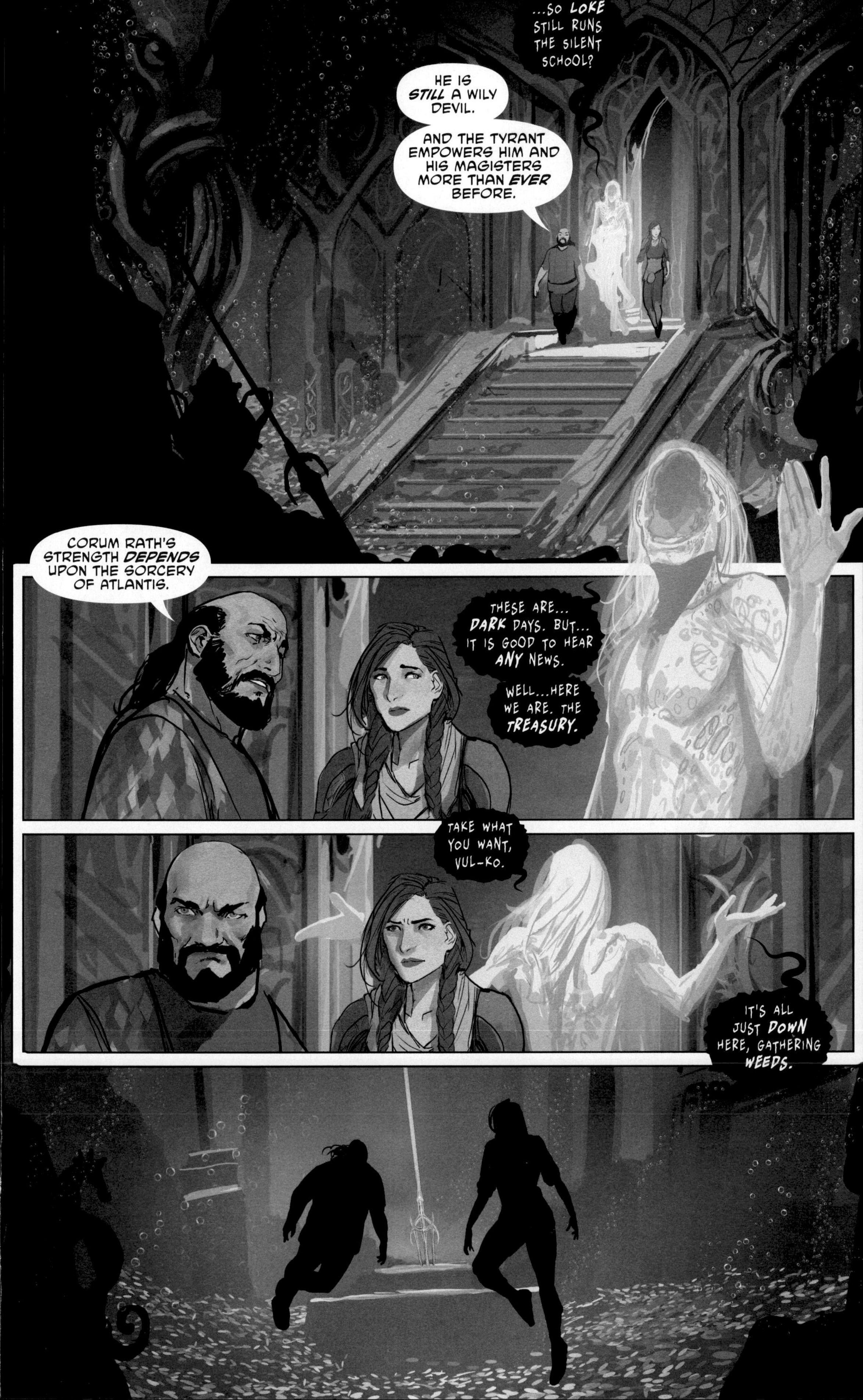
...SO LOKE STILL RUNS THE SILENT SCHOOL?
HE IS STILL A WILY DEVIL.
AND THE TYRANT EMPOWERS HIM AND HIS MAGISTERS MORE THAN EVER BEFORE.
CORUM RATH'S STRENGTH DEPENDS UPON THE SORCERY OF ATLANTIS.
THESE ARE... DARK DAYS. BUT... IT IS GOOD TO HEAR ANY NEWS.
WELL...HERE WE ARE. THE TREASURY.
TAKE WHAT YOU WANT, VUL-KO.
IT'S ALL JUST DOWN HERE, GATHERING WEEDS.

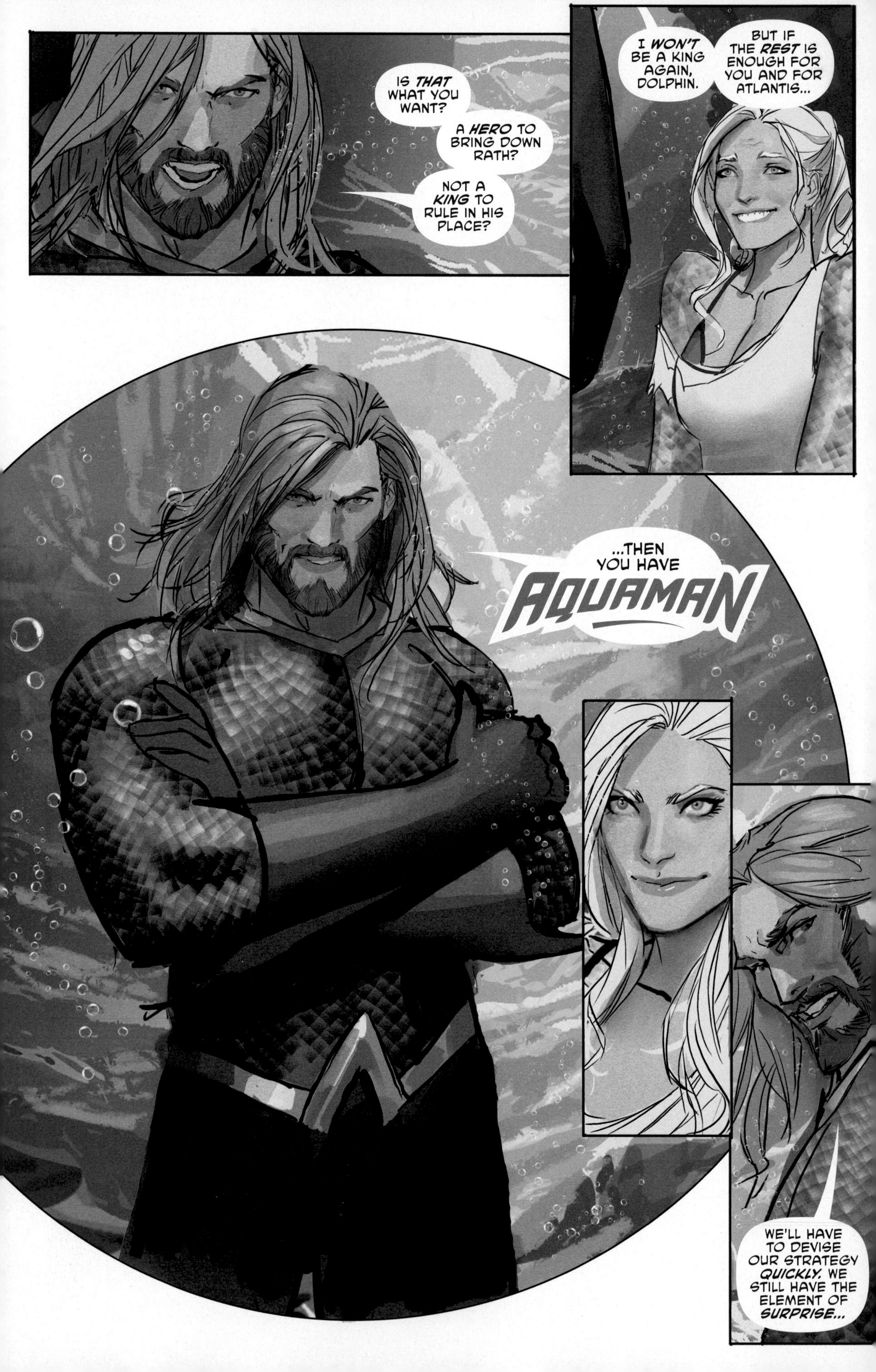
IS THAT WHAT YOU WANT?
A HERO TO BRING DOWN RATH?
NOT A KING TO RULE IN HIS PLACE?
I WON'T BE A KING AGAIN, DOLPHIN.
BUT IF THE REST IS ENOUGH FOR YOU AND FOR ATLANTIS...
...THEN YOU HAVE AQUAMAN
WE'LL HAVE TO DEVISE OUR STRATEGY QUICKLY. WE STILL HAVE THE ELEMENT OF SURPRISE...

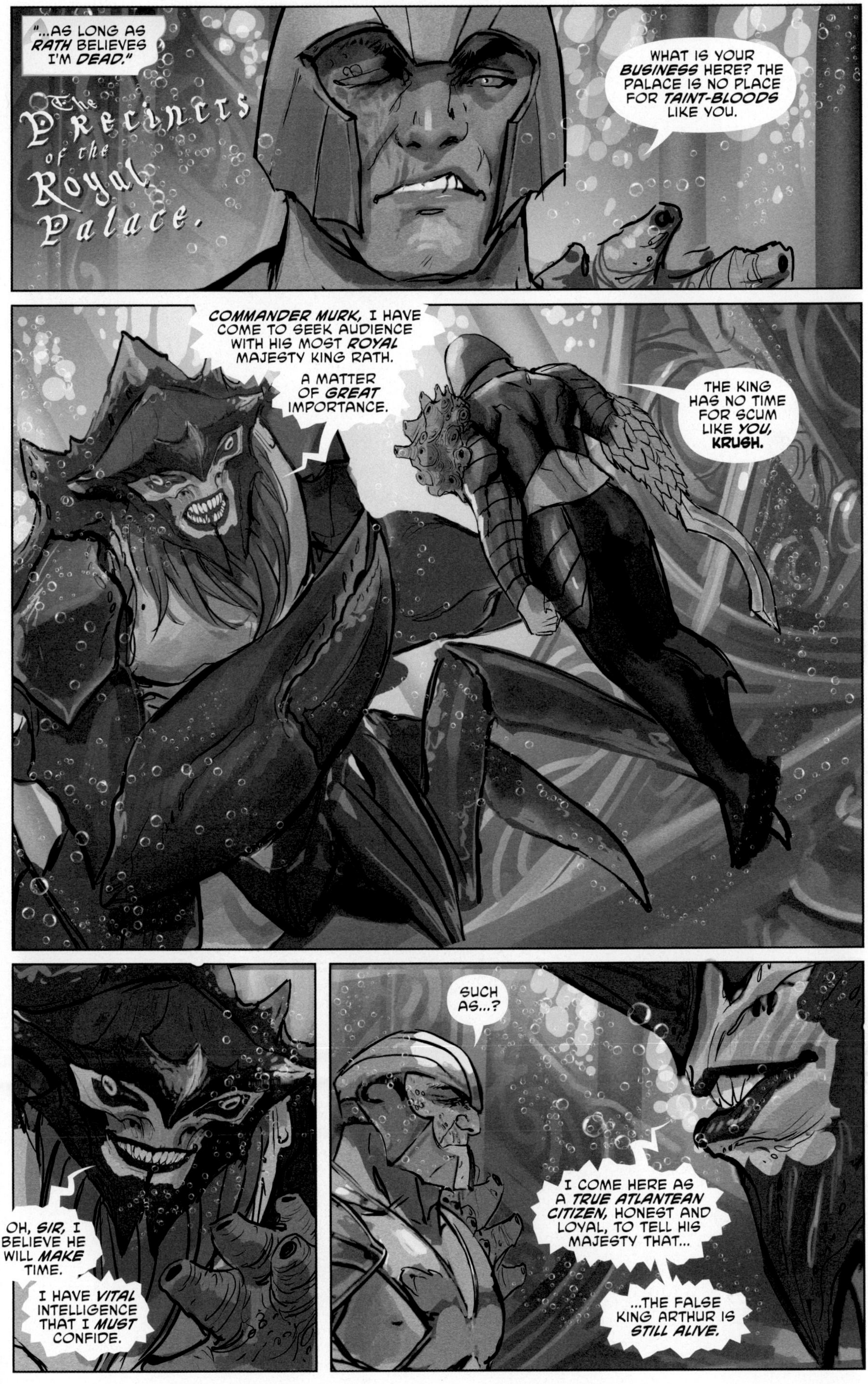
"...AS LONG AS RATH BELIEVES I'M DEAD."
The Precincts of the Royal Palace.
WHAT IS YOUR BUSINESS HERE? THE PALACE IS NO PLACE FOR TAINT-BLOODS LIKE YOU.
COMMANDER MURK, I HAVE COME TO SEEK AUDIENCE WITH HIS MOST ROYAL MAJESTY KING RATH.
A MATTER OF GREAT IMPORTANCE.
THE KING HAS NO TIME FOR SCUM LIKE YOU, KRUSH.
OH, SIR, I BELIEVE HE WILL MAKE TIME.
I HAVE VITAL INTELLIGENCE THAT I MUST CONFIDE.
SUCH AS...?
I COME HERE AS A TRUE ATLANTEAN CITIZEN, HONEST AND LOYAL, TO TELL HIS MAJESTY THAT...
...THE FALSE KING ARTHUR IS STILL ALIVE.

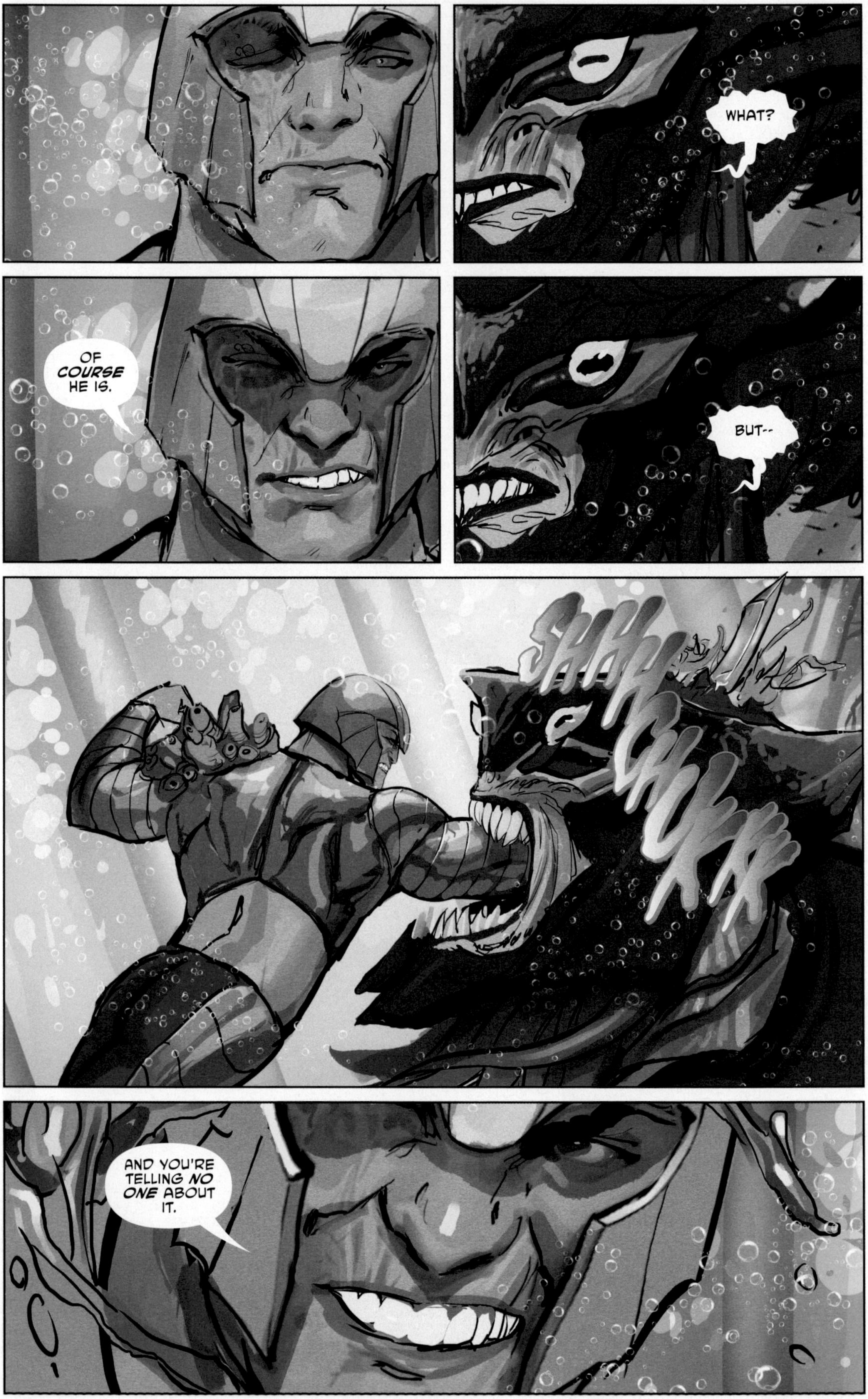
WHAT?
OF *COURSE* HE IS.
BUT--
SHHHCHUKK
AND YOU'RE TELLING *NO ONE* ABOUT IT.

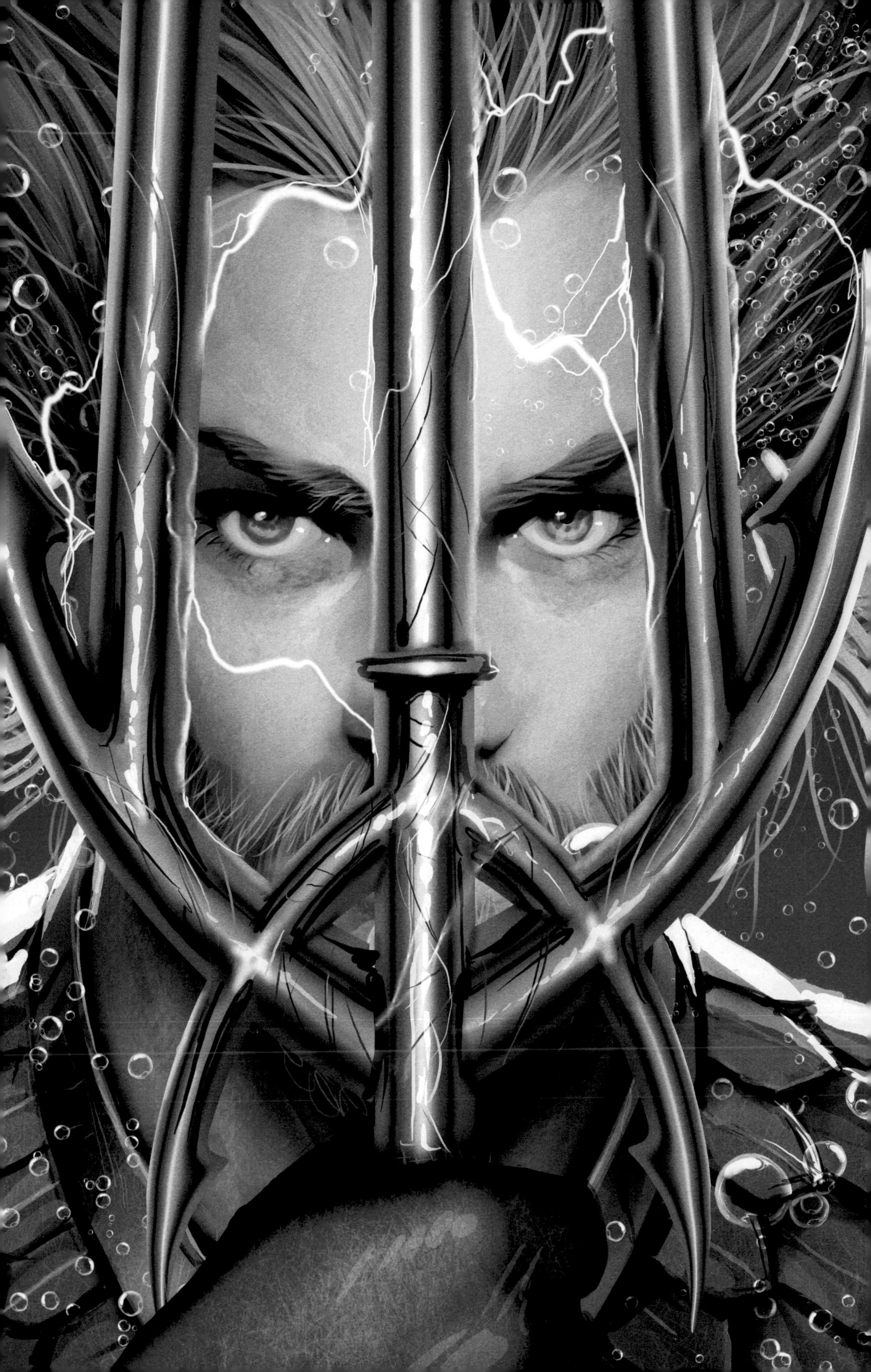

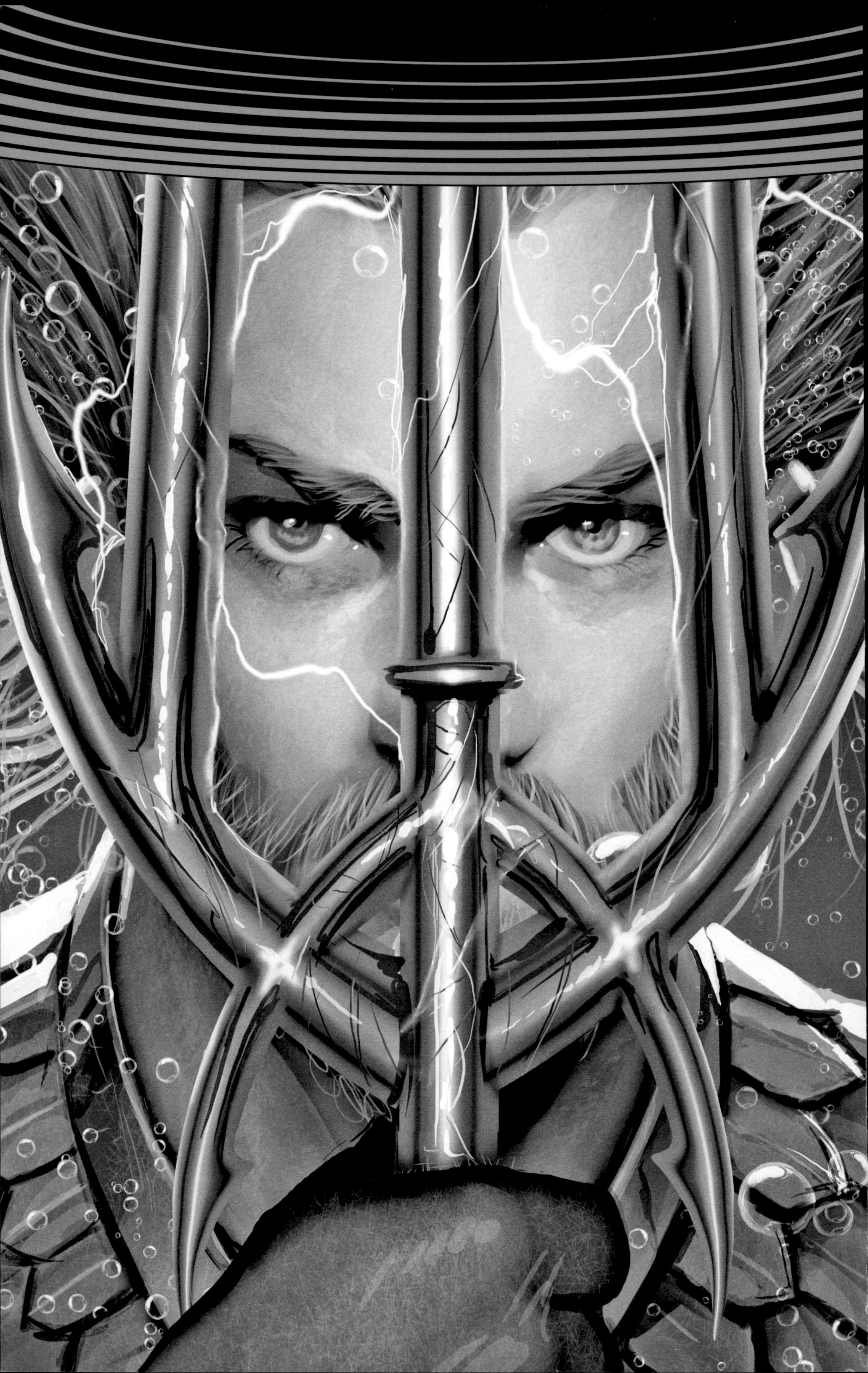

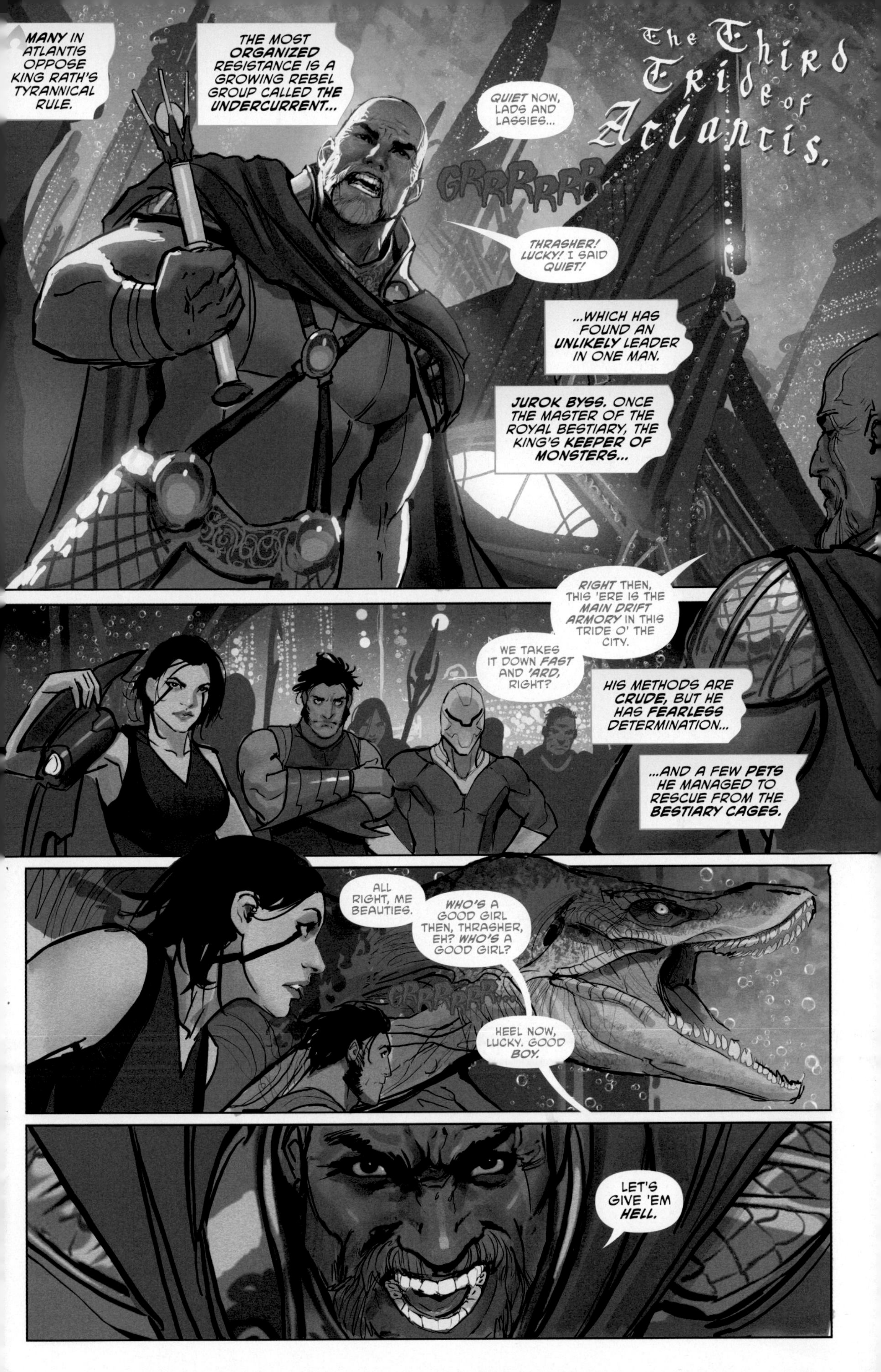

MANY IN ATLANTIS OPPOSE KING RATH'S TYRANNICAL RULE.
THE MOST ORGANIZED RESISTANCE IS A GROWING REBEL GROUP CALLED THE UNDERCURRENT...
The Third Tride of Atlantis.
QUIET NOW, LADS AND LASSIES...
GRRRRRR
THRASHER! LUCKY! I SAID QUIET!
...WHICH HAS FOUND AN UNLIKELY LEADER IN ONE MAN.
JUROK BYSS. ONCE THE MASTER OF THE ROYAL BESTIARY, THE KING'S KEEPER OF MONSTERS...
RIGHT THEN, THIS 'ERE IS THE MAIN DRIFT ARMORY IN THIS TRIDE O' THE CITY.
WE TAKES IT DOWN FAST AND 'ARD, RIGHT?
HIS METHODS ARE CRUDE, BUT HE HAS FEARLESS DETERMINATION...
...AND A FEW PETS HE MANAGED TO RESCUE FROM THE BESTIARY CAGES.
ALL RIGHT, ME BEAUTIES.
WHO'S A GOOD GIRL THEN, THRASHER, EH? WHO'S A GOOD GIRL?
GRRRRRR...
HEEL NOW, LUCKY. GOOD BOY.
LET'S GIVE 'EM HELL.

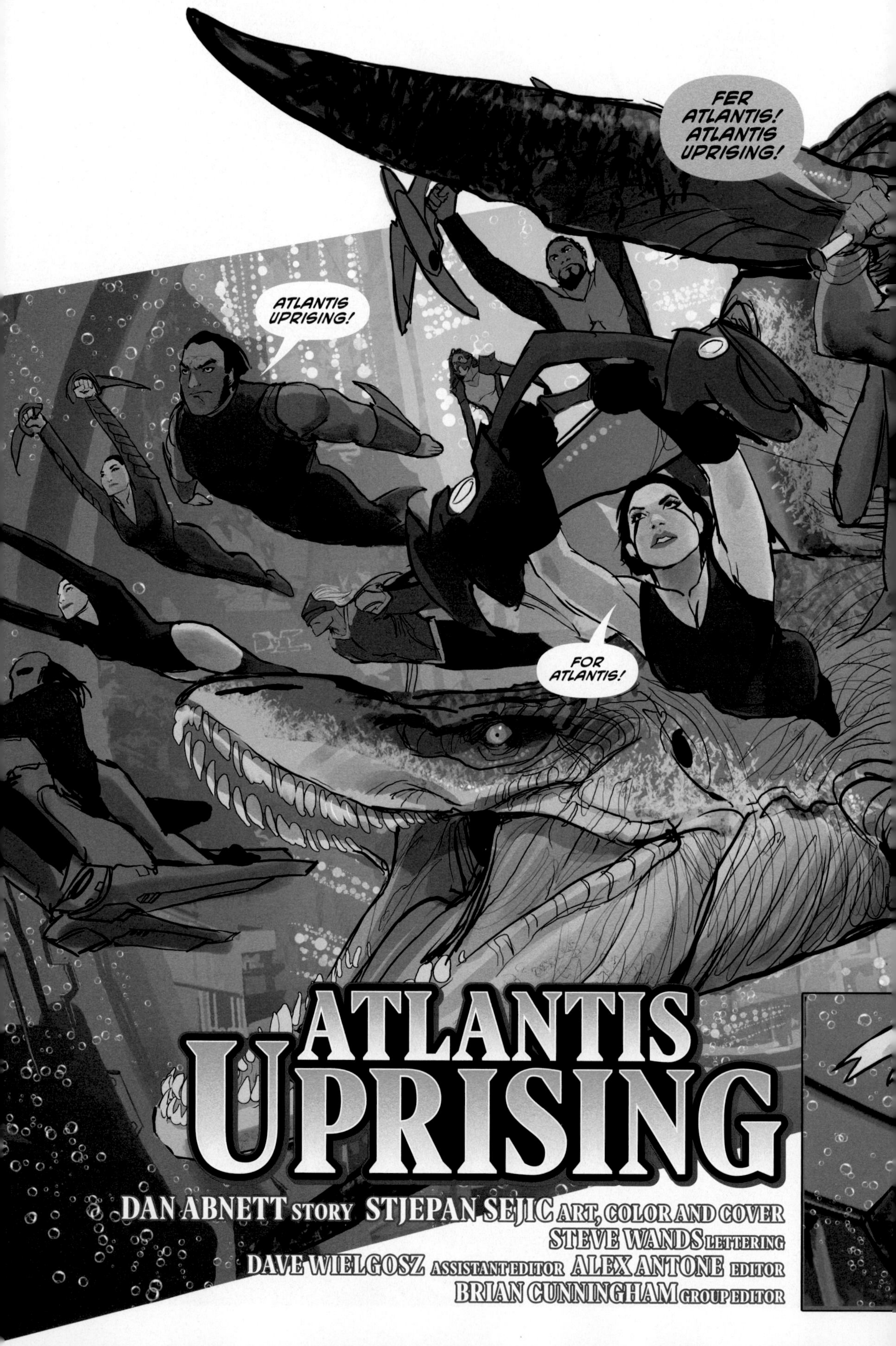
FER ATLANTIS! ATLANTIS UPRISING!
ATLANTIS UPRISING!
FOR ATLANTIS!
ATLANTIS UPRISING
DAN ABNETT STORY STJEPAN SEJIC ART, COLOR AND COVER
STEVE WANDS LETTERING
DAVE WIELGOSZ ASSISTANT EDITOR ALEX ANTONE EDITOR
BRIAN CUNNINGHAM GROUP EDITOR

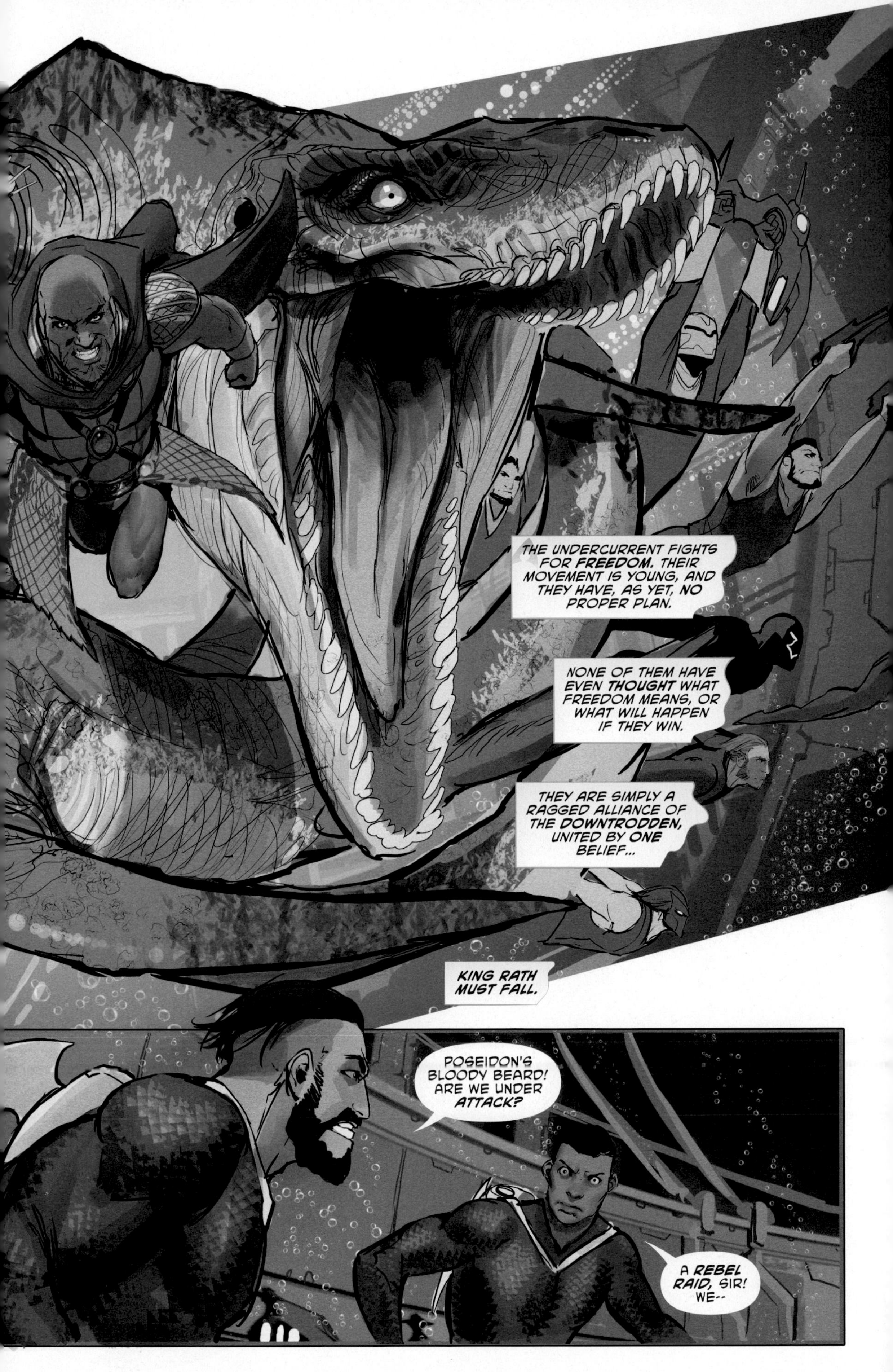

THE UNDERCURRENT FIGHTS FOR FREEDOM. THEIR MOVEMENT IS YOUNG, AND THEY HAVE, AS YET, NO PROPER PLAN.
NONE OF THEM HAVE EVEN THOUGHT WHAT FREEDOM MEANS, OR WHAT WILL HAPPEN IF THEY WIN.
THEY ARE SIMPLY A RAGGED ALLIANCE OF THE DOWNTRODDEN, UNITED BY ONE BELIEF...
KING RATH MUST FALL.
POSEIDON'S BLOODY BEARD! ARE WE UNDER ATTACK?
A REBEL RAID, SIR! WE--

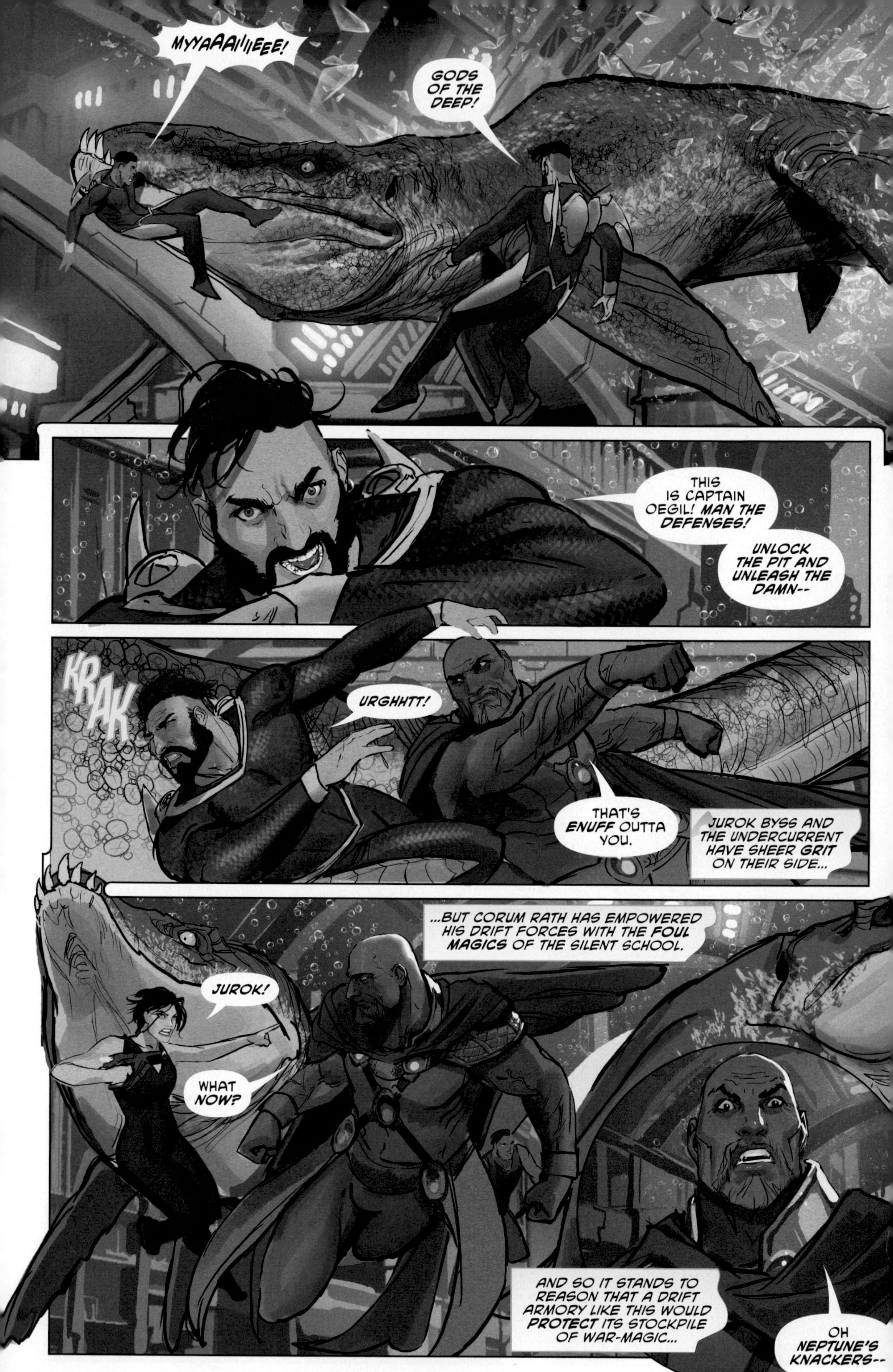
MYYAAAIIIIEEE!
GODS OF THE DEEP!
THIS IS CAPTAIN OEGIL! MAN THE DEFENSES!
UNLOCK THE PIT AND UNLEASH THE DAMN--
KRAK
URGHHTT!
THAT'S ENUFF OUTTA YOU.
JUROK BYSS AND THE UNDERCURRENT HAVE SHEER GRIT ON THEIR SIDE...
...BUT CORUM RATH HAS EMPOWERED HIS DRIFT FORCES WITH THE FOUL MAGICS OF THE SILENT SCHOOL.
JUROK!
WHAT NOW?
AND SO IT STANDS TO REASON THAT A DRIFT ARMORY LIKE THIS WOULD PROTECT ITS STOCKPILE OF WAR-MAGIC...
OH NEPTUNE'S KNACKERS--

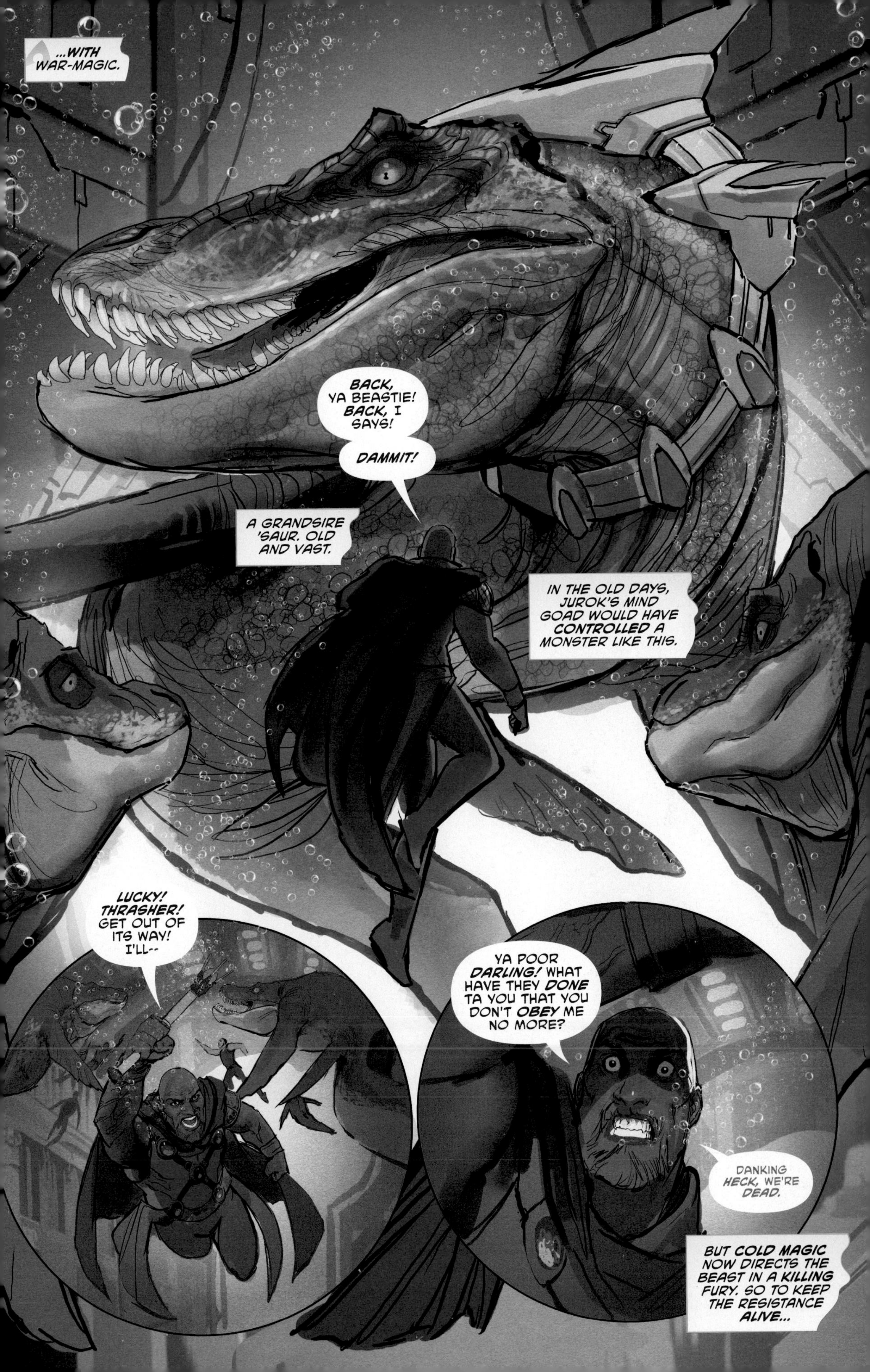
...WITH WAR-MAGIC.
BACK, YA BEASTIE! BACK, I SAYS!
DAMMIT!
A GRANDSIRE 'SAUR. OLD AND VAST.
IN THE OLD DAYS, JUROK'S MIND GOAD WOULD HAVE CONTROLLED A MONSTER LIKE THIS.
LUCKY! THRASHER! GET OUT OF ITS WAY! I'LL--
YA POOR DARLING! WHAT HAVE THEY DONE TA YOU THAT YOU DON'T OBEY ME NO MORE?
DANKING HECK, WE'RE DEAD.
BUT COLD MAGIC NOW DIRECTS THE BEAST IN A KILLING FURY. SO TO KEEP THE RESISTANCE ALIVE...

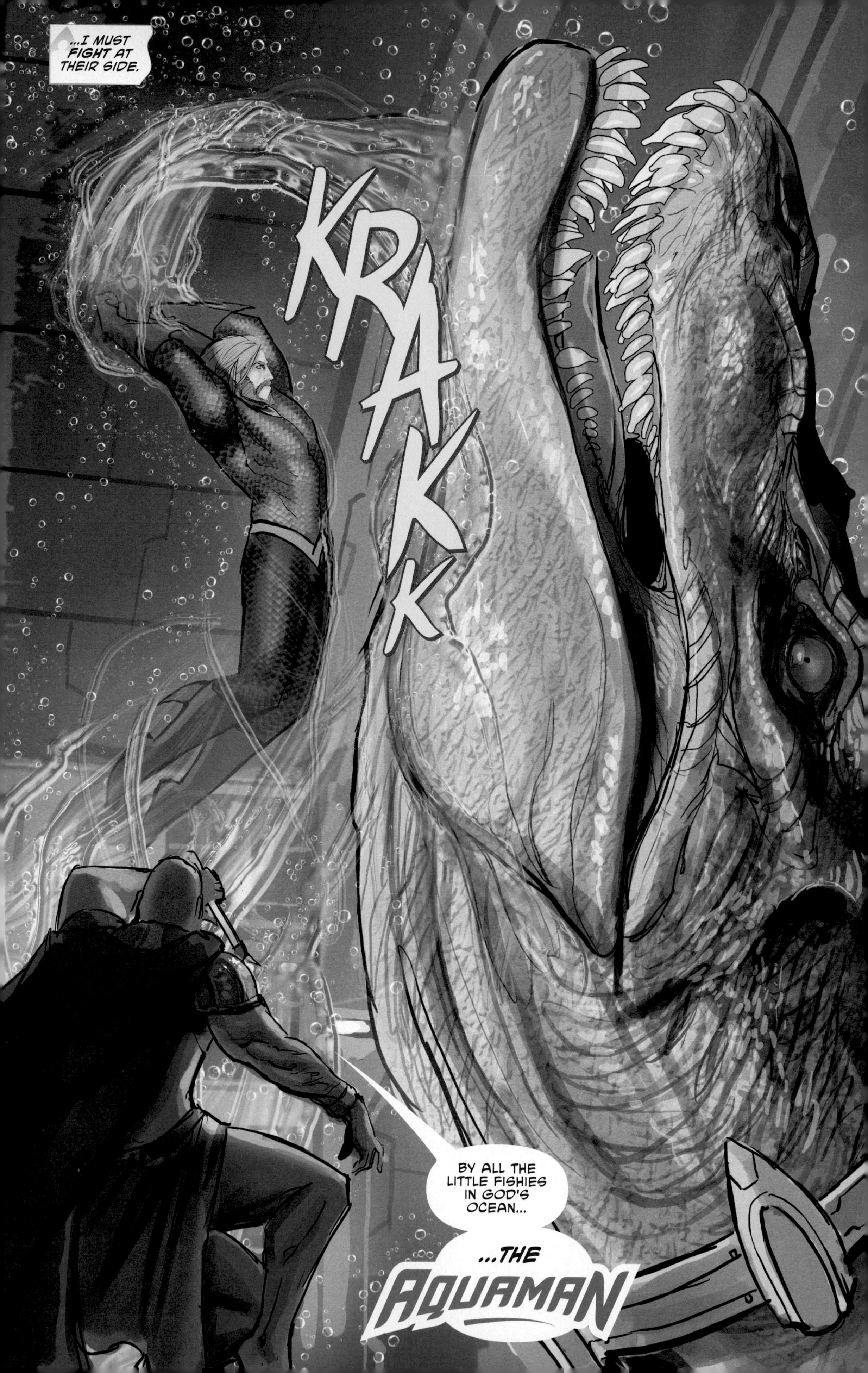
...I MUST FIGHT AT THEIR SIDE.
KRAKK
BY ALL THE LITTLE FISHIES IN GOD'S OCEAN...
...THE AQUAMAN

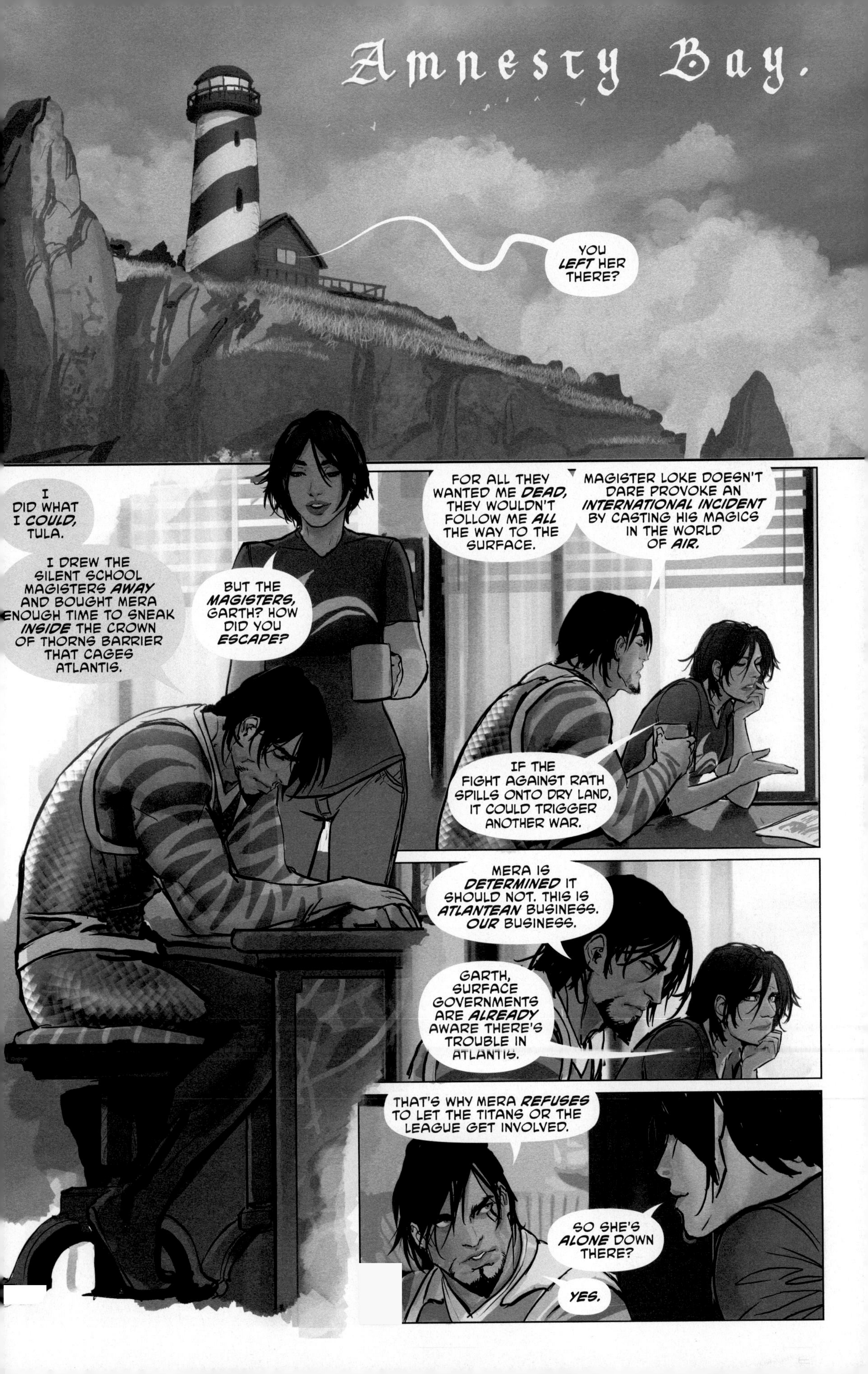
Amnesty Bay.
YOU LEFT HER THERE?
I DID WHAT I COULD, TULA.
I DREW THE SILENT SCHOOL MAGISTERS AWAY AND BOUGHT MERA ENOUGH TIME TO SNEAK INSIDE THE CROWN OF THORNS BARRIER THAT CAGES ATLANTIS.
BUT THE MAGISTERS, GARTH? HOW DID YOU ESCAPE?
FOR ALL THEY WANTED ME DEAD, THEY WOULDN'T FOLLOW ME ALL THE WAY TO THE SURFACE.
MAGISTER LOKE DOESN'T DARE PROVOKE AN INTERNATIONAL INCIDENT BY CASTING HIS MAGICS IN THE WORLD OF AIR.
IF THE FIGHT AGAINST RATH SPILLS ONTO DRY LAND, IT COULD TRIGGER ANOTHER WAR.
MERA IS DETERMINED IT SHOULD NOT. THIS IS ATLANTEAN BUSINESS. OUR BUSINESS.
GARTH, SURFACE GOVERNMENTS ARE ALREADY AWARE THERE'S TROUBLE IN ATLANTIS.
THAT'S WHY MERA REFUSES TO LET THE TITANS OR THE LEAGUE GET INVOLVED.
SO SHE'S ALONE DOWN THERE?
YES.

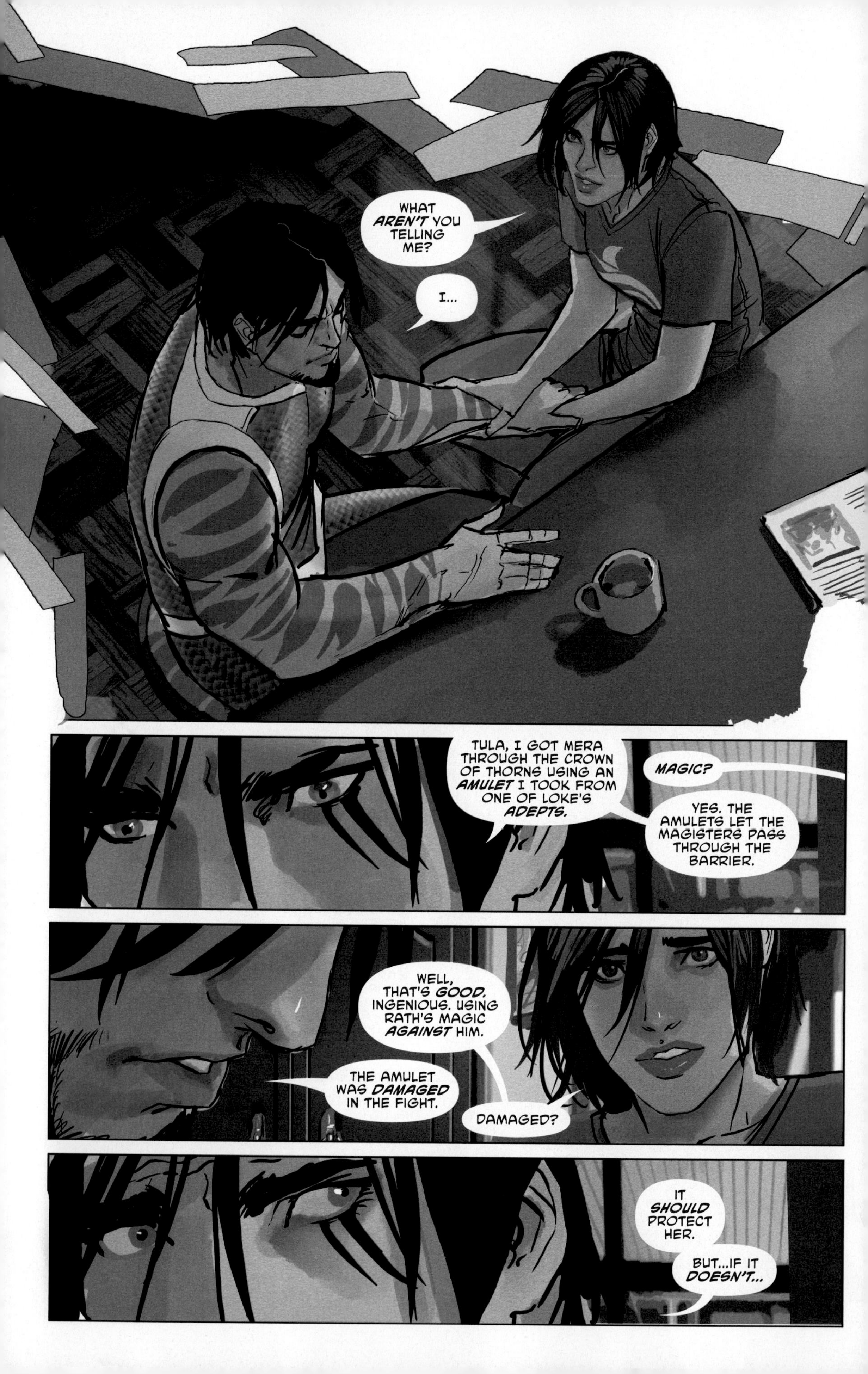
WHAT AREN'T YOU TELLING ME?
I...
TULA, I GOT MERA THROUGH THE CROWN OF THORNS USING AN AMULET I TOOK FROM ONE OF LOKE'S ADEPTS.
MAGIC?
YES. THE AMULETS LET THE MAGISTERS PASS THROUGH THE BARRIER.
WELL, THAT'S GOOD. INGENIOUS. USING RATH'S MAGIC AGAINST HIM.
THE AMULET WAS DAMAGED IN THE FIGHT.
DAMAGED?
IT SHOULD PROTECT HER.
BUT...IF IT DOESN'T...

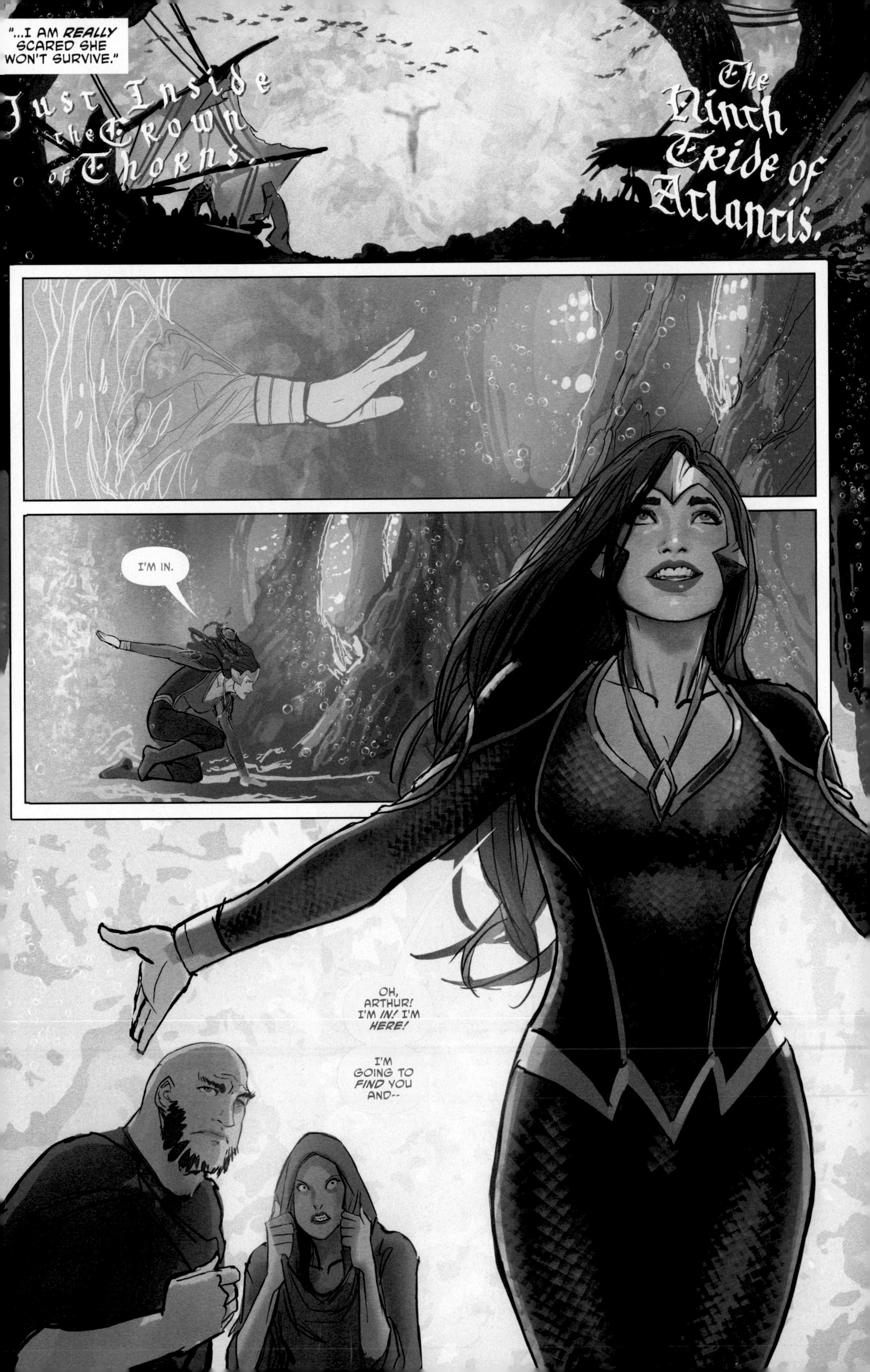

"...I AM REALLY SCARED SHE WON'T SURVIVE."
Just Inside the Crown of Thorns.
The Ninth Tride of Atlantis.
I'M IN.
OH, ARTHUR! I'M IN! I'M HERE!
I'M GOING TO FIND YOU AND--

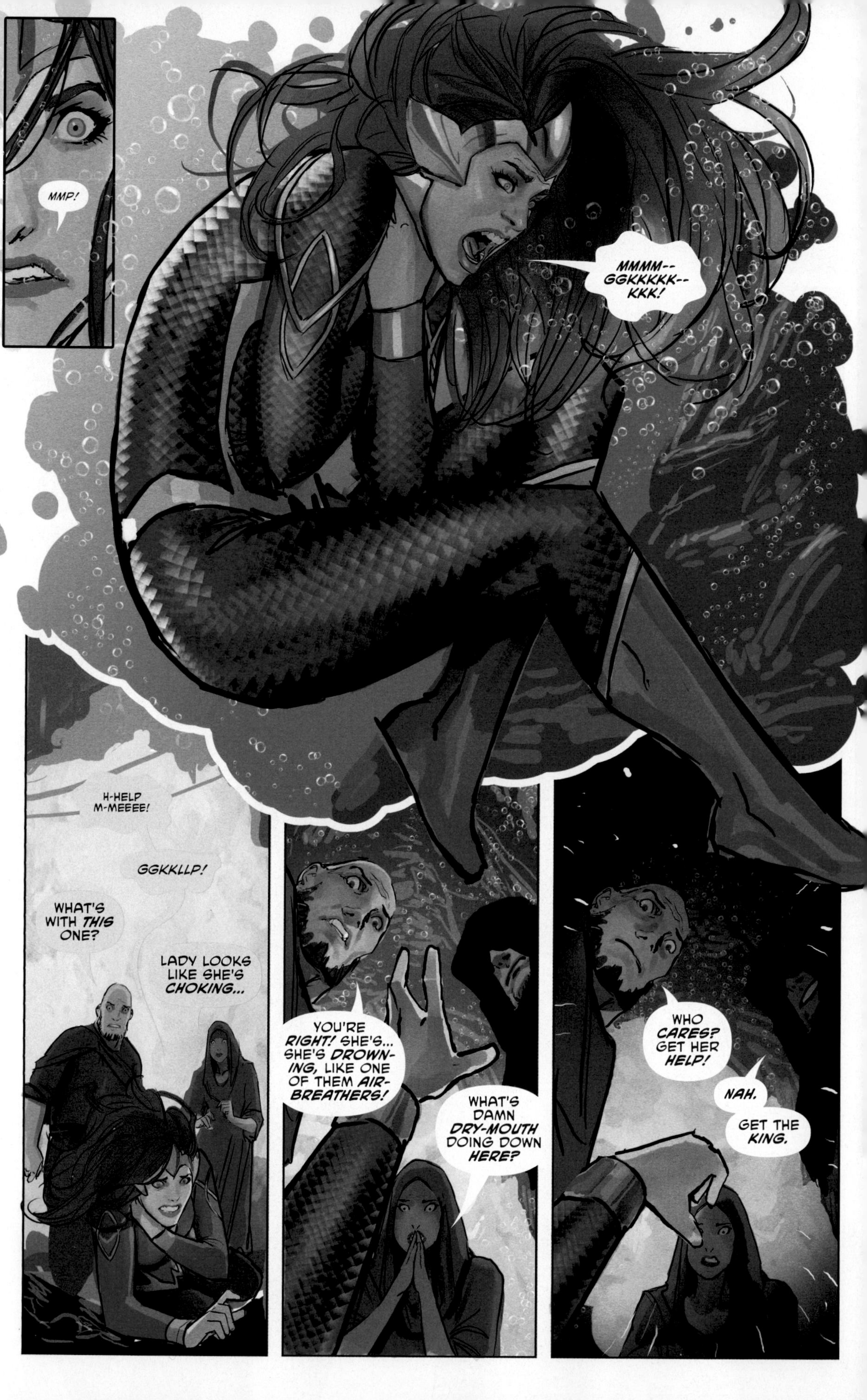
MMP!
MMMM--
GGKKKKK--
KKK!
H-HELP
M-MEEEE!
GGKKLLP!
WHAT'S
WITH THIS
ONE?
LADY LOOKS
LIKE SHE'S
CHOKING...
YOU'RE
RIGHT! SHE'S...
SHE'S DROWN-
ING, LIKE ONE
OF THEM AIR-
BREATHERS!
WHAT'S
DAMN
DRY-MOUTH
DOING DOWN
HERE?
WHO
CARES?
GET HER
HELP!
NAH.
GET THE
KING.

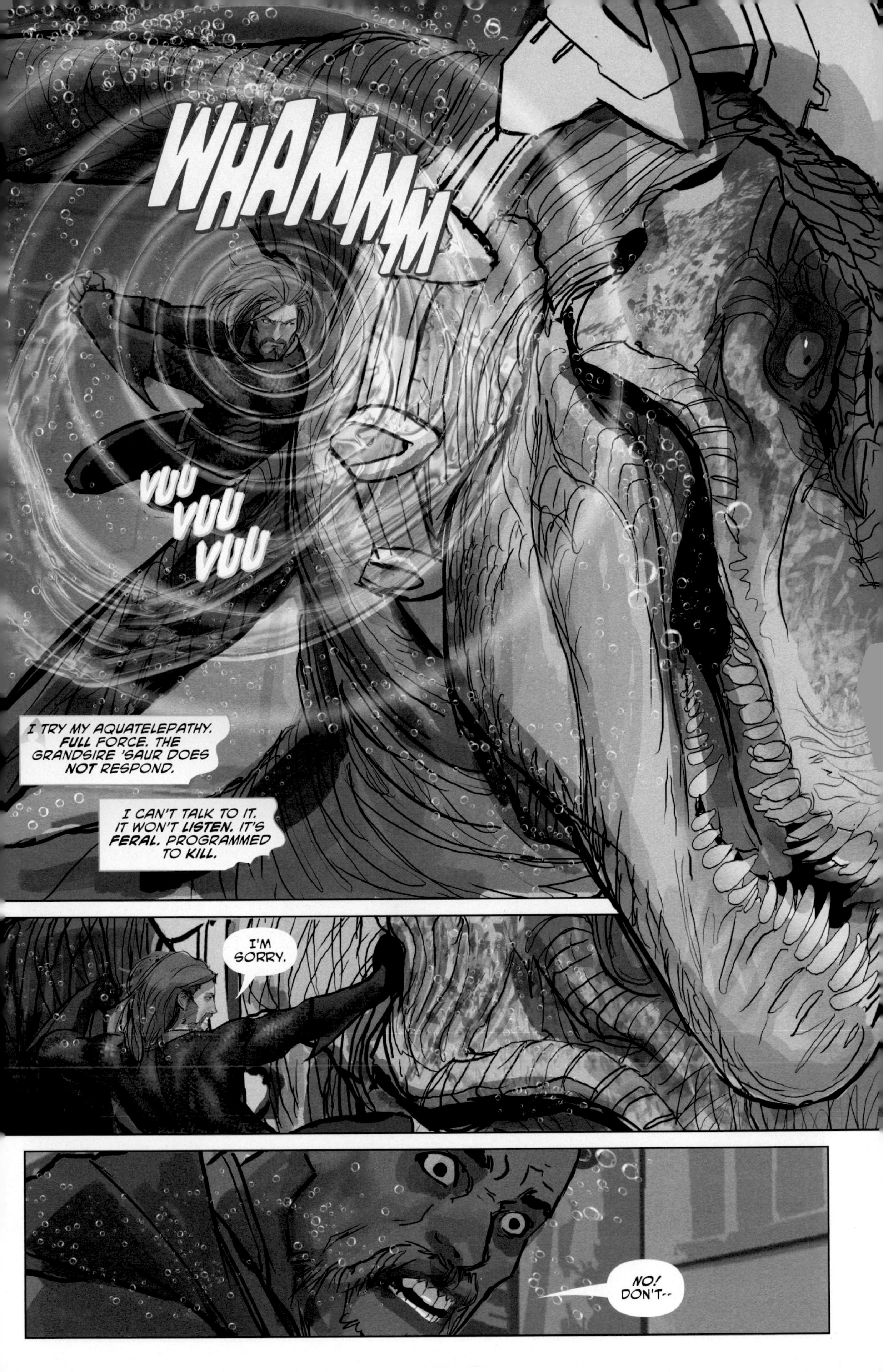
WHAMMMM
VUU VUU VUU
I TRY MY AQUATELEPATHY. **FULL** FORCE. THE GRANDSIRE 'SAUR DOES **NOT** RESPOND.
I CAN'T TALK TO IT. IT WON'T **LISTEN.** IT'S **FERAL.** PROGRAMMED TO **KILL.**
I'M SORRY.
NO! DON'T--

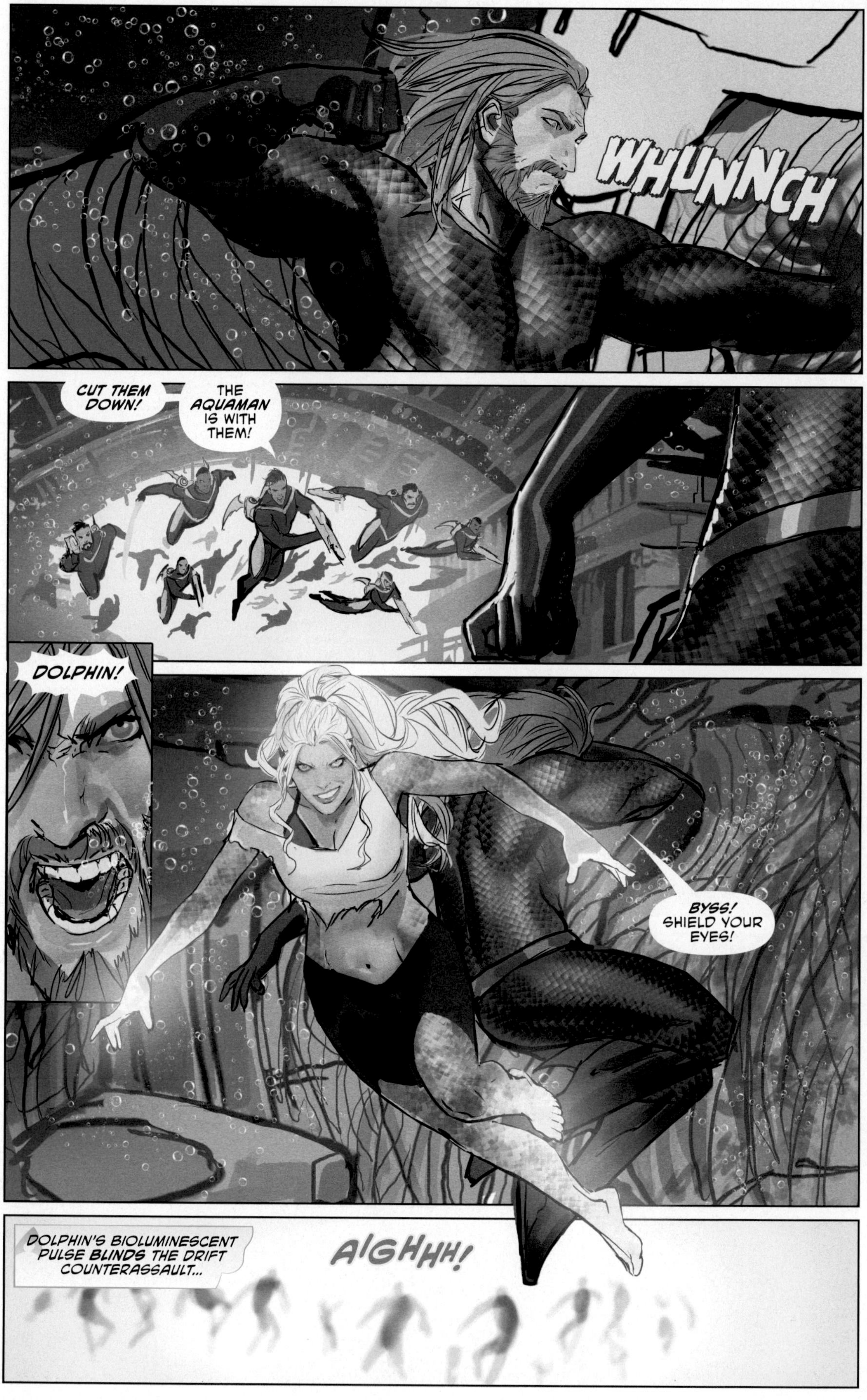
WHUNNCH
CUT THEM DOWN!
THE AQUAMAN IS WITH THEM!
DOLPHIN!
BYSS! SHIELD YOUR EYES!
DOLPHIN'S BIOLUMINESCENT PULSE BLINDS THE DRIFT COUNTERASSAULT...
AIGHHH!

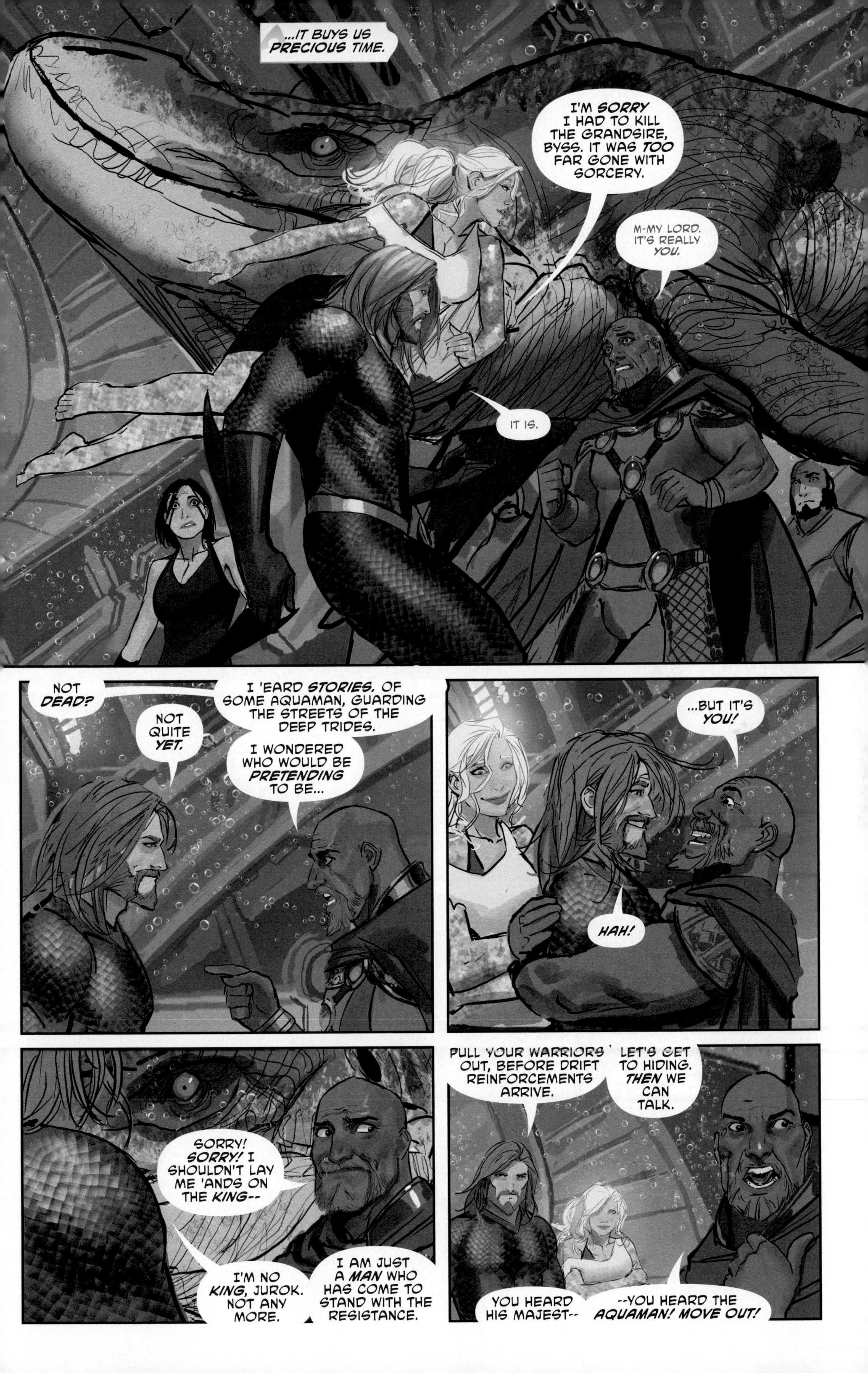
...IT BUYS US PRECIOUS TIME.
I'M SORRY I HAD TO KILL THE GRANDSIRE, BYSS. IT WAS TOO FAR GONE WITH SORCERY.
M-MY LORD. IT'S REALLY YOU.
IT IS.
NOT DEAD?
I 'EARD STORIES. OF SOME AQUAMAN, GUARDING THE STREETS OF THE DEEP TRIDES.
NOT QUITE YET.
I WONDERED WHO WOULD BE PRETENDING TO BE...
...BUT IT'S YOU!
HAH!
SORRY! SORRY! I SHOULDN'T LAY ME 'ANDS ON THE KING--
I'M NO KING, JUROK. NOT ANY MORE.
I AM JUST A MAN WHO HAS COME TO STAND WITH THE RESISTANCE.
PULL YOUR WARRIORS OUT, BEFORE DRIFT REINFORCEMENTS ARRIVE.
LET'S GET TO HIDING. THEN WE CAN TALK.
YOU HEARD HIS MAJEST--
--YOU HEARD THE AQUAMAN! MOVE OUT!

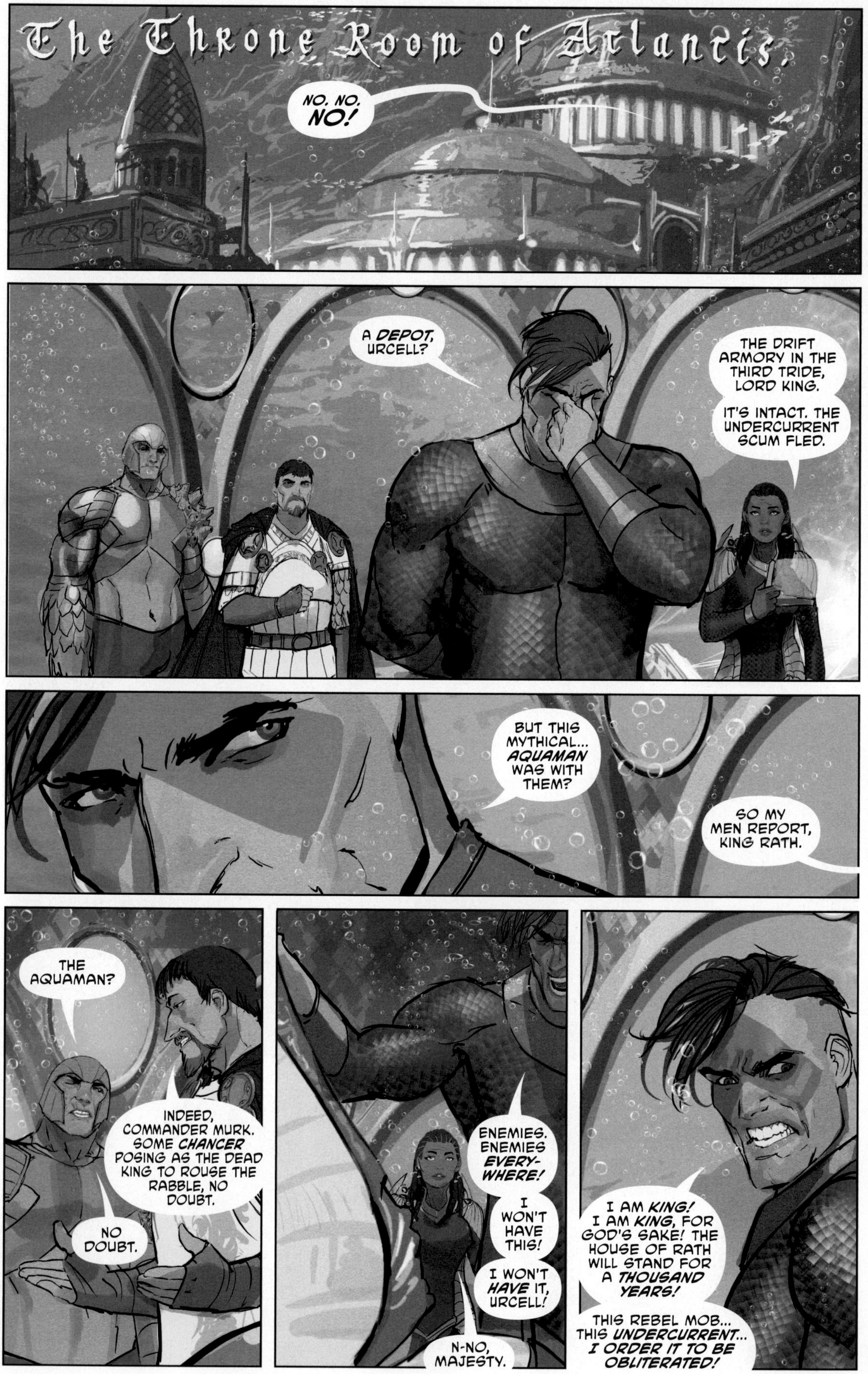
The Throne Room of Atlantis.
NO. NO. NO!
A DEPOT, URCELL?
THE DRIFT ARMORY IN THE THIRD TRIDE, LORD KING.
IT'S INTACT. THE UNDERCURRENT SCUM FLED.
BUT THIS MYTHICAL... AQUAMAN WAS WITH THEM?
SO MY MEN REPORT, KING RATH.
THE AQUAMAN?
INDEED, COMMANDER MURK. SOME CHANCER POSING AS THE DEAD KING TO ROUSE THE RABBLE, NO DOUBT.
NO DOUBT.
ENEMIES. ENEMIES EVERY-WHERE!
I WON'T HAVE THIS!
I WON'T HAVE IT, URCELL!
N-NO, MAJESTY.
I AM KING! I AM KING, FOR GOD'S SAKE! THE HOUSE OF RATH WILL STAND FOR A THOUSAND YEARS!
THIS REBEL MOB... THIS UNDERCURRENT... I ORDER IT TO BE OBLITERATED!

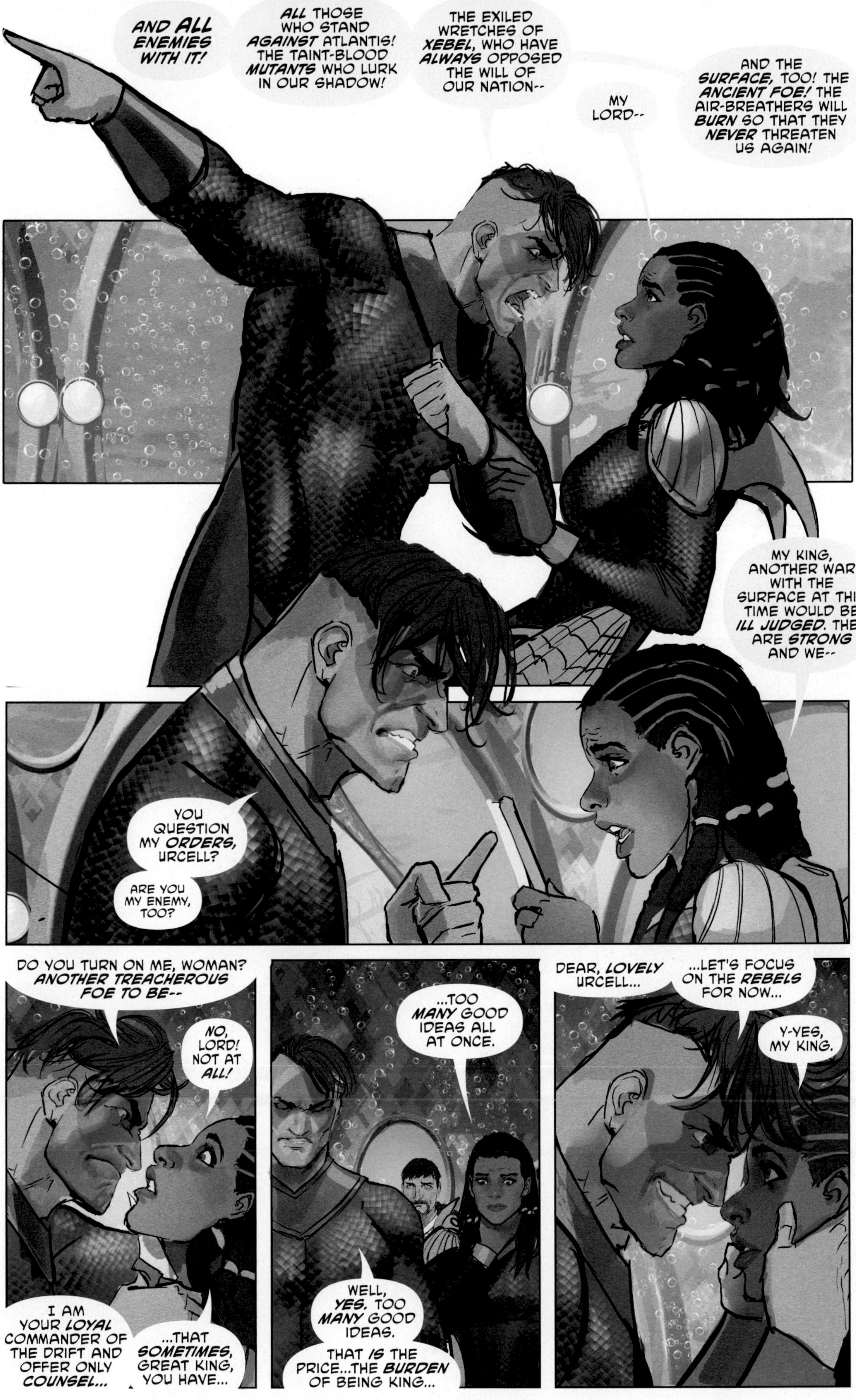
AND ALL ENEMIES WITH IT!
ALL THOSE WHO STAND AGAINST ATLANTIS! THE TAINT-BLOOD MUTANTS WHO LURK IN OUR SHADOW!
THE EXILED WRETCHES OF XEBEL, WHO HAVE ALWAYS OPPOSED THE WILL OF OUR NATION--
MY LORD--
AND THE SURFACE, TOO! THE ANCIENT FOE! THE AIR-BREATHERS WILL BURN SO THAT THEY NEVER THREATEN US AGAIN!
MY KING, ANOTHER WAR WITH THE SURFACE AT THIS TIME WOULD BE ILL JUDGED. THEY ARE STRONG AND WE--
YOU QUESTION MY ORDERS, URCELL?
ARE YOU MY ENEMY, TOO?
DO YOU TURN ON ME, WOMAN? ANOTHER TREACHEROUS FOE TO BE--
NO, LORD! NOT AT ALL!
I AM YOUR LOYAL COMMANDER OF THE DRIFT AND OFFER ONLY COUNSEL...
...THAT SOMETIMES, GREAT KING, YOU HAVE...
...TOO MANY GOOD IDEAS ALL AT ONCE.
WELL, YES. TOO MANY GOOD IDEAS.
THAT IS THE PRICE...THE BURDEN OF BEING KING...
DEAR, LOVELY URCELL...
...LET'S FOCUS ON THE REBELS FOR NOW...
Y-YES, MY KING.

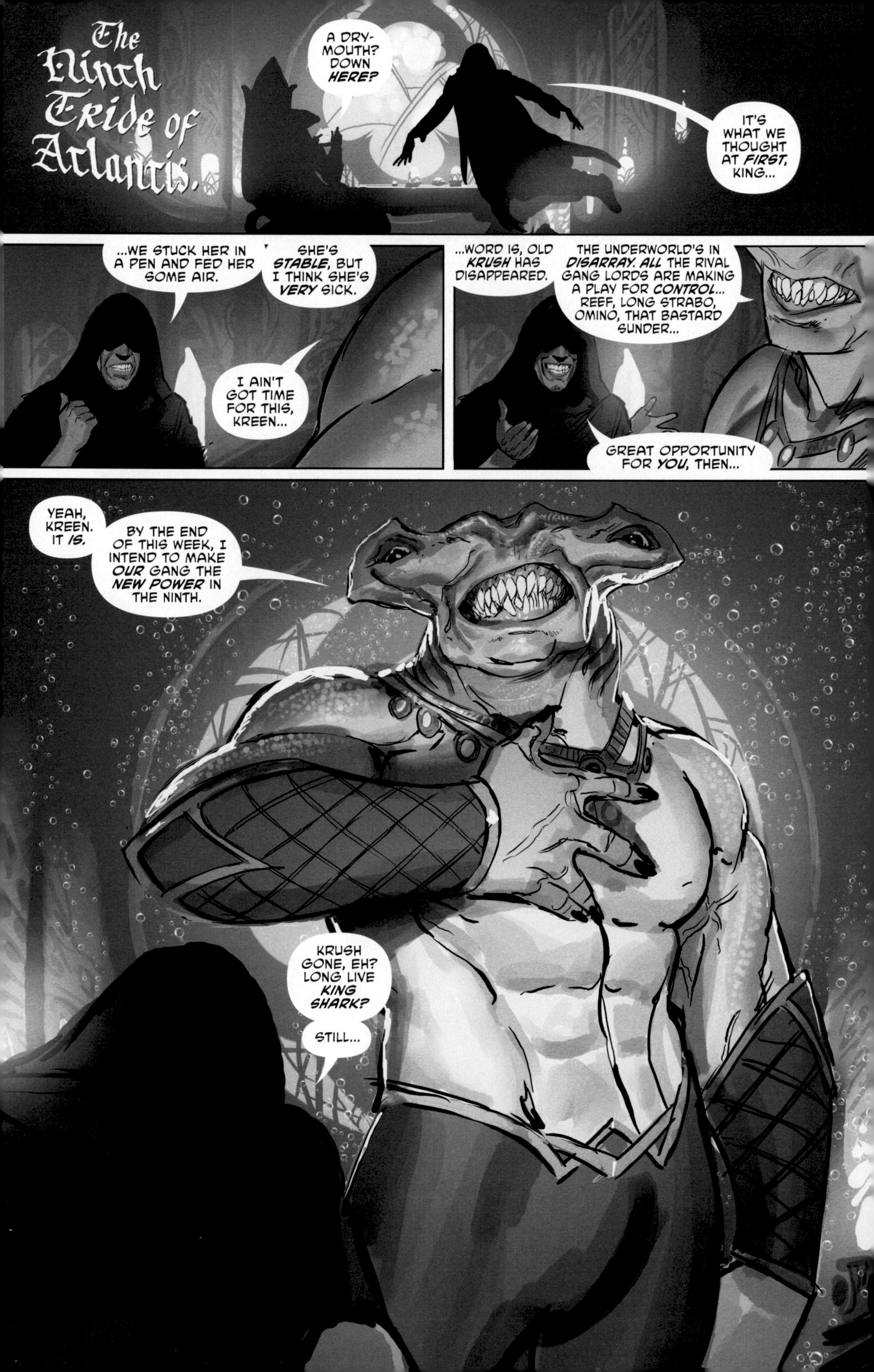

The Ninth Tride of Atlantis.
A DRY-MOUTH? DOWN HERE?
IT'S WHAT WE THOUGHT AT FIRST, KING...
...WE STUCK HER IN A PEN AND FED HER SOME AIR.
SHE'S STABLE, BUT I THINK SHE'S VERY SICK.
I AIN'T GOT TIME FOR THIS, KREEN...
...WORD IS, OLD KRUSH HAS DISAPPEARED.
THE UNDERWORLD'S IN DISARRAY. ALL THE RIVAL GANG LORDS ARE MAKING A PLAY FOR CONTROL... REEF, LONG STRABO, OMINO, THAT BASTARD SUNDER...
GREAT OPPORTUNITY FOR YOU, THEN...
YEAH, KREEN. IT IS.
BY THE END OF THIS WEEK, I INTEND TO MAKE OUR GANG THE NEW POWER IN THE NINTH.
KRUSH GONE, EH? LONG LIVE KING SHARK?
STILL...

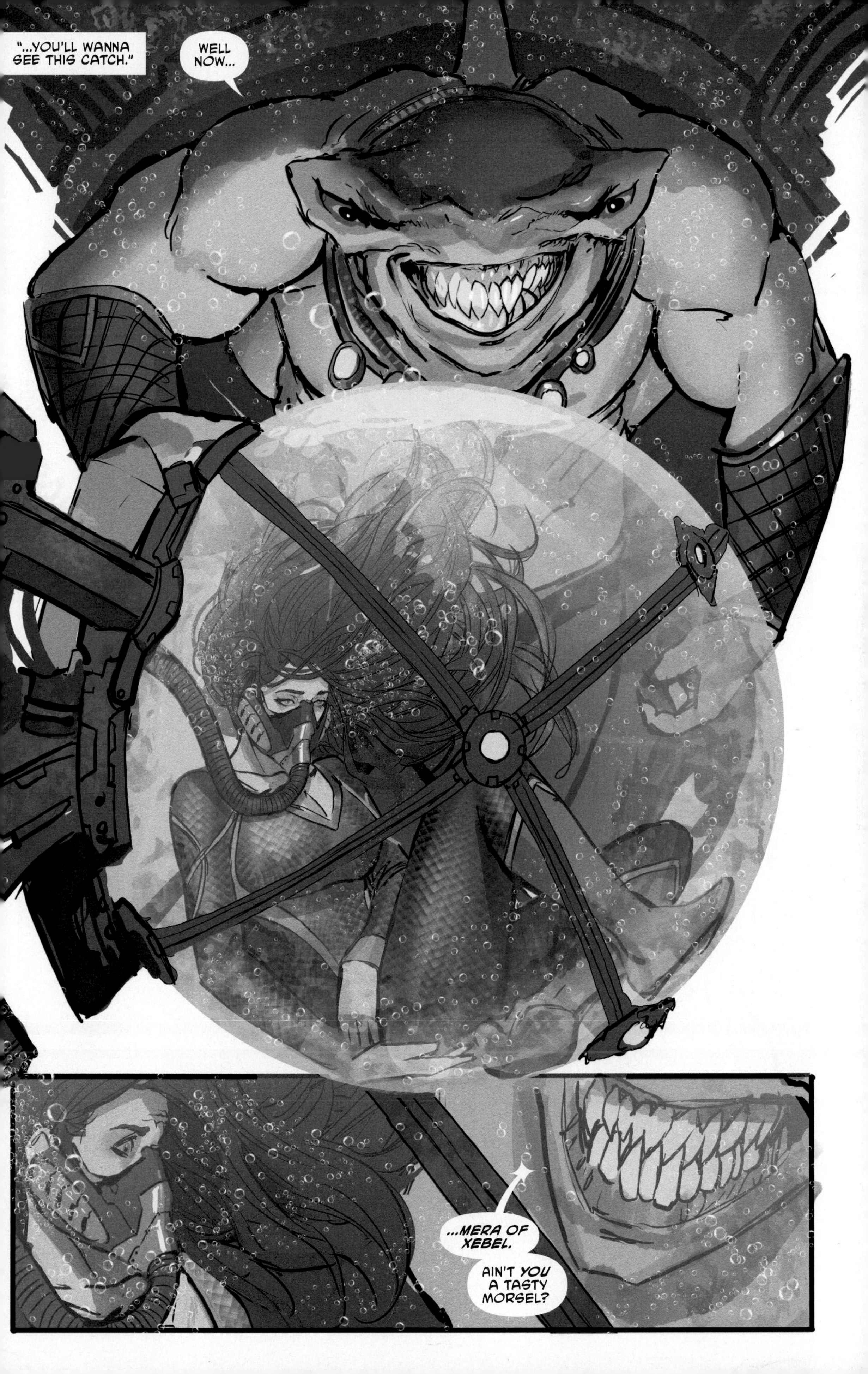
"...YOU'LL WANNA SEE THIS CATCH."
WELL NOW...
...MERA OF XEBEL.
AIN'T YOU A TASTY MORSEL?

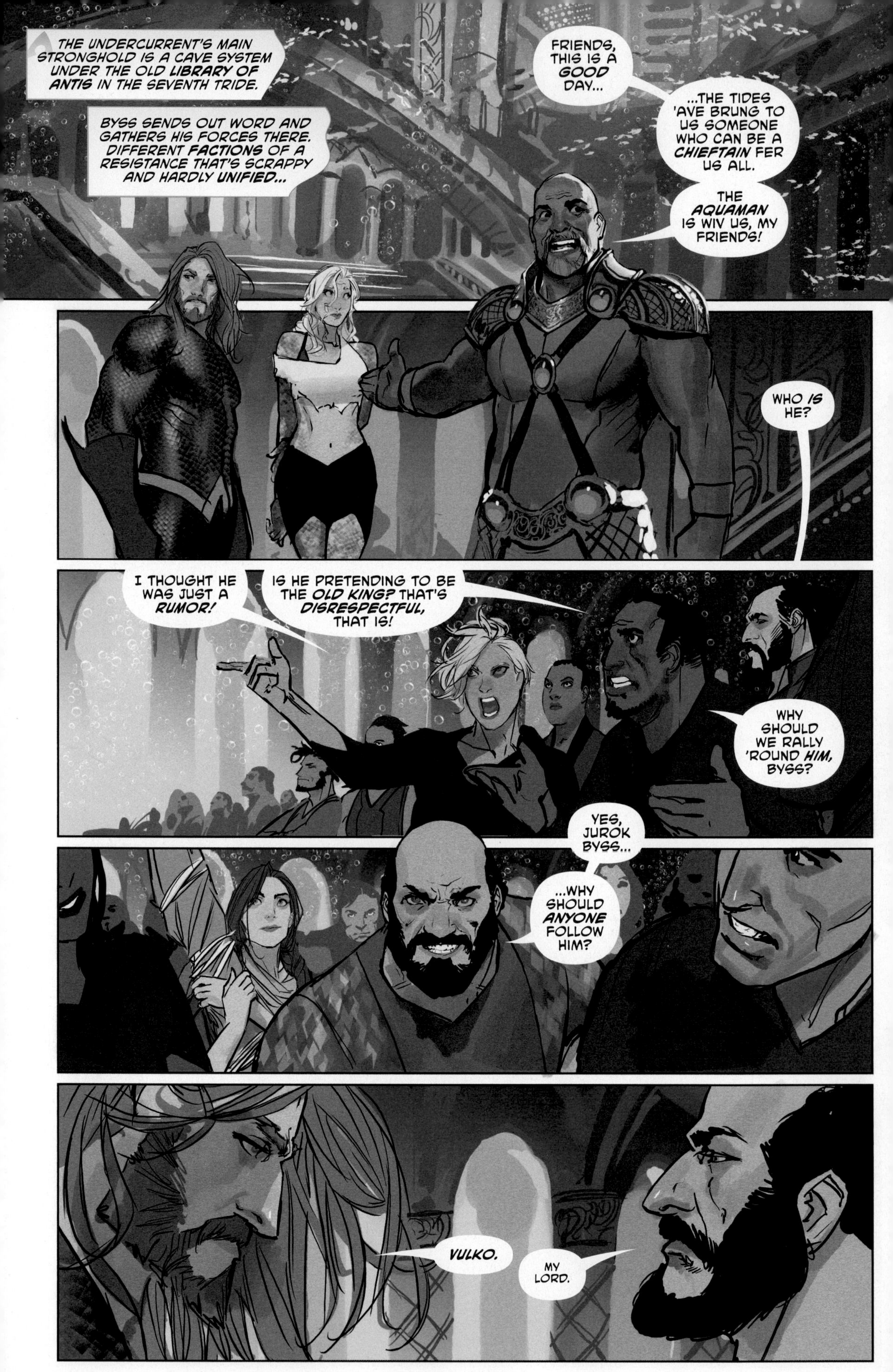
THE UNDERCURRENT'S MAIN STRONGHOLD IS A CAVE SYSTEM UNDER THE OLD LIBRARY OF ANTIS IN THE SEVENTH TRIDE.
BYSS SENDS OUT WORD AND GATHERS HIS FORCES THERE. DIFFERENT FACTIONS OF A RESISTANCE THAT'S SCRAPPY AND HARDLY UNIFIED...
FRIENDS, THIS IS A GOOD DAY...
...THE TIDES 'AVE BRUNG TO US SOMEONE WHO CAN BE A CHIEFTAIN FER US ALL.
THE AQUAMAN IS WIV US, MY FRIENDS!
WHO IS HE?
I THOUGHT HE WAS JUST A RUMOR!
IS HE PRETENDING TO BE THE OLD KING? THAT'S DISRESPECTFUL, THAT IS!
WHY SHOULD WE RALLY 'ROUND HIM, BYSS?
YES, JUROK BYSS...
...WHY SHOULD ANYONE FOLLOW HIM?
VULKO.
MY LORD.

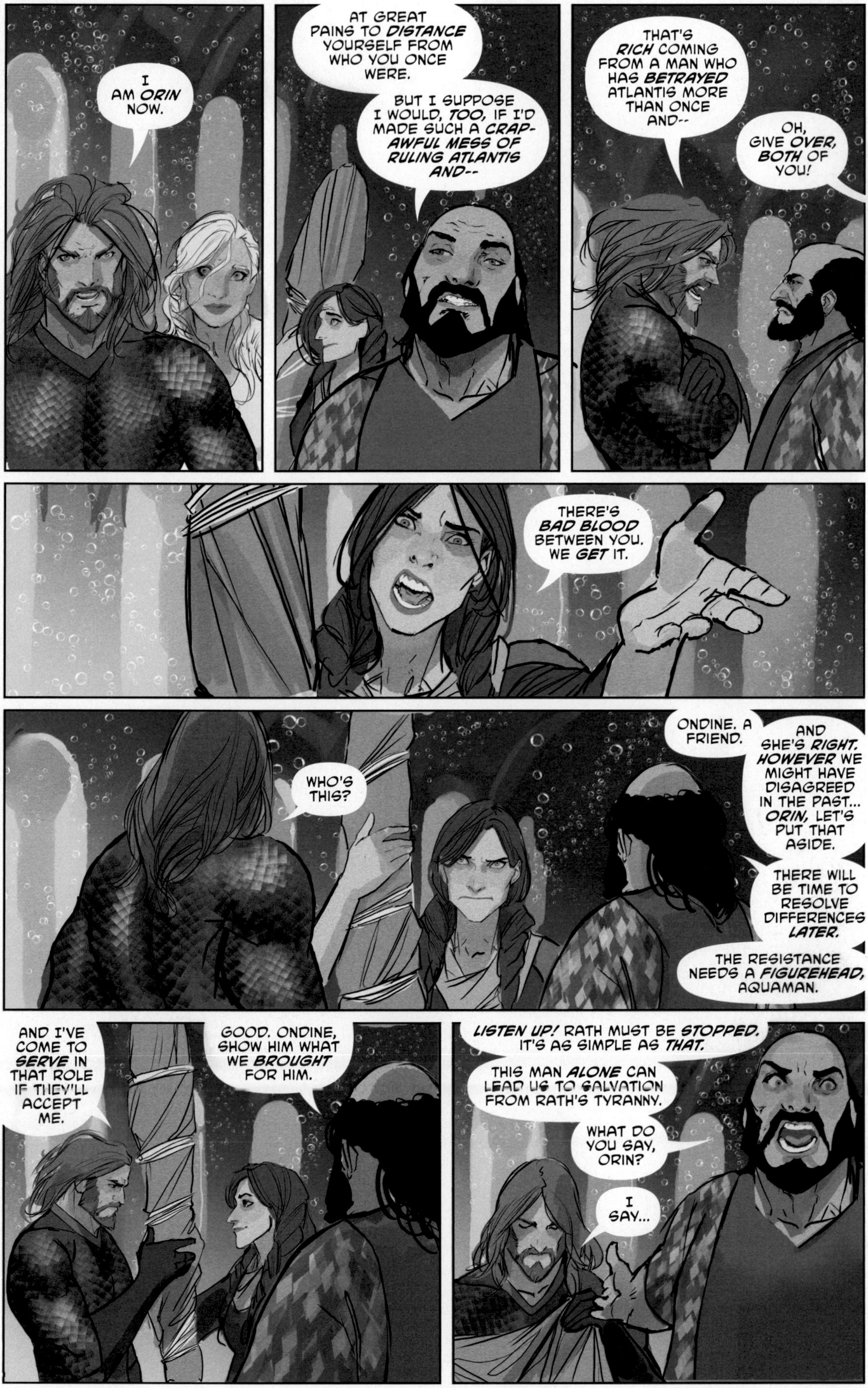
I AM ORIN NOW.
AT GREAT PAINS TO DISTANCE YOURSELF FROM WHO YOU ONCE WERE.
BUT I SUPPOSE I WOULD, TOO, IF I'D MADE SUCH A CRAP-AWFUL MESS OF RULING ATLANTIS AND--
THAT'S RICH COMING FROM A MAN WHO HAS BETRAYED ATLANTIS MORE THAN ONCE AND--
OH, GIVE OVER, BOTH OF YOU!
THERE'S BAD BLOOD BETWEEN YOU. WE GET IT.
WHO'S THIS?
ONDINE. A FRIEND.
AND SHE'S RIGHT. HOWEVER WE MIGHT HAVE DISAGREED IN THE PAST... ORIN, LET'S PUT THAT ASIDE.
THERE WILL BE TIME TO RESOLVE DIFFERENCES LATER.
THE RESISTANCE NEEDS A FIGUREHEAD, AQUAMAN.
AND I'VE COME TO SERVE IN THAT ROLE IF THEY'LL ACCEPT ME.
GOOD. ONDINE, SHOW HIM WHAT WE BROUGHT FOR HIM.
LISTEN UP! RATH MUST BE STOPPED. IT'S AS SIMPLE AS THAT.
THIS MAN ALONE CAN LEAD US TO SALVATION FROM RATH'S TYRANNY.
WHAT DO YOU SAY, ORIN?
I SAY...

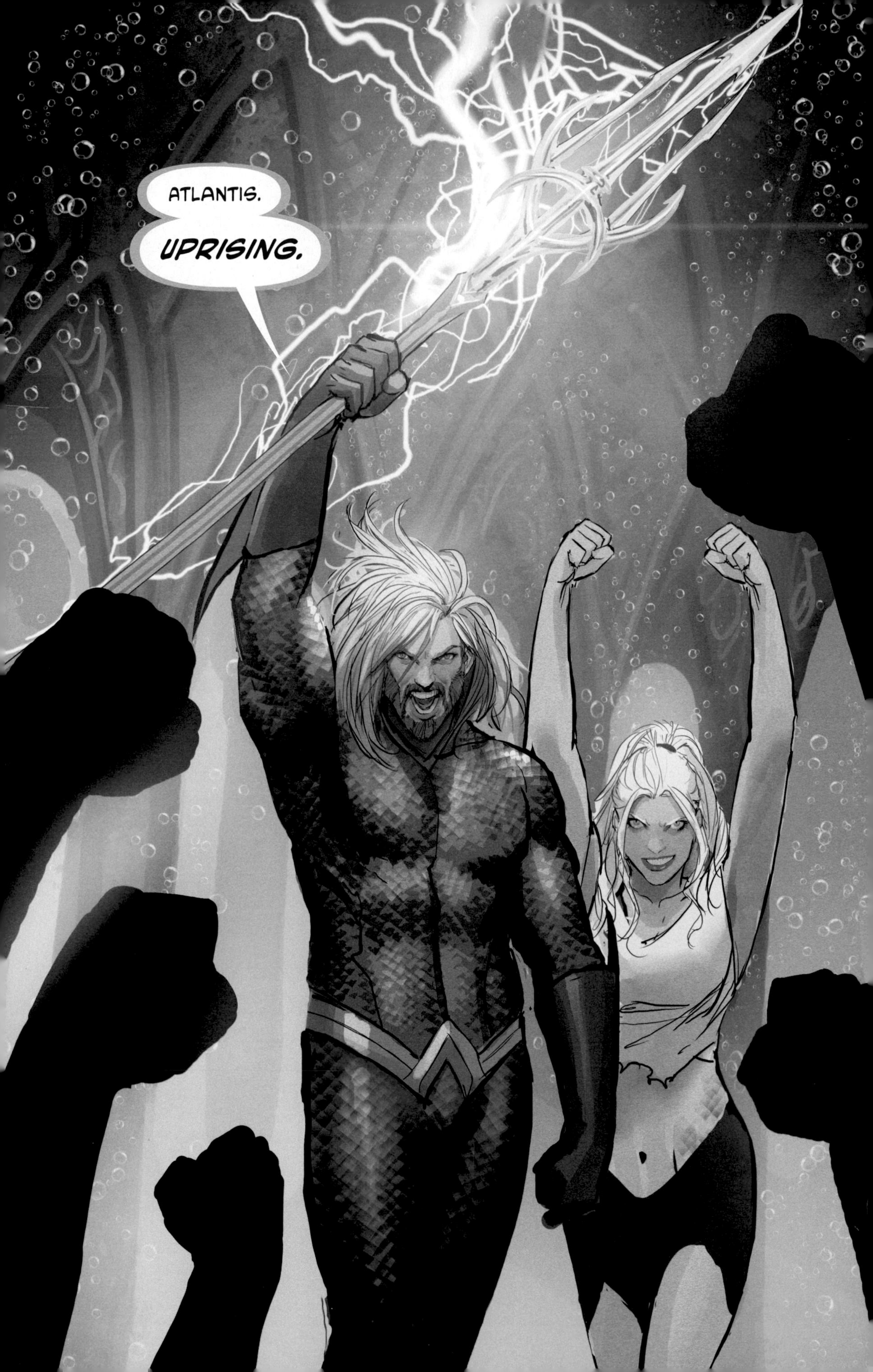
ATLANTIS.
UPRISING.

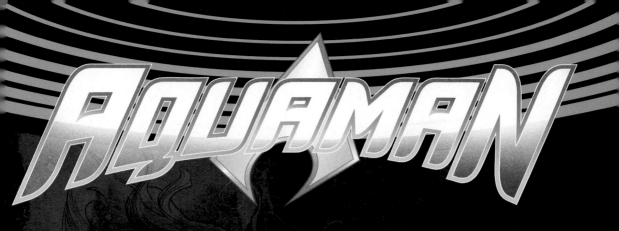

AQUAMAN

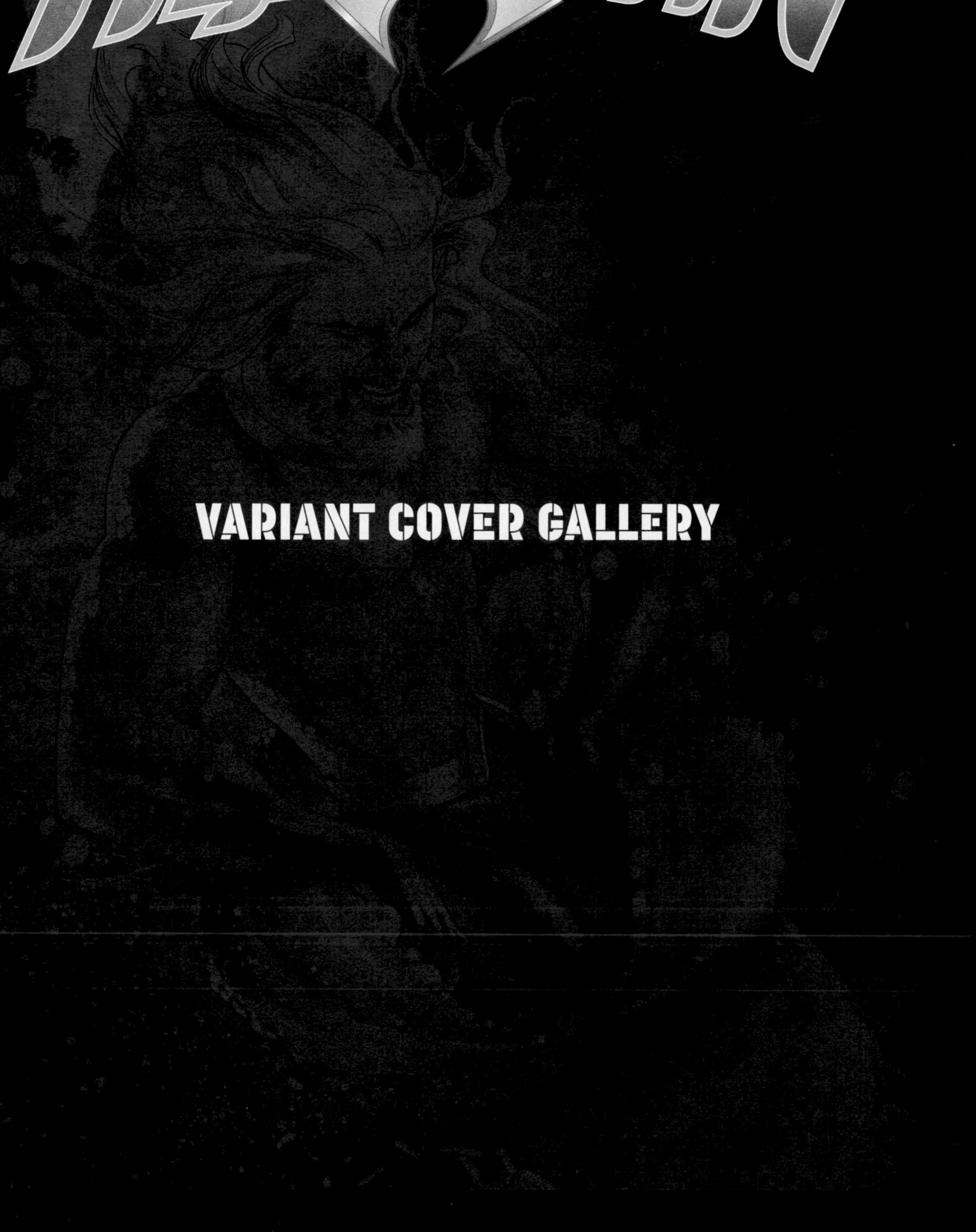

VARIANT COVER GALLERY

AQUAMAN #25 variant cover by JOSHUA MIDDLETON

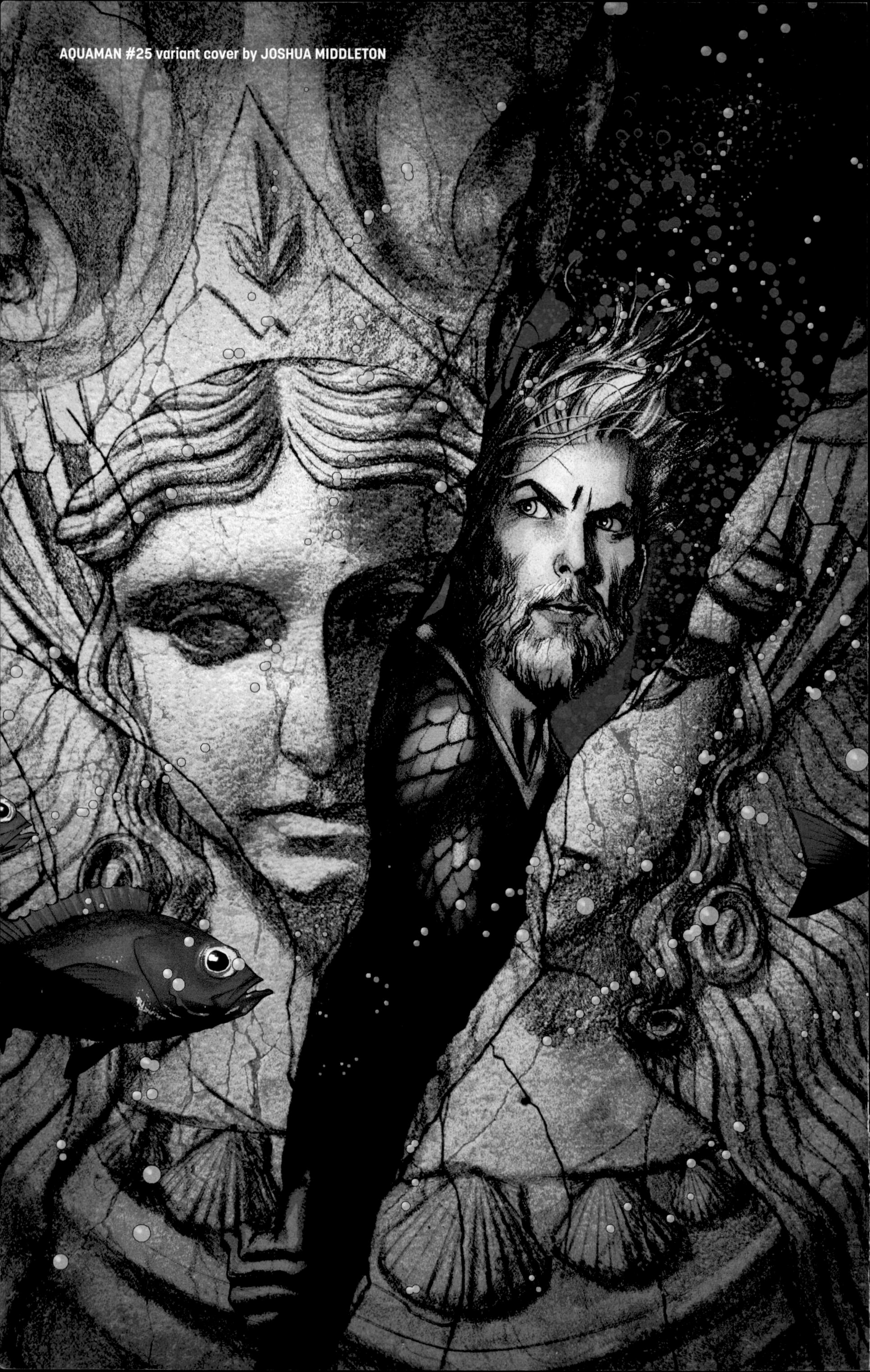

AQUAMAN #26 variant cover by JOSHUA MIDDLETON

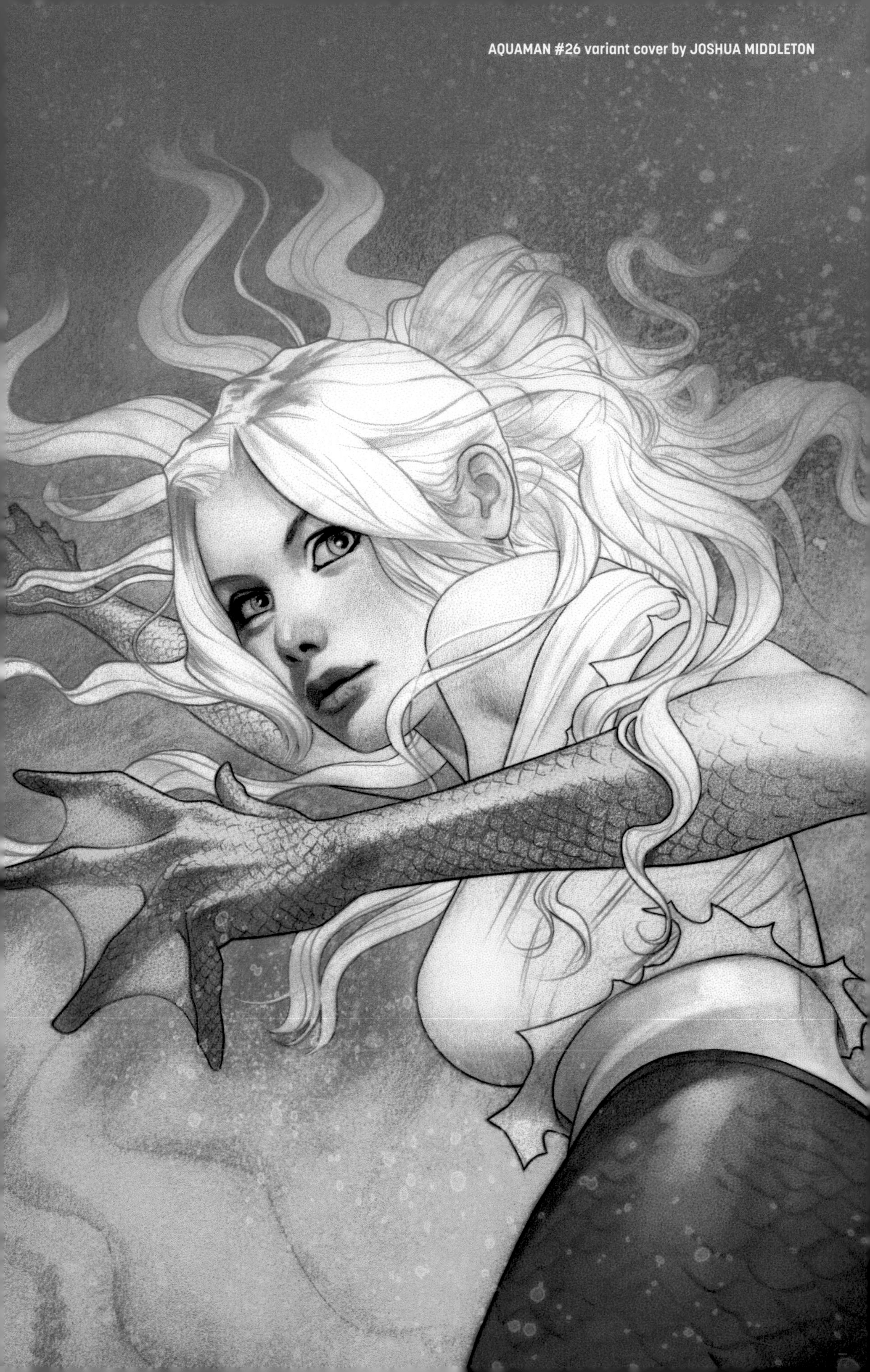

AQUAMAN #27 variant cover by JOSHUA MIDDLETON

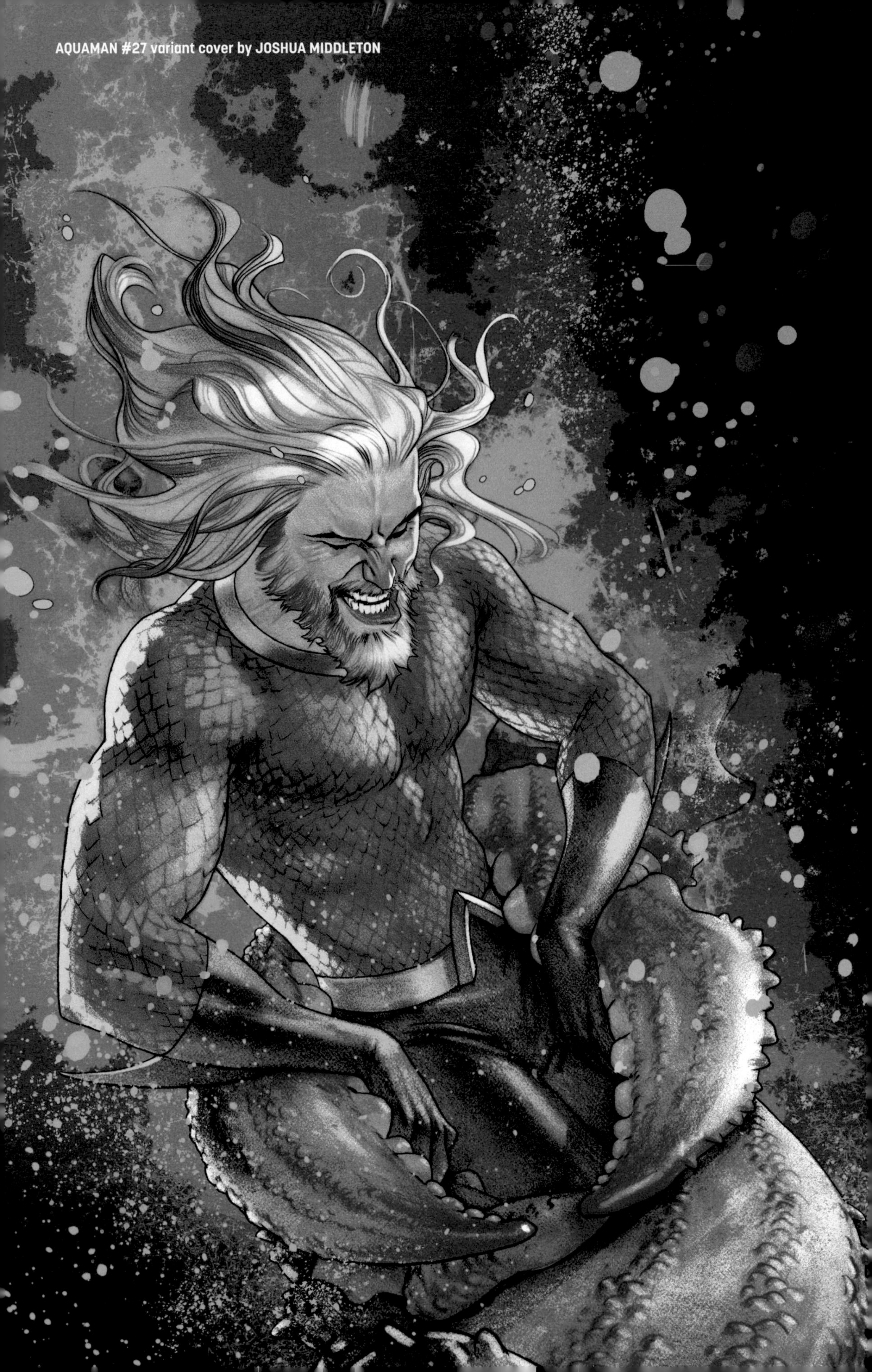

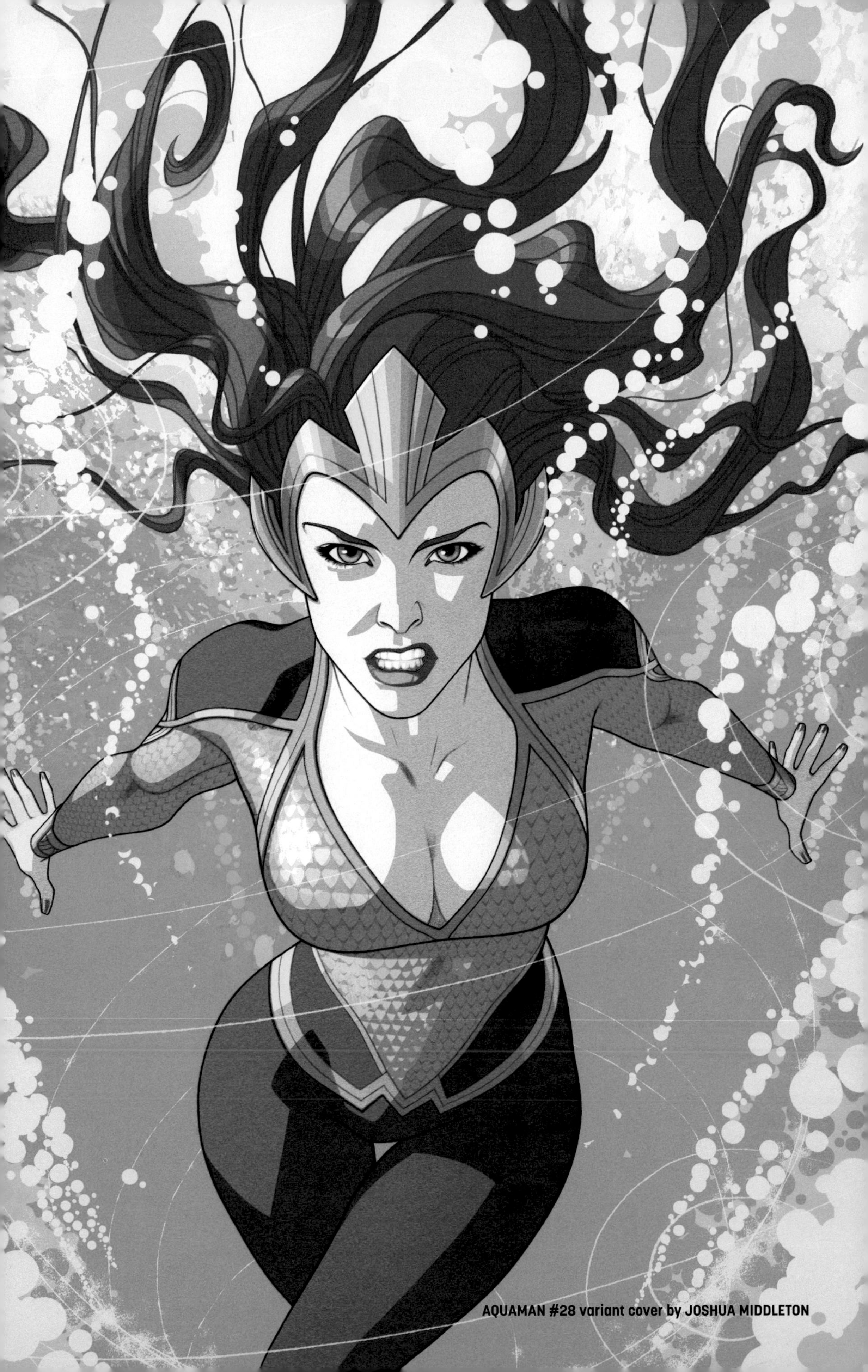

AQUAMAN #28 variant cover by JOSHUA MIDDLETON

AQUAMAN #29 variant cover by JOSHUA MIDDLETON

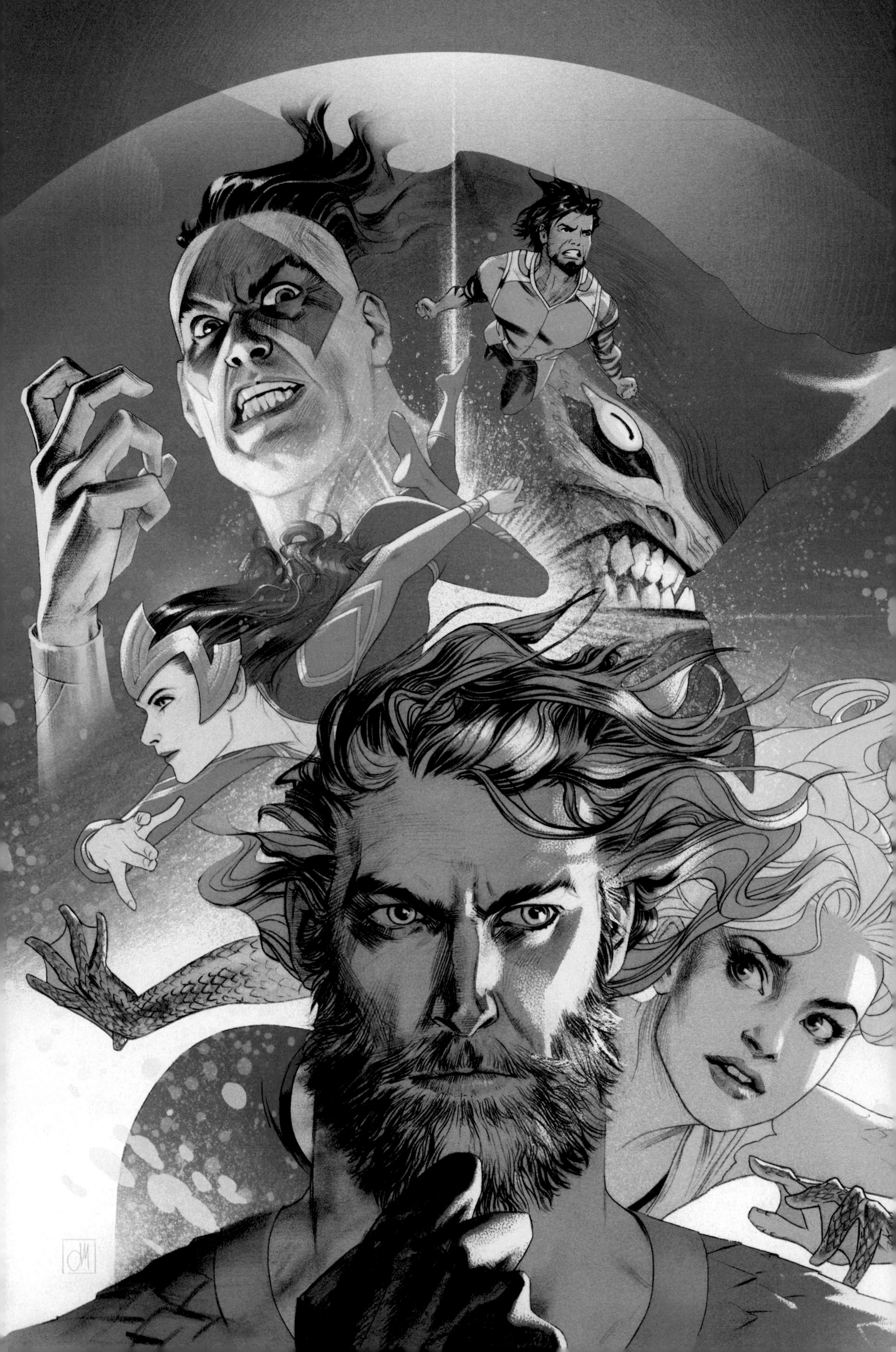

AQUAMAN #30 variant cover by JOSHUA MIDDLETON

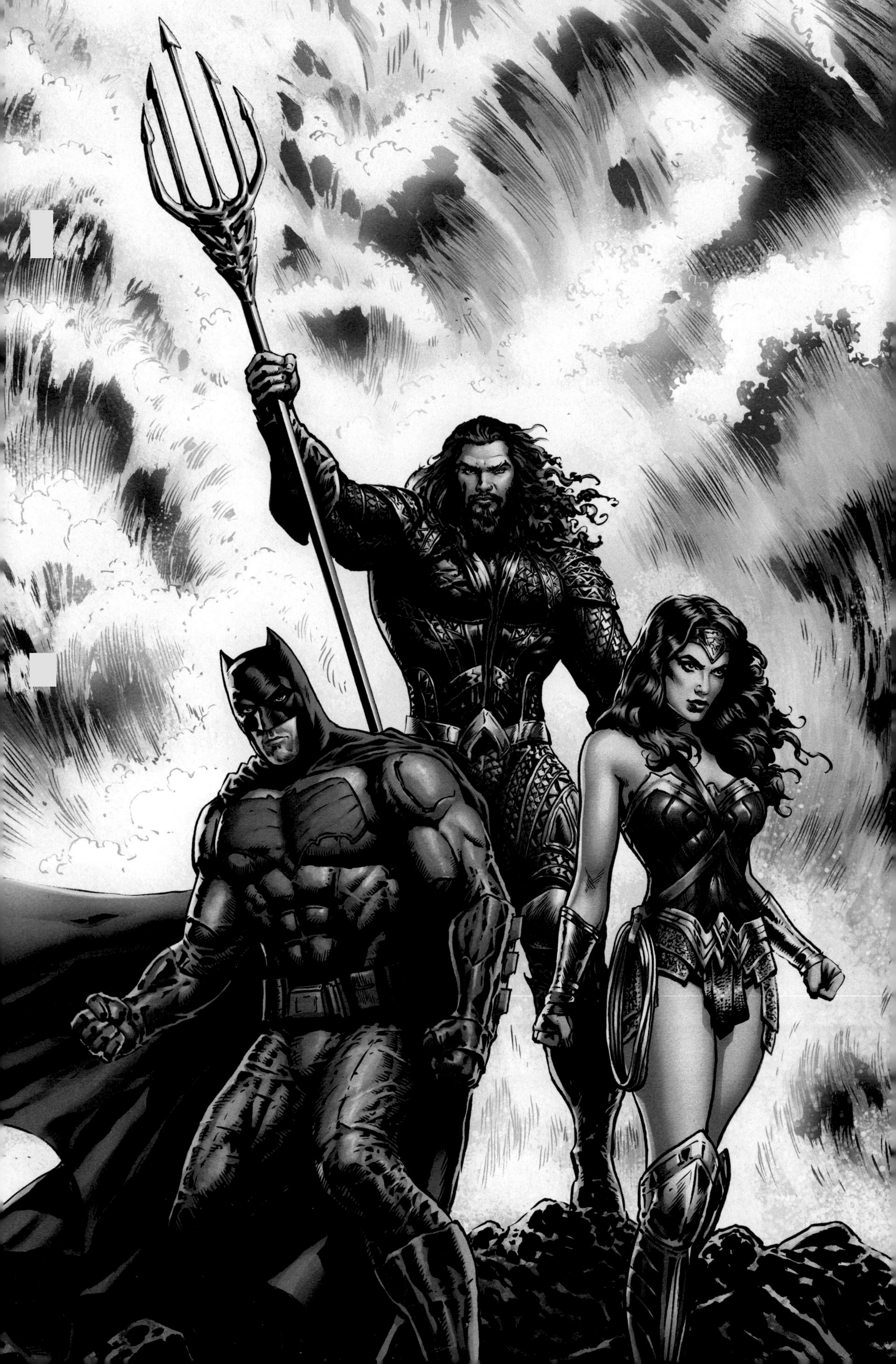

> "AQUAMAN has been a rollicking good ride so far… The mythology Johns has been building up here keeps getting teased out at just the right rate, like giving a junkie their fix." — **MTV GEEK**

> "With Reis on art and Johns using his full creative juices, AQUAMAN is constantly setting the bar higher and higher." — **CRAVE ONLINE**

AQUAMAN
VOL. 1: THE TRENCH
GEOFF JOHNS
with IVAN REIS

AQUAMAN VOL. 2:
THE OTHERS

AQUAMAN VOL. 3:
THRONE OF ATLANTIS